THE WORLD ATLAS OF
Revolutions

Saturn
by Francisco Goya
(Madrid, Prado Museum)

THE WORLD ATLAS OF
Revolutions

by
ANDREW WHEATCROFT

SIMON AND SCHUSTER
New York

For
James Manderston Wear

¡*Venceremos*!

Text copyright © 1983 by Andrew Wheatcroft
Copyright in cartography © 1983 by Hamish Hamilton Ltd

Published by Simon and Schuster
A Division of Gulf and Western Corporation
  Simon and Schuster Building
  Rockefeller Center
1230 Avenue of the Americas
New York, NY 10020

SIMON AND SCHUSTER and colophon
are trademarks of Simon & Schuster

Cartography by **Malcolm Porter**
assisted by Duncan Mackay
Picture research by Anne-Marie Ehrlich
Jacket design © 1983 Robert Anthony, Inc.

10 9 8 7 6 5 4 3 2 1

Library of Congress Cataloging in Publication Data

Wheatcroft, Andrew
  The World Atlas of Revolutions
    1. revolutions—maps   2. coups d'etat—maps
I. Title
  G1035.W5   1983   912'.132242   83–675888
    ISBN 0–671–46286–5   0–671–87207–0 (paperback)

Contents

		Page
Introduction		8
Acknowledgments		10
To the reader		12

Part 1: THE WORLD TURNED UPSIDE DOWN

NORTH AMERICA 1765–75:
'Shots that rang round the world' — 14

FRANCE 1789–95:
In the name of liberty — 21

IRELAND 1798:
The travails of the Irish — 30

SPAIN 1808–14:
The little war — 34

GREECE 1821–27:
'That Greece might still be free' — 38

SPANISH AMERICA 1808–30:
'Those who serve the revolution plough the sea' — 42

EUROPE 1848–49:
'The springtime of the peoples' — 46

INDIA 1857–59:
The wind of madness — 50

ITALY 1860:
Garibaldi: the revolutionary as hero — 54

CHINA 1850–1911:
The end of old China — 58

JAPAN 1865–80:
The earthquake of change — 62

MEXICO 1810–1920:
A century of revolution — 66

ARABIA 1900–35:
Ibn Saud and the sword of Islam   70

Part 2:   THE SEIZURE OF POWER

PARIS 1871:
The crucible   74

RUSSIA 1905:
The proving ground   78

RUSSIA 1917:
The Russian revolution   85

PETROGRAD 1917:
The take-over   89

RUSSIA 1917–21:
The civil war   93

TURKEY 1918–35:
The rebirth of Turkey   96

EUROPE 1918–23:
'Bolshevism is gaining ground everywhere'   100

ITALY 1919–25:
The 'dynamic minority' – Mussolini and the Fascists   104

GERMANY 1923–35:
The vocabulary of violence   108

SPAIN 1936:
The holy war – Spain's twin revolutions   112

Part 3:   FREEDOM, NOW!

INDIA 1905–47:
Violence and non-violence   118

SOUTH EAST ASIA 1945–62:
Bandits or freedom fighters?   122

KENYA 1950–56:
Mau Mau   126

ALGERIA 1949–62:
Algérie française   130

INDO CHINA 1945–75:
A thirty years' war   134

CYPRUS 1955–60:
The struggle for *enosis*   140

Part 4: THE REVOLUTIONARY MIRAGE

CHINA 1923–76:
Forging the Communist revolution 144

CUBA 1956–60:
Revolution in one country 154

LATIN AMERICA 1960–82:
The failure of revolution 158

SOUTHERN AFRICA 1960–82:
The last redoubt 164

UNITED STATES 1963–82:
'We shall overcome, some day . . .' 170

ETHIOPIA 1974–82:
Revolutionary chauvinism in world power-politics 174

IRAN 1978–82:
The power of militant Islam 178

AFGHANISTAN 1975–82:
The tradition of resistance 182

MIDDLE EAST 1934–82:
The matter of Palestine 186

IRELAND 1920–82:
The static revolution 190

THE WORLD 1960–80:
The military option 194

THE WORLD 1900–:
The uses of terror 196

Sources 200

Select bibliography 201

Photographic sources 205

Index 205

Introduction

I HAVE intended to write a book on revolutions since a day in the spring of 1963, when I came across a bullet-scarred wall in the grounds of the University of Madrid, a mute testimony to the events of the Civil War more than twenty-five years before. Since then I have read and collected material in a desultory way, talked to people who have experienced the course and consequences of modern revolutions, and tried where possible to separate fact from fiction, not always an easy matter with material of so sensitive a nature. The main difficulty I encountered was in trying to pin the events which were being described, either in print or by word of mouth, to the ground on which they took place.

In pursuing this mild obsession, I was accused by many friends and colleagues of trying to treat revolutions as a set of physical events, to ignore the metaphysics of revolution – the wild elation, the sense of comradeship, the adrenalin of combat – and to detach events from their causes, rendering the whole process of revolution incomprehensible.

So my attempt in this book, to make the revolutions I have chosen *more* comprehensible, may seem ill-fated from the start. However, the form in which they are presented forces the reader to take a fresh look at sometimes over-familiar events. In an atlas, by using a series of graphic images and conventions, it is possible to present a simultaneity of events, something which can never happen within the sequence of a simple text. It is possible to look at a map and to form your own patterns within the information presented. There is no tyranny of precedence as with the printed page, of an idea imprinting itself before the next one can be absorbed. There are, equally, some things which can never be done successfully in graphic form alone. The amount of information which can be presented is limited by the demands of clarity, nor is it easy to present development and movement as it is with a written narrative. A combination of the two forms goes some way towards providing a solution.

I have also presented each revolution over a timespan which brings out its essential character. In the case of Spain, I have looked at the revolution in the perspective of the ferment of July to September 1936, rather than in the longer term of the Civil War. In this case I am more concerned with the antecedents of the outbreak than its later course. On the other hand, in Indo China, the course of the war, or wars, over thirty years, forged the pattern of the revolution, and it is essential to consider the way in which the war was fought on the ground.

The motive for choosing these particular revolutions is of necessity idiosyncratic. Some are obvious, like the Russian and Chinese revolutions. Others are curious, like the creation of Arabia by Ibn Saud. Still others are looked at with an unusual approach: Spain in 1936 as a pair of revolutions, rather than a rising of the right and a revolution of the left. Above all, I have tried to present the variety of revolutionary experience – limited by the notion that it seems unwise to talk about 'revolutions' much before the last quarter of the eighteenth century. For all its inadequacies on many scales of revolutionary content, I believe the American Revolution was the first revolution of the western world. For a full discussion of the whole subject of what is and is not a revolution, I would refer readers to those books cited in the bibliography.

This book has been designed so that it is possible to use the maps without having read the text. I have written as fully as space permits on the background and the causes of the events the maps depict, but they are two independent entities. Nor have I sought to present that most tedious of literary exercises, the concise, balanced, and judicious résumé. The book does not, I hope, have a particular political bias one way or the other, but I have not sought to be aloof and detached from the events described. In human terms, most of the revolutions I have considered added more to the sum of misery than they alleviated, for reasons which most revolutionaries are unwilling to admit. In the words of Federica Montseny, who lived through the revolution in Spain after a life spent in its anticipation,

The revolution, in which uncontrollable forces operate imperiously, is blind and destructive, grandiose and cruel; once the first step has been taken and the first dyke broken, the people pour through like a torrent through the breach, and it is impossible to dam the flood. How much is wrecked in the heat of the struggle and in the blind fury of the storm! Men as we have always known them, neither better nor worse, . . . they reveal their vices and their virtues, and while from the hearts of rogues there springs a latent honesty, from the depths of honest men there emerges a brutish appetite – a thirst for extermination, a desire for blood – that seemed inconceivable before.

La Revista Blanca, 30 July 1936

Like Goya's terrifying picture of Saturn, the revolution devours its own children, and tramples the rest of mankind to death in the process.

A. J. M. W.
Hagg Newhall, 1983

Acknowledgments

IN writing this book I have incurred a great many debts of gratitude to those scholars into whose specialist fields I have wandered, to those with a detailed first-hand knowledge of current revolutions which they have passed on to me, and to those friends who have survived the bombardment of my thoughts on revolution. To take the last case first, Norman Stone and Jonathan Steinberg will know how much I have relied upon their friendship and support, and I cannot fully express my thanks to them. To Neil Parsons, who has led me through the complexities of Southern Africa, I am similarly grateful. Marc Ferro will recognize that what he has told me in the past has not gone unheeded, while Alistair Horne will see that the last seven years have produced many changes to the scheme we first discussed then. Richard Luckett has proved stalwart, as ever. And, *fons et origo*, I would like to thank Professor Sir John Plumb, who forced me to see that everything is grist to the mills of history. I hope that he may see in this book a tribute to the breadth of vision which he has conveyed to so many whom he has taught.

I would also like to express my gratitude to Professor Michael Balfour and Jean-Marie Benoist who have helped me to clarify my ideas, to Sir Isaiah Berlin who has given me some invaluable insights into Imperial Russia, and to Professor Geoffrey Best, who has made me think more precisely about the moral dimension of revolutionary terror. Dr Robin Bidwell has answered my questions about Arabia, and Professor Martin Blinkhorn added a new insight into Spanish matters. Professor John Brewer advised me on some of the early drafts, and Geoffrey Brown has confirmed a number of technical military points. I enjoyed talking to Professor Charles Carlton on patterns of violence in Northern Ireland and to Raymond Carr about the Spanish Civil War and its antecedents. Charles de Chassiron has given me his first-hand knowledge of one area mentioned in this book, and Professor Marcus Cunliffe has put me straight about the American Revolution. Christian and Gerry Jo Cranmer not only entertained me splendidly at Roundtop, but helped me to understand the way revolutionary war developed as a consequence of the terrain. Christian also gave me much detailed and unique information for which I am very grateful. With David Damant I have had many fruitful conversations about revolutions and militarism, evidence for which lies in these pages. Thanks to Dr Raymond Dawson, I have got a clearer perspective on China, and I hope I have not distorted what he told me. Marc Dragoumis was very revealing about revolution in Greece, and from Christopher Duffy I have gained great insight not only into the role of fortification in modern revolutions, but on the development of revolution in Afghanistan.

Talking to Professor John Erickson both at the War and Society conference in 1972 and many times subsequently has coloured my whole thinking about Russia in this century. Dr Erich Gabriel in Vienna has helped me considerably in relation to Austrian history as has Dr John Gooch with Italian matters. Stella Goldman helped me to meet many useful people with first-hand experience, as did Jay Gould, Stephanie Grant, and Richard Hartill. Pepe Heredia helped me to know Granada better, and Don Joaquin Hidalgo Diaz gave me a wonderful perspective on the outbreak of the Civil War in Andalucia. Professor Eric Hobsbawm has always been a good friend and I have learned much from him. Dr Richard Holmes has talked through France in 1871 with me, and Professor James Joll has managed to combine counsel and criticism immaculately. John Keegan who has been both collaborator and friend over the years has also taught me how to look at military institutions. From a meeting with the late Lord Kinross I gained even more insight into Turkey than is contained in his magisterial life of Ataturk. Dr Jonathan Kitchen has forced me to think more clearly about the categories of revolution, while Professor Martin Kitchin opened my eyes to an aspect of German history. Professor F.S.L. Lyons talked to me about Ireland, while Dr Adrian Lyttelton enriched my thinking about fascist Italy. Professor Walter Laqueur has fired my enthusiasm over the question of revolutionary terror, and much else besides. Ahmed Malik advised me on matters dealing with Malaya, and I have also benefited from Dr Tim Mason's forthright views on the workers in the Third Reich. Dr Joaquin Maura has widened my notions on the role of the left in Spain in this century, as has 'Mencho'. Trevor Mostyn has discussed the Middle East with me, to my benefit. Chukumeweku Osuji poured scorn on my notions of Africa, something both chastening and very helpful. Dr Richard Overy has allowed me to see his as yet unpublished work on Nazi Germany, and suggested many avenues of exploration. Pat and Judy Palaveda looked after me in Atlanta, and also gave me some insight into the race question in the south. Professor Richard Pipes sowed some very fertile seeds about the nature of Russian government and society, while the late Derek Pitt helped me to think constructively about the role of revolutions. Jasper Ridley will recognize how much I have drawn on his ideas, very freely given. Professor George Rudé proved as enlightening in person as in print, and I am grateful to him. Dr Avi Schlaim has been a a perceptive critic, while Professor Simon Schama is a friend who has always listened and enlightened. Dr Dieter Senghaas helped me think more coherently about the structural function of the military in society, while Professor John Shy pointed out the lacunae in my thinking about the American revolution. Dr Christopher Smith has argued many points of detail, and usually ended by convincing me, while my great-uncles, the late Otto and Paul Veit, gave me great insights both of the Far East and of Europe before 1940. Lloyd Wiggins has collected source material for me and discussed the anatomy of a race riot, which I found most illuminating. Professor Stuart Woolf has talked to me about Italy, to my advantage. To all of them I would express my warmest thanks, with the usual caveat that they are in no way responsible for the use I have made of their advice and information.

The fact that this book is an atlas creates a special set of debts. In the first place, without the pioneering work of Martin Gilbert and his outstanding series of atlases, it would not have existed. He has shown how the highest standards of scholarship can make the historical atlas a new type of history book, as I discovered when working with him on his *The Arab–Israeli Conflict*. I am happy to acknowedge how much stimulus I have gained from him. In this atlas, all the cartography has been carried out by Malcolm Porter, and working with him has been both a delight, and an education in what can and cannot be achieved in a graphic presentation.

There are a number of institutions whose help I would like to acknowledge: the Librarian and staff of the University Library Cambridge, and in particular those of the Map Room; the staff of the London Library; the Director of the Lincolnshire Library Service, Raymond Carroll, and his staff. In particular, I would like to thank Stephen Moore and the staff of Boston Library, who have unfailingly responded to my requests for arcane material. The Heeresge-schichtliches Museum and the Kriegsarchiv in Vienna proved most helpful, and I am also grateful to the Facultad de Filosofia y Letras, Universidad de Madrid, and to the Universidad de Granada for their patience and assistance. The University of Texas at Austin demonstrated the truth of their reputation for friendliness and efficiency during my stay there.

Finally, I would like to acknowledge the help with translation from the Russian given to me by Norman Stone and Don Thom, and from the Czech by George Brusa. I should also like to express my thanks to Christopher Sinclair-Stevenson and Clare Alexander of Hamish Hamilton, for their confidence in the project, and to Julian Evans who has saved me from many silly errors. I am also grateful to Alice Mayhew of Simon and Schuster. My research assistant, Wendy Baxter, has managed to impose some order out of the chaos of my working material, and I would like to thank Artemis Wheatcroft who has nagged me into a more orderly approach while organizing matters for herself and to my benefit. Finally, to my wife Janet, who has suffered more from this book than all my previous work, and who has had to put up with an absentee husband or one preoccupied while present. Yet she has also been able to read and comment on the material, and to advise me. I think she appreciates the extent of my gratitude.

To the reader

A FEW technical points should be noted. All the maps are orientated north–south, except where an azimuth is shown to indicate north. All the projections used are standard, except in a few cases where special projections have been adopted to obtain better coverage of an area within the page. Russia is a case in point, where the graticule lines have been shown to provide a point of fixed reference. In maps such as those dealing with the American colonies and Spanish America, the maps have been orientated to make an historical point. The American colonies were dependent not on the interior of North America but on Europe. They have been given an Atlantic perspective which also emphasises the linearity of the colonies. In the case of Spanish America, political and physical geography are at cross-purposes. From the point of view of a Spaniard or *criollo*, Spanish America is the band of territory shown on this map. Brazil was a vast irrelevancy. Roads and railways have been shown where they have a special relevance. Similarly, borders and boundaries are included only as necessary. Where, as in the case of Europe after the First World War, I wanted to emphasise the spread of opposition across the whole area, national borders have been deliberately omitted. In general, I have tried not to distort geographical fact unless it is essential to do so in making an historical or political point.

The literature on revolutions is enormous, and I have read as widely as I can. The select bibliography carries a warning label as it includes a number of books with a very obvious political bias, but which contain important information. I have selected those books which themselves lead the reader deeper into the literature of the subject. I have also tried to cite the sources for each quotation or point of factual information, again in the hope that the reader may want to move further into the subject. I have not attempted to explain the scholarly controversies which many of the events have spawned. I have followed my own path through them and leave others to judge whether I have gone astray. Where a source is oral information the source has been included in the acknowledgments, but many people have asked that their names should not be related to any piece of oral data and I have observed their wishes.

Place names have changed over time, and I have tried to follow a consistent but not a rigid policy. As a rule, I have used the form most commonly used at the time the map describes, or that which is most commonly used in the west. Hence, I have used Cawnpore rather than Kanpur, and Peking rather than Beijing. Where, as in the case of Vietnam, place and province names alter depending on which side you support, I have tried to strike a reasonable balance, or have omitted contentious information which is not essential.

The content and the approach of the maps is a matter of choice and judgment on my part. I would very much welcome readers' suggestions for additional maps, or comments on details of any errors or obscurities which the present maps contain.

Part 1:

'O liberté, O liberté ! que de crimes on commet en ton nom !'

('O Liberty, O Liberty, what crimes are committed in thy name!')

Mme Roland,
before her death on the guillotine, 1793

Part 2:

'A revolution is not a dinner party, or writing an essay, or painting a picture, or doing embroidery; it cannot be so refined, so leisurely and gentle, so temperate, kind, courteous, restrained and magnanimous. A revolution is an insurrection, an act of violence . . .'

Mao Tse Tung,
Report on an investigation of the
Peasant Movement in Hunan,
March 1927

Part 3:

'I do not carry innocence to the point of believing that appeals to reason or respect for human dignity can alter reality. For the Negro who works on a sugar plantation in Le Robert, there is only one solution: to fight. He will embark on this struggle and he will pursue it, not as the result of a Marxist or idealistic analysis but quite simply because he cannot conceive of life otherwise than in the form of a battle against exploitation, misery and hunger.'

Frantz Fanon

Part 4:

'Lächelnd scheidet der Tyran
Denn er weiss, nach seinem Tode
Wechselt Willkür nur die Hände
Und die Knechtschaft hat kein Ende.'

'The tyrant dies smiling
For he knows, after his death
Despotism will merely pass
Into other hands, and
slavery is endless.'

Heinrich Heine,
1797–1856

Part 1

THE WORLD TURNED UPSIDE DOWN

NORTH AMERICA 1765–75

The American Revolution: 'Shots that rang round the world'

THE moment of inception for the American revolution was the afternoon of Tuesday 30 January 1649, when at a little after two o'clock, the people of England cut off the head of their King, Charles I. It was in England and Scotland that the idea of revolution was born and reverenced, where injustice and oppression could be righted by a violent overthrow of the political system. Charles's son, James, did not end on the executioner's block as his father had done, but he too was pushed from his throne by his people, who thereafter described his flight as a Glorious Revolution. It was this tradition of violent resistance to authority which the settlers from Britain carried to the new lands across the Atlantic, to the colonies of America.

The world of these colonies was utterly unlike anything which Europe had created. No one would take all the risks implicit in the long journey across the ocean, and brave the dangers from the savage natives and wild animals which filled the New World, unless they had good reason to leave the Old World. Colonists were more ambitious, more religious, more turbulent, indeed given to excess in all things: they were adventurers, existing on the margin of whichever social stratum had produced them. The men and women who became rich in the colonies may have had the veneer of good manners and taste which followed London, Dublin and Edinburgh; but beneath the surface they were as rough and insubordinate as their social inferiors, and quite as ready to resort to their fists, a gun or the knife to settle an argument. If the veneer of civilization covered only part of American society, it also had a very restricted territorial extent. The part of the colonies which mirrored most closely the structures and values of the Old World was the thin coastal strip from Georgia to New England. Here were concentrated the cities and the bulk of the population, and, inevitably, both economic and political power. All the lines of communication ran along the line of the coast; up-country, in the mountains and on the borders of Indian lands, the cities and Euro-

pean values of the leaders of Boston, New York, Philadelphia and Charleston were a world away, not the short span of miles that they seemed on a map.

There were thirteen colonies which were eventually to form the United States of America. In reality, all that united them was hostility to Britain. Some colonies were more antagonistic to the mother country than others, and skilful ministers in London would seek to set one colony against another on the principle of divide and rule. The real centres of opposition were located in the commercial classes of New England, Virginia and Pennsylvania which opposed British attempts to regulate trade with the colonies for the benefit of British merchants. The supreme success of the opposition in America was to persuade sufficient of their fellow countrymen that British rule in North America posed a dire threat to them.

Americans had developed a tradition of righting wrongs by violent means. In the hill country of the Carolinas, bands known as 'regulators' established a rough and ready system of justice when the authorities on the coast failed to respond to their demands for redress of grievances. In the cities, riot – a fine old British tradition – was systematized for political purposes. It is not surprising that the centres of violent unrest before the outbreak of the revolution should feature prominently in its early days. The ingredients for a violent overthrow, a renewal of the tradition of 1649 and 1688, were all present in the colonies. There was an articulate and determined group willing to accept a revolution in fulfilment of their ends. There were the channels of influence and propaganda which allowed them to disseminate their views throughout the colonies, as the circulation and readership of radical pamphlets and newspapers reveals. There were arms and equipment and a sufficient degree of training in the colonial militia to provide the genesis of an armed force. And there were causes in plenty, sparks to ignite the powder, provided by an insensitive and largely inept government too far away to control the situation even if they had

had the capacity to do so. The events of the spring of 1775 surprised no one.

The British army had garrisoned the colonies, partly to protect them from an external threat – as the French colonies in Canada had been – and partly for internal political control. By the mid-1760s the threat from the French had ended with their expulsion from Canada, but the fear of the Indians remained. The French had used Indian allies during the Seven Years War (1759–63), and they realised that the colonies provided easy pickings. In 1763 the Ottawa tribe under Chief Pontiac ravaged the frontier west of Niagara; in 1774 the Shawnee rose on the borders of Virginia and Kentucky. While the comfortable citizens of Boston and New York might seem far distant from the night terrors and scalping raids to the north and west, fear was real and pervasive.

New Yorkers remembered how in 1753, Chief Hendrick of the Mohawk had stood before the governor and said: 'Brother, by and by you'll expect to see the Nations (the Six Nations of the Iroquois) down here (in New York City) . . .'[1] The image of sudden death, of mutilation and torture, was repeated in newspapers, and in pamphlets and broadsheets. It gave point to the theory of a people in arms, defending themselves against a largely unseen enemy, a point made more strongly by the utter failure of the British garrison to protect the colonies from these incursions. The purpose of these troops came increasingly to be seen as the repression of liberty rather than protection.

The doctrine of self-help was born out of need.

Continued on page 18

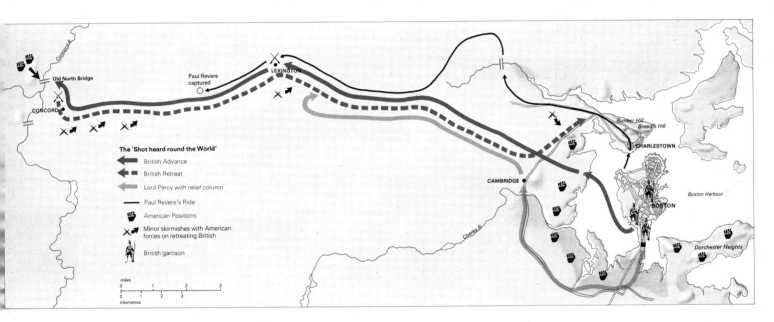

The 'Shot heard round the World'

- ← British Advance
- ← - - British Retreat
- ← Lord Percy with relief column
- —— Paul Revere's Ride
- ✊ American Positions
- ✗↗ Minor skirmishes with American forces on retreating British
- 🧍 British garrison

miles 0 1 2 3
kilometres 0 1 2 3

The British commander, General Gage, was hamstrung by the need to confirm his orders with London: by the time he received an answer the situation had changed. His principle, outlined in September 1774, was: 'To avoid any bloody Crisis as long as possible unless forced into it by the rebels themselves'.[2] His tactic was to launch surprise patrols to capture arms and supplies – with some success. What he wanted to achieve was a carefully prepared coup. At the time the leading revolutionaries were all in the Boston area: had he acted then, the policy would have succeeded. But they soon realized their danger and withdrew to Concord.

The letter from the government ordering the seizure of the Massachusetts provincial congress was dated 27 January; it arrived in Boston on 14 April. Gage acted on 19 April, trying as far as possible to achieve surprise. About 700 grenadiers and light infantry were sent secretly by sea to Somerville, in the hope that the Americans were watching the usual land route over the fortified Boston Neck. But their departure was observed, and messengers were sent to alert the colonial militia – among them Paul Revere. The military equipment at Concord was taken away and the leaders prudently removed themselves. To buy time, the militia were ordered to oppose the advancing British at Lexington. A skirmish took place, with dead on both sides, and

the British force advanced on Concord, found nothing and retired. By now the whole countryside was roused against them, and they retreated under a steady hail of sniper fire. A relief column with artillery met them at Lexington, and they made a somewhat undignified retreat back into Boston. The Americans occupied the commanding heights above Boston, having suffered only 93 casualties to 273 British losses. Two months later, with General Gage having received reinforcements, the British again attempted a stroke to break the Americans' will. The battle of Bunker's Hill (17 June 1775) achieved the reverse: although the position was taken, at the cost of huge British casualties – over a thousand lost from an attacking force of 2200, the colonial militia demonstrated that they could stand against regulars, at least behind field fortifications. In March 1776 the British evacuated Boston and sailed off to Halifax, Nova Scotia. Four months later, on 4 July, the colonies made their formal Declaration of Independence.

The Americans benefited from the most priceless gift to any revolutionaries: operating at long range from the political centre of their enemies – what a soldier would term 'interior lines'. They also rapidly came to dominate in the propaganda war, both internally and outside the country.

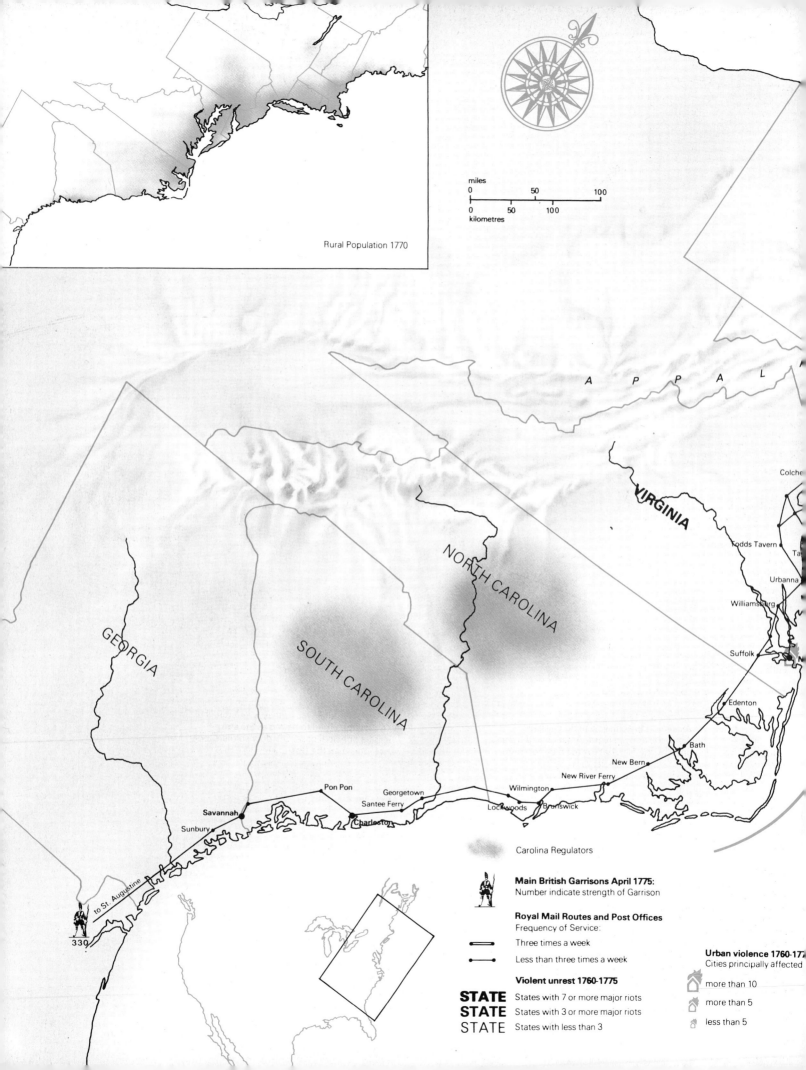

Rural Population 1770

miles
0   50   100
0   50   100
kilometres

APPAL

VIRGINIA

Colche

Todds Tavern   Ta

Urbanna

Williamsburg

Suffolk

NORTH CAROLINA

SOUTH CAROLINA

GEORGIA

Edenton

Bath

New Bern
New River Ferry
Wilmington
Pon Pon   Lockwoods   Brunswick
            Georgetown
            Santee Ferry
Savannah
Sunbury   Charleston

to St. Augustine

330

Carolina Regulators

Main British Garrisons April 1775:
Number indicate strength of Garrison

Royal Mail Routes and Post Offices
Frequency of Service:

────── Three times a week

●────● Less than three times a week

Violent unrest 1760-1775

STATE States with 7 or more major riots

STATE States with 3 or more major riots

STATE States with less than 3

Urban violence 1760-177
Cities principally affected

🏠 more than 10

🏠 more than 5

🏠 less than 5

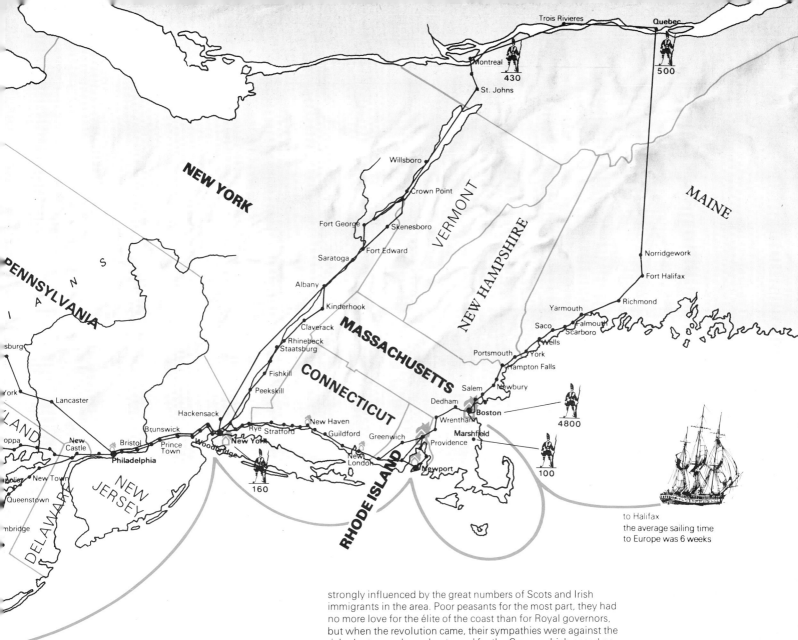

to Halifax
the average sailing time
to Europe was 6 weeks

'America' in 1775 was only the eastern strip of the continent, and looked to Europe rather than inland. So the colonies have been given an Atlantic orientation; communication with Britain by sea was generally routed to Halifax before undertaking the long voyage across the ocean. Average sailing times were about six weeks, slower for a number of ships travelling together, and faster for a single vessel aiming to achieve a rapid passage. Communications between the army in North America and home were further handicapped by the fact that the main depot for the army in North America was at Cork in Ireland, while political decisions would be made in London. At several points during the revolution, the failure to achieve a speedy decision and to communicate it to the commander in Boston gave the initiative to the Americans.

Each of the colonies had a different character, determined by its social make-up and the conditions of its foundation. In revolutionary terms, the most coherent opposition was to be found in the cities, and in New England. In other states, loyalism to the Crown was more pronounced, particularly in rural areas of the southern colonies, in Maryland, Virginia, the Carolinas, and in the areas of New York and New Jersey along the Potomac. But 'loyalism' was a less coherent force than 'revolution', and it depended for its effectiveness on a British army in the field. Where it was most important was in raising a number of detachments of irregular horse, of men who knew the country and had the mobility lacking in the British army, which had scant cavalry. It is also notable that not all the violent incidents shown on this map should be equated with opposition to the Crown. The 'regulator' movement in the Carolinas was strongly influenced by the great numbers of Scots and Irish immigrants in the area. Poor peasants for the most part, they had no more love for the élite of the coast than for Royal governors, but when the revolution came, their sympathies were against the rich planters and merchants, and for the Crown which posed no threat to them.

During the war with the French and Indians, the British army had established garrisons through most of the frontier area; thereafter, they began to concentrate their forces in the populated areas. The consequence was increasing friction between the colonists and the 'lobsters', as they referred to the Redcoats. This latent hostility turned to hatred as the army settled upon Boston as its principal base. Off-duty soldiers took on work at lower wage rates than the Bostonians, and the constant reiteration of military ceremonial — parades, patrols — made their presence all the more obvious. The final concentration of British forces in Boston took place in September 1774 when General Gage withdrew his garrisons from New York, New Jersey, Philadelphia, Halifax and Newfoundland. Together with a large naval squadron under Admiral Graves, Boston became a garrison town. But despite the threat posed by British armed might, the demonstration of power only served to rally waverers to the revolutionary cause, as they saw all the grim warnings about oppressive power being enacted before their eyes.

All the cities were linked by an effective system of post roads and communications following the easy land route along the coastline. Inland, and especially as the land rose towards the Appalachians, communications were much more haphazard. But news and information could be carried rapidly between the principal centres of population, and most particularly in the revolutionary heartland, where a service operated three times a week. In addition, the post roads could be used by other riders to spread the news or carry information and rumour.

Troops and resources from Britain were never sufficient, so each state raised its own militia, on the British model of a part-time yeomanry. It was formed and equipped out of provincial taxes, and is the most notable example of the colonists' passion for corporate activity. Committees, clubs, social and political organizations, all provided channels of communication and of primary organization. In times of peace, these ad-hoc bodies fulfilled a social function, providing mutual support, and it is striking that the areas where this sense of practical community was strongest – in Massachusetts, and New England generally – were also those where the armed revolution took hold most strongly. In the language of later revolutionary writers, the town meeting, the political club, the militia, even the ladies' quilting bee, became a *focus* through which the issues of the revolution could

be communicated, and propaganda could find an audience. In a society where literacy was limited, and the means of communication restricted by distance, the importance of oral communication and face-to-face contact was paramount. The idea of the revolution was spread by preachers in their pulpits, by newspapers and pamphlets read to the illiterate in taverns, and by rumour.

The effects of this communalism, especially when coupled with a ready resort to violence, made opposition to the prevailing prejudices difficult and dangerous. For every firebrand committed to the principles of the revolution, there were many half-hearted followers. But the majority in many regions which had no love for the revolution and its adherents kept

Continued on page 20

All the symbols of British tyranny in North America: gallows, tea, and the loyalist or excise-man tarred and feathered by 'patriots'. They have hung him on his own gallows, cut him down and are forcing him to drink the tea all Americans shunned. The '45' on the hat refers to No. 45, *The North Briton*, emblem of the British resistance to Royal autocracy. There were close links between British and American radicals

Spreading the news

John Adams, one of the architects of the American Revolution, wrote later to Thomas Jefferson with his view of the Revolution:

'What do we mean by the revolution? The war, that was no part of the revolution. It was only the effect and consequence of it. The revolution was in the Minds of the People, and this was effected from 1760 to 1775 in the course of fifteen years, before a drop of blood was shed at Lexington.'[5]

The coverage of the colonies by the press was remarkable, as was the complex set of links with opposition figures in Britain. Frequently the colonists' interpretation of events was current in London before the government was even informed as to what had taken place: merchants in Virginia and Boston communicated directly with London, Liverpool and Bristol. Similarly, the colonists were quickly made aware of resistance to the 'tyranny' of the Crown towards its subjects in Britain. Each radical printing press, and every radical newspaper – such as the *Pennsylvania Journal* – had a wide audience. Thus when the news of Lexington and Concord was transmitted down the post roads, with the radicals' interpretation of the events, it was repeated and magnified down the line. So too were rumours of British atrocities towards those who had fallen into their hands: there were stories of 'savage Barbarity exercised upon the bodies of our unfortunate Brethren who fell. . . . Not contented with shooting down the unarmed, aged and infirm, they disregarded the Cries of the wounded, killing them without Mercy, and mangling their Bodies in the most shocking manner.'[6] It was utterly untrue, but it served its purpose, and hardened revolutionary purpose in New York, Pennsylvania, Virginia and the southern states.

Without the channels of information and propaganda, without the skill of the radical pamphleteers and journalists (far superior to those whom the Crown patronized), it would have been virtually impossible to achieve a co-ordinated response to British actions, and to effect the change in the Minds of the People to which John Adams refers.

The Thirteen Colonies which formed the United States of America, in order of accession:
Delaware
Pennsylvania
New Jersey
Georgia
Connecticut
Massachusetts
Maryland
South Carolina
New Hampshire
Virginia

New York
North Carolina
Rhode Island
(Vermont achieved statehood in 1791, while Maine, included in these maps, was a district of Massachusetts and the subject of many border disputes with Canada, until finally admitted to the Union in 1820)

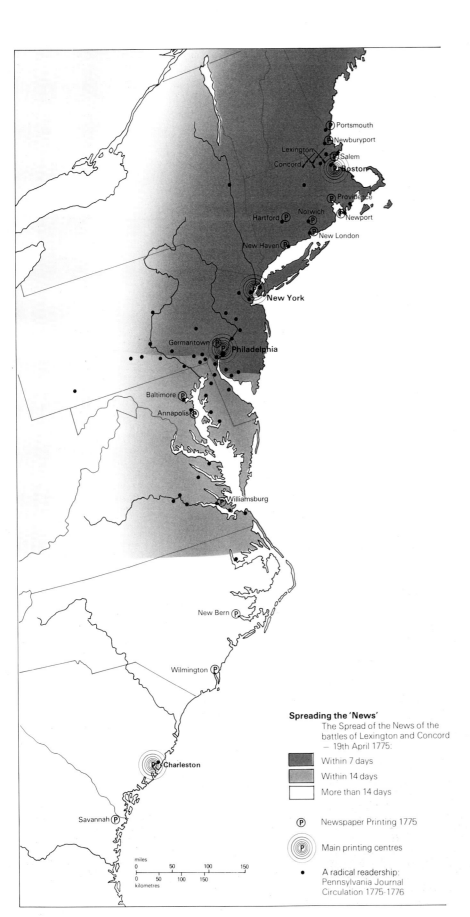

Portsmouth
Newburyport
Lexington
Concord
Salem
Boston
Providence
Hartford
Norwich
Newport
New London
New Haven
New York
Germantown
Philadelphia
Baltimore
Annapolis
Williamsburg
New Bern
Wilmington
Charleston
Savannah

Spreading the 'News'

The Spread of the News of the battles of Lexington and Concord – 19th April 1775:

Within 7 days

Within 14 days

More than 14 days

(P) Newspaper Printing 1775

(P) Main printing centres

• A radical readership: Pennsylvania Journal Circulation 1775-1776

miles
0   50   100   150
0   50   100   150
kilometres

The Timetable of Revolution

1700–60

Massive increase in population, mostly by immigration, to 1·5 million. Similar increase in commerce: exports and imports totalled £3.1 million annually (1761–70)

1754–9

Conflict with French on borders of Canada led to all-out war. War ended by Peace of Paris 1763, with massive increase in British domain in Canada.

1763–5

New British Prime Minister Grenville determined to tighten control of colonies and extract full tax yield. Range of new duties, including (1765) extension of British requirement for all documents, including newspapers and pamphlets, to pay tax.

1765–7

Stamp Act provoked violent response in America, linked with agitation in Britain led by John Wilkes. New Prime Minister Rockingham repealed act, but Parliament restated legal right to tax colonies.

1767–73

Wide range of import duties imposed on colonial trade. Repeated violent resistance plus widespread evasion forced abolition of all duties save 'symbolic' duty on tea. Continuing expansion of anti-Government associations, like the Sons of Liberty. Pamphlet war against British 'tyranny', like so-called Boston 'Massacre', Jan–March 1770, when troops fired on mob.

1773–4

Tea Act (May 1773) passed to establish monopoly of tea trade for East India Company, 16 Dec 1773. Party of Bostonians 'disguised' as Indians emptied cargo of 'monopoly' tea into harbour. Culmination of violent anti-excise attacks: excise vessel *Gaspee* burnt, Rhode Island 1772. Government riposted by suspending provincial assembly, strengthening garrison, and closing Boston Port to trade. Created unity among warring mob factions in town. Concerted action among merchants and landholders, culminating in first Continental Congress in Philadelphia, Sept–Oct 1774.

1774–5

Massachusetts, the focal point: almost whole of British army in America being concentrated in Boston. First Massachusetts Congress held. Established body of 'minutemen', ready to serve at a minute's notice. Elected Committee of Safety and voted supplies for army of 15,000. British acted to seize cannon and warlike stores. General Gage ordered secret pre-emptive strike on Concord, and supposed arms dumps. Colonial minutemen resisted British advance at Lexington and Concord, and militia and civilians harried British forces returning to Boston.

silent through self-interest. Loyalism to King and the British connection was a risky business. The targets for the communal violence were predominantly the hate-figures of any society – the excise men and tax gatherers, the press gangs, absentee landlords – but armed resistance to them was given the dignity of the defence of liberty. In 1774 the Continental Congress of the colonists declared a total embargo on trade with Britain, and set up a committee in every 'county, city, and town' to serve notice on all opponents 'that all foes to the rights of British-America may be publicly known and universally contumned as the enemies of American liberty. . . .'

But to mount an embargo, tar and feather a loyalist, and tip tea into Boston harbour (the famous Boston Tea Party), were acts of bravado, taunts to authority only, and did nothing much towards the actual seizure of power. British authority was based on a still substantial army-in-residence, although much less so than it had been during the war with France. It was well-officered, and its morale was good. Moreover, the effect of the stream of provocative acts from the revolutionaries in Boston had resulted in a concentration of British forces in Boston as a punishment levied on the inhabitants. This provided more ammunition for the Crown's opponents, since the soldiers had a bad reputation in Boston, but it rendered any armed uprising infinitely more perilous. There can be little doubt that the leaders of the revolutionary party were willing to undertake a rebellion; but most of their possible adherents required a sense of right and justice in their cause to take up arms. The tenor of the propaganda for a decade had been popular

rights against an intrusive Royal authority, a campaign which found its echoes in Britain and which harked back to the Civil War of the seventeenth century. Meetings, pamphlets, newspapers, caricatures, and scurrilous rumours were all used to foment the impression that the Royal authorities were determined to enslave the colonists. When the Governor of Massachusetts, Thomas Gage, ordered the Bostonians to disarm in June 1775, the following appeared in the *Pennsylvania Evening Post*: 'To the vilest Tool of the most profligate and tyrannical Administration that ever disgraced a Court . . . are you not ashamed to throw out such an insult upon human understanding, as to bid the people disarm themselves till you and your butchers murder and plunder them at pleasure . . . ?' The American propagandists presented the core issue as they saw it:

'We have seen the humble Petitions of these Colonies to the King of Great Britain repeatedly rejected with Disdain. For the Prayer of Peace he has tendered the sword – for Liberty, chains; for Safety, Death! He has licenced the Instruments of his hostile Oppressions to rob us of our Property, to burn our Houses and to spill our Blood. He has invited every barbarous Nation [the Indian menace again] whom he could hope to influence to assist him in prosecuting those inhuman Purposes. Loyalty to him is *now* Treason to our Country.'[3]

The revolutionaries played a single tune: Now was the time, death and disaster would befall all who fell back. There was no way forward but armed struggle. As Tom Paine declared in *Common Sense*: 'Reconciliation is now a fallacious dream.'[4]

In the name of liberty

NO country in Europe contains within its borders as many contrasts in landscape and terrain as France. It comprises Atlantic France and Mediterranean France, the France of the sandy Camargue and arid *maquis*, of the lush rolling fields of Normandy, the France of ravines, marshland, mountains, open plains. Politically, it has meant throughout history that France has been a mosaic of different habits, attitudes, and aspirations. The rulers of the nation centred in Paris, whether monarchs or republicans, have always fought against this tendency. So there was not one but many French Revolutions, each the product of local circumstances as well as national issues. Most attention is generally focused on the Revolution in Paris. The assumption is made that the horrors of Paris, the elation of the revolutionaries who tore down the Bastille, or the grim satisfaction of those who watched the guillotine at work, were representative of the nation as a whole. Yet there were parts of France not more than a few days' journey from Paris where there were no executions, no Terror, no revolutionary transformation of life at all. Elsewhere, as in Lyon and the South, the revolution was waged with a ferocity that often overtook Paris.

Of the 26 million French men and women in the 1780s all but a fifth lived outside the towns and cities; and in the towns many of the inhabitants were first-generation immigrants from the countryside. The oppressive nature of the Ancien Régime was seen with full force only in the countryside, where the extent of feudal privileges enjoyed by the nobility and the clergy was felt, rightly or wrongly, to be increasing. In a world where prices were rising, free peasant labour or the nobles' freedom from taxation were increasingly valuable, and many nobles sold their rights over their peasantry to businessmen who then exploited these rights to the full as a commercial proposition. Taxes on basic items, such as salt, caused widespread resentment in those regions where the tax was highest. Rural discontent expressed itself, as it always had, in riot, usually of limited extent and duration and restricted to specific grievances. The price and shortage of bread in the period immediately before the outbreak of the revolution produced numerous violent outbursts. However, external circumstances provided a focus for discontent and brought it to bear on the centres of power in the court at Versailles. The French support for the United States had been immensely costly, quite beyond the capacity of the economic and taxation system, and in an attempt to achieve some form of financial stability, the King, Louis XVI, was forced to summon an assembly of 'notables' (the nobles, clergy and leading officials) to demonstrate public support for a wide range of financial expedients. This limited exercise in public participation of November 1788 led directly to the summoning of the elected body known as the Estates General, last called together in 1614. It was the incapacity of the government to operate successfully within the traditional resources allocated to it which allowed the intervention of a popular element: the revolution stemmed directly from institutional failure.

The political system was capable of absorbing widespread social unrest, even civil war, so long as it did not reveal itself to be both vulnerable and fallible. The intrusion of public opinion in 1788 and 1789 could not be restricted to the issues which the government laid down for discussion.

Much more was expected of the Estates General than the narrow financial proposals advanced by the government. The delegates came primed with the notions of freedom and liberty, with the doctrines of Rousseau which had been discussed in the flood of pamphlets emanating from Paris and the other great cities. Attempts to muzzle the Estates, such as the suggestion from the Parisian lawyers (*parlement*) that the precedents of 1614 should be followed to the letter and the Estates should be split into three sections – Nobles, Clergy and The Rest – were thrust aside. The Estates met on 5 May 1789; by 17 June, the Third Estate, comprising all those who were not elected by the nobles or the clergy, had declared themselves to be a National Assembly. Three days later, barred from meeting by Royal command (the King did not like the turn events had taken), they came together in the Tennis Court of the palace, and there took the famous Tennis Court Oath: that they would remain in session until an acceptable constitution was granted. To the King's attempts to curb them, they retorted in the words of the Comte de Mirabeau, the inspiration behind the assembly, 'We are here by the will of the people and . . . we shall not stir from our seats unless by force, at the point of a bayonet'.[1]

Force was not an option which the Crown could invoke, for behind the delegates at Versailles lay the turbulent masses of Paris only a dozen miles away. When the King, early in July 1789, ordered a concentration of troops around Paris, he found that many of the soldiers were also infected by the same seditious sentiments which fired the delegates to the National Assembly.

Nevertheless the threat of military intervention prompted an astonishingly vigorous response in Paris. The working-class areas of the south and south-east of the city organized their populations for resistance. Gun shops were looted, and arms of all sorts collected at strategic points; clashes with troops in the streets of Paris became increasingly frequent. The 'respectable elements' of Paris responded with equal radical vigour: an independent council for the government and defence of Paris was established in the Hôtel de Ville, and a body of militia – the National Guard – organized. Throughout the Revolution, as at its outset in Paris, the two elements – the power of the people in the streets, and the political leadership – existed in parallel, though not always in harmony. Sometimes the street dictated the pattern of events, sometimes the leadership; but a barometer of revolutionary fervour gradually emerged. Most 'revolutionary' were the *sans-culottes* of Paris (their name, proudly borne, denoting that they did not wear the knee-breeches of the well-to-do), and the politicians who espoused their cause, to be closely followed by the urban working-class revolutionaries of the great provincial cities. Next came the broad spread of provincial opinion represented in the National Assembly by the delegates from the regions of France. Last came the feeling of the countryside which looked to the revolution merely for the redress of grievances – for the ending of their feudal obligations, and for a redistribution of land. For the peasants, the revolution, like all external interventions in their lives, was an alien force. It was from the peasants of the west and the south that the armies of counter-revolution were to be formed. From the first days, however much the revolutionary leaders might preach that they 'represented the nation' they were aware that they were an isolated minority, and that their revolution was threatened from all sides. This was no illusion: the cry 'the country in danger', used to justify the most barbarous excesses, was true beyond question, as the history of later decades was to prove.

The course of the revolution moved forward in spurts, the famous *journées*, days of mass action in the streets. Of these the most symbolically important was the destruction of the Bastille fortress on 14 July 1789, the culmination of weeks of violent outbursts. It marked more than anything else that the dynamic of the revolution lay with the actors rather than the talkers. The news of the assault on the Bastille spread rapidly through France, where it served to catalyze an urban revolution which was already under way. The news arrived at Dijon, for example, on 17 July, and the people surged into the streets seizing the armouries, the nobles and the clergy. At Montauban, Lyon, Barry and Laval, and in many other towns they took control of the town council, fearing a Royal coup against the revolution. Throughout the whole of France a great wave of uncertainty gripped town and country alike. Rumour ruled everywhere, linking fears of hunger from the growing grain shortage with fears of reaction from the established orders. As early as 20 May, a pamphlet published at Orléans had declared: 'The princes, linked in a common bond with the nobility, the clergy and all the *parlements* . . . have bought up all the grain in the kingdom; their abominable intentions are to prevent the meeting of the Estates General by spreading famine through France and to make part of the people die of hunger . . .'[2] In the countryside, there were rumours that brigands and beggars, the outcasts of society, had been suborned by the hated nobles and clergy to ravage the land: everywhere communities responded by acting on their own initiative. This reaction, known

The Fear and the Terror

The panic which swept France in July and August 1789, known as the Great Fear, and the Reign of Terror of 1793–4 are at two poles of political expression: the first, an anarchic, undirected popular spasm, the second, the deliberate and directed exercise of revolutionary power, to exterminate the enemies of the French Republic. But both share common characteristics. Except in Paris, the Terror was primarily – like the Fear – the product of local circumstances. The level of executions was highest in those areas where the threat was greatest. In the west, the area known as the Vendée, where civil war raged, most executions took place in the *départements* of Loire Inférieure, Vendée, and Maine et Loire. Similarly, the *départements* of Gard, Bouches du Rhône, Var and Vaucluse, were nests of counter-Revolutionary activity. As in so much else, Lyon led the way in a frenzy of revolutionary justice, led by the *représentant en mission*, of the Committee of Public Safety in Paris, Joseph Fouché, who had the prisoners mown down by cannon fire when the guillotine proved too slow: in the Vendée at Nantes a similar problem was resolved by mass drownings of the unfortunate victims. On the frontiers to the north, many were killed for supposed collaboration with external enemies. But the overall effect was patchy, depending on the efficiency and fanaticism of the *représentant*, the zeal of the local revolutionaries, and the availability of victims: in the south, the land of the blood feud, old scores were frequently paid off in the name of revolutionary justice. The Great Fear produced some acts of violence against people, but mostly against property, in particular, burning the manorial documents which recorded the feudal duties a peasant owed his master. There is also a pattern which shows up clearly but is difficult to explain, between the two sets of events. The lines of the Fear and the incidence of the Terror observe certain common paths, and most interestingly, both avoid that area of central France south of Paris, the peaceable zone of Loiret, Yonne, Cher, Aube, Loir et Cher. Figures show that many of the victims of the Terror from these areas were taken before the tribunals in Paris, and met their end on the guillotine there, but the overall numbers are very low.

The Terror represented in the most dramatic way the intrusion of Paris into the provinces. Perhaps more pervasive in their effects were the *levée en masse*, of 1793, creating a popular army for the defence of the nation by universal conscription, and the decrees against the Church, and (ultimately) in 1794 against Christianity itself. Other intrusions, such as the new revolutionary calendar of October 1793, which replaced the old system with one based on the Revolution and reason – months named after their climatic conditions, a week ten days long – was met with traditional Gallic disregard in much of France.

The revolution failed to meet the demands of the countryside, lightening their burdens in name only – the 'abolition' of feudal duties – but imposing many new ones. The arbitrariness of the Terror and the insane blood-fury of the leaders in Paris turned the provinces away from the revolution. It was the provincial deputies to the Convention (the sovereign legislature erected in the emergency of September 1792) who made possible the end of the Terror by voting down Robespierre and the extremists in July 1794.

Continued on page 25

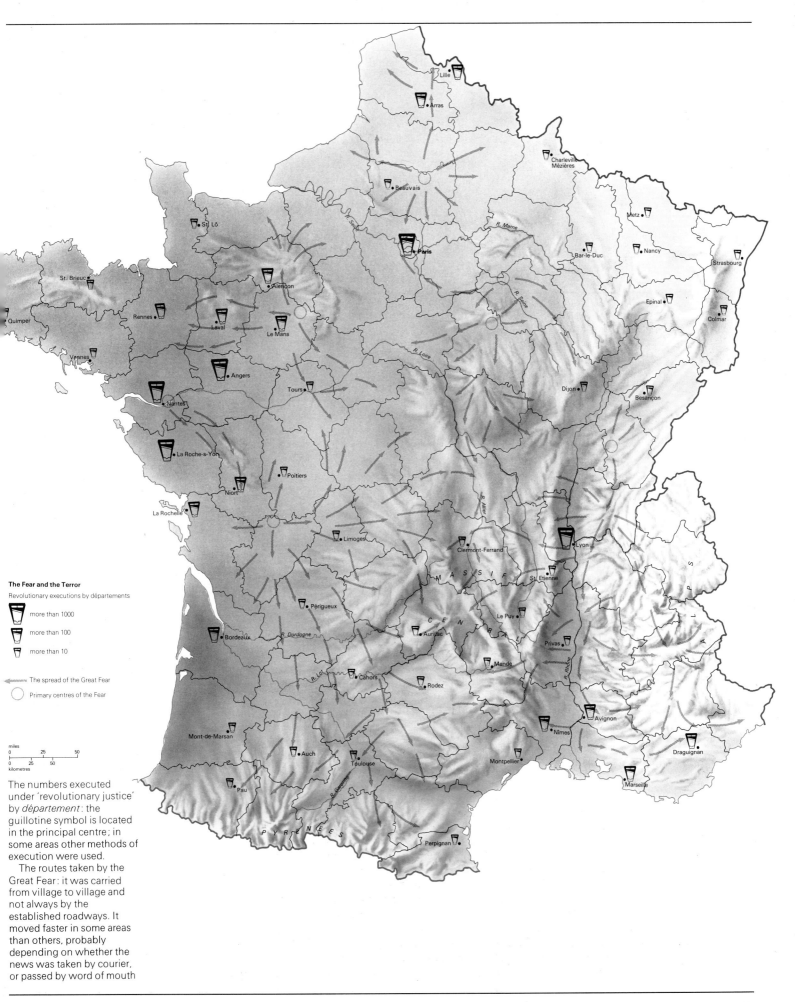

The Fear and the Terror

Revolutionary executions by départements

- more than 1000
- more than 100
- more than 10

→ The spread of the Great Fear

○ Primary centres of the Fear

miles
0   25   50

kilometres
0   25   50

The numbers executed under 'revolutionary justice' by *département*: the guillotine symbol is located in the principal centre; in some areas other methods of execution were used.

The routes taken by the Great Fear: it was carried from village to village and not always by the established roadways. It moved faster in some areas than others, probably depending on whether the news was taken by courier, or passed by word of mouth

Lille
Arras
Charleville-Mézières
Beauvais
Metz
Bar-le-Duc
Nancy
St. Lô
Paris
Strasbourg
St. Brieuc
Alençon
Epinal
Colmar
Quimper
Rennes
Laval
Le Mans
Dijon
Besançon
Vannes
Angers
Tours
R. Loire
Nantes
La Roche-s-Yon
Poitiers
Limoges
Clermont-Ferrand
Lyon
Niort
R. Allier
St. Etienne
La Rochelle
MASSIF
Le Puy
Périgueux
CENTRAL
Aurillac
Privas
R. Dordogne
Mende
Bordeaux
R. Lot
Cahors
Rodez
R. Rhône
Avignon
Mont-de-Marsan
Nîmes
Draguignan
Auch
Toulouse
Montpellier
Marseille
Pau
R. Garonne
PYRÉNÉES
Perpignan

14 July 1789: the crowds
surge into the Bastille,
carrying with them the
cannon to batter down its
gates

collectively as the Great Fear, raced through much of France, reaching even into the recesses of the Massif Central. But it was not a unified mass-movement. Each locality reacted to an immediate perceived threat: in some zones, the revolutionaries of the cities – Lyon, Marseille – pushed out into the countryside and provincial towns to spread the gospel of the Parisian revolution. They found many converts, but usually only those already predisposed towards the revolution. The bulk of the population remained fearful and apathetic.

In the first year of the revolution many of the more moderate reforms were achieved. France became a monarchy with a constitution, the French Catholic Church officially severed its links with Rome, hereditary titles were declared void, and feudal rights renounced. Nor was there any inevitability that it would move further. At every stage when the king seemed to embrace the cause of the revolution for public consumption, he attracted wild support; at every stage he succeeded in dispelling this latent good will. More and more he came to be equated with France's foreign enemies, an impression fostered by unwise liasons with *émigrés* and the constant reminder of the foreign links of his abhorred wife, the Austrian Marie-Antoinette. But to the ardent revolutionaries who made up the Paris *sections* (as the districts of the capital were now described), and the members of the Cordeliers Club and the Jacobin Club, stagnation spelt the end of their hopes. 'Peace will set us back,' declared Madame Roland, an archetype of the revolutionary, 'we can be regenerated by blood alone.' Terrified of the dangers within and without France, they pressed for continuing revolution. In March 1792 war was declared against Austria and Prussia, but the many failures in the war pointed to treason at all levels in the army and society at large. As the foreign armies came closer, the sense of emergency generated hysteria: on 17 August a vast mob, many from the revolutionary *sections* located in the former Faubourgs St. Marcel and St. Antoine, together with the armed contingents from the provinces which had arrived to defend Paris, stormed the palace of the Tuileries. The royal residence in Paris was felt to be a nest of traitors and Austrian sympathizers, and the 20,000 enraged citizens, after a short battle, massacred over 500 of the defending Swiss guard. This mass bloodletting, where the bodies were mutilated in a bestial fashion, was the first frenzied slaughter of the revolution; within three weeks, from 2–7 September, worse was to follow. The prisons of Paris were invaded, and the supposed enemies of the state found inside, cut down or tortured to death. The fury of the attackers, the perverted glee which they took in the suffering of their victims, produced a sense of outrage. But from that point, the mass shedding of blood and the antecedents of the Terror of 1793–4 may be dated.

The war emergency had placed the conduct of affairs in the hands of radical revolutionaries, who were dedicated to a centralized and unified revolutionary state. In this, party labels – whether they were called Girondins, Dantonists, Robespierrists, Hebertists – mattered little. All believed that the more that resistance was shown, the more instruments of terror should be used to enforce compliance. (In the end the Terror turned on its creators, becoming the instrument of their own jealousy, fear and powerlust.) The incidence of executions during the reign of Terror corresponds in the main to where the revolution was felt to be most endangered. In the west, war was being waged in the Vendée against an overt peasant and royalist rebellion; on the northern frontier, executions of supposed sympathizers with the Prussians and Austrians were numerous. But much the most interesting pattern, other than Paris itself, was in the south, where the revolution was an excuse to pay off old scores. Near Nîmes, where there was a sizeable Protestant minority, religious prejudice against the Catholic majority made many Protestants fervent advocates and beneficiaries of the revolutionary cause. As the cause of the revolution waned in 1795, they were among the early victims of a counter-terror which ravaged the south. Paris, however, remained the main theatre of the revolution. There the king (21 January 1793) and later his wife (16 October 1793) were guillotined, to be followed by thousands of others – former nobles and clerics, fallen revolutionary idols, and, in numerical terms the huge majority, the humble and poor. The very theatricality of the Parisian revolution, the constant pressure from below of the articulate *sans-culottes*, allowed those leaders – pre-eminently the 'incorruptible' Maximilian Robespierre, the architect of the Terror – to mistake the cheers of the gallery for the authentic voice of the French people. Nowhere was this more strongly seen than in the campaign against Christianity, which, in the end, was to bring the advance of radical revolution to a halt and to put it into reverse.

The clerical hierarchy had been traditionally unpopular in France, and the abuses of the church were a scandal. But there was little mass feeling against religion *per se*, and earlier attempts to bring the church to heel, through making them agents of the state, had provoked unrest in the more traditional regions. For Robespierre, the Church, or rather, the Christian God, represented the last bastion of the old order. In this he was right, for the Church was the only effective representative of authority in the rural communities, and a seedbed for counter-revolution. Having failed to manipulate the faithful, he decided to abolish their faith, and replace it with a more truly rational and revolutionary creed, that of the the Supreme Being. This bizarre mish-mash of the beliefs of the Age of Reason, to be enforced by the instruments of the Terror, the Revolutionary Tribunals,

Continued on page 29

Paris in the Revolution

This map is based on the first-ever 'bird's eye' view of Paris commissioned by the Controller of Finances, Turgot, in 1774. The city is surrounded by a ring of customs posts linked by a ten-foot wall, erected in 1785 with the aim of increasing tax revenue on goods entering and leaving the capital. Inside it were suburbs formerly outside Paris, the *faubourgs*, Saint-Victor, Saint-Marcel, Saint-Jacques, and Saint-Germain to the south, Saint-Antoine to the east, and Saint-Martin and Saint-Denis to the north. By 1789, the customs barrier was yielding over 40% of the national customs duties: it was much hated by Parisians. The population enclosed by this boundary was in excess of 600,000, a number growing all the time as peasants crowded into the city hoping to escape from the rigours of rural life. The newcomers tended to concentrate in the working-class *faubourgs* of the south and south-east: of those who were later to be accorded the title of 'conqueror of the Bastille' over 60% were first-generation Parisians, and most of them gave addresses in the *faubourg* Saint-Antoine. The character and attitude as well as the class make-up varied from area to area of Paris. The engine room of the revolution was the districts on the southern outskirts, Saint-Marcel, Saint-Victor and Saint-Antoine; those which eventually were to turn the tide against the excesses of the revolution were to be found on the Right Bank of the Seine, in the *faubourg* Saint-Honoré and to the north. But the revolutionary zeal of the *sans-culottes* dominated all the *sections* (as the new organization of the city was termed) while the revolution was at its zenith and unity was preserved. The popular will of the *sections* was expressed by representatives in the Revolutionary Commune, which governed Paris, or by mob rule in the streets. All the stages of the revolution, from rioting against the customs barriers and the troops in early July 1789, the storming of the Bastille on 14 July, the march of the people to Versailles in October 1789,

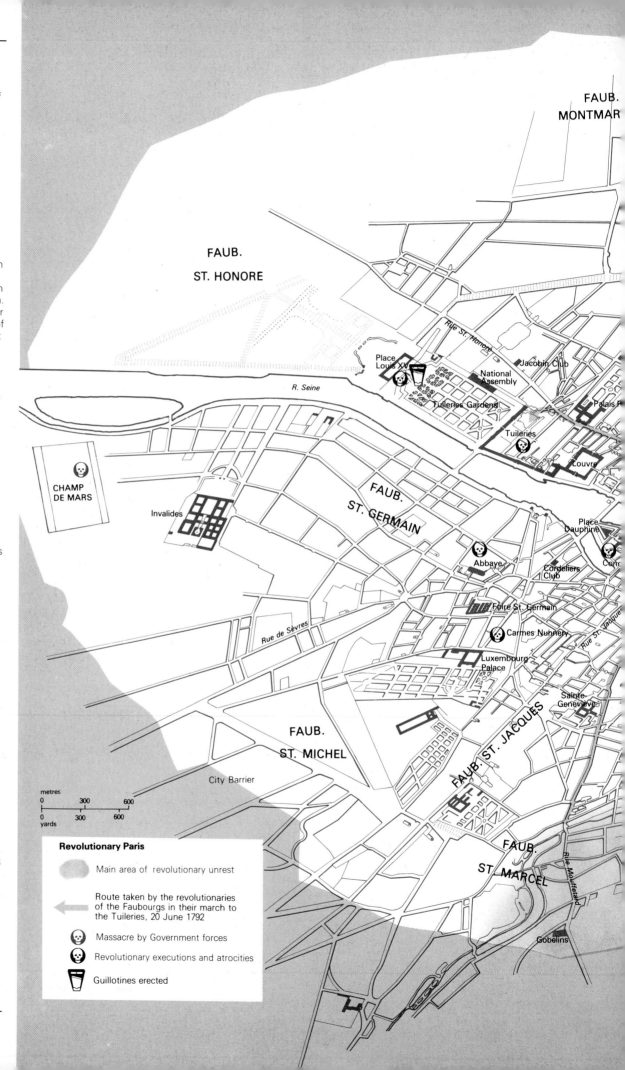

Revolutionary Paris

Main area of revolutionary unrest

Route taken by the revolutionaries of the Faubourgs in their march to the Tuileries, 20 June 1792

Massacre by Government forces

Revolutionary executions and atrocities

Guillotines erected

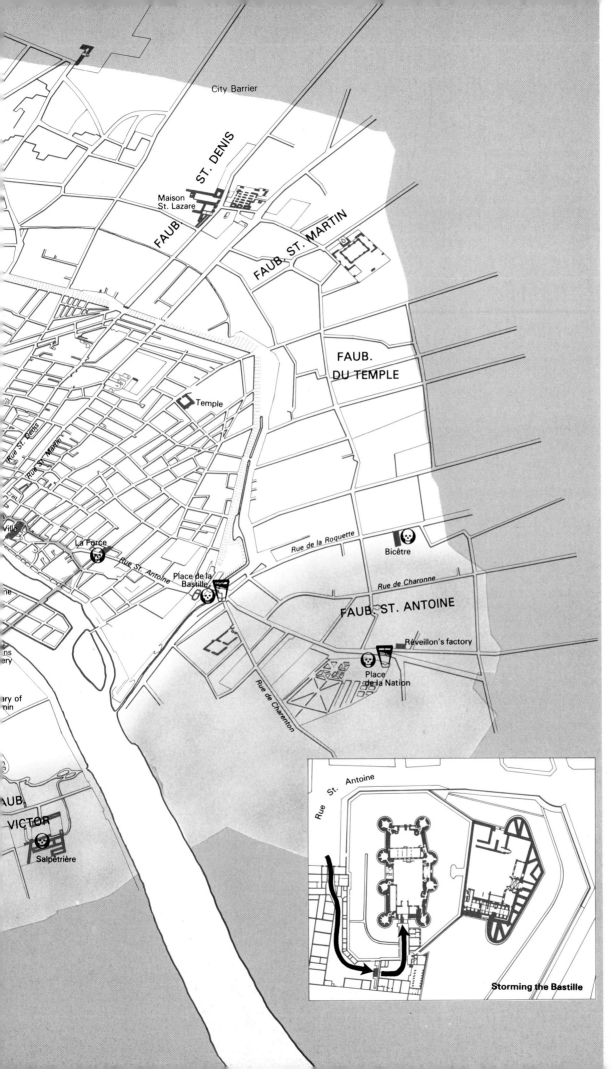

Storming the Bastille

the 'massacre' of the Champs de Mars in July 1791, the storming of the Tuileries in August and the assault on the prisons in September 1792, were demonstrations of the power of mass action. But the Parisian revolution was largely introspective, dominated by the attitudes of the humble members of the *sections* and the politicians who claimed to speak for them. There is no doubt that the people of the revolutionary *faubourgs* were in advance of their leadership, pressing them onwards towards more far-reaching changes. Yet like all manifestations of mass feeling, its mood was fickle and its sense of practical unity fragile. In the end Paris no longer spoke for the nation, and the radical Parisian revolutionaries did not even speak for the whole of the capital when it came to the test on 27 July 1794, 9 Thermidor of Year Three of the Revolution.

The Storming of the Bastille

Foolishly, the military authorities decided to store gunpowder in the old fortress of the Bastille, symbol of royal power in Paris. Dense crowds gathered outside early in the morning of 14 July demanding the gunpowder, and the removal of artillery from its battlements which dominated Paris. The crowds pushed in from the Rue Saint-Antoine into the outer courtyards, always left unguarded. Only when the governor saw the drawbridge guarding the inner courtyard being lowered did he fear an assault and opened fire, killing 98 and wounding 73. Infuriated, the former royal *Gardes Françaises* brought up cannon from the Invalides, fought their way in and prepared to batter down the gates. At this point the governor, de Launay, panicked and gave the order to surrender. A few of the garrison were murdered in the aftermath; the victors found few victims of royal oppression inside the grim walls. Like much else, the Bastille was a paper tiger, but as a revolutionary symbol it was immensely potent, and the news sped through France.

27

The Counter Terror

The French revolution spanned the period from July 1789 to July 1794; until September 1792 the country was, notionally, a constitutional monarchy, and at times Louis XVI did attempt rather feebly to exercise a restraining influence. By contrast, the counter-terror which was unleashed in the wake of the events of 9 Thermidor (27 July 1794) lasted for over a decade, and affected the political shape of French society for generations thereafter. The Terror had been bureaucratized and was by its own lights justified and systematic — the atrocious events at Nantes and Lyon were put down to the extremity of the emergency. But on the whole it was not marked by excesses of mindless brutality like the assaults of September 1792 on the prisons of Paris. But the counter-terror or 'white terror' unleashed by the royalists on the south and south-east of France sought to terrorize by bestiality. Gangs of murderers roamed the small towns and countryside of the Midi (the south of France) murdering and mutilating anyone with revolutionary connections. In some places Protestants and Jews suffered in consequence of the ultra-Catholic nature of many of the murder gangs. Whole families and clans were exterminated, often in pursuit of old village feuds long antedating the revolution. Many of the revolutionaries from the provinces who had either gone to Paris, or fled there, were returned for 'justice' to the south. The memory both of the Red Terror of the revolution and the counter-terror of the *égorgeurs* and *sabreurs* (from their habitual use of the knife on their victims) lasted through families for generations, becoming reflected in voting patterns for left or right, in attitudes for and against Vichy France generations later.

The Counter Terror

- Principal areas of counter Terror
- Death routes
- Centres of counter Terror

The Timetable of Revolution

1789

5 May Estates General met for first time since 1614, to rescue France from financial collapse.

20 June Tennis Court Oath by Third Estate (commoners) to remain in session until grievances redressed.

12–17 July Rising tension in Paris: riots against customs barrier and troops, culminating in:

14 July Storming of the Bastille.
Mid July–August Spread of the Great Fear — rural riots and provincial revolutions.

5 October March of over 10,000 to Versailles demanding an end to bread shortage. Forced Royal family to return with them to Paris.

1790

Consolidation of the revolution. Formation of political clubs including Society of the Friends of the Constitution better known as Jacobins.
Formation of provincial 'federations' to support the revolution: born from sense of regional autonomy.

19 June Attacks on privilege: Titles declared void; nobles renounced their feudal rights (August 1789).

12 July Clergy 'nationalized' via Civil Constitution: church property rights already annexed — November 1789.
Reaction: mutinies in navy and army suppressed. Bread riots continued.

27 Nov Civic oath imposed on the clergy. Many refused to take it.

1791

20 June King and his family flee in secret to join *émigrés* over German border; taken prisoner at Varennes and returned to Paris.
Increasing radical pressure:

17 July 'Massacre' of the Champ de Mars: mob out of hand fired on by National Guard. Impatience of *sans-culottes* with slow pace of change.
Rise of more radical party — Girondins — within the assembly, and voices urging war as only solution to threat from royalist *émigrés* and their allies — Austria and Prussia.
Royalists promote counter-revolution in the Vendée in western France, and the Midi to the south.

1792

20 April War declared against Austria. Prussia immediately entered as well.
War emergency catalyzed revolution. Volunteer armies arrived from the *fédérations*, notably Marseilles.

17 August Mass action by Parisians and *fédérés*: march on Royal Palace of Tuileries, and massacre of Swiss Guards defending it. King universally held to be in league with Austria.

19 August Defection of hero of 1789, Lafayette, to Austrians. Foreign armies entered France. France now under control of revolutionary government.

2 Sept Fortress of Verdun fell to Prussia: Paris believed open to invasion. Prisoners in Parisian jails slaughtered.

20 Sept Military tide turned by victory at Valmy. Same morning, National Convention met in Paris, replacing the Assembly, lineal descendant of the National Assembly of 1789. Convention purged of possible royalist sympathizers, and took dictatorial powers. The legislative instrument of revolutionary government.

21 Sept Monarchy abolished.

6 Nov Victory at Jemappes. Revolutionary armies carried war to the enemy.

the Committees of Public Safety and General Security, was launched in a great ceremony on 8 June 1794. Although the ceremony was generally seen as an exercise in self-glorification for Robespierre, it was also hoped that it might herald the end of the Terror. When it was clear that the reverse was true, and that the Terror was to be intensified, with the passing of the law of 10 June which abolished the right to defend a case brought before the Revolutionary Tribunal, the largely silent mass of the Convention turned against Robespierre, and denounced him. When his supporters in the National Guard commanded by his nominee Hanriot tried to release him, the Convention responded by calling in militia loyal to them from other *sections*. These events, of 9 Thermidor in the new revolutionary calendar, were followed the next day (28 July 1794) by the end of Robespierre on the guillotine, to be followed by many members of the radical Commune of Paris, the organizational expression of *sans-culottisme*.

From Thermidor onwards, although the revolutionaries of Paris would come onto the streets on many occasions in an effort to rekindle the radical spark, direct action was ineffectual. On 1 and 2 April 1795 a *journée* was countered with armed might, after marchers from the Faubourg St. Antoine had invaded the Tuileries where the Convention was sitting. In the tumult a deputy was killed and the government responded with a threat to bombard the Faubourg unless his killer was handed over.

The revolution which had begun with the fall of the Bastille in July 1789 effectively ended in this reaction of 1795; in the south of France, a counter-terror was unleashed which was to last for a decade. The various constitutional arrangements made after Thermidor led by slow steps towards Bonapartism, for the army was the only force in the state which could ultimately secure *any* government against revolution from below. Thus, while the French Revolution of 1789–95 provided the paradigm for many later revolutionaries, indeed created the revolutionary tradition in Europe and beyond, it also showed that the obverse face of the coin was military domination of the state, rule by a new Caesar.

1793
21 Jan King executed.

10 March Revolutionary tribunal established to apply 'revolutionary justice'.
War with rebels in the Vendée.

26 March Committee of Public Safety established; with the Committee of General Security, the executive arm of the revolution.
Provincial revolts by *fédérations* against the dictatorship of Paris. Revolution beset on all sides by enemies. Response: reign of Terror.

16 Oct Execution of Queen Marie-Antoinette.

31 Oct Revolution within the revolution: execution of radical Girondins by more radical Jacobins, under Robespierre. Reign of Terror operative throughout France under control of representatives of the Convention.

1794
5 April Execution of Danton, last threat to Robespierre.

8 April Festival of Supreme Being marked abolition of Christianity.

10 June Abolition of right of defence before revolutionary tribunals.

26 July Robespierre called for mass purges in speech to Convention.

27 July (9 Thermidor). Fearing extent of Robespierre's purge, moderate and largely silent majority in Convention voted him down, and ordered his arrest, summoned loyal militia from *sections* to oppose National Guard led by Robespierrists. Robespierre shot in struggle, jaw shattered.

28 July Robespierre executed, radical revolution put into reverse. Purge of Robespierre faction, and abolition of Commune in Paris, power-base of radical *sans-culottes*.

12 Nov Jacobin Club closed.

1795
April and May
Failure of radical elements in Paris to regain position.

22 August Convention approved the Constitution of Year III, re-establishing government in hands of non-radicals and the affluent.

6 Oct Directory of Five took over executive authority, after royalist counter-coup defeated by 'a whiff of grapeshot' at the hands of artillery officer Napoleon Bonaparte.

The travails of the Irish

THE hatred the peasants of Ireland bore for their English overlords was the product of centuries of exploitation, of oppression under Elizabeth I and of the 'Godly slaughter' which Cromwell wrought on a guiltless Irish Catholic population in 1649. Upon that memory, of the massacres of Drogheda, Wexford, and Clonmel, and a host of minor injustices, was built a more immediate and ardent sense of grievance. Catholic Irishmen were forced to pay tithes to support a Protestant church which they abhorred. Ireland was delivered into the hands of Scotsmen and Englishmen. Economic power belonged to a Protestant minority, and frequently the profits of trade in Ireland were diverted to support absentee owners in London. In short, the province felt a deep sense of inferiority and resentment, almost a mirror image of the grievances which pushed the American colonists into revolution. As in America, their sense of outrage, most forcefully urged by an urban and educated class, was given point by armed force. A Volunteer militia was formed to defend Ireland during the war of the American Revolution, but like the Americans, the Volunteers turned to demand redress of their grievances. They were successfully bought off by the sort of concessions, both economic and political, which a wise British administration would have conceded to the Americans in 1775–6. The 'constitution of 1782' provided cosmetic freedoms, but did little or nothing to satisfy the deep sense of injustice felt by the bulk of the Irish nation. For them the new independent Irish Protestant Parliament was a body representing their oppressors.

In the nine years between the outbreak of the French Revolution and the rising of the Irish people in 1798, the process of gradual but grudging reform was continued. But Irish Catholics, both the peasantry and the Catholic aristocracy, saw how first the Americans and latterly the French had gained liberty, and made active plans for violent action. In France the Irish revolutionaries, led by Wolfe Tone – a Protestant – found a base from which to work: they achieved a promise of armed French intervention to support an internal rising. The 'United Irishmen' thus had a mass movement at their back with, the government believed, almost 280,000 men arming and training for war. They possessed a coherent political programme and an able leadership not only in Dublin but with agents throughout the country.

Plans were made throughout 1796 and 1797 in the most elaborate detail, designed to contain the British garrison and to control all the major lines of communication within the country. But all this skilful revolutionary activity was vitiated by the simple fact that the central organizing body in Dublin, the Supreme Executive, was penetrated by government informers. In a swoop on a house in Bridge Street, on 11 March 1798, the government secured the Directory for the province of Leinster, and then quickly scooped up most of the Supreme Executive of the 'United Irishmen'. With sixteen of their leaders in custody, the energy went out of the movement. The government declared martial law on 30 March 1798, and this was used to unleash a terror campaign. Atrocities were committed by soldiers in the provinces around Dublin to a horrifying degree; the practical justification was the huge quantity of arms yielded by these methods. The terror campaign lasted through April and May, breaking the unity and co-ordination of the revolutionary movement as more of the leaders were captured. But it also served to harden the feeling among the mass of the membership that they had little to lose by rebellion. When the outburst finally came on 24 May 1798, it surged upwards from the masses, directed at best by local leaders, but largely out of control, and without much of the careful co-ordination determined by the Supreme Executive.

The British military leadership saw no real reason to fear the Irish; they rather regarded them with contempt. The numerous violent incidents which preceded the outbreak – the murder of magistrates, intimidation, house burning and the like, required no *military* skill. It came as a shock when they discovered that not only were they vastly outnumbered by the United armies, as they had expected, but that Irish peasants would attack with desperate and lunatic courage, regardless of losses. The peasants also took their revenge on Protestants where they could, matching the barbarities of the troops. Within a few days of the outbreak, the British government had lost control of most of the counties around Dublin. Where they did win a victory, as at Tara Hill, or Kilcullen Bridge, the rebels simply withdrew and the violence burst out somewhere else. By decapitating the movement, as they had done with the seizure of the Supreme Executive, the option of coming to terms with the United Irishmen had gone. None of the new leaders could speak for the movement as a whole, and the government's only recourse was to mass its resources, and bring each independent unit of the revolutionary armies to battle. Yet time was not on their side, for the knowledge that the French intended to invade was reinforced by captured documents. With a trained French army, experienced in the revolutionary wars in Europe, facing the second-rate British forces which comprised the garrison of Ireland, the issue was not in doubt. If the internal revolution could not be suppressed before the French arrived, Ireland would be lost.

The scale of the rising, both in the south of the country, and later in the province of Ulster, staggered the British government in London. A member of the Viceroy's staff in Dublin wrote to the Chief Secretary for Ireland, 'there was never in any country so formidable an effort on the part of the people'. The Viceroy, Lord Camden, declared: 'The organizing of this Treason is universal.'[1] Moreover, there were less than 10,000 regular infantry in the whole of Britain, and the Viceroy believed that it would take that number to subdue the Irish. The rebels had taken the town of Wexford and proclaimed a republic: ominously, a committee of public safety on the French model was established. But while they could win victories in the field, and even survive defeat, there was no sense of objectives. The Wexford republic talked grandly of 'We the people associated and united for the purpose of procuring our just rights . . .', but how these were to be achieved was quite unclear. One school of thought held that the Wexford army should march on Dublin, but they had no means of co-ordinating activity with the other armies outside their own province. The revolution was degenerating into provincialism, held together more by fear of the British than by common aims. The first task of the new British Viceroy, Lord Cornwallis, was to capitalize on divisions among the rebels by allowing the rank and file to surrender without reprisals. His principal objective was to conserve his forces for countering a French invasion force, rather than squandering his reserves in endless skirmishes with desperate peasants. Not all his field commanders had such an acute

political sense. General Lake in County Wexford, and General Asgill in Counties Carlow, Kilkenny and Queen's, perpetuated the same policy of brutality which, although it seemed to work in the short term, made the outbreak liable to recur once the troops were removed. The common people had little confidence in their leaders, who, save the priests like Father Philip Roch, were a feeble crew with little stomach for the cause. In August 1798 Cornwallis offered a general amnesty, and the last remains of resistance petered out. The war had lasted for some three months, and left well over 25,000 dead including 2000 Protestant civilians and Catholics loyal to the Crown. The numbers of arms recovered – over 48,000 muskets, 70,000 pikes (a most effective weapon), and 22 cannon – were evidence of the scale of the armed uprising. It was at this point, with the revolution quelled and peace being restored, that the French arrived.

They landed on 23 August 1798 at Killala in County Mayo in the far west, hitherto unaffected by the fighting. One thousand landed, with some 7000

The rough Irish rebels repel the British charge on their camp at Vinegar Hill. The war was marked by many atrocities on both sides

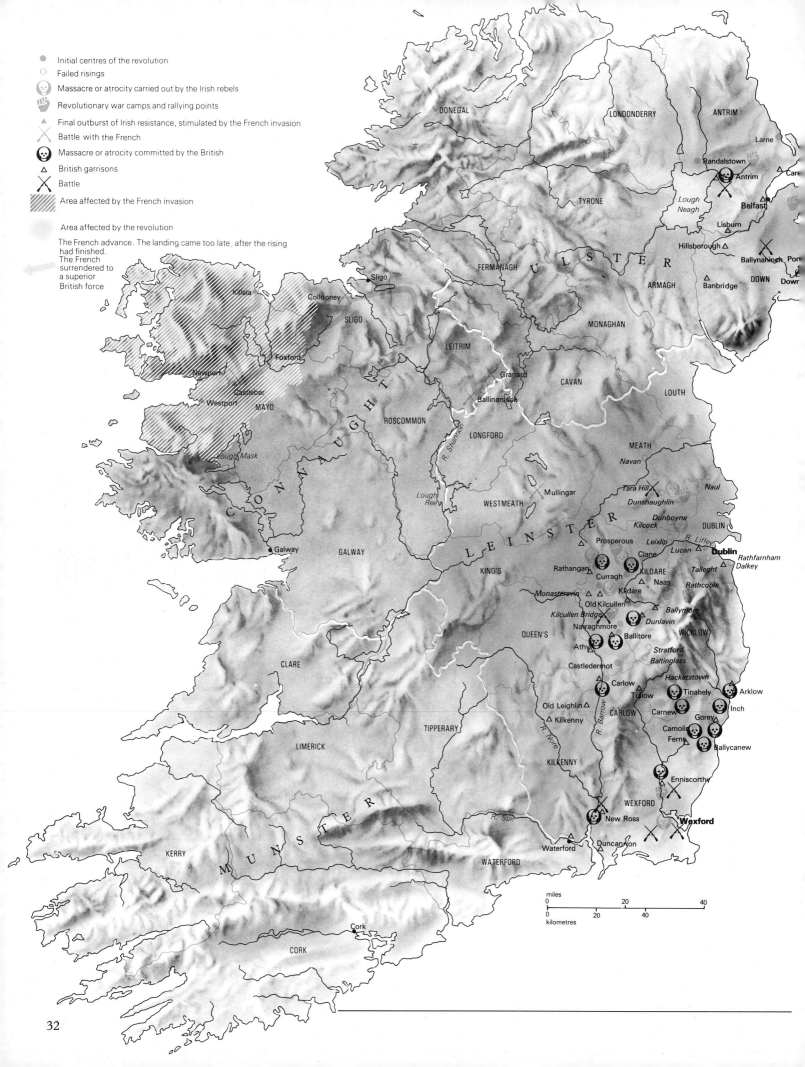

Initial centres of the revolution
Failed risings
Massacre or atrocity carried out by the Irish rebels
Revolutionary war camps and rallying points
Final outburst of Irish resistance, stimulated by the French invasion
Battle with the French
Massacre or atrocity committed by the British
British garrisons
Battle

Area affected by the French invasion

Area affected by the revolution

The French advance. The landing came too late, after the rising
had finished.
The French
surrendered to
a superior
British force

DONEGAL

LONDONDERRY

ANTRIM
Larne
Randalstown
Antrim   Carn
Belfast
Lough
Neagh
Lisburn
Hillsborough   Ballynahinch   Por
Banbridge   DOWN   Down

TYRONE

FERMANAGH   U L S T E R

ARMAGH   MONAGHAN

Killala
Sligo
Collooney
Newport   Foxford
Castlebar
Westport   MAYO
Lough Mask

SLIGO
LEITRIM
Granard
Ballinamuck
ROSCOMMON   LONGFORD
CAVAN   LOUTH

C O N N A U G H T

MEATH
Navan
Mullingar   Tara Hill   Naul
Lough   Dunshaughlin
Ree   WESTMEATH   Dunboyne
Kilcock   DUBLIN
L E I N S T E R   Leixlip   R. Liffey
Prosperous   Lucan   Dublin
Clane   Rathfarnham
Galway   KING'S   Rathangan   Curragh   KILDARE   Tallaght   Dalkey
GALWAY   Monasterevin   Kildare   Naas   Rathcoole
Old Kilcullen   Ballymore
Kilcullen Bridge   Dunlavin
Naraghmore   WICKLOW
QUEEN'S   Ballitore
Athy   Stratford
Baltinglass
Castledermot   Hacketstown
Carlow   Tinahely   Arklow
CLARE   Tullow   Inch
Old Leighlin   Carnew
Kilkenny   CARLOW   Gorey
Camolin   Ferns   Ballycanew
LIMERICK   R. Barrow
R. Nore
TIPPERARY   Enniscorthy
KILKENNY
WEXFORD
New Ross
M U N S T E R   R. Suir   Wexford
Waterford   Duncannon
WATERFORD
KERRY

Cork
CORK

miles
0   20   40
0   20   40
kilometres

32

more to come. Wolfe Tone arrived with the first group, under General Humbert, while Napper Tandy, the other leading United Irish leader with the French, was to come with the relief force. Over 7000 Irishmen rose to support the invasion, mostly from Counties Westmeath and Longford, and the British feared that the whole revolutionary movement would come to life once more. But the French had come too late, and as poor timing and ill-fortune had dogged the first stages of the revolution, so it continued to the end. The British army defeated the United Irishmen at Granard. Humbert, without the French relief army he had expected, faced over 5000 British troops with only 850 men at Ballinamuck, fought for half an hour and then surrendered. The few remaining rebels near the French landing at Killala were soon disposed of.

The aftermath of the war was marked by hangings, transportation to Australia, and a general repression. Violent resistance continued with disturbances in Galway and Clare in following years.

Political violence remained (and remains) a notable characteristic of Irish political life. But the revolution and the horrors which it brought were not what had been planned. A number of the leaders of the United Irishmen under sentence of death persuaded the government to allow them to emigrate in exchange for a full description of the planning of the revolution. In it they detailed an entirely plausible and practical plan for the seizure of power and the achievement of independence, based on the alliance with France and a well-controlled mass rising. They believed that the untried leadership which had succeeded them had been panicked into premature action, and had launched not a revolution but a peasant revolt. But

what is remarkable about the events as they turned out was the speed with which the peasant host adapted, learned to face regular troops, grasped the skills of using artillery. Whether the huge mass of the rebel forces, men, women and children living off the land and in the open through a warm summer, could have survived the rigours of winter, is open to doubt. But equally, had the French forces arrived as planned, with effective Irish leaders – Tone and Napper Tandy – and powder and shot for the rebel muskets and cannon, independent Ireland would have been won.

No quarter was given on either side. Protestants were the immediate victims of the rebels, as were any of the King's soldiers who fell into their hands. Here a 12-year-old drummer boy is killed by the fearsome Irish pikes

The little war

BY December 1807 the armies of France had no equal in Europe, and Napoleon regarded his Spanish allies with utter contempt. His decision to end the 'dirty intrigues' which had split the Spanish Royal family into squabbling factions was made firstly out of a desire to relieve a minor irritation and, as a by-product, to tighten the economic blockade of England in the Iberian peninsula. His method was not new: he simply replaced the lawful Bourbon dynasty, whose leading members he enticed to a meeting in Bayonne, with a trusted follower of his own, in this case his brother Joseph.

The events of May 1808 in Madrid, when the Spanish people unexpectedly revealed their capacity to resist, are known most graphically from the two great paintings of Goya: the mob rising in a spasm of unrestrained fury to massacre any Frenchman or suspected Spanish collaborator, and the French response of the firing squad and a ferocious general repression. These two qualities – an almost insane viciousness on the part of the Spaniards defending their country from the invader, and a willingness by the French commanders to match terror with terror – were to characterize the entire six years of the conflict. The events in Madrid were largely spontaneous, and they were echoed in similar risings, variously calling for constitutional liberty or the return of the Bourbons, through every part of Spain. Some, like the patriot Calvo de Rozaz, declared: 'The Spaniard must now know that he is not struggling so gloriously against the aggressor in order to place his independence . . . once more at the mercy of a capricious Court'[1] (1809). But liberty was a word much in the mouths of the French, and many Spaniards dedicated to reform believed that co-operation with the new regime was a better means to achieve progress than trusting to the quarrelling Bourbon princes. Perhaps more representative of the bulk of the nation were the staunch royalists who complained against those who were 'spreading new ideas and doctrines unknown to our forefathers', and 'launching flanking attacks on the divine religion of our ancestors'.[2] But from the outset of the war against the French, there was no agreement, no common understanding as to the political objectives of the 'little war'. Each band, each little group of fighters fought for its own cause, sometimes acknowledging the theoretical authority of the 'representatives of the nation' established in the many juntas which sprang up throughout the country, and latterly in the central junta established in one of the few cities free from French control, Cadiz. This junta, which was transformed into first a Regency, and latterly, in 1810, into a Cortes, was out of touch, issuing endless instructions for the conduct of the war against the French and tables of procedure and organization which bore no resemblance to the situations of the guerrilla bands of the *sierras*.

The regular Spanish army, as Napoleon was aware, was a feeble entity, badly led. In the first few months after the Madrid rising it achieved some success against the second-rate troops which had been sent to accomplish the occupation of Spain, notably on the plain of Jaén at Bailén, where a French army of 20,000, exhausted and dispirited after their long march south from Madrid, surrendered to 30,000 Spaniards (on 19 July 1808). But matters were very different when Napoleon himself came south with an army of battle-tried soldiers in November 1808. The Spanish generals, by now intoxicated with the spirit of Bailén, saw one French army as being much like another. They were quickly proved wrong. In the space of a few months, their armies had ceased to exist, in any organized sense, as effective military units. The most determined and energetic of the soldiers left to join the many resistance groups which had sprung up in almost every area of the country, and in particular strength in the mountains of the south, in the Basque country of the north, and in the highlands of Castille and Aragon.

These were the traditional lands of the brigand and the fugitive from justice. The tradition of violent resistance to central authority was well established in rural Spain: even the word *guerrilla* ('little war'), Spain's greatest contribution to the vocabulary of war, had been in use for centuries to describe the state of internal war endemic in much of the countryside of Southern Spain. In short, Spaniards were practised in the art of the *guerrilla*.

Spanish successes in the 'little war' were built on French mistakes. In February 1810, while Joseph was seeking to win over his new subjects by making a progress through the south (after he had been reimposed on his throne by force of his brother's armies), the French were seeking to impose a more draconian military rule in the north. Many of the uncommitted turned against Joseph and the French armies for the simple reasons of their barbarity and their callous insensitivity towards Spaniards. In one village, Arenas de San Pedro near Talavera, where some French troops were captured and mutilated by the women of the village, three regiments were sent to obliterate the village and its inhabitants. In the words of an eyewitness, 'sharpshooters amused themselves by running after the fleeing Spaniards and shooting them down like hares at a hunt. I have seen men burst out laughing when their victims fell into the grass.'[3] Women and children were slaughtered and the village finally burnt to the ground. Such instances could be multiplied at will, for as an English prisoner noted, 'it is a general order that the inhabitants of a place where such a crime is committed are to be put to the sword without exception of age or sex, and their habitations burned to the ground; nor is any enquiry ever made into the provocation which may have occasioned their excess'.[4] The acts of the Spaniards were often even more bestial, and there does seem to have been some conscious desire to use the weapon of terror against the French soldiers. As a device, it achieved some success, for not only did it prompt the response in kind which did so much to alienate the body of the population, but also produced a terrible erosion of morale. It was a common catch-phrase among French soldiers that war in Spain spelt 'death for the soldier, ruin for officers, fortune for generals'.[5] French soldiers were less and less willing to expose themselves to danger, preferring to seek the protection of fortresses or even field fortifications. Although Napoleon was determined that the way to defeat the guerrilla was to harry the bands of irregulars with mobile flying columns, it was never possible to use any more than a tiny proportion of the occupying forces in this way.

Over the years 1809–13, the guerrilla bands expanded and came to dominate most of the land outside the cities. In one or two cases, such as Saragossa and Gerona, there was an urban resistance to the French, but it had no hope of anything other than temporary success. It is often suggested that the true motive force for the liberation of Spain from the French was the Anglo-Spanish force based in Portugal from 1808. This was the army which undoubtedly beat the French in the field and forced its withdrawal across the frontier in March 1814. But as Sir Basil Liddell Hart has observed, while the army under Sir Arthur Wellesley caused some 45,000 casualties to the French, the deaths at the hands of the guerrillas were ten to twenty times that number. Their action made Spain, in his words, 'a desert where the French stayed only to starve'.[6] There was no means by which the French armies could preserve their lines of communication from attack, and as the years went on, the economic cost of the Spanish involvement was the most substantial drain on the French government. Nor should it be assumed that had Napoleon himself taken the Spanish imbroglio in hand, as he did in 1808, his superior genius would have resolved the problem. His only experience of irregular war had been against the rebels in the Vendée during the Revolution. But in these flat lands of western France, bounded by the Atlantic, it had been possible to adopt a strategy of containment and pursuit. In the mountains and plains of Spain, a vast land in which a guerrilla could strike, run and hide, the same approach had no chance of succeeding. It remained a stock French response, as in Algeria from 1840–7, but the conditions of Spain, with its capital city deep inland, and any foreign army dependent on long lines of supply, ruled out any military solution to the problem of the 'little war'.

The forces ranged against the French could agree

From Goya's *Disasters of War*, a frighteningly accurate image of the horrors of the guerrilla war in Spain

on nothing except their desire to remove the intruder. The prime mistake made by the French themselves was their contempt for Spain and its inhabitants and their neglect of any political approach. The majority of the 'political nation' leaned towards the ideals of the Enlightenment and away from the authoritarianism enshrined in Bourbon rule. Many became active supporters of the French – the *afrancesados* – and many more might have followed the same path. As the extreme reactionary Blas Ostolaza sourly remarked in the Cortes of Cadiz in 1811, there were many policies advanced by Spaniards which were 'deceitfully dubbed liberal . . . (and) coincide with the revolutionary principles of Robespierre, the greatest enemy of the people'.[7] The lessons of the war of liberation in Spain were not learned outside Spain; within they were learned too well. From the Carlist Wars of the 1840s and the 1870s, through to the Civil war of 1936–39, the Spaniards resorted to the *guerrilla* with practised ease, as well as to the tactics of terrorism. The success of these tactics against the French, the very terminology of the 'war of liberation', sanctified the notion of violence within political life in Spain.

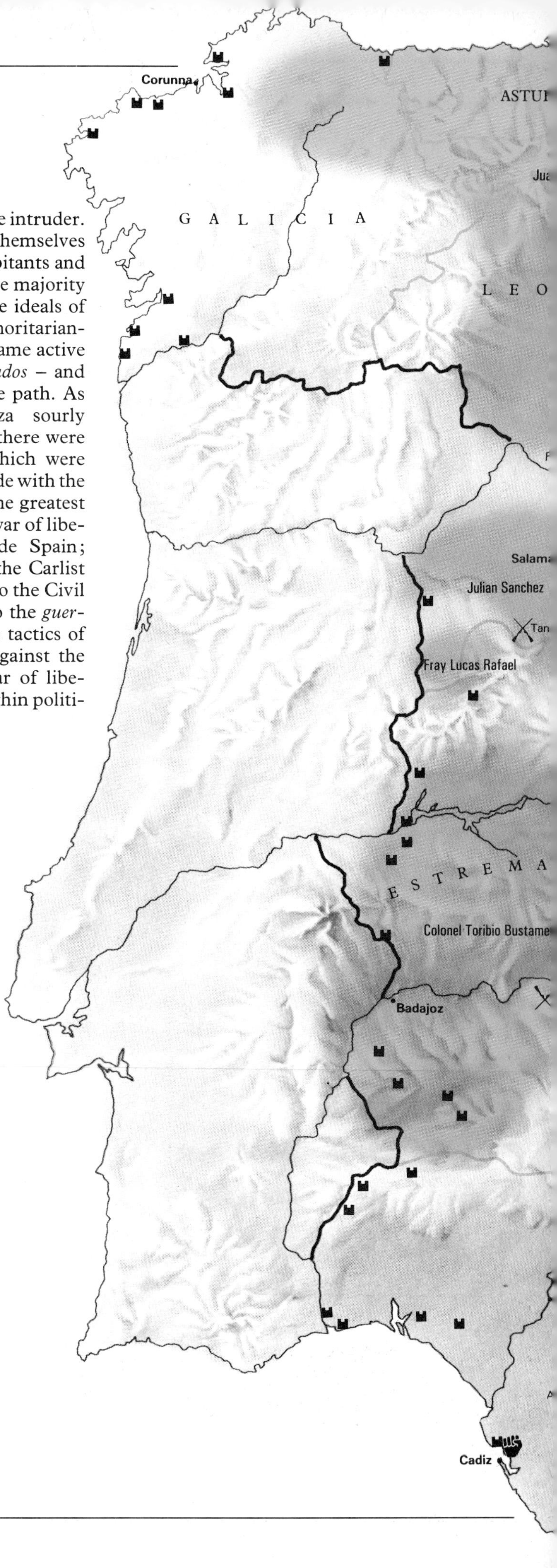

Corunna

ASTUI

Jua

GALICIA

LEO

Salama

Julian Sanchez

Tan

Fray Lucas Rafael

ESTREMA

Colonel Toribio Bustame

Badajoz

Cadiz

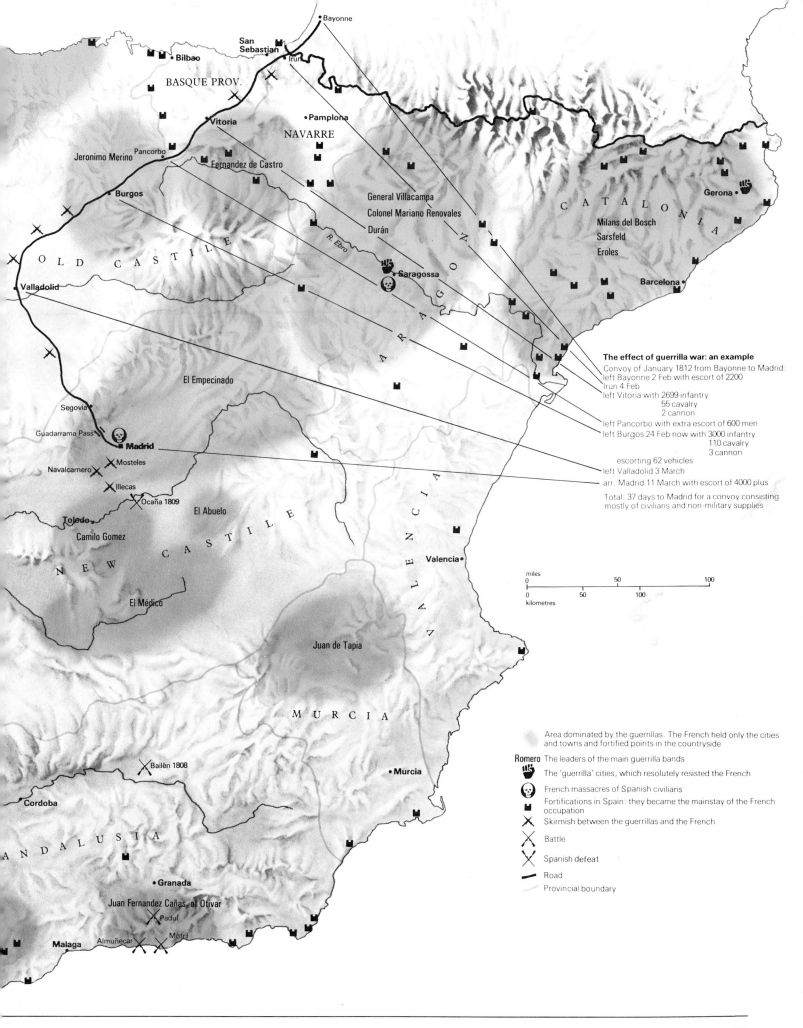

Bayonne

San Sebastian

Bilbao

Irun

BASQUE PROV.

Vitoria

Pamplona

NAVARRE

Jeronimo Merino

Pancorbo

Fernandez de Castro

Burgos

CATALONIA

Gerona

General Villacampa

Colonel Mariano Renovales

Durán

Milans del Bosch

Sarsfeld

Eroles

R. Ebro

O L D   C A S T I L E

A R A G O N

Saragossa

Barcelona

Valladolid

El Empecinado

The effect of guerrilla war: an example
Convoy of January 1812 from Bayonne to Madrid:
left Bayonne 2 Feb with escort of 2200
Irun 4 Feb
left Vitoria with 2699 infantry
     55 cavalry
     2 cannon
left Pancorbo with extra escort of 600 men
left Burgos 24 Feb now with 3000 infantry
     110 cavalry
     3 cannon
   escorting 62 vehicles
left Valladolid 3 March
arr. Madrid 11 March with escort of 4000 plus

Total: 37 days to Madrid for a convoy consisting
mostly of civilians and non-military supplies

Segovia

Guadarrama Pass

Madrid

Mosteles

Navalcarnero

Illecas

Ocaña 1809

Toledo

El Abuelo

Camilo Gomez

N E W   C A S T I L E

El Médico

V A L E N C I A

Valencia

miles

0   50   100

0   50   100

kilometres

Juan de Tapia

M U R C I A

Bailén 1808

Murcia

Cordoba

Area dominated by the guerrillas. The French held only the cities
and towns and fortified points in the countryside

Romero The leaders of the main guerrilla bands

The 'guerrilla' cities, which resolutely resisted the French

French massacres of Spanish civilians

Fortifications in Spain: they became the mainstay of the French
occupation

Skirmish between the guerrillas and the French

Battle

Spanish defeat

Road

Provincial boundary

A N D A L U S I A

Granada

Juan Fernandez Cañas, of Otivar

Padul

Malaga   Almuñecar   Motril

'That Greece might still be free'

IN 1810, writing at Symrna on the coast of Asia Minor, George Gordon, Lord Byron, epitomized in two lines the land of Greece which he had recently seen for the first time. The reality of Greece had shaken his hitherto exclusively literary notion of the country:

Fair Greece! sad relic of departed worth!
Immortal, though no more; though fallen, great![1]

Byron responded to Greece with a paradox, as well he might, for nineteenth-century Greece embodied only the faintest trace of its classical heritage. The population was mixed with strong Turkish, Slav and Albanian elements, while the country was a backwater with all the more enterprising spirits in Constantinople, in the service of the Ottoman empire, in trade or in self-exile in Europe or Russia. The national industry was banditry. Some of the bandits had been recruited by the Turkish rulers of Greece as a militia. Others merely preyed on travellers, and engaged in a desultory warfare with other bandit groups. The militia were known as *armatoli*, the bandits as *kleftes*; to the outsider they were indistinguishable. The only real voice of order was the Orthodox Church. Throughout their empire, the Ottomans had adopted a policy with non-Moslem subject peoples of allowing them relative independence provided they pay their taxes.

The Turks used the upper echelons of Greek society as administrators, for which the Greeks proved peculiarly talented, and the capital city of Constantinople had a large Greek population –

within which were to be found numerous fanatics devoted to the idea of a free and independent Greece. It was the Greeks of the diaspora who provided the intellectual leaven for the independence movement. The most ardent fighters for independence were on the islands of the Aegean, however. While on the mainland there was a system of Turkish administration, the islanders came under the much lighter hand of the Turkish admiralty. With their fishing boats and trading vessels, they provided the network of communication essential to any independence movement. A secret society, the *Filikia Etaria* (Friendly Society), began to enlist members to fight for Balkan independence, promising the support of the Greek Orthodox patriarch and of the Emperor of Russia. In fact, they had no promise of support from any powerful body. The Sultan soon got news of the conspiracy from his Pasha at Jannina. But Ali Pasha was a byword for cunning and duplicity. His aim was to achieve an independent state in Greece for himself and his family and by the end of 1821 the Sultan was at war with his own Pasha, to the delight of the Greeks who watched the Ottoman armies tear each other to pieces.

The Greek *etaria* decided to act while the Turkish forces were engaged in an internecine struggle. In January 1821, far to the north, a small force of 4500 liberators crossed the river Pruth into Turkish territory, and after a few engagements withdrew again. Much more significant was the start of the rising in the Peloponnese. Since the beginning of the year, recruits and arms had been landed in the very south of the peninsula, in the wild country of the Mani peninsula. On 6 April the bishop of Patras declared at the monastery of Agia Lavra, near Kalavrita, that Greece would take her freedom; in the space of a few weeks the whole of the Peloponnese was awash with blood, as the Greeks launched a war of racial hatred against any Moslems they could find. In the region north of the Mani peninsula, indescribable atrocities were committed, and 15,000 Turks were slaughtered. The remainder of the 40,000 fled into the towns and fortresses which the Ottomans still held.[2] The war of liberation was marked by an extreme savagery which was uncommon by the nineteenth century. The Turks responded in kind. Greeks were flayed alive, roasted over slow fires, or burned to death in their churches. The Turks could rarely catch the guerrilla fighters, for kleftic warfare was based on sniping and the ambush. They vented their fury on the villages, often those which were notionally clients of the Turkish administration. Both Greeks and Turks were gripped by a blind hatred.

The revolution was launched in a spirit of optimism, and in the belief that external help would soon arrive. An appeal had already been sent to all the courts of Europe on 9 April, invoking 'the aid of all the civilized nations of Europe.... Greece, our

A contemporary Greek image of the war with the Turks. The white-clad Greeks fight with black chested Turks. In the background on the hill, a Greek has been impaled, a standard Turkish punishment, while in the foreground the artist gives an accurate impression of the Greek warriors

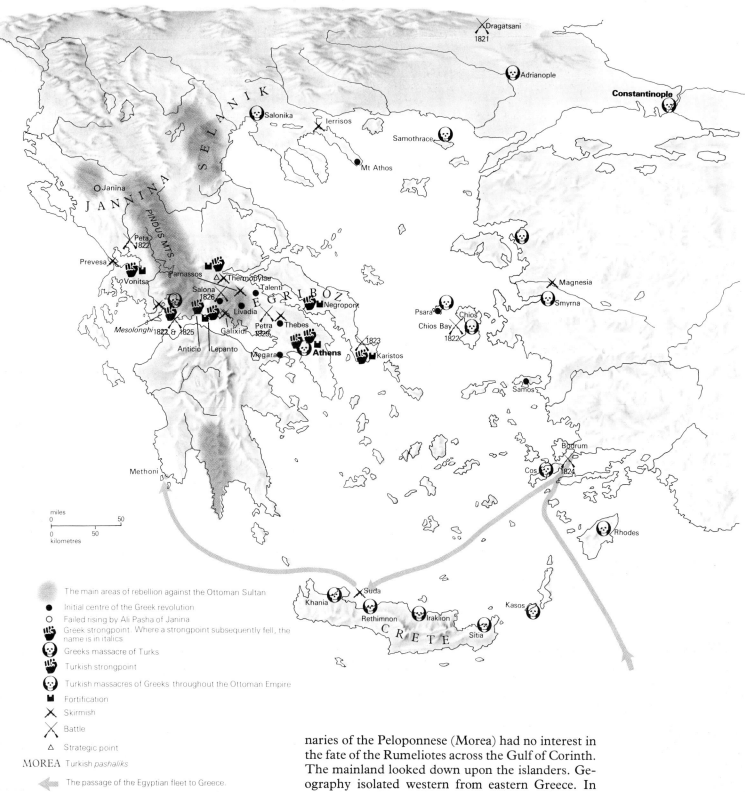

Dragatsani 1821

Adrianople

Constantinople

Salonika

Ierrisos

Samothrace

Mt Athos

SELANIK

Janina

JANNINA

PINDUS MTS

Peta 1822

Prevesa

Vonitsa

Parnassos

Thermopylae

Talenti

Salona 1826

Livadia

EGRIBOZ

Negropont

Magnesia

Smyrna

Psara

Chios

Mesolonghi 1822 & 1825

Galixidi

Petra 1826

Thebes

Chios Bay 1822

Anticio

Lepanto

Megara

Athens

Karistos

1823

Samos

Methoni

Bodrum

Cos 1824

Rhodes

miles
0 — 50

0 — 50
kilometres

Kasos

Khania

Suda

Rethimnon

Iraklion

Sitia

C R E T E

The main areas of rebellion against the Ottoman Sultan

● Initial centre of the Greek revolution

○ Failed rising by Ali Pasha of Janina

Greek strongpoint. Where a strongpoint subsequently fell, the name is in italics

Greeks massacre of Turks

Turkish strongpoint

Turkish massacres of Greeks throughout the Ottoman Empire

■ Fortification

✕ Skirmish

✕ Battle

△ Strategic point

MOREA Turkish *pashaliks*

The passage of the Egyptian fleet to Greece.

mother, was the lamp that illuminated you; on this ground she reckons on your active philanthropy. . . .' The invocation went unheeded and even Russia, of whom they expected so much, provided nothing. The Greek revolutionaries were on their own.

There were many fragments in the revolutionary cause, and the enthusiastic spirit of unity soon evaporated. Local issues predominated. The revolutio-

naries of the Peloponnese (Morea) had no interest in the fate of the Rumeliotes across the Gulf of Corinth. The mainland looked down upon the islanders. Geography isolated western from eastern Greece. In 1822 Ali Pasha at last received his just deserts, and his head was dispatched to Constantinople in a sack. The Turkish armies were now free to turn their full attention to the Greeks. However, success demanded co-ordination between the eastern and western Turkish armies, separated by the central mountain spine, and the navy which was to support their advance. They were never able to achieve it. In 1823 the Sultan planned a combined military and naval assault on

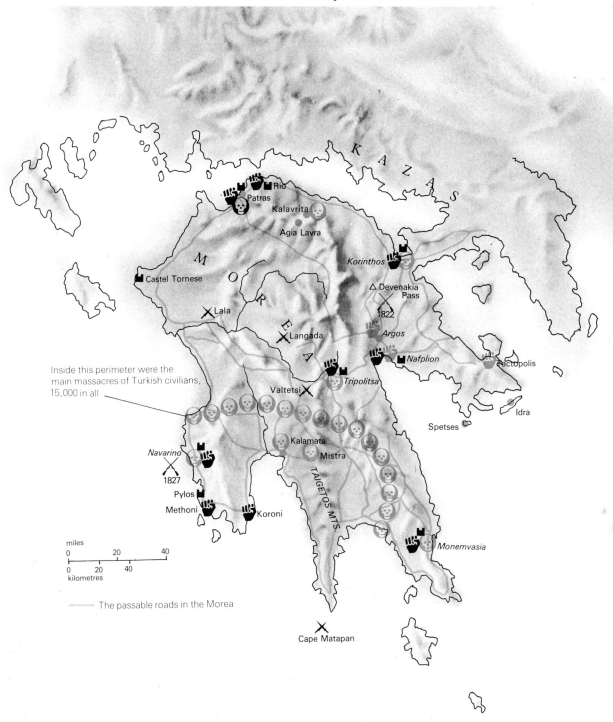

Inside this perimeter were the
main massacres of Turkish civilians,
15,000 in all

miles
0   20   40

0   20   40
kilometres

—— The passable roads in the Morea

the western Peloponnese with a huge artillery train of 1200 guns. Fortunately for the Greeks, these were lost in a huge fire in Constantinople, which destroyed the arsenal and much of the city as well. The fleet managed to reinforce the few fortresses which the Turks still held, but spent most of its time in aimless cruising, with an occasional descent on one of the islands. No real progress was made towards the recovery of sovereignty in Greece.

Progress was eventually made by internationalizing the conflict.[3] In 1825, having failed to gather sufficient resources himself, the Sultan Mahmud called in the Egyptian army, the best trained and led force in the Ottoman empire. On 24 February 1825 Ibra-

him Pasha landed at Methoni with 4000 infantry and 500 cavalry; a month later, he had added another 6000 infantry and plentiful artillery. On the way, his forces had overwintered on Crete and ravaged the island. On the northern coast of the Gulf of Corinth, international support for the Greek cause could be seen in the base at Mesolonghi. The Philhellenes, with Byron as their most notable member, raised money and troops throughout Europe. Even governments despised by the Philhellenes for their passivity became alarmed at the prolonged struggle and began to think in terms of an imposed solution. While they deliberated, the military advantage lay with the Turks and Egyptians. In April 1826 Mesolonghi fell to Ibrahim, and in August, Reshid Pasha with his Turkish army captured Athens. But it was a war of attrition and of the 24,000 Egyptian troops dispatched to Greece since 1825, only 8000 remained fit for battle. On the Greek side, despite the efforts of the volunteers from Europe, hope of success had almost died, and the endless bickering among the Greek factions grew stronger.

The resolution of the Greek issue was imposed from outside. The Turkish position was untenable if they lost control of the sea. In two naval battles, at Salona and Navarino, two Turkish fleets were destroyed, in the first case by a fleet led by Lord Cochrane, and in the second by the combined fleet of the European powers who had come to impose a settlement. Navarino was a mistake on the allies' part, but its effect was catastrophic for the Ottoman cause. Sixty Ottoman and Egyptian ships were sunk, and 8000 lives were lost. No ships were sunk in the allied fleet, and only 176 were killed. Once the European powers became embroiled in the Greek question and were determined to impose a settlement which favoured the Greeks, there was no hope for the Ottomans. The war continued, with the balance of advantage shifting to the Greeks and their allies. Russia went to war with Turkey in the spring of 1828, while the French sent a detachment to aid the Greeks in the Peloponnese. Not until September 1829 did the Turks at last concede and accept an independent Greece at the Peace of Adrianople, although the problems of Greece did not end there. The allied powers wanted the new state to be a monarchy, but it proved impossible to find a suitable candidate. Civil war broke out among the various interests, and it was not until January 1833 that the new king, Otho (son of the king of Bavaria), disembarked at Nafplion.

The settlements ultimately resolved less than they should have. The monarchy failed, the borders satisfied neither Greek nor Turk, and the European powers, having involved themselves in the affairs of the Eastern Mediterranean, returned to it again and again, an itch which demanded to be scratched. Greece had to wait until almost a century after the war of liberation to achieve 'natural' frontiers, and the Turks equally as long to rid themselves of the Greek presence in Smyrna and other cities of Anatolia. Even the issue of Cyprus was a continuation of the struggle of Greek and Turk, a racial and religious war seemingly without end.

The siege of the Acropolis by the Greeks, 1821. The Turks were all massacred after their surrender in 1822

'Those who serve the revolution plough the sea'

THE French take-over in Spain in 1808 induced a crisis of authority in the Spanish lands of south America. Joseph Bonaparte *might* be confidently proclaimed 'King of Spain and the Indies'. But the effect of the invasion was to catalyze opposition to foreign rule which had been dormant in America for a generation. Americans of Spanish descent saw themselves as exploited and patronized by Spanish newcomers whose only asset was their unimpeachable birth in the mother country. As in the colonies of north America, the various domains had developed cultural and social patterns quite unlike those of Spain itself. There was pressure from those who had become rich and successful in the Americas, for whom the monopoly of political power by the Spanish-born was irksome, to achieve a limited independence from Madrid's excessive paternalism. These were the tentative revolutionaries who laid claim to their independence in the years after 1808. But from this same group – the *criollos*, those of Spanish blood but born in America – were to come the true revolutionaries, like Simon Bolivar, Jose de San Martin, Bernadino Rivadavia.

From the outset, there was a tone of stridency underlying the process of the revolution. While the leaders of the *criollos* in Buenos Aires were debating political abstractions, in the highlands of the future Bolivia in May 1809, at Chuquisaca and La Paz, power was being seized from the Spanish authorities, and the issues stated unambiguously: 'Now is the time to organize a new system of government, founded upon the interest of our country which is downtrodden by the bastard policy of Madrid. . . . Now is the time to raise the standard of revolt in these unfortunate colonies.'[1] However, the real question which would dominate all the revolutionary activity of two decades (1808–28) was raised immediately. Every territory of the vast area which made up Spanish America contained a cocktail of different races and interest-groups: Spaniards born in the mother country (*peninsulares*); Spaniards born in America (*criollos*); those of mixed race– *mestizos, pardos, castas, coyotes, cholos, zambos* – all indicating the precise admixture of European, Indian and Negro blood; and, at the base of the social pyramid, the vast body of the exploited, Indians tied to permanent servitude and Negro slaves. No successful revolution could exist on the basis of support from the *criollos* alone, for they represented a small and largely urban minority. Supporters of the Spanish crown found it easy to construct a counter-revolution from among the many groups who looked on *criollo* supremacy with even less pleasure than they had on Spanish rule. Beyond the racial and social interest-groups lay an equivalent variety of regional and local interests. Spanish rule had grouped territories into viceroyalties usually based on the pattern of the original conquest. In the ferment of revolution each area laid claim to its own independence. The revolution which began in Buenos Aires in the years 1808–10 proclaimed a unitary state of all the territories which had made up the viceroyalty of the Rio de la Plata (Argentina in colloquial speech); up-country, towns and provinces connected with the coast only by administrative accident saw things differently and demanded *their* freedom. Elsewhere, the tide of revolution washed away the bases of political organization which had to be built anew.

The pattern of the revolution developed slowly, at the extremities of the sub-continent. A post-Spanish regime was quickly and painlessly established in Buenos Aires, and despite endless squabbles with provincial separatists and royalist incursions from the interior, the revolution there was never seriously threatened. The Rio de la Plata provided a base for the revolution in Chile and, eventually, in Peru. In the north in Venezuela the revolution was much more bloody and less certainly accomplished, but there too, at the hands of the genius of revolutions, Simon Bolivar, a base was created from which he moved forward to free the lands which were to become Colombia, Ecuador, and Bolivia. Both Bolivar and San Martin, who led the liberation of Chile from his base in Mendoza province (Argentina), had a strategic vision which allowed them to see beyond local problems to revolution on a continental scale. San Martin took his small army across the Andes in January 1817, together with the exiled Chilean revolutionaries, headed by Bernardo O'Higgins, who had already suffered defeat at the hands of the Spaniards (Rancagua, 1814). In the space of one spring, and a single battle in February 1817, the Army of the Andes was able to take the capital, Santiago, and to hold it against royalist armies sent south from Peru. San Martin however lost to the royalists in March 1818 and this struggle for the possession of Santiago, fought out at nearby Maipú (April 1818), was desperately close. To secure the revolution it was necessary to attack the source of Spanish power in America, the viceroyalty of Peru. San Martin opted for a seaborne landing, made possible by the destruction of the Spanish command of the sea. The speed and daring with which the small Chilean navy had obliterated the powerful Spanish forces and captured the Spanish base at Valdivia (1820) came from the inspirational command of Thomas Cochrane. Cochrane, Earl of Dundonald, was to become a hero of three wars of independence – Chile, Brazil and Greece.

The Army of the Andes, now 4500 men, sailed from Valparaiso in August 1820, to Pisco. Here San Martin set up his base and sought to rally Peruvian opposition to Spain, while Cochrane (always happier with direct action), besieged the Spanish port of Callao. The combination of San Martin's waiting game and Cochrane's impetuosity brought success: town after town rallied to the cause and in July 1821 the Spaniards (cut off from relief), abandoned Lima and retreated into the mountains.

San Martin's victories, although dramatic, were also largely illusory. He had destroyed the Spanish domination of the towns but he could not control the countryside. The whole history of the conquest of the Americas had demonstrated that a small group of determined men could take control of the centres of power; but from Pizarro onwards, the difficulty lay in the deep recesses of the country. In Peru the concentration of wealth and resources lay along the coastal strip. Inland the war was waged by guerrilla bands, some for the revolution, some against. It was this style of warfare which Bolivar, after a sequence of revolutions and counter-revolutions in the towns and valleys of the coast, had been forced to adopt in his struggle far to the north. There revolution had slipped into a social and racial war. In Venezuela, over sixty percent of the population was wholly or partly black. Many upper-class Venezuelans feared independence, believing that 'in revolutions they would run the risk of losing their slaves',[2] as the traveller and explorer Alexander von Humboldt observed. They also had memories of the great slave rebellion of 1795. Bolivar, a great aristocrat and landowner, saw that the revolution would have to encompass a social transformation, removing what he described as 'the dark mantle of barbarous and profane slavery'. He stated categorically that it was 'madness that a revolution for liberty should try to retain slavery'.[3] Against him were ranged not merely the forces of Spain but all those elements of *criollo* society unwilling to stomach such heresy; and, allied with the freebooting cavalry of the plains of Venezuela, they overcame the revolution in a bloodbath. Bolivar fled by sea to the port of Cartagena and eventually to Jamaica. Gradually, after an abortive return to Venezuela over the summer of 1816, he devised an approach which led to victory. In December 1816, against much opposition, he established his base in the lands south of the Orinoco, as far as possible from the civilization of the coast. Other revolutionary groups fought back in Barcelona, Cumana, and Maturin, but Bolivar, with his sanctuary at Angostura, eventually led the republican revolution. A year after he set up his Orinoco base, he and his troops made a long and dangerous march to the plains of the Apure river, where he forged an alliance with Jose Antonio Paez, who led the fierce horsemen of the plains. These *llaneros* had been the key element in the defeat of the revolution of 1814; Bolivar now promised them what they wanted, plunder. What he needed above all was victory, and it continued to elude him. In May 1819 he decided on a momentous stroke: to attack the Spanish at their weakest point, across the Andes in the viceroyalty of New Granada (the future Colombia). In Venezuela he had both army and much of the existing landed interest ranged against him. In New Granada he faced only a complacent Spanish army largely untried in battle.

Bolivar's 'long march' proved a triumphant success. In the space of six weeks in July and August 1819, he shattered the royalist armies, and after the battle of Boyacá (7 August 1819) he entered Bogota as liberator. Flushed with the success of the campaign, he returned to Venezuela and the hard struggle for victory. It was 24 June 1821 before he won a final battle with the Spanish army at Carabobo and entered Caracas. But now his aspirations had grown to encompass the final reduction of Spanish power in the south. He returned to Bogota and fought his way south towards Quito, hoping to win Ecuador for his new dream of a united state of Gran Colombia before San Martin could claim the land for Peru. These vaunting dreams of a new liberal empire built out of the ruins of the Spanish domains were not rooted in reality. After his final move to the south, in 1823, when he arrived in Lima, Bolivar began the

A later impression of Simon Bolivar gives an exact impression of the many groups and races who made up his army

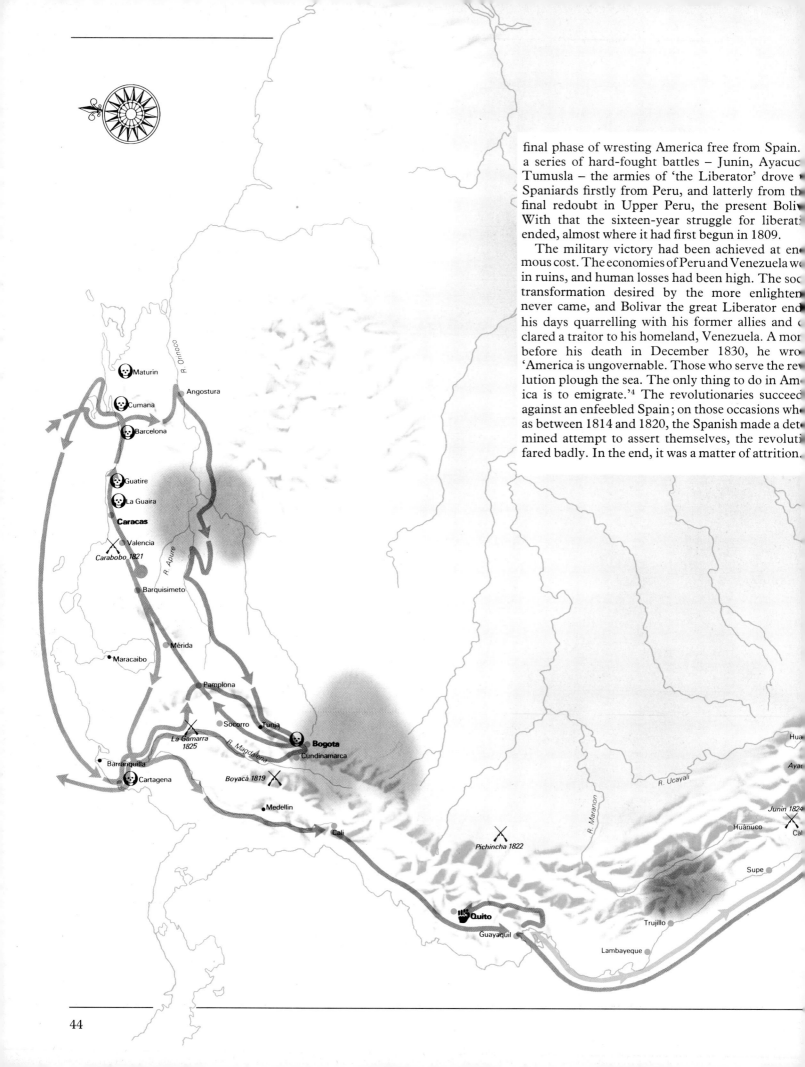

final phase of wresting America free from Spain. a series of hard-fought battles – Junín, Ayacuc Tumusla – the armies of 'the Liberator' drove Spaniards firstly from Peru, and latterly from th final redoubt in Upper Peru, the present Boliv With that the sixteen-year struggle for liberati ended, almost where it had first begun in 1809.

The military victory had been achieved at en mous cost. The economies of Peru and Venezuela w in ruins, and human losses had been high. The soc transformation desired by the more enlighten never came, and Bolivar the great Liberator end his days quarrelling with his former allies and clared a traitor to his homeland, Venezuela. A mon before his death in December 1830, he wro 'America is ungovernable. Those who serve the rev lution plough the sea. The only thing to do in Am ica is to emigrate.'[4] The revolutionaries succeed against an enfeebled Spain; on those occasions wh as between 1814 and 1820, the Spanish made a det mined attempt to assert themselves, the revoluti fared badly. In the end, it was a matter of attrition.

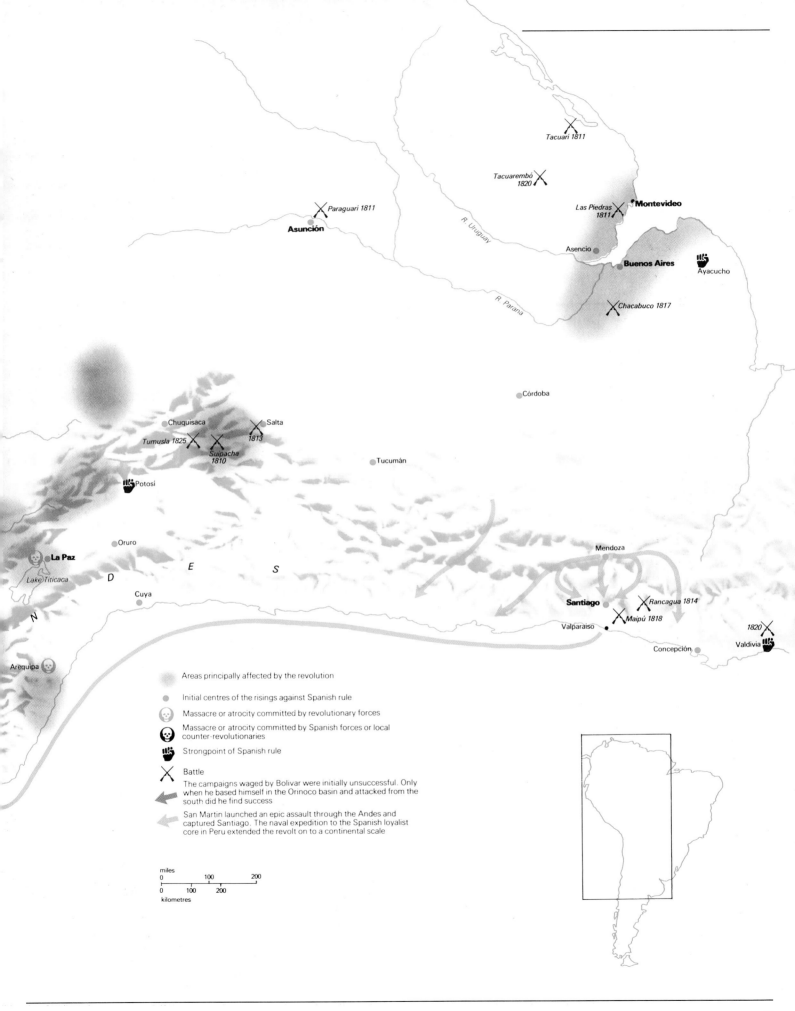

Tacuari 1811

Tacuarembó 1820

Paraguari 1811

Asunción

R. Uruguay

Las Piedras 1811

Montevideo

Asencio

Buenos Aires

R. Parana

🖐 Ayacucho

Chacabuco 1817

Córdoba

Chuquisaca

Salta

Tumusla 1825

1813

Suipacha 1810

🖐 Potosi

Tucumán

Oruro

Mendoza

☠ **La Paz**

D   E   S

Lake Titicaca

Cuya

Santiago

Rancagua 1814

N

Valparaiso

Maipú 1818

1820

Concepción

Valdivia 🖐

Arequipa 💀

Areas principally affected by the revolution

Initial centres of the risings against Spanish rule

💀 Massacre or atrocity committed by revolutionary forces

☠ Massacre or atrocity committed by Spanish forces or local counter-revolutionaries

🖐 Strongpoint of Spanish rule

✕ Battle

The campaigns waged by Bolivar were initially unsuccessful. Only when he based himself in the Orinoco basin and attacked from the south did he find success

San Martin launched an epic assault through the Andes and captured Santiago. The naval expedition to the Spanish loyalist core in Peru extended the revolt on to a continental scale

miles
0   100   200
0   100   200
kilometres

'The springtime of the peoples'

IN the years of 1846 and 1847, there was famine in Europe. The potato crop, staple diet of the peasants in Ireland, Silesia, northern France, the Low Countries, and parts of Germany and Scotland, was afflicted with a blight which turned it into a black mush. There was a cattle plague in Hungary and devastating floods along the Vistula. Cities like Salzburg, where the bread flour was being eked out with clover, experienced a massive inrush of those who could no longer find a living in the countryside. In Vienna refugees from Styria, Bohemia and Silesia brought with them typhus, which spread rapidly in the overcrowded conditions. In Paris the country-people massed in the eastern districts of the city.[1] In both town and country the hunger sparked bread riots and attacks on food shops and those thought to be hoarding or profiteering. Wherever the hunger struck, social tensions were magnified, and the authorities became increasingly edgy. Police reports in Vienna, on the shanty towns of the dispossessed which had grown up on the outskirts, stressed the volatility of the population, the startling rise in crime, and the overall sense of social decay. From Paris official reports expressed the same concerns.

The stereotype of the revolutionary of 1848, with broad-brimmed hat, beard, long hair, and a generally raffish air, is that of the student, and students did indeed play a significant part in the revolutions. Throughout Europe there was overproduction by the universities. In Prussia the number of law students rose by almost a third in the years after 1841, and there was no hope of work for them. The same pattern was visible in other disciplines.[2] Students were trapped, since they had few of the skills which would qualify them for the better grades of manual work; they were discontented, articulate, receptive to ideas, and as marginal to the society in which they lived as the dispossessed living in squalor and poverty.

At a time when communications throughout Europe were still poor, the revolutionary impulse spread with remarkable speed. The Parisian uprising of February 1848 began the general process. Within the space of a few weeks France, Germany, the Habsburg Empire, had all been thrown into political turmoil, and on the periphery Ireland and Romania experienced a faint echo of the shock wave. Even in England where there was no rising, it was expected that the Chartist movement for political reform would take a revolutionary turn. So serious was the danger felt to be that Queen Victoria and Prince Albert, with their newborn daughter and remaining children, left London hurriedly for the safety of the Isle of Wight.

It was in the countryside where the greatest danger of a true social revolution lay. The peasants' demands were a universal chorus – land and freedom. In some areas like southern Italy and southern Germany, they had already begun to riot and occupy the great estates. In the Habsburg empire, memories of the peasant rising in Galicia in 1846, when the peasants had massacred their landlords, were still fresh. The agricultural catastrophe of 1846–47 meant that the countryside was everywhere in an ugly mood, and the urban revolution could catalyze a rural revolt on a vast scale. In the Austrian domains where the peasant problem was at its most sensitive the peasants' demands were met in full. Labour service was abolished, as were all the dues and payments attached to peasant lands, and Hungarian peasants who had lived as villeins for generations became freeholders.

Each of the revolutions had its own character, but there were certain elements in common which led to initial success. The first and most important was governmental failure. In almost every case the authorities caved in to the revolutionaries at the first blow. In Vienna, after a day of rioting in the Inner City on 13 March 1848, the Emperor Ferdinand declared, 'Tell the people that I agree to everything.'[3] In Paris, Louis Philippe, who had come to the throne of France as a consequence of the revolution in 1830, seemed resigned to the outcome. King Frederick William of Prussia disregarded his generals' advice to crush the revolution in Berlin, and drove around the city sporting the black, red and gold colours of the revolution. Even in Prague, where the Habsburg administration had a firm grip, concessions were made. The best that could be said for this course of action was that it was a tactical withdrawal, like Radetsky's removal of Austrian troops from Milan when the scale of the opposition became clear. The second element of importance was that the revolution should have mass support across the class boundaries. In Vienna the revolution broke out on a Monday, 'Saint Monday', which many workers took as an unofficial holiday each week. Observers noticed many faces in the crowd who had obviously come in from the shanty towns. In Paris, after the clash on the Boulevard des Capucines when over forty people were shot, the workers tore up the cobble-stones – over a million of them – cut down several thousand trees and blocked the streets of Paris with over 1500 barricades.[4]

The apparent ease with which the Paris revolution was accomplished in February 1848 acted as a stimulus to revolution elsewhere. It emboldened the reluctant middle classes to come out onto the streets, and it helped to foster that sense of paralysis which gripped the rulers of Europe. But only where revolutionary spirit fused with nationalist fervour, as in Italy and Hungary, did this enthusiasm last more than a few days. Elsewhere revolutionary zeal was spasmodic. In Vienna the demonstrations lasted over the thirteenth and fourteenth of March, then there was relative calm until early May,[5] when the revolutionaries tightened their grip and the Imperial family withdrew to the safety of Olmutz. Month by month, the number of those willing to come out onto the streets in support of the revolution was reduced. As

From Alfred Rethel's *The Dance of Death Again*, a hard-nosed view of the reality behind the revolution of 1848. Death was the only victor

each of the interest groups – the peasants, the middle classes – achieved redress of its grievances, it lost interest in the revolutionary cause. In Germany and Austria the opening of the Frankfurt Parliament was greeted with elation; in fact it was a meaningless gesture. As the revolution lurched leftwards, the middle classes deserted the cause, justifying the remark by the architect of Italian nationalism, Count Cavour: 'If the social order were to be genuinely menaced . . . the most enthusiastic republicans . . . would be the first to join the ranks of the conservative party.'[6] By the summer of 1848 the revolution had lost its mass character, leaving only a hard core of workers, some students, and a handful of professional revolutionaries. In June the forces of the new French republic, under General Cavaignac, destroyed the Paris revolution. Over 1500 were killed in the battles for the barricades of eastern Paris, plus some 3000 more in the reprisals which followed, and 4500 were imprisoned.[7] In the same month, the same process was begun in the Habsburg empire. The briefest of cannonades brought the surrender of Prague on 16 June; and in the following months the Austrian general Windichgrätz made his preparations to retake Vienna. At the end of October, with 70,000 troops surrounding the city, he began his bombardment. A planned surrender went awry, and he was forced to take the city by storm. At 5.00 pm on 31 October, his troops broke through the Burg Tor in the old city walls, and fought their way to the Royal palace and

the city centre.[8] At dusk all the city gates were locked and guarded, and the troops hunted the revolutionary leaders. In all there were 2000 arrests and over 3000 killed in the final assault and its aftermath. Of the survivors, nine of the leaders were executed, and nine sentenced to imprisonment.

Two main centres of the revolution remained after the fall of Vienna. In Hungary and Italy the revolution had become a war of national liberation. In both cases, the Habsburg armies were ultimately successful, although it was August 1849 before the Hungarian armies surrendered at Világos, and the fortress of Komárom held out until October. The cause of the Italian revolutionaries was doomed when their powerful ally, the Kingdom of Piedmont, was decisively beaten at the battles of Custozza (July 1848) and Novara (March 1849). In the summer of 1849 the Roman Republic, defended by Garibaldi, fell to a French army; Garibaldi was lucky to escape with his life. The last redoubt of the revolution in Italy, the Republic of Venice, surrendered to the Austrians in August. The victors took their revenge. In northern Italy and Hungary, General Haynau organized a massive plan of repression. In Hungary he had over 500 sentenced to death, and it was only through the intervention of the new young Emperor Franz Joseph that no more than 114 of these actually went to the gallows. The terror launched by Haynau, known as 'the cold vampire', poisoned relationships between Austria and Hungary for a generation.

NORWAY

SWEDEN

SCOTLAND

DENMARK

IRELAND

Ballingarry July 48
Killenaule
July 48   Mullinahole
July 48

WALES

ENGLAND

HOLLAND

HANOVER

Berlin
1-2 Mar/11-13 Mar 48

Poznan
10 Apr 48

WESTPHALIA

P R U S S I A

BELGIUM

R. Rhine

Solingen Mar 48

P Cologne Mar 48

HESSE

Nassau Mar 48

Leipzig
Apr/May 49

Dresden
3 May 49

SAXONY

× Frankfurt
31 Mar/4 Apr 48

Prague
1-2 Mar/12 June 48

Paris
22-24 Feb 48

B A V A R I A

Olmutz

Cracow
18 Mar 46/

Rastatt

Liptovsky Mikula

F R A N C E

Baden
Mar/Apr 48

WÜRTTEMBERG

Munich
29 Feb/2 Mar 48

Vienna
29 Feb/13 Mar 48

E M P I R E

P Konstanz Apr 48

Pressburg 3 Mar 48

Nagysa

Kandern

Komárom

SWITZERLAND

A U S T R I A N

Linz
Apr 48

Graz
Apr 48

Pest 29 Feb 48

Mor   Buda

Szolnok

Lyons
Feb 48   SAVOY

17 Mar/18 Mar 48
Milan   Peschiera
Legnano   Verona

Padua Dec 47

Turin P

Novara Pavia
Dec 47

Brescia

Venice 18 Mar/21 Mar 48

Mantua

P I E D M O N T

Custozza

Ferrara

O T T O M A N   E M P

Bologna
Aug 48

Livorno
Aug 48   TUSCANY

PAPAL
STATES

MONTENEGRO

CORSICA

Rome
16 Nov 48

KINGDOM
OF
SARDINIA

Gaeta

Naples
Jan/Feb 48

K I N G D O M   O F   T H E   T W O   S I C I L I E S

miles
0   100   200
0   100   200
kilometres

Palermo   Areas already in rebellion when the revolution broke out in Paris

The area principally affected by revolution in 1848. The focus of
attention switched to the nationalist rising in Hungary after the fall
of Vienna in October 1848. The tiny rising in Ireland was the only
direct consequence of 1848 in the British Isles

Initial centre of the revolution, and the date news was received of
revolution in Paris or Vienna

Local rallying points of the revolution

P   Initial centres of revolutionary appeals and propaganda

P   The twin fountain-heads of the revolution

Reprisals by governments against the revolutionaries, leading to
many deaths

Fortification

Skirmish

Battle

The railway was only beginning to speed communications
in limited areas. Most news travelled by traditional means

*Palermo
Jan 48*   Messina

48

G

A few months before the revolution, Alexis de Tocqueville, the great political philosopher, gave the French Chamber of Deputies this warning. 'We are sleeping on a volcano. . . . Do you not see that the earth trembles anew? A wind of revolution blows, the storm is on the horizon.'[9] Tocqueville might have claimed a degree of prescience, but he later admitted that his speech was mostly empty rhetoric. The wind blew down governments in its path, but they sprang back again. Nor did the revolutions leave much sign of their passing. They had seemingly come without warning and were gone in a moment. In 1848 people played at revolution like a game, albeit a risky one. Only at the end, when all the casual crowd had departed, did it turn into a bloody and unpleasant business. The great tradition of coming onto the streets to seek redress of grievances, a refinement of rioting, began to die away. The middle classes had become too scared, while the workers began to discover that industrial strikes were a much more effective way of achieving their ends. Only a few 'revolutionaries' remained, of whom Garibaldi was the archetype. Most became folk heroes, at least among the working classes and the peasants. But the day of the romantic revolutionary was ended in Europe. Future revolutions – the Paris Commune of 1871, Russia in 1905 and 1917 – would be in deadly earnest.

The final attack on Vienna in October 1848 by the army of Prince Schwarzenburg. Cobbles have been used to make the barricades, useful because they enabled revolutionaries to create instant defences

The wind of madness

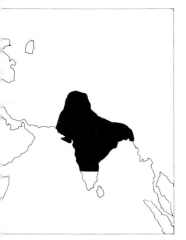

IN the spring of 1857, northern India experienced a unique set of events. 'No one seems to know the meaning of it,' wrote Dr Gilbert Hadow to his sister in England. 'It is not known where it originated, by whom or for what purpose. . . . The Indian papers are full of surmises as to what it means. . . . It is called the chuppaty movement.'[1] A man would arrive by night with five chuppaties (or sometimes another object), give them to the watchman of a village, and tell him to make four more. He was then to pass them to the next village with the same instructions. They were sent to Hindu and Moslem villages alike, and sometimes they could be carried up to 200 miles in a single night.[2] The mystery of the chuppaties has never been solved, but what the incidents prove is the existence of a channel of communication spread across northern India far more pervasive than anything which the government possessed. If an official wished to communicate with any part of India, he had the choice of a letter, which was slow, a messenger, who would be faster where trunk roads existed, or the telegraph to those few locations which were on the telegraph line. The entire railway 'network' amounted to only a few miles of track, and where communication with the villages or rural towns was concerned, this was a matter of chance. As what the British described as 'the Mutiny' developed, the rebels were often better informed than the government. Sita Ram, a *sepoy* loyal to the British, described how he returned to his village on leave: 'I arrived at my own village without hearing anything out of the ordinary on the road, but shortly afterwards we heard that the troops of Meerut and Delhi had risen and killed their officers. . . . It was such an extraordinary story that I refused to believe it, considering it a story invented to inflame the mind of the populace, but the rumour gathered strength daily.'[3] He went to see the Deputy Commissioner 'who asked me a number of questions to discover how much I knew and what effect it was having on the minds of people in my district. Finally, the *sahib* admitted that he had heard the rumour . . . but that reports were very vague.' His village in Oudh province was hundreds of miles from Delhi and Meerut to the north west, and off the main trunk road. Clearly rumour was a better source of information than official channels.

The events in India do not constitute a revolution or even the first evidence of a movement for national liberation. There were few common objectives, other than destroying the British and all their innovations. There was no concerted planning, or evidence of any central direction of a conspiracy. What *is* amply clear is the facility with which a mass movement was gathered together. The focal point of the rising was the sepoy army, who had their own set of grievances against the British. It spread almost immediately into society at large, which shared only some of the same feelings of resentment. It encompassed both Hindu and Moslem, as well as all classes within society, but it was localized in its influence. Physically, the limits of the unrest were vast, inevitable given the size of the sub-continent, but it was restricted to north and central India. South India remained free from the contagion. So did a number of groups within the affected area. The Sikhs, and the Gurkhas of Nepal continued to serve the British, and were principal instruments in the suppression of the rising. The causes of the rising were specific, and consisted of a set of events which were independent of each other, but which taken together provided evidence of a British plan to destroy Indian religion and culture. Mistrust had grown between the British and their Indian subjects so that the worst possible construction was placed on any British action. The British issued a denial that they had '"any intention of hurting their (the sepoys') feelings or breaking their caste." However, the very reading out of this order was seized upon by many as proof that the *Sirkar* had broken our caste, since otherwise the order would never have been issued. What was the use of a denial if it had not been the Government's intention originally to break our caste?'[4]

What affected the troops and then the civil population was what was described as 'a wind of madness', a hot insistent summer breeze that drives men to insanity. The sepoys in the garrison at Meerut, the first to rebel, were convinced (rightly) that new cartridges which they had to bite contained animal fats offensive to Moslems and Hindus alike. They linked this, which would cause them to be shunned by their co-religionists, with the efforts of missionaries and a number of senior officers to evangelize for Christianity. It was widely known that education in schools and even the receipt of charity was dependent on learning to read the Bible or attending Christian worship. Equally resented was the high-handed British attitude towards landholding and inheritance, which had been 'reformed' in such a way as to bring it under control of British rather than customary courts. In every respect, the British administrators had become more intrusive than any conqueror in the past, and their interventions were seen, not unnaturally, as part of a concerted plan. In reality, they were the piecemeal response of energetic and high-minded British officials determined to make more efficient and 'useful' the whole government of India which had wallowed in corruption and inefficiency for centuries. The British who had come in the eighteenth century to plunder had stayed to reform, to build and to improve. Their good intentions were fatal.

In military terms, the position of the British was weak. There were only some 21,000 British troops in India, while the sepoy armies of Bengal, Madras and Bombay were in excess of 277,000.[5] Nor were the British located so that they could easily put down any rising. The first tremors of mutiny came in Dum Dum, the arsenal near Calcutta, where the rumours concerning the cartridges were started. Throughout the spring there were disturbances, at Barrackpur, Berhampur, Ambala and Lucknow, and at Meerut where on 10 May 1857 the sepoy Light Cavalry and Native Infantry rose and murdered all the British they could find.[6] The cavalrymen rode from the camp to spread the news to other garrisons, while the remaining mutineers marched to Delhi, the old capital of the Moghul empire. The mutiny spread during the whole of May and on into June. The British seemed powerless to resist, and everywhere rumours spread of the atrocities committed by the rebels upon British men and women, and indeed children too. The events were certainly horrific. At Cawnpore, the remnants of the garrison, given safe conduct down the Ganges by boat, were fired upon and massacred. The women and children who survived were butchered, and their bodies thrown down a well. But as the British recovered their nerve, and the forces in Calcutta under Colonel Neill advanced to Allahabad, the incidents were magnified in rumours now created by the British. Neill and other officers initiated a campaign of racial terror, hanging almost any Indians on whom they could lay their hands in an orgy of vengeance. Worse still were the parties of civilian irregulars. When the British reached Cawnpore, and saw the results of the atrocities committed there, they became frenzied. Neill devised special forms of execution which, depending on whether he was Moslem or Hindu, would damn the victim eternally. He forced prisoners to lick up the blood from the floor of the small house where the women and children had been killed. Stories were invented that women had

been raped and tortured, their white womanhood ravaged by 'black faced curs', and children deliberately and slowly tortured.[7] In fact most of the atrocities were committed in the heat of the moment, or in panic, rather than by deliberation. This did not stop the British from instituting a policy of terror, aided by those like the Sikhs who hated both Hindus and Moslems. One officer came across a party of Sikhs roasting a sepoy over a slow fire; it was not an isolated incident. There was an official campaign to restore death by torture, hanging being too swift for those who had committed *Vile Acts*. There were exceptions to this bloodthirstiness, but not many.

If there was one common theme which had linked all the risings, military and popular, it was a determination to rid India of the British. This determination hardened as the violence of the British response became clear. Sita Ram tells of a broadsheet 'printed on yellow paper and said to have been issued by the king (of Delhi)'. It called for sepoys 'to fight for their religion and drive the detested foreigners out of the country'. He added: 'Every man who heard it believed every word of it. Even I was impressed by it.'[8] The news of British actions was passed by word of mouth, while written bulletins were read to those who could not read. The risings were suppressed one by one, a task made difficult by the many small forts and towns held by the rebels. When the fortress at Jhansi was taken in April 1858, the Indian leader Tantia Topia took to the jungle and wild country. He eluded his pursuers until February 1859, and with his death on the scaffold at the town of Sipri on 18

The massacre at Cawnpore, an amalgamation of a number of the atrocities which took place in the city. On the river the boats evacuating the garrison are being bombarded, while on the terrace bodies are being thrown down a well. The print indicates the horror with which the British received the news of the murder of women and children, and explains the lust for vengeance which filled the British troops. The British commander made his Indian captives lick up the dried British blood of the slaughtered women and children before they were hanged

April 1859, the military aspect of the risings was ended. The British government in London imposed a settlement which was not ungenerous. The East India Company, which had ruled India until the mutiny, was abolished, and the continent was to be ruled directly by the British authorities. All remaining rebels were pardoned, provided they had committed no crime, and the sanctity of religious freedom was guaranteed. The process of reform proceeded even faster than before.

The new regime created in time a class of educated Indians, and it was in this group that the later movement of Indian nationalism took root. By the turn of the century, groups inspired by the memory of the risings of 1857–9 were turning again to violence as a means of expelling the British, but they were small and largely ineffective. The mainstream of Indian nationalism turned towards political and economic pressure, and eventually to the Gandhian technique of provocation and civil disobedience.

But in this final movement of resistance to the British, which finally achieved their withdrawal a century after the 'wind of madness', can be found the same pattern of 'rousing the masses' as in 1857–9. The means of political action in a pre-literate society remained the same, a hidden network of communication by rumour and word of mouth.

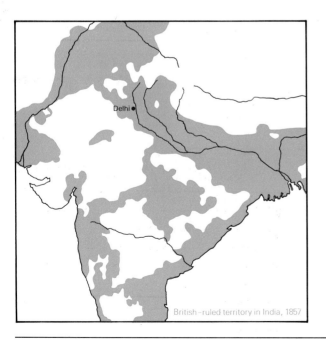

British-ruled territory in India, 1857

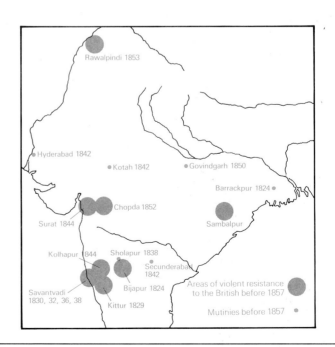

Rawalpindi 1853

Hyderabad 1842

Kotah 1842

Govindgarh 1850

Barrackpur 1824

Chopda 1852

Surat 1844

Sambalpur

Kolhapur 1844

Sholapur 1838

Secunderabad 1842

Savantvadi 1830, 32, 36, 38

Bijapur 1824

Kittur 1829

Areas of violent resistance to the British before 1857

Mutinies before 1857

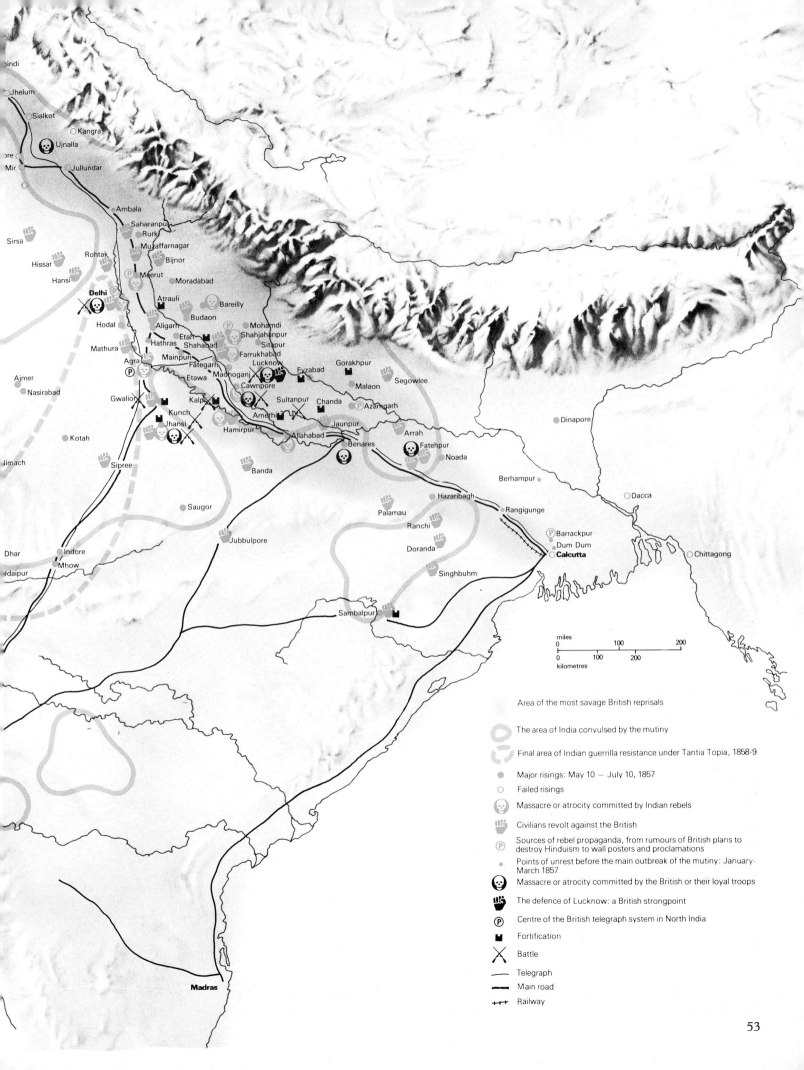

Garibaldi: the revolutionary as hero

GIUSEPPE Garibaldi possessed the supreme quality in a revolutionary – good luck. On any rational grounds, many of his greatest exploits had no chance of success. His years of training had been spent in aiding the infant revolutions in South America. He was 28 when he sailed from Marseille to Rio de Janeiro, and over 40 when he returned to aid the Italian struggle for freedom. He had achieved his greatest success when he was able to use his skills as a seaman, a guerrilla of the ocean. Born in 1807, it was 1840 before he fought his first substantial engagement on land, at Taquari in Brazil. His capacity to rouse his men to achieve seemingly impossible objectives won him his greatest battle in South America, at San Antonio in 1846, when 200 of his Italian Legion plus a few Uruguayans smashed an enemy column of over 1000. Even so, this was little more than a lengthy skirmish, and when he returned to Europe with a handful of the Italian Legion, his reputation was larger than his experience warranted. The sea-captain from Nice was already being hailed as the archetypal revolutionary.

To authority Garibaldi posed a threat. After the King of Piedmont, Charles Albert, had met him he wrote to his minister of war: 'If there were a naval war he might be employed as a leader of privateers, but to employ him otherwise would be to dishonour the army.' He hoped that 'the self-styled general and his disciples' could be bought off: 'The best would be if they went off to any other place. . . .'[1] This view of Garibaldi as a danger rather than an asset ran through the whole of his relationship with the leaders of Italy whom he so loyally followed. Even at the height of his success in 1860, they distrusted him. In 1848, the year of his return, he was fobbed off with a minor campaign around Lake Maggiore in the north. Yet when, in the following year, he was called upon to defend the hard-pressed Roman Republic, under the guidance of his political mentor Mazzini, he responded with instant energy. On 27 April 1849 he rode into Rome after a forced march from the north. Beside him rode a black Uruguayan and some sixty of his Italian Legion who had followed him from Montevideo and the South American campaigns: all wore the red shirts that became a symbol of the Garibaldini. In total his forces amounted to about 1300 men. He inspired the whole of the defending force with a spirit approaching elation, a feeling which grew to adulation when he threw back the attacking armies, first of the French and then of the King of Naples, at Velletri. But the odds were too great, and by the third week in June 1849, he recognized the battle was lost. 'I regard Rome as having fallen' was his laconic statement. By 2 July all the city's defences had fallen to the French and Garibaldi decided to carry on a guerrilla war in the countryside. He drew up his small army in St Peter's Square and made an epic declaration which added another star to his incandescent reputation: 'This is what I have to offer those who wish to follow me: hunger, cold, the heat of the sun; no wages, no barracks, no ammunition; but continual skirmishes, forced marches and bayonet fights. Those of you who love your country and love glory, *follow me*.'[2] It was irresistible, and over four thousand streamed after him out of the Porta San Giovanni.

In the event, his hopes of a continuing struggle were futile, and he was lucky to escape, after many adventures, to the coast. His wife Anita died during their flight. His defence of Rome was epic and became more so with each re-telling. When war came again in 1859, he volunteered as he had eleven years before. Although he was now too famous to be ignored he was fobbed off with a minor command and the rank of general in the Sardinian army. In his distinguished blue uniform, he looked an unlikely revolutionary, as the Parisian Dupont discovered. 'A felt hat, a ferocious countenance, imbedded in a mass of dishevelled hair . . . a naked sabre in his hand; such is the personage of the legend. He may have appeared in this condition ten years ago, under the walls of Rome, but times have changed and Garibaldi with them.'[3] Superficialities misled him, for Garibaldi in his fifties had lost none of the passions of his youth. The war of 1859 had made some progress towards the liberation of Italy, but Garibaldi was more convinced than ever that the failing structure of power needed only one further violent push to bring it down. He began to wear the red shirt again, and to collect arms for an expedition to Sicily to strike a new blow for a united Italy. He sailed from Quarto on 5 May 1860, with little over 1000 men. No one, least of all the government of Sardinia, gave him any hope of success. They were glad to see the back of a turbulent and disruptive influence.

From the moment the expedition left, it seemed to have a charmed existence. On 11 May, as the Garibaldini sailed towards Marsala, the two Neopolitan warships which could have blown them out of the water left to patrol the south. He landed his troops and sent an advance party to seize the telegraph office. They found a message had already been sent that an invasion was in progress, and the telegraph relay station at Trapani was asking for confirmation of this disturbing news. They quickly sent a correction that it was an error, and the 'invaders' were only merchant ships discharging stores. 'Idiots' came the reply. Then the Neopolitan ships returned and began to shell the red shirts. But almost all of them had disembarked; had the shelling begun a few minutes earlier, many would have been killed. Good fortune continued once they moved inland. When they met a force of Neapolitan soldiers at Calatafimi, the Garibaldini swept through them in a bayonet charge, despite their stronger position. The Sicilians, who hated the intruders from Naples, began to turn against their overlords. There was considerable violence on the Bronte estates near Mount Etna, and as Garibaldi

approached the capital Palermo, the people drove the Neapolitan soldiers from the streets back into the citadel. By 6 June, Garibaldi had sent columns through the island to mop up the remaining groups of enemy soldiers, and accepted the surrender of 20,000. The only garrison which still resisted him were 5000 at Messina. The Thousand had overcome The Twenty-Five Thousand.

He quickly reduced the Messina garrison and shipped them out of the island, but he was anxious to move on. He had already been forced to suppress the peasant rising at Bronte, and he knew the volatility of the Sicilians. But while he had entered Sicily by stealth, the whole world was now expecting his move forward on to the mainland. A naval squadron guarded the Straits of Messina, and troops were massed to defend the coastline. His first exploratory thrust across the sea was a failure. 200 men put ashore near Scilla met a larger Neapolitan force and had to retreat into the hills of Aspromonte. But this feint attracted the enemy to the narrowest part of the straits in the north. On 18 August after a brief foray to Sardinia to collect more troops, Garibaldi drove south from Messina to Taormina where 3360 troops had been collected. That night they sailed in two steamers to Melito, south of Reggio di Calabria. Garibaldi was always at his happiest on the deck of a ship,

and the seaborne assault was his most practised tactic. On the morning of 19 August, the Garibaldini took Reggio by storm. The ships guarding the straits now moved quickly south, and his remaining 1500 troops crossed the straits in fishing boats. He had wrong-footed them twice. By now the peasants of the countryside were rising to support him, and the armies of the King of Naples shrunk daily through desertion. By 5 September he had arrived at Salerno, where 20,000 people greeted him, and he was invited to take possession of Naples. The railway ran from Salerno, and so he arrived at Naples by train, a conquering hero under the guns of the Carmine fortress. Yet so great was the sense of demoralization that the royalist garrison made no attempt to resist him. From 7 September to 8 November 1860, Garibaldi was Dictator of Naples.

On 11 September, the Sardinian army moved south through the Papal States with the intention of linking with Garibaldi. He, by this time, had moved forward to Caserta to confront the remainder of the Neapolitan army gathered on the Volturno River. He was also faced with the need to garrison Naples, and to send troops against royalist peasants in the Ariano, where they were massacring anyone thought to be sympathetic to the revolution. In all he had 20,000 men against 50,000 in the Royal army. In the battle

Garibaldi leaving for the expedition to Sicily on the night of 5 May 1860. The Thousand, as his revolutionaries became known, actually numbered 1089 and were mostly North Italians

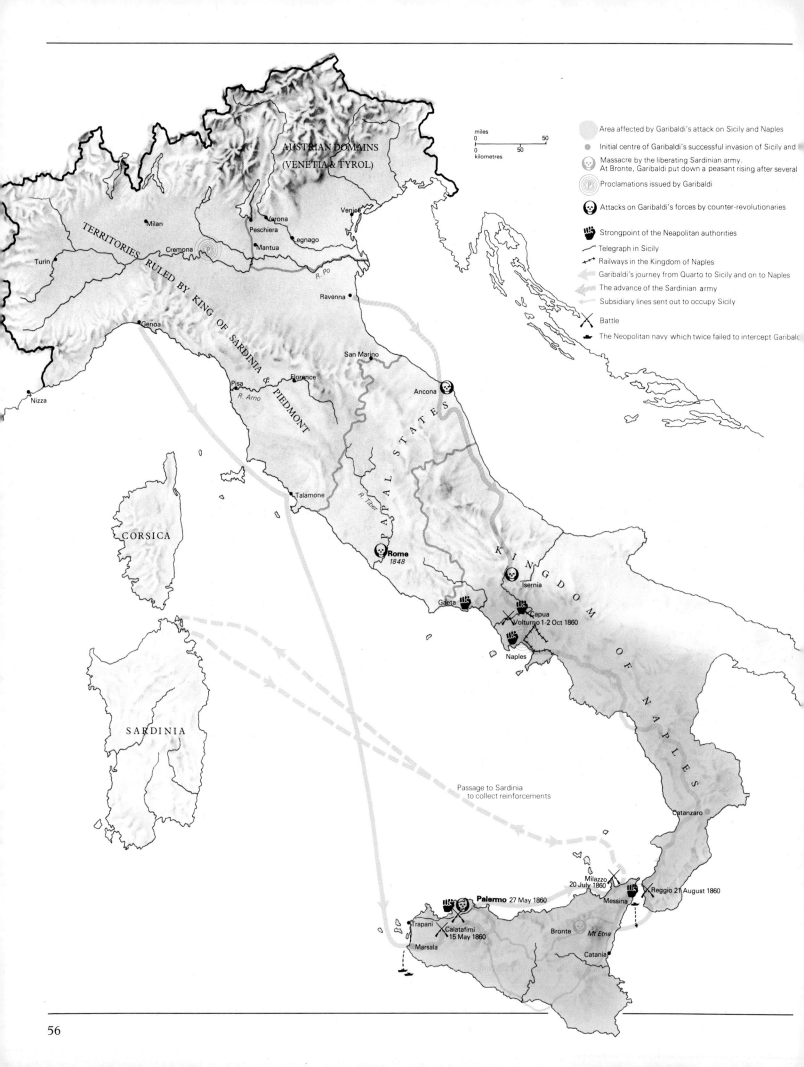

AUSTRIAN DOMAINS
(VENETIA & TYROL)

Milan

Verona
Peschiera
Legnago
Mantua

Cremona ⓟ

Turin

R. Po

TERRITORIES RULED BY KING OF SARDINIA & PIEDMONT

Genoa

Ravenna

Nizza

San Marino

Pisa
Florence
R. Arno

Talamone

R. Tiber

Ancona ☠

CORSICA

☠ **Rome**
1848

P A P A L   S T A T E S

Isernia ☠

Gaeta ✊

✊ Capua
✕
Volturno 1-2 Oct 1860

✊

Naples ✊

SARDINIA

K I N G D O M   O F   N A P L E S

Passage to Sardinia
to collect reinforcements

Catanzaro

Milazzo
20 July 1860 ✕

Reggio 21 August 1860

✊ Messina

✊ ⓟ **Palermo** 27 May 1860

Trapani
✕ Calatafimi
15 May 1860

Bronte *Mt Etna*

Marsala

Catania

miles
0 _____ 50
0 _____ 50
kilometres

⬤ Area affected by Garibaldi's attack on Sicily and Naples

● Initial centre of Garibaldi's successful invasion of Sicily and

☠ Massacre by the liberating Sardinian army.
At Bronte, Garibaldi put down a peasant rising after several

ⓟ Proclamations issued by Garibaldi

☠ Attacks on Garibaldi's forces by counter-revolutionaries

✊ Strongpoint of the Neapolitan authorities

⌒ Telegraph in Sicily

⊢ Railways in the Kingdom of Naples

⟵ Garibaldi's journey from Quarto to Sicily and on to Naples

⟸ The advance of the Sardinian army

⟶ Subsidiary lines sent out to occupy Sicily

✕ Battle

⊢ The Neopolitan navy which twice failed to intercept Garibald

which followed in the first days of October, Garibaldi stopped the royalist advance on Naples, but their army was left largely intact. He could not advance any further from the coast without endangering his line of retreat. He was forced to await the advance of the Sardinians under king Victor Emmanuel. On 25 October the two armies met near the village of Marganello, a meeting celebrated both in words and heroic painting. From that moment, Garibaldi was pushed progressively into the side lines. Rewards were heaped upon him – a full general's rank, a castle and a private steamer – all of which he refused. When he asked for political office, as first Governor of Naples which he had so recently ruled as Dictator, he was denied it. All that was left was to return to his home on Caprera, and await a new call to arms.

It had all been too easy. As he believed, the pack of cards had collapsed, and the power of the Kingdom of Naples fallen at the first push. Yet he could have been stopped on the shore at Marsala, and limped home in defeat. The Garibaldi legend grew year by year, strengthened by his extraordinary human warmth and resolute simplicity. He came to be seen as the archetypal revolutionary hero, honourable and chivalrous, daring and inventive. Even in his sixties and seventies, the visual image of Garibaldi never aged: he was always seen as the young hero described by Dupont. Yet all his enterprises had been hit or miss affairs, the same story of volunteers flocking to the colours, arms hurriedly assembled, of a campaign won at the point of a bayonet in the nick of time. It was thrilling, but not a good model to follow.

Garibaldi in action in July 1860. The artist sketched the picture 'on the spot'

The end of old China

THE Emperors of China ruled because they possessed 'the mandate of heaven'. An unsuccessful monarch could be held, by his failures, to have lost the mandate, and the Dragon Throne would lie vacant ready to be taken by some successful general.[1] The alien Manchu rulers had taken and held the throne in 1644 because they were strong enough to do so: by the nineteenth century, as the Chinese Empire received a succession of humiliations at the hands of the Western barbarians, it seemed that the Emperor Hsien-feng who came to the throne in 1851 no longer possessed divine favour. At his accession, the Western powers had gained rights of trade through a number of treaty ports, reluctantly conceded by the Treaty of Nanking in 1842. More significantly, the Manchu faced internal rebellion on a scale unknown for centuries. The Chinese had never accepted their rule willingly, seeing them as an evil imposed by providence. Numerous secret societies had flourished, the most notable being the White Lotus Society of Honan province, which had been pushed southwards by Manchu pressure after a major rebellion in 1775.[2] China south of the Yangtze, and in particular the coastal cities and provinces of Kwantung and Fukien, received an infusion of refugees from the north, violently anti-Manchu in their attitudes, and practised in the arts of conspiracy and subversion.

The tension between the regions of China has determined the course of much (some would say all) of Chinese history. The rebellions against the Manchu in the middle of the nineteenth century took place on the periphery, at the points inaccessible to the power of the central authority. Moreover, they had their origins among social and racial groups on the margin of Chinese society. The opposition of Moslem peoples to efforts of Chinese officials who wished to impose the State religion upon them resulted in a major uprising in Kansu and Shensi. Far to the south in the hills of Kweichow, a non-Chinese tribe, the Miao, in 1854 began a long-running irregular war against the Chinese authorities which was not finally put down until the early 1880s.

But neither of these called in question the existence of the Manchu state, as did the most significant of the rebellions, that of the Taiping, the 'Heavenly Kingdom of Great Peace'. It was a movement which gathered together all the discontents of southern China and expressed them in a fundamental repudiation of traditional society. The pressures of floods, bad harvests, and famine were not new, and the usual response was an attempt by the local authorities to alleviate the worst of the problems, backed by armed force if resentment turned to violence. But by 1850 not only were the economic problems magnified by an exceptional rise in population which put pressure on scarce resources, but there was a collapse of confidence in the capacity of the authorities. Much of this loss of face could be attributed to the humiliation of the Manchu at the hands of the Europeans and the exceptional measures which the war had brought about. 'It is well known that, previous to the war (1842) the appearance of the insignia of a Mandarin ... could disperse the most turbulent crowd in Canton, the most turbulent city in the empire ... during the war arms were so generally distributed that loose characters of all kinds got possession of them, while at the same time respect for the government had been destroyed by the manner in which its immense pretensions had been broken through by the despised Barbarians.'[3] The author, Thomas Meadows, writing in 1856, saw for himself the early stages of the revolution in southern China. The Taiping emerged from a minority community, the Hakka. These 'guest settlers' had come from northern China to Kwangsi and Kwangtung during the first millennium AD; they were still regarded by the Chinese of the south as outsiders, with their own dialect and communities. The inspiration behind the movement was a young man called Hung Hsiu-ch'uan from near Canton, who became a village schoolteacher in Kwangsi. He came from a peasant family and as he began to spread his new creed – a mixture of half-understood Christian teaching joined to the usual peasant complaints against landlords and the authorities, he gained a following among both Hakka and southern Chinese. The 'Society of God Worshippers' quickly gathered to it many of those forces which opposed Manchu rule, attracted by its proclamation of the Kingdom of God on Earth and a radical revolution within society. The God Worshippers called for the abolition of private property, redistribution of the land, equality of the sexes, and a puritan attitude towards opium, tobacco, drink and 'graven images'. The leaders, now styled 'kings', declared themselves a new dynasty, and stated, 'Our Heavenly King [the former schoolteacher] has received the Divine Commission to exterminate the Manchu, to exterminate all idolators generally, and to possess the Empire as its True Sovereign. . . . We command the services of all and we take everything. All who resist us are rebels and idolatrous demons, and we kill them without sparing; but whoever acknowledges our Heavenly King and exerts himself in our service shall have full reward.'[4] The Taiping matched their words with a fanaticism in battle which made them difficult to defeat. The Taiping armies, which grew from the ten thousand with which they had set out from Kwangsi, headed north to the great cities of central China. Wuchang and Hankow were besieged and fell, to the accompaniment of immense slaughter of all who would not join the movement. The Taiping pressed on towards Nanking, the traditional eastern capital, which was taken in 1853. Now they controlled the heart of China, an army numbered in the hundreds of thousands, and vast wealth. The mandate of heaven did seem, as they claimed, to have been passed to them.

The reasons for the failure of the Manchu were not hard to find. They had lost a costly and devastating war against the Europeans and they had never held the south of China as firmly as the north. Furthermore, their soldiers were fighting what amounted to a colonial war. The Governor of Kwangsi admitted: 'Our troops have not a vestige of discipline; retreating is easy to them, advancing difficult; and, though repeatedly exhorted, they remain as weak and timorous as before. . . .'[5] The standing of the Manchu government was dealt a further blow when war with the European powers, which flared up from 1856–8, and again during 1860, led to the sack of Peking and the humiliation of the Emperor. In August 1861 he died at Jehol, leaving a young son. After considerable palace intrigue, his favourite concubine, who had been created Dowager Empress on his death, emerged as the most powerful voice in the state. Although the Taiping claimed that they 'held the Empire in an iron grasp . . . [their] troops more numerous than the streams',[6] their position was less strong than it seemed. Factions had formed, with a state of civil war existing between the subsidiary kings. Nor was their control over the whole of their vast territory entirely secure. Wuchang had briefly been lost in 1855, while there were constant attacks on the Taiping forces in Chekiang province. The Taiping response was invariably annihilation of all who opposed them: in Chekiang 10,000 were put to the sword to avenge an attack on some Taiping soldiers near Ningpo. In consequence, they soon came to be seen not as liberators but as worse tyrants than the Manchu. Although they had launched an attack towards Peking during 1853 and 1854, which reached as far as Tientsin, they failed to carry on to the capital and cut off the head of the 'Tartar dog', the Emperor. In the province of Hunan, a local governor Tseng Kuo-Fan rallied the peasants against the Taiping and, with two other competent generals, rallied the Manchu forces against the God Worshippers. In 1861 Tseng Kuo-Fan was appointed supreme commander in Kiangsu, Anhwei, Kiangsi and Chekiang, and with the aid of the small 'Ever Victorious Army' led by Charles 'Chinese' Gordon, the future hero of Khartoum, the Imperial armies pressed the Taiping back towards Nanking. In 1864 the city fell, as Tseng Kuo-Fan reported to the Dowager Empress: 'The . . . creek was filled with bodies. Half the false kings, chief generals, heavenly generals and other heads were killed in battle, and the other half either drowned themselves in the dykes . . . or else burned themselves. The whole of them numbered about 3000 men . . . [the soldiers] searched through the city for any rebels they could find and in three days killed over 100,000. Not one surrendered. . . .' The final remnant of the Taiping was exterminated on the borders of Anhwei and Chekiang.

The war which raged for over a decade produced a strong reaction among the peasants. Some joined the Imperial armies of Tseng Kuo-Fan and Li Hung Chang, while others, in the worst affected province of Anhwei, had taken matters into their own hands and were defending themselves from all the armies, Taiping and Imperial. The Nien Fei, begun in the borderlands of Honan and Anhwei, a poor sandy area, banded together by villages and built rough fortifications to defend themselves. Since it was an area where horses were widely used, the Nien soon created mobile raiding bands which probed deeply to the north and west. In 1853 the Yellow River changed course, ruining agriculture in Anhwei and Shantung, and in consequence, many who had nothing else to lose joined the Nien bands. The Imperial forces found the Nien more difficult to pin down than the Taiping, and it required fifteen years of painstaking battles to destroy the nodules of resistance in the fortified villages and to track down the roving guerrilla bands. Nor was it accidental that the epicentre of the final great popular movement of the century, the rising of the Righteous Harmonious Fists (better known as the Boxers), developed in a marginal area between provinces and in an area deeply affected by the Nien rising.

The Boxer rising has always been marked, in Western eyes, by its hatred of foreigners. In this it shared common ground with the other great popular movements of the century. The Taiping had begun, in its pseudo-Christian spirit, by welcoming Europeans, but by 1860 it described them as 'foreign devils'. The Nien and the Boxers railed against the Manchu and the gentry; only after the Boxers had been taken up by the Imperial authorities and received encouragement to act against European influences did their movement acquire its quality of xenophobia. Their special hatred was reserved for missionaries and their

A contemporary Chinese print of the Taiping attack on Shanghai. It accurately shows that they have removed their top-knots, symbol of Manchu domination, and grown their hair

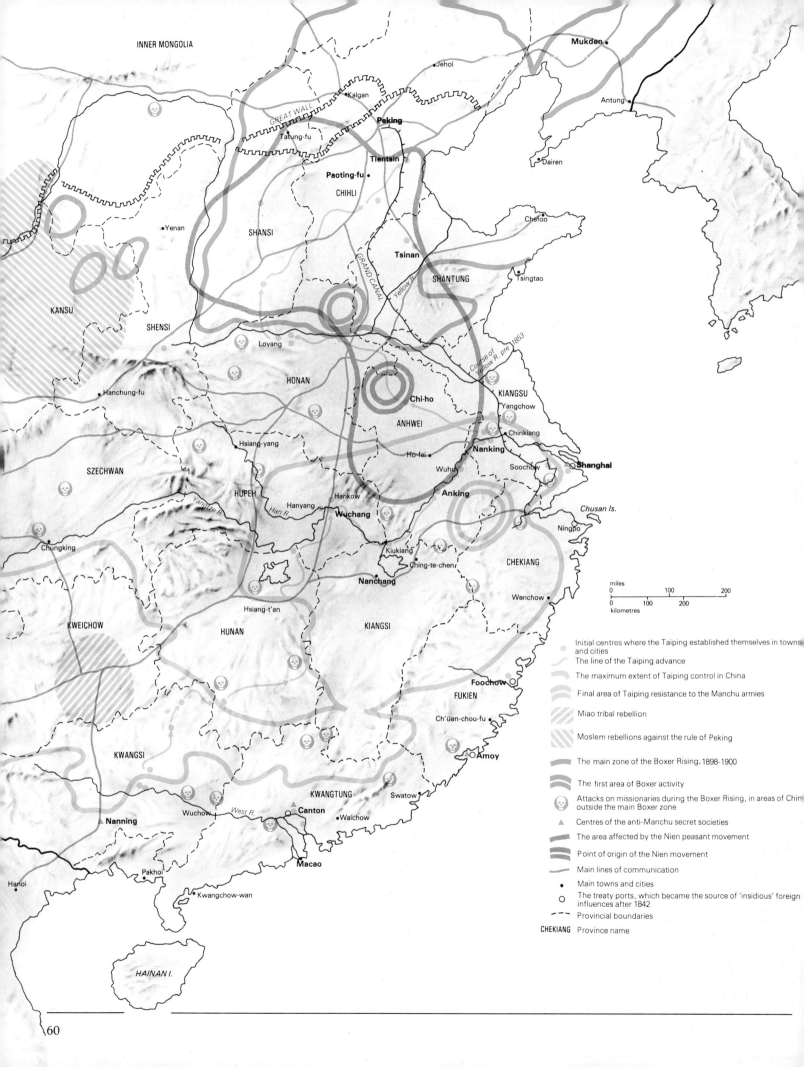

INNER MONGOLIA

Mukden

• Jehol

• Kalgan

GREAT WALL

Tatung-fu

Peking

Antung

Tientsin

Paoting-fu •

CHIHLI

• Dairen

• Yenan

SHANSI

• Chefoo

GRAND CANAL

Tsinan

Yellow R.

SHANTUNG

• Tsingtao

KANSU

SHENSI

Loyang •

*Course of
Yellow R. pre 1853*

• Hanchung-fu

HONAN

Chi-ho

KIANGSU

Yangchow

ANHWEI

Chinkiang •

• Hsiang-yang

Ho-fei •

Nanking ×

SZECHWAN

Soochow

Shanghai ○

HUPEH

Wuhu •

Chusan Is.

Han R.

Hankow

Hanyang

Anking

Ningpo •

Wuchang

• Chungking

Yangtze R.

Kiukiang •

• Ching-te-chen

CHEKIANG

Nanchang

KWEICHOW

HUNAN

Hsiang-t'an •

KIANGSI

Wenchow •

miles
0   100   200
0   100   200
kilometres

Foochow ○

FUKIEN

KWANGSI

Ch'üan-chou-fu •

Amoy ○

KWANGTUNG

Swatow •

Nanning

Wuchow •

West R.

▲ **Canton**

• Waichow

• Pakhoi

Macao

Hanoi •

• Kwangchow-wan

HAINAN I.

Initial centres where the Taiping established themselves in towns
and cities

The line of the Taiping advance

The maximum extent of Taiping control in China

Final area of Taiping resistance to the Manchu armies

Miao tribal rebellion

Moslem rebellions against the rule of Peking

The main zone of the Boxer Rising, 1898–1900

The first area of Boxer activity

Attacks on missionaries during the Boxer Rising, in areas of Chin
outside the main Boxer zone

Centres of the anti-Manchu secret societies

The area affected by the Nien peasant movement

Point of origin of the Nien movement

Main lines of communication

Main towns and cities

The treaty ports, which became the source of 'insidious' foreign
influences after 1842

Provincial boundaries

CHEKIANG   Province name

60

The final destruction of the Taiping in Nanking. The captured leaders are carried off for execution 'by a slow and painful process'

Chinese converts, and attacks on missions, with frequent murder and mutilations, extended far beyond the area dominated by the Boxers in the north. The progressive domination of China by the Western world, through commercial treaties conceded under the muzzle of a gun and the division of China into 'spheres of influence' like some conquered country, was deeply wounding to all Chinese. Nationalism grew as a force, drawing on the same regional resources as the Taiping. Southern and central China provided the main support of the illegal nationalist movement which developed from the 1890s. The secret societies of the coastal provinces, now known as Triads, were once again active in the anti-Manchu movement. Under the leadership of a young doctor, Sun Yat Sen, born as a peasant in Kwangtung, the nationalists were united in the 'Society of Sworn Confederates', devoted to nationalism and the end of Manchu rule, republicanism, and land reform. By 1910, there were renewed rebellions against the Manchu in Hunan, as well as demonstrations against the government in Szechwan. In October 1911, there was a much more profound rising in Hankow and Wuchang, the great Yangtze cities. Provincial governors in the south, by now more concerned with their own survival than that of the dynasty, made no very effective efforts to suppress it. Even the general summoned to suppress the revolution, Yuan Shih-Kai, ended by making common cause with it against the

dynasty in Peking. On 29 December 1911 a provisional government was set up in Nanking with Sun Yat Sen as President, and by February the dynasty renounced its rights to the throne of China and declared the republic to be the lawful form of state. The mandate had been passed.

By the end of Manchu rule, the state had been at war with internal enemies for almost thirty years. For much of the period since 1850 Peking exercised no control over much of eastern or southern China, while her finances and armies were ruined by conflict with the western powers. The separation between north and south, Manchu and Han Chinese, became a more dramatic fragmentation in the years after the revolution of 1911, when China turned to rule by warlords. In the context of the longer span of Chinese history, the end of domination by the north represented not the end of old China, but a reversion to an earlier time, the China of the Five Dynasties and the Ten Kingdoms which destroyed the Tang dynasty in the last years of the first millennium AD. Within the span of Chinese history, the rule of the Manchu was an inconsequential moment.

The earthquake of change

JAPAN had been a stable and largely static society since the victory of the Tokugawa family over all their adversaries between 1600–50 ended a state of internal war which had lasted for centuries. The Tokugawa became in fact, if not by law, hereditary *shogun*, holding the supreme power in the state in trust for a venerated and wholly powerless emperor. It was a society based on clan and feudal loyalties, and many of those families which the Tokugawa had all but crushed in their drive for power remained hostile in succeeding centuries. While the economic and military power of the *shogun* remained concentrated in the rich plains around Yedo (Tokyo), their hereditary enemies remained most powerful in the extremities of the islands, especially in Kyushu and across the straits of Shimonoseki in Choshu. These were poor lands compared with the rich rice plains which made up much of the Tokugawa heartland. Favours, court office, and patronage went to the members of the extended Tokugawa family and their loyal vassals, *fudai*, faithful among the faithful.

The stability of the system depended on control, and both social and economic legislation was fiercely enforced in Japan. Contact with the outside world was strictly controlled through the small Dutch and Chinese merchant communities in Nagasaki; it was only through the ports of the south that innovation appeared in Japan. Christianity, for long thought dead after the most vicious persecutions, survived in deepest secrecy in Kyushu. In 1841, after the defences of Nagasaki had been modernized by a local magistrate, Takashima Shuhan, a demonstration of the new techniques of fighting so terrified the shogunal authorities that Takashima was eventually banished and imprisoned. But it was impossible to suppress all the experiments in gun-founding and technology which were taking place in the domains in Kyushu. They lay outside the direct feudal control of the *shogun*, and although in later years, the Tokugawa encouraged technical and military reforms in their own lands, they had lost a crucial lead.

The entry of foreign trade on a substantial scale after the Perry expedition of 1854 caused considerable social dislocation. Conservative elements were affronted by the habits and lack of manners displayed by the foreigners, and there was a steady stream of violent incidents. This placed the shogunal authorities in a dilemma. Failure to punish the offenders would rouse the anger of the foreign governments, while a repressive attitude would be interpreted by Japanese as cringing submission to the barbarians. In 1853, the *shogun* Ieyoshi died, leaving only an ailing son Iesada, who became *shogun* until his death five years later. He had no son, and the Tokugawa were faced with a succession crisis. In the bitter intrigues which followed, the family was split between two candidates, and the success of one, who took the name Iemochi, was the signal for the suppression of those who opposed him. A new port was built at Yokohama near Yedo, designed to bring the profits of foreign trade from the south-west into the Tokugawa domains, but it also brought the problems of xenophobic Japanese attacks on foreign diplomats and traders under the *shogun*'s direct protection. A coalition was in the process of forming. The clans of the west, faced with a direct attack on their interests, began to make common cause against Yedo. The Tokugawa family and their client lords were no longer united as they had been in the past, and many, especially those from the ultra-nationalist Tokugawa fief of Mito, were appalled at the growing contact with foreigners. In addition the Emperor Komei in distant Kyoto was a convinced xenophobe, and was willing to lend his support to schemes against the Tokugawa shogunate and the foreigners.

Hatred of the outsider was a convenient rallying point, but it was also used as a device to embarrass the shogunal authorities. In 1863–5 nationalists had bombarded Western shipping in the straits of Shimonoseki, and had promptly been destroyed by naval gunfire. The same scene was enacted at Kagoshima. The inadequacy of Japanese armaments was immediately laid on the *shogun*'s shoulders. The rallying cry of the opposition gradually changed from 'Expel the foreign barbarians' to 'Enrich the country, strengthen the army'.[1] The clans of Choshu now came out in open rebellion; they possessed as their trump card new military units composed both of traditional *samurai* and commoners, but armed with modern firearms. The shogunal authority could not rally enough support from other clans to mount a full-scale assault on Choshu, despite the unpardonable crime of the Choshu forces in invading the Imperial town of Kyoto.

In fact, the intransigence of the extremist elements in Choshu made clear that a confrontation between the Tokugawa and their enemies was at hand. More moderate clans in Choshu and Satsuma joined in a common army, which ostensibly aimed to 'free the emperor', the time-honoured cue for rebellion. In this moment of crisis Iemochi died, to be succeeded by the failed candidate of 1858, Yoshinabu. He had the complete confidence of the emperor and was ideally placed to rally support in the emperor's name and crush the rebellion. But on 30 January 1867, only twenty days after Yoshinabu was proclaimed *shogun*, the Emperor Komei died, leaving a young son to succeed him, Prince Sachi, then aged 14. The whole matter of a regency threw the political issues seemingly settled by Yoshinabu's succession back into play: until regents were appointed and his offices confirmed, his power was, formally, only temporary. On 3 January 1868 displaying a precocious flair for statesmanship, the new Emperor, decided 'to return to the old monarchy in order to lay the foundations for the restoration of national power'. He abolished the traditional offices associated with the shogunal power system and proposed a new, quasi-parliamentary structure.

It was carried out under the eyes of a large army assembled from the non-Tokugawa fiefs – Satsuma, Choshu, Echizen, Nagoya, Tosa and Hiroshima.[2] The political decision was confirmed by the defeat of the shogunal army south of Kyoto on 27 January, a foregone conclusion since many of his allies had already deserted Yoshinabu for the Satsuma–Choshu coalition.

The decrees of January and the new administration which followed represented a complete revolution in the structure of government. In the years that followed power was centralized to a degree unthinkable under the *shogun*. The feudal structure of local government was abolished in 1871, with fiefs becoming provinces and feudal lords being transformed into civil governors, often in the new western uniform of tail-coat and top hat. In the same year the *samurai* were permitted to cease wearing the two swords, badge of their class; in 1876 the permission became a prohibition against the wearing of swords. While the territorial lords, *daimyo*, found new opportunities in the new political system, a position sweetened by the substantial financial concessions given to them, their followers the *samurai* lost heavily under the new arrangements. They formed a discontented and dangerous force in the new state, and only a proportion of them could be absorbed into the new army. Their prestige and status was dealt a further blow by a law of universal conscription in 1873 which abolished the by-now slightly theoretical right they possessed to be the sole bearers of arms. The sword decree proved the final humiliation, and after many minor *samurai* revolts, there was a major rising in Satsuma in 1877. An army of 40,000 began to march on Yedo, now

The Meiji revolution: a contemporary Japanese view of the contrast between the new units armed with European style equipment and the traditional *samurai* warriors

Traditional Samurai fighting
'the new army' at
Kumamoto, 1876

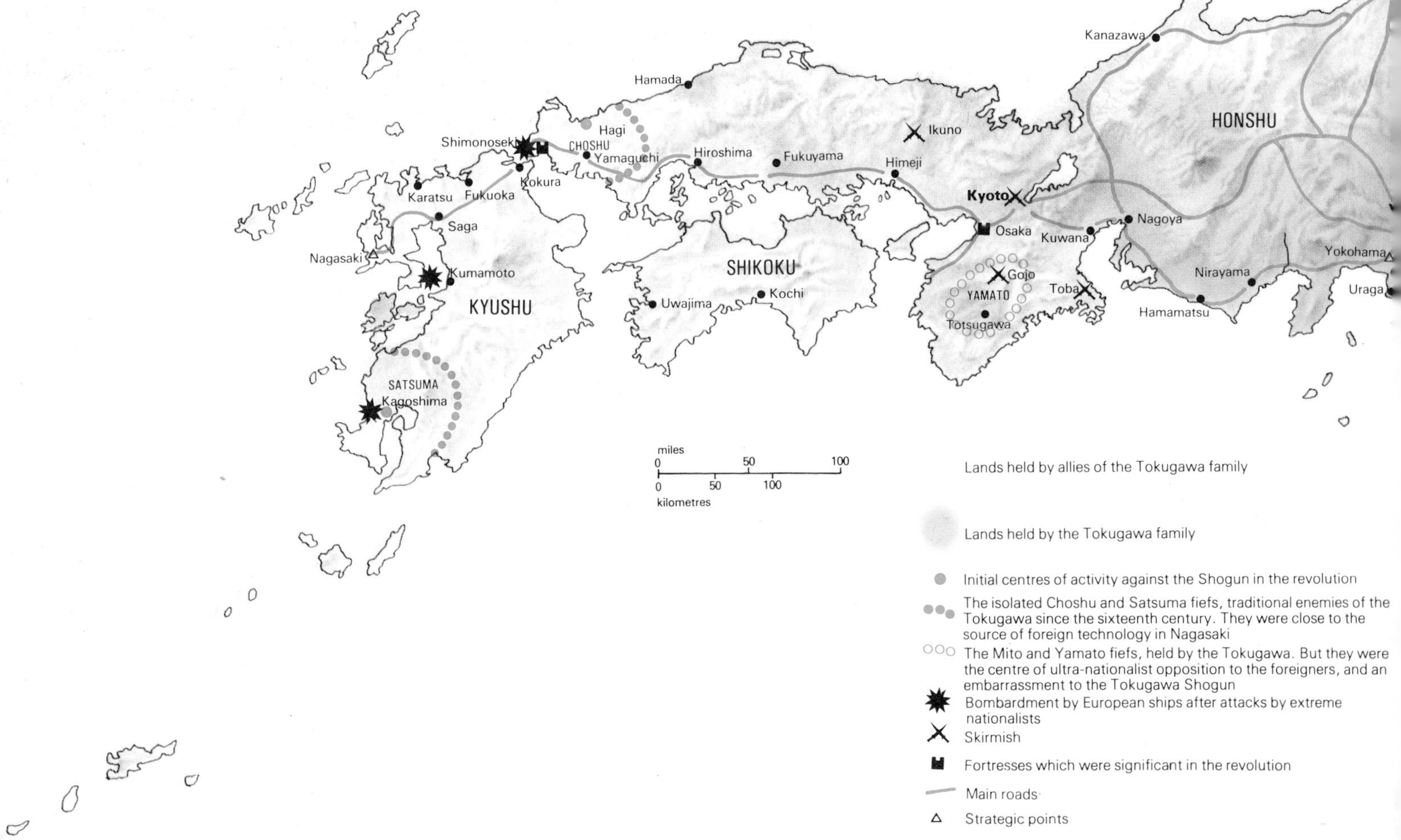

Kanazawa

HONSHU

Hamada

Shimonoseki   Hagi
CHOSHU   Yamaguchi
Kokura   Hiroshima   Fukuyama
Karatsu   Fukuoka   Himeji
Saga   Kyoto✕   Nagoya
Nagasaki   Osaka   Yokohama
Kumamoto   Kuwana   Nirayama
                        SHIKOKU   Gojo   Uraga
KYUSHU   YAMATO   Toba   Hamamatsu
                        Uwajima   Kochi   Totsugawa

Ikuno

SATSUMA
Kagoshima

miles
0   50   100
0   50   100
kilometres

Lands held by allies of the Tokugawa family

Lands held by the Tokugawa family

● Initial centres of activity against the Shogun in the revolution

●●● The isolated Choshu and Satsuma fiefs, traditional enemies of the
    Tokugawa since the sixteenth century. They were close to the
    source of foreign technology in Nagasaki

○○○ The Mito and Yamato fiefs, held by the Tokugawa. But they were
    the centre of ultra-nationalist opposition to the foreigners, and an
    embarrassment to the Tokugawa Shogun

✹ Bombardment by European ships after attacks by extreme
    nationalists

✕ Skirmish

◼ Fortresses which were significant in the revolution

— Main roads

△ Strategic points

EZO
(HOKKAIDO)

Morioka

called Tokyo, but they delayed to besiege the provincial stronghold at Kumamoto. A government army, including many of the reformed units which had been hurriedly retrained under the last *shogun*, marched west and finally besieged the rebels after six months of fierce fighting in the coastal fortress of Kagoshima. There the leaders and many of their followers died by their own hands, in accordance with the traditional rite of *seppuku* or *hara-kiri*. With the destruction of the *samurai* army – many of whom had been the instrumental cause of the 1868 revolution's success – the path forward was clear to the construction of a modernized state.

The intricacies of the revolution are myriad. In part its success was circumstantial: timely death among the main protagonists played an important part. So too did the patterns of alliance between the clans, many of which were traditional enemies. The main engine of change was the pressure placed upon a static and inflexible system by the contact with the West. The intrusion of western trade, politics, and economics – Japan was rapidly drained of gold by an unrealistic exchange rate – were more than the feudal structure of government could bear. The rule of the Tokugawa depended first of all on competence which they generally possessed, but equally the capacity to maintain an alliance system within their clan and its clients. At a crucial point, the fragile structure collapsed, thrown down in an earthquake of change.

A century of revolution

THE revolutions of Latin America sprang from a conflict *within* white society. The *criollos*, born in the Americas, fought the *peninsulares*, those born in Spain itself, for domination of the new world. The Indians, those of mixed blood, and the negro slaves, stood on the sidelines, occasionally snatching an advantage when they could. They had no more feeling for the new republics than they had had for the old Spanish Empire. It was irrelevant to them. In Mexico, once the brightest jewel of the Spanish crown, there was the same struggle between the possessing classes as occurred to the south, but beyond that there was a much deeper social transformation. The dispossessed, the small landholders, the Indians made insistent demands for a real transformation of society. In consequence, the Mexican revolution lasted not two decades but for over a century.

Mexicans possessed a symbol of their aspirations. In the Black Virgin of Guadalupe was a religious and nationalist symbol associated with a shrine which predated the introduction of Christianity. The first generation of revolutionaries against Spain were drawn from the *criollos* – Miguel Hidalgo, Jose Antonio Torres – or were *mestizos* (those of mixed blood) like Jose Maria Morelos, but both were clear that they led a revolution of the people. Hidalgo and Morelos were country priests, trusted by the people. When, on 16 September 1810, Hidalgo proclaimed a rebellion at Sunday mass in the village of Dolores (the *grito de Dolores*), there was a mass rising of the poor against the rich. His Indian horde sacked the town of Guanajuato, and massacred the inhabitants. The revolt became, in the words of an eye witness, 'a Monstrous Union of religion with assassination and plunder, a cry of death and desolation'.[1] Hidalgo allowed his Indians to pillage, seeing it as a rapid means of redressing social injustice, but he attracted few followers outside the area known as the Bajío. Eventually, the established orders of society united against him. His horde of eighty thousand Indians was beaten in pitched battle, and Hidalgo was executed far to the north in Chihuahua. The Indians were suppressed with considerable cruelty; but terror was not sufficient to crush the revolution. Morelos continued to wage a guerrilla war for 'our holy revolution' with an army composed exclusively of the dispossessed. One of his former prisoners described it thus: 'None of them comes from a decent family . . . there are Indians, Negros, mulattos, and delinquents, fugitives from their homelands'. In November 1810, he declared that the people would 'no longer be designated as Indians, mulattos or other castes, but all will be known as *Americans*'. In 1813 he issued a decree abolishing slavery and called for a radical re-distribution of property. Eventually in 1815 he, like Hidalgo, was tracked down and executed as a heretic and traitor. After his death, guerrilla warfare was continued in the south, but in general the counter-revolution was triumphant.

With the defeat of the popular revolution the *criollos* achieved independence from Spain on their own terms. The pressure from below was contained, by force where necessary. The new state continued to be run as before, on behalf of the great interest groups, the Church, the landowners and, latterly, the army. In mid-century, the power of the conservative forces was fragmented, allowing the election of Benito Juarez, an Indian from Oaxaca as president. While not a revolutionary in the tradition of Hidalgo and Morelos, he was determined to break the power of the Church, as well as defending Mexico from outside intervention. Although he succeeded against the French invaders, and executed their 'Emperor of Mexico', Maximilian of Austria, he could not contain the native forces of reaction. Before his death in 1872, he faced repeated military risings led by Porfirio Diaz, who was eventually elected president in 1877. With Diaz, conservativism was once again in the ascendant. He held office from 1877–80 and again from 1884–1911, and developed so effective a system of political fraud and manipulation that it became known as 'porfirismo'. By 1910, the centenary of the *grito de Dolores*, Hidalgo had become a national hero of the war of independence; of his aims and ideals, less was said. Even in 1910, the peasant was tied as effectively to the land and his master as he had been a century before. Diaz was due for re-election in 1910. 'Porfirismo' did its work and the dictator was returned triumphantly for another term. His opponent was a landowner from the northern province of Coahuila called Francisco Madero. The president was now in his eighties, and in a poor position to resist the revolution that Madero now called for in San Luis Potosí. Madero was a man of peace, with an unshakeable faith in the power of law. His programme was based on secular education, free elections, and a reduction of the power of the Church. He was not a radical, but many of those who answered his call to rise against the dictatorship were, in the tradition of Hidalgo and Morelos. South of Mexico City, the peasants of the state of Morelos had already set in motion a thorough-going rural revolution under the leadership of Emiliano Zapata. The forces of reaction conspired to defeat Madero, who went down after a whole series of military rebellions. The new dictator was General Victoriano Huerta, who had Madero shot on 22 February 1913. In classic revolutionary style, Madero dead was more use to the revolution than Madero alive, for he became a symbol of liberty against military tyranny.

In the revolutionary wars which followed no quarter was given or expected. Huerta was opposed by a temporary alliance of groups united only by their hatred of the new military dictator. Foremost among them was Venustiano Carranza, the governor of Madero's home state of Coahuila, who inherited the Constitutionalist position of Madero. He would, for example, not declare himself as President but only

The face of the revolution in Mexico. The camera has caught a typical scene – the execution of captured enemy fighters (1914)

'First Chief of the Constitutionalist Army in charge of the Executive Power'. At the other end of the spectrum were 'Pancho' Villa, a peasant from Chihuahua, and Emiliano Zapata from Morelos. Once Huerta was beaten, the revolution continued with Villa and Zapata, a somewhat unlikely alliance of north and south ranged against the forces of respectability surrounding Carranza. The war which lasted from 1913 to 1917, and intermittently to 1920, was dominated by the railway map of Mexico, and by the capital, Mexico City. On the revolutionary side, Zapata was much better placed than Villa and the Constitutionalist generals to attack Mexico City. Morelos was in easy striking distance, and Zapata had adequate forces. But the peasant revolution which he led had the narrowest of objectives. He, and they, were only interested in the fate of their own state, and were reluctant to move beyond its borders. The brunt of the fighting was borne by Villa's men, with their power in the north. The lines of communication between the two elements of the radical revolution were dangerously over-extended. By contrast, support for the Carranza group was strong in the eastern provinces around Veracruz; as the war dragged on, these logistical factors assumed more and more importance.

The two factions occupied and re-occupied the capital for a few days at a time, using it as a sounding board for their political ideas. The Revolutionary Convention which opened on 1 October 1914 in Mexico City was transferred to Aguascalientes. It became more and more radical, exposing the rift which lay within the revolution. 'That which we have been wont to call our independence,' declared a radical named Diaz Soto, 'was no independence for the native race, but for the creoles alone. . . . We are making a great revolution today to destroy the lie of history. . . .'[2]

The battleground of the revolution covered only part of the republic. The provinces of Oaxaca and those to the east were untouched by the war. There was no fighting in Sonora (in the north west). In the main the revolution of 1910–20 was fought over much of the same ground as in 1810–15. The armies fought five times for Mexico City, and the war was waged back and forth for crucial railway junctions and centres of communication. All the armies lived off the land, Villa's more energetically than the others; but he did not have the advantage of a seaport at his back, as did the Constitutionalists. Veracruz was their greatest asset. Villa was dependent on whatever supplies

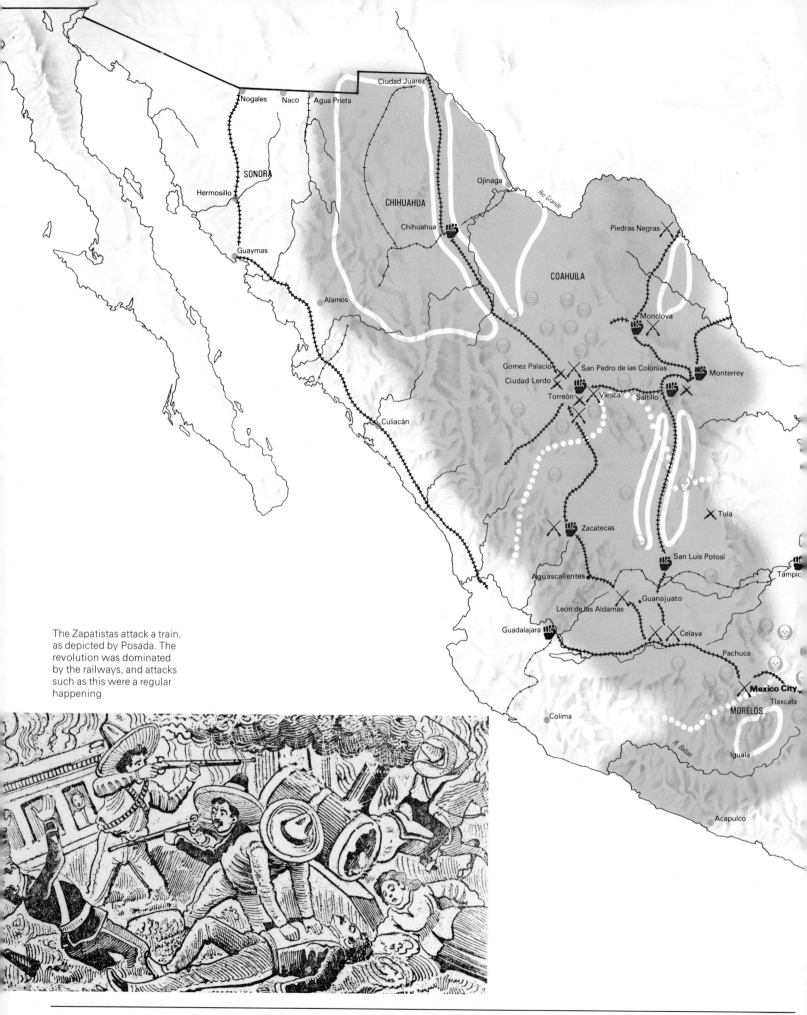

The Zapatistas attack a train, as depicted by Posada. The revolution was dominated by the railways, and attacks such as this were a regular happening

SONORA

Nogales
Naco
Agua Prieta
Ciudad Juarez

Hermosillo

CHIHUAHUA

Ojinaga

Rio Grande

Guaymas

Chihuahua

COAHUILA

Piedras Negras

Alamos

Monclova

Gomez Palacio
Ciudad Lerdo
Torreón
San Pedro de las Colonias
Viesca
Saltillo
Monterrey

Culiacán

Tula

Zacatecas

San Luis Potosi

Támpic

Aguascalientes

Guanajuato

Leon de las Aldamas

Celaya

Guadalajara

Pachuca

Mexico City

Colima

Tlaxcala

MORELOS

R. Balsas

Iguala

Acapulco

The maximum area dominated by the forces of Villa and Zapata at the height of their power

The revolutionaries united against Huerta: the main areas of revolutionary strength, while Huerta held the railways and the main towns

The area most affected by the revolution of 1810

● Initial centres of the 1910 revolution against Huerta

Area of massacre or atrocity

The rallying point for Carranza's Constitutionalist forces

Strongpoint of Huerta's forces, holding strategic railheads and communications centres

✕ Skirmish

✕ Battle

The strategic railway lines

Other railway lines

could be passed over the Texan border, which could be closed at will by the United States government. When military pressure became too strong for him, he pulled all his troops back into the northern fastness of Chihuahua. The territory controlled by Villa's Army of the North and Zapata's Liberating Army of the South seemed much greater than that of their opponents, but this advantage was illusory. Villa in particular fancied his abilities as a general and a strategist, but against more skilful soldiers, like Alvaro Obregón, he revealed himself as inept. Both Villa and Zapata ended as they had begun, not as generals of armies, but as guerrilla leaders.

The radicals failed on the military plane, and the Constitutionalists triumphed. Villa resumed a life of banditry, while Zapata was murdered by his enemies. But as the revolution was 'institutionalized' under Lázaro Cardenas and his Party of Institutionalized Revolution (PRI) after 1934, the radical objectives for land, secularization and social justice became official policy. It was a hollow victory, achieved at the cost of countless lives lost in the 'killing zone' during the revolution, and antagonisms which persist to the present day.

Ibn Saud and the sword of Islam

WAR in the desert was as much ceremony as combat. The economy of the desert tribes of Arabia was founded upon raiding and sporadic warfare, defence of territory and the pursuit of blood feuds. Pitched battles were almost unheard of, and even death in battle a comparative rarity. Two groups would meet in the desert, trade insults and war cries, a few shots would be fired and the weaker party would retire. Often the shots would be omitted, for ammunition was costly. The element missing in this casual fighting was any cause or conviction. The tribes looked upon war as a way of life, not the means to any end. Yet it was these same tribes which had provided the manpower for the great Islamic expansion into Asia and Europe in the century after the death of the Prophet Mohammad.

Militant sects were common in Islam, and they had the power to convert natural belligerence into a fanaticism never to be found among the desert tribes. In the eighteenth century, a militant ascetic created a great following in the heart of Arabia. Mohammad Ibn Abdul Wahhab allied himself by marriage with the Saud family of central Arabia, and the Wahhabi armies swept from the interior to seize the holy city of Mecca in 1807. The spirit of Wahhabism declined because it had no form or direction, rather like the various dervish movements of Sudan and Anatolia. But they were dormant rather than extinguished. In the hands of a war leader, the spirit of the *jihad* (holy war) could be roused with astonishing ease. Colonial powers, the French in Africa, the British in India, and the Russians in Central Asia, were acutely aware of the dangers latent in the Islamic tribes. What they feared most was a leader who could transform a horde into an army of the True Faith which would sweep all before it. In Arabia at the turn of the twentieth century, the Saud family produced such a leader in Abdul Aziz ibn Abdul Rahman al Saud, better known as Ibn Saud. His achievement lay not only in rousing the spirit of militancy – this was not difficult – but also in taming and directing that spirit to political ends. The revolution in Arabia lay in the creation of a united state from an ant-heap of squabbling tribes and factions. His instrument was the Wahhabi army, the Brotherhood of the *Ikhwan*. The final stage of the revolution saw the destruction of the *Ikhwan* who eventually challenged his political and economic goals for the new state. Ibn Saud's revolution, then, was doubly successful, as he destroyed the instrument by which he had achieved power, cauterizing the wound and leaving the body of Arabia stable.

Ibn Saud began with nothing. His family had been exiled from their traditional home in Riyadh when the Rashid tribe, based on Hail to the north, began a campaign of expansion to the south. In 1900, with only a handful of followers, he recaptured Riyadh in a night attack. His father, the Emir of Nejd (the 'heart of Arabia'), resigned his position to his son, and Ibn Saud set about winning over the desert tribes to the south of Riyadh. The coup of recapturing Riyadh was an epic feat, which immediately became the subject of desert legend. News of this success spread with great speed through the desert, as news always does, and a number of the smaller tribes rallied to his banners. The larger tribes awaited the outcome of the struggle between the Rashidi and the Saudi. The conflict between them followed exactly the traditional pattern of desert warfare, with raids and counter raids. Even the encounters usually called 'battles', as at Dilam, south of Riyadh (1902), were little more than skirmishes. Ibn Saud was fighting close to home, while the Rashidi were operating far from Hail in hostile terrain. The balance of the war went to the Saudi, and more of the larger tribes came in on his side. In 1906 Ibn Saud moved forward towards Hail, and at Rowdhat Muhanna, the Rashidi were beaten, with their chief, Abdul Aziz ibn Mutaib al Rashid being killed. It was a lucky victory, and could easily have gone the other way.

With the neutralization of the emirate of Hail, Ibn Saud continued to rally the tribes to his side, declaring himself the true inheritor of the Wahbabi tradition. He created a dedicated and fanatical army, much larger than that of any other ruler in the peninsula, but one which was difficult to command, for the tribesmen were still dominated by the mores of raiding and pillage. His technique was to create permanent encampments around wells and in oases, and to allocate specific territories to the tribes. Disputes were to be adjudicated through his courts and not by recourse to arms. The first of these settlements at Artawiya in 1913 was a considerable success, and the inhabitants of Artawiya formed the first of the *Ikhwan*. The settlements were run on the strictest Kora-

nic principles, and were described as *hijrah*, 'domains of the righteous'. From the *hijrah*, which eventually totalled more than 150, he could rally a large force of fanatical warriors at will. In 1913 he turned his army on the town of Hofuf, in the Hasa district, which held a Turkish garrison of 1200 men. During the years of the First World War, Ibn Saud concentrated on the final reduction of the Hail emirate. By 1919, when the Emir of Hail was murdered by his cousin, the Rashidi were willing to accept the rule of Ibn Saud. The only remaining competitor was Hussein, *sherif* of Mecca, and ruler of the Hejaz. The ally of Lawrence of Arabia, he had inherited a trained army and much British equipment. On paper, the Hejazi army was far stronger than the forces of Ibn Saud. But Hejazi advances into the interior were complete failures, while the Saudi made a rapid conquest of the province of Asir, south of Hejaz. In 1924 the *Ikhwan* came out of the desert to storm the city of Taif, which they put to the sword. They swept on towards Mecca, and in October 1924 Ibn Saud entered the holy city. The Hejazi retreated in panic behind the walls of Jidda and Medina. In December 1925 Jidda fell after a prolonged siege, and on 10 December 1926, Ibn Saud was proclaimed King of Hejaz.

The *Ikhwan* army was capable of defeating any threat from within Arabia, but they were no longer willing simply to return to the *hijrah* at Ibn Saud's behest. He now needed to consolidate the new state and unite its various fragments. He had already seen the power of western technology when he had visited the British army at Basra during the First World War, and he knew that communications were the key to success in Arabia. He began to establish radio con-

nections throughout the kingdom and buy modern armaments and vehicles. All of these were deemed non-Islamic by the *Ikhwan*, who now began to extend their intense puritanism to the towns of the kingdom. Anyone they deemed a heretic was liable to immediate death. For a time, Ibn Saud tried to divert their attention, but their incursions became intolerable. At the point when they decided to raid over the border into Iraq, which invited a violent response from the British forces stationed in Iraq, he decided to move against them. In two campaigns during 1929, he gathered an army of about 30,000 tribesmen, and he caught the *Ikhwan* army on 30 March. The advantage in fact lay with the *Ikhwan*, for they were all battle-hardened while Ibn Saud had mostly local levies. But within half an hour, the mobile machine-gunners of Ibn Saud's army had put them to flight, at which point his horsemen swept in and slaughtered the stragglers. It was a vindication of the policy of modernization. He moved quickly to the east where another tribe had risen against his authority, and after putting down the revolt, north again to attack another fragment of the *Ikhwan* on the Iraqi border. By the end of the year the military power of the *Ikhwan* was broken.

Religious fanaticism was a weapon which Ibn Saud used, but he was not prepared to see his new state become fossilized in a theocratic form. Unlike Ataturk, who was at best an agnostic, Ibn Saud was a devout Moslem, and the revolution he created was contained within a strictly Islamic context. What he sought, often by careful manipulation of the Islamic courts, the *ulema*, was a pragmatic fundamentalism. In its externals, his state remained strictly Koranic, but it was capable of accepting an economic transfor-

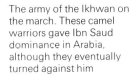

The army of the Ikhwan on the march. These camel warriors gave Ibn Saud dominance in Arabia, although they eventually turned against him

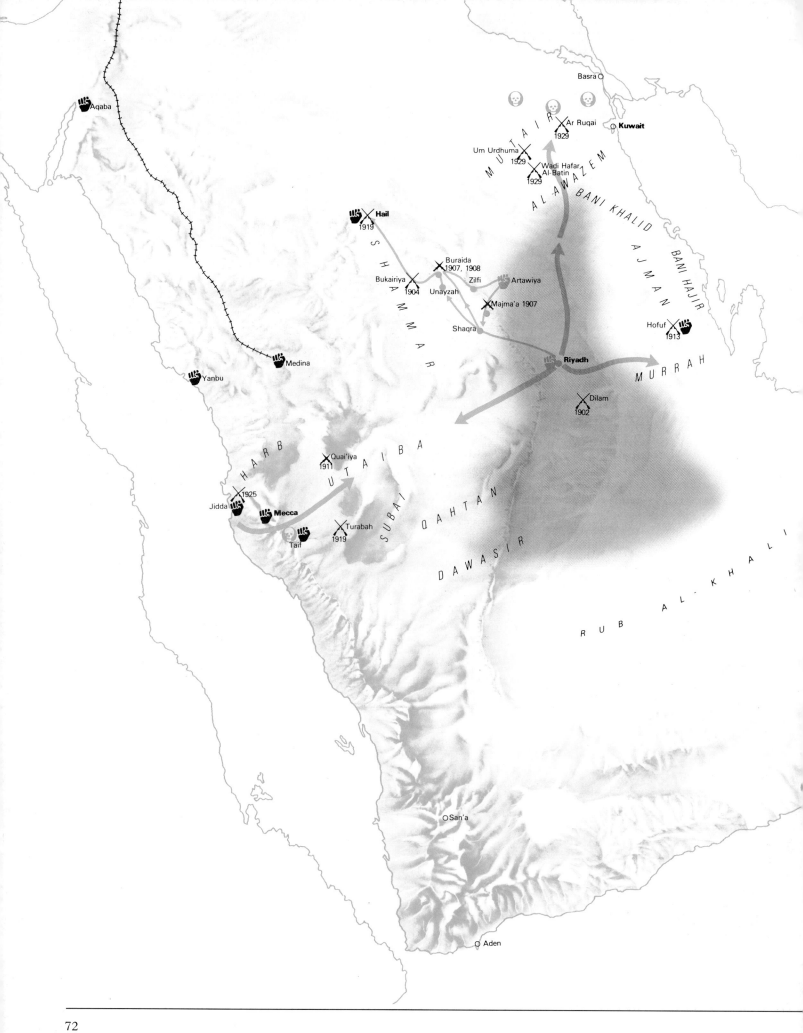

Basra ○

Kuwait ○

Ar Ruqai
1929

Um Urdhuma
1929

Wadi Hafar
Al-Batin
1929

MUTAIR

AL-AWAZEM

BANI KHALID

AJMAN

BANI HAJIR

Aqaba

Hail
1919

SHAMMAR

Buraida
1907, 1908

Bukairiya
1904

Zilfi

Artawiya

Unayzah

Majma'a 1907

Shaqra

Hofuf
1913

Medina

Riyadh

MURRAH

Yanbu

Dilam
1902

Quai'iya
1911

UTAIBA

SUBAI

QAHTAN

HARB

Jidda
1925

Mecca

Taif

Turabah
1919

DAWASIR

RUB   AL-KHALI

San'a ○

Aden ○

miles
0   200   200
0   100   100
kilometres

The core area of the Saudi revolution in Arabia

Initial targets of Ibn Saud's expansion

Wahhabi strongpoint of the Saudi revolution

Massacre or atrocity carried out by the Ikhwan

Strongpoint of the forces opposed to the Saudis

Skirmish

Battle

Ibn Saud's first campaign to control the Ikhwan,
formerly the basis of his power
Ibn Saud's final moves against the Ikhwan and
the tribes which supported them

Mecca to Damascus railway

Muscat

mation (even before the oil boom) as well as a social transformation. He moved where possible by stealth and diplomacy. He did not execute the leaders of the *Ikhwan* who fought against him, for that would only have established the pattern of blood feud which had divided Arabia for centuries. But he ensured that power rested with those tribes and their leaders who had remained loyal to him. The tribes respected him for his cunning and his openness. His council (*majlis*) was always available to any tribesman who wished to petition him.

He described himself with complete precision in the old Arab proverb, 'A viper is soft to the touch, but if it turns upon you, its fangs are deadly.'[1]

War in the desert: on campaign against the Turks in eastern Arabia, 1911

Part 2

THE SEIZURE OF POWER

PARIS 1871

The crucible

IT took the Prussian armies a scant six weeks in the summer of 1870 to crush the armies of France and topple the empire of Napoleon III. On 19 September, General von Moltke completed his encirclement of Paris and laid siege to the city, but it was 1 March 1871 before the German triumph was complete, and the victors marched ceremonially through the streets of the French capital. The defence had not been a military success so much as a triumph for the idea of the 'people in arms'. Parisians believed that the starvation, the German bombardment and the spirit of popular unity had created a new social and political order. An officer who experienced the siege described this new atmosphere: 'When you know Paris, she is not a town, she is an animated being, a natural person, who has her moments of fury, madness, stupidity, enthusiasm.'[1] The product of this

Paris, 1871: National Guardsmen stand in the Place Vendôme behind a barricade of cobble stones. Many of the Paris barricades were much more massive affairs

highly charged atmosphere was the Commune of 1871, which ruled Paris from 19 March 1871 to its bloody end in the last days of May 1871. The Commune became a landmark in the history of revolutions, the seizure of power by the people in a great European city. Like the fall of the Bastille, it became a symbol for future revolutionaries, more and more revered as it receded into history.

For future revolutions the Commune has had an entirely malign influence, laying a false path along which many have wandered. As an image of defiance it is seductive. The people in arms did establish a counter-state, a revolution of, admittedly, brief duration. The white terror has obliterated the atrocities carried out by the Communards: when over 20,000 were shot in the relentless 'cleansing' carried out by the national government, the hundreds who were killed by the Commune dwindle into insignificance. All became martyrs for future generations of the left. To deprecate the Commune has become an act of impiety to those who are annually commemorated by a pilgrimage to the Père Lachaise cemetery, whose walls became an execution ground in May 1871. The events in Paris pioneered the idea of urban revolution in a way which no previous rising had done. The ultimate failure of the Commune was put down to technical flaws in its conduct. The Communards did not appreciate the effects which the rebuilding of Paris had had on the techniques of street fighting. It was no longer the city of 1848. The new boulevards were too wide to be blocked by barricades, too easily outflanked by attacks launched along parallel streets. Only in the working-class districts to the east and the unreconstructed enclaves around Montmartre were the old tactics still effective. Nor did the military leaders of the Commune manage to enforce the central direction of the defence of the city. Street fighters were happy defending their own quarter, but felt distinctly uneasy on the barricades in the west end of the city. In a crisis, they tended to abandon their positions and return home. Because of this unfamiliarity with the terrain over which they fought, they were often at a disadvantage when faced by troops working with the street map. For the Communards, western Paris was enemy country.

Some of the inadequacies of the Communards were military and technical, others were political. Paris was isolated from the provinces, not only by the effects of the siege, but by a difference in attitudes. Parisians looked down on provincials, who were in turn horrified by the insane radicalism of the capital. There was no political programme, no notion as to how revolutionary Paris would inspire the nation to follow suit. It was fuelled by memories of the past, of 1789 and 1848. Families which had been persecuted under the revived monarchy had 'come out' in 1848, and they did so again in 1871. The insurrection in the streets provided its own logic, quite separate from any analysis of the real world around. As the troops of the Versailles government were pouring into the city, the chairman of the Commune, Adolphe Assi, roused the people of Paris thus: 'Enough of militarism! No more General Staffs with badges of rank and gold braid at every seam! Make way for the people, for the fighters with bare arms. The hour of revolutionary warfare has struck!'[2] The Commune spurned professionalism in the art of war, believing that the left imbibed the skills of street warfare at the breast. The Commune lost because of its amateurism, and paid the price.

The malign lesson of the Commune is that cities are soft targets for a revolution. In the first hours of the revolution, when the troops of the national government attempted to neutralize the National Guard in Paris, by removing their artillery, they were defeated by the people pouring in their thousands into the streets. The revolutionaries did not seize power by force of arms, but by walking into the buildings abandoned in panic by the forces of order. Although there was more violence in both 1789 and 1848, the process was identical: the authorities lost their nerve. But while it is easy to take control, it is hard to galvanize a city sufficiently to resist a further coup. Paris, a large city by the standards of the time, was impossible to defend except by conventional military means. The Prussians had never put it to the test, being content with a little shelling and starvation. The only alternative was a scorched earth policy, a defence building by building, destroying what could not be held. It was not a strategy which the Communards contemplated.

The Commune ended with what was known as 'the bloody week'. The armies of the national government based at Versailles entered the city through an undefended point near the Point du Jour on Sunday 21 May. Over the next seven days, the army fought its way forward, sometimes advancing rapidly as they did in the south, sometimes meeting a strongpoint as they did around the Place Vendôme and the Hôtel de Ville. What they feared most was that the Com-

mune would destroy the city rather than yield it. When a few buildings were set on fire along the Rue Royale to clear them of Versailles army snipers, it was thought that the Communards intended to fire the whole city. Wild rumours began to circulate of *pétroleuses*, women armed with fire bombs sent to burn Paris to the ground. There was no evidence that such a plan ever existed, but many women were shot out of hand by the army in their panic. Nor did they stop with the *pétroleuses*. Communards caught with arms, or with gunpowder marks on their clothes, were summarily executed. One chimney sweep on his way home blackened with soot met the same fate, despite his protested innocence. As the week wore on the army's bloodlust rose, and by the time the soldiers reached the final redoubt, around Père Lachaise, the Buttes Chaumont, and the Belleville suburb, they were determined to destroy working-class resistance for ever. Execution squads were set up at convenient points, and prisoners were 'processed' with only the semblance of a trial. The disposal of the bodies became a terrible problem. The smoke from the bodies burnt in Buttes Chaumont hung over Paris, impregnating clothing with a sickly smell. Elsewhere mass graves were dug. Even after all this effort by the army, overwhelmed by the efficiency of their repression, the city of Paris had to dispose of 17,000 bodies. Nor were the executions in Paris the end of the reprisals. Many thousands were taken for trial and sentence to Versailles, more than 40,000 by some counts. In the words of Marshal MacMahon, the liberator of Paris: 'Today the struggle is ended; order, work and security will be reborn.'[3]

Urban uprisings are easy to start, but they are hard to win. The lessons of the Commune obsessed Lenin,

Paris in flames. There were wild rumours that the Communards and National Guard intended to burn Paris rather than surrender

evening 23 Ma[y]

R. Seine

evening 22 May

Montmartre
cemetery

Bvd de Clichy

Parc
Monceau

early
morning 22 May

Arc de Triomphe

Place de la
Madeleine

Opéra

Rue Royale

Rue Florentin

Place Vendôme

Place de la
Concorde

Tuileries

Palais Royal

Les Halles

Rue de Rivoli

Porte de la Muette

Champ
de Mars

Rue de Lille

Rue de l'Université

Bvd Raspail

Croix Rouge

St Germain

Palais de Justice

Préfecture
de Police

Ecole Militaire

R. Seine

Saint Sulpice hospital

Dupleix barracks

Luxembourg
gardens

Panthéon

Ste Pélagie
prison

early morning 22 May

evening 22 May

Buttes aux [C]

evening 23 May

evening 24 May

evening 25 May

evening 26 May

evening 27 May

Buttes Chaumont

evening 27 May

Rue Haxo

La Roquette prison

Père Lachaise cemetery

...azas prison

evening 26 May

...rleans

...anne d'Arc

evening 25 May

not only because he knew his history better than many revolutionaries, but because he also had the evidence of the suppression of the Moscow Revolution in 1905. Yet modern revolutions cannot succeed unless they are capable of taking over the cities. The increasing complexity of urban society makes it vulnerable to insurrection, but also impervious to total control. Even at the height of the Commune, the middle classes pursued the normal course of their lives, albeit a little fearfully. On the day before the army attacked, an English resident Edward Child recorded in his diary that he was 'at . . . church at 11 . . . breakfasted *au* Café du Helder . . . afterwards strolled to the Champs Elysées. . . . Lovely day.'[4] In the Commune, the old traditions and elements of the new were mixed. From this crucible emerged a formula which proved successful in October 1917 in Russia – and nowhere else since that date.

Advance by the Army of Versailles

Areas of heaviest fighting

Areas fired by the Communards

Principal Communard barricades

Atrocities committed by the Communards

Main locations of the reprisals and mass executions carried out by the Army of Versailles

The proving ground

THE New Year and the feast of the Epiphany were always a time of friendship and goodwill in Russia when children were over-indulged, and a general air of cheerful optimism prevailed. The New Year of 1905 was no exception. It was true that the country was at war with Japan and was not doing well, but the war was far distant at the end of the Trans-Siberian railway and although the Russian bear was slow to rouse, no one really doubted that the armies would triumph in the end. The war had been accompanied by considerable social discontent, and 1904 had seen political assassinations, demonstrations and strikes, and a general sense of disquiet. But even these negative factors had begun to diminish after an Imperial edict on 12 December made minor but significant concessions, giving the impression that the Czar and the government would become less intransigent. Thus it was barely credible news that on Sunday 9 January, a large but peaceful procession in St Petersburg which was making a well-advertised march to present an appeal to the Tsar had been received by volleys of well-aimed rifle fire from crack regiments of the garrison or troops specially brought in for the occasion. This had happened not once but in places all over the capital. It could not possibly have been an accident, and the death toll, according to official figures, of more than a hundred and almost three hundred wounded, was raised to some 4600 by other reports.[1] The consequence of this sour new year was to be an army and a navy dissolving into mutiny, and a Russian empire with its towns and cities in open rebellion, and much of the countryside in the grip of a vast peasant uprising.

The 'revolution' of 1905 was not one but many movements of protest which formed temporary alliances against the common Czarist enemy. Yet the government did not perceive this fragmentation, which was a profound weakness in the revolutionary movement. They saw only the collapse of the social base in the midst of the war, and disaffection springing up like rampant weeds. Their sense of paralysis is not surprising since the situation was unique in Russian history; but the cause of autocracy was unlucky in having Nicholas II as the man to face the crisis. His father Alexander III would have reacted, in the manner of Ivan the Terrible, with exemplary severity. This was in fact Nicholas' own inclination, for he was determined to retain his autocratic rights intact. The orders which had led to Bloody Sunday sprang directly from this determination. But he was also shamed by the consequences of his decision. 'God, how sad and grim,' he had recorded in his diary on Sunday night. So he decided to attempt both concession and coercion at the same time. To his opponents this tremulous dithering merely signalled that autocracy had faltered; it was time to strike a further blow.

The Czar and the government believed it was all a conspiracy, in which simple but good-hearted Russians were misled by 'ill-intentioned leaders',[2] as Nicholas asserted in his manifesto to the people of 18 February. But the eruption was largely spontaneous, born of a deep anger at the autocratic system. Cities all over Russia came out in protest as they received the news of Bloody Sunday. More organised action followed almost immediately as workers left their factories *en masse*. Moscow was first on the day after the massacre, followed by Warsaw, Kharkov, Vilna, Kovno and Helsingfors on 11 January. The news was spread along the telegraph system, which the government was able to control through censorship. But it could not control the trains running all over Russia from Moscow and St Petersburg. Railwaymen passed the news from station to station. On 12 January the wave of strikes hit Riga, Kiev, Voronezh, Mogilev, and Libau. By the seventeenth it had reached Batum, and by the next day Tiflis, and with it much of Caucasia was in turmoil. By the end of January almost half a million workers were on strike, plus many students and members of the 'intelligentsia', i.e. the educated élite of the country. The protest was particularly strong in those marginal areas of the empire which were Russian only by right of possession. The minorities were active in the moves against the central government, but here, as with the conventional political parties, it was the people who were in advance of their leaders. The sudden crisis took everyone by surprise. The active revolutionaries in exile abroad had no real notion of what was going on in Russia, although Trotsky of the Social Democratic party and a few others re-entered Russia illegally to play their part. For the most part the leadership sat back and fantasized. Lenin, the thirty-five-year-old leader of the Bolshevik faction of the Social Democrats (SD), began to take an active interest in the arts of street fighting. The Socialist Revolutionary party, who were stronger on the ground in Russia, particularly among the peasants, had already developed an organization to carry out political assassinations, but they too were bemused by the new situation. The revolutionaries encouraged strikes, printed pamphlets, agitated and exhorted the workers to insurrection, but without any sense of what should be done to convert popular feeling into popular revolution. Everyone had come out against the autocracy, even quite conventional and right-wing parties, and this was not the material from which a socialist revolution could be fashioned.[3]

The most dangerous threat to the government came from the dominant role of the All Russian Union of Railway Employees and Workers. The centre of the railway network was the Moscow group of stations and railway yards, and these were dominated by the Menshevik wing of the Social Democratic party. The key line in Siberia, which was the lifeline to the troops fighting the Japanese, had many union branches dominated by the Bolshevik wing of the SDs. Between them, the two wings of the SDs

The Cossacks attack the people in St Petersburg after a march led by Father Gapon. This was the catalyst of the 1905 Revolution

could enforce paralysis throughout Russia, so long as they could carry the union membership with them. But because their membership was small and dispersed through the towns and cities of Russia, the socialists were reliant on support from a broad spectrum of opinion. They thus created events and demonstrations around which opposition could rally. May Day, the traditional worker's holiday, was made an occasion for widespread protest strikes and marches carried through to 2 May. By such means as these they were able to reinforce the sense of purpose which had quickly ebbed in the masses. The strikers of January had mostly returned to work by April, but over 200,000 again came out in response to the May Day appeal. The support for action was there, but it was difficult to sustain for long periods. However, one factor which served to harden antagonism was the growing number of clashes between troops and strikers, which resulted in many deaths and injuries. Nor were the troops themselves immune. In June the flagship of the Black Sea fleet, the battleship *Potemkin* came out in mutiny in Odessa. In the space of twenty-four hours on 15/16 June 1905, Odessa erupted into revolution. Over 2000 were killed within a few days.[4] More sinister still, the rural areas which had been relatively quiet now began to grow increasingly turbulent. By the late autumn, it seemed that the worst fears of the landlords and nobility might be realized with a peasant war in the countryside. Concessions by the government failed to have little more than a temporary effect in the slide

towards chaos. In October another and even more effective strike movement was organized, and by 16 October the entire railway system was at a standstill. More cities were involved than ever before. On 17 October the Czar made what he believed was the ultimate concession. He agreed to an elected *Duma* (parliament), and to a limit being set on his autocracy. At that point, he thought, his back was to the wall.

But the sacrifice of autocracy had not been in vain. The decree succeeded in convincing the disaffected establishment – the intelligentsia, the dissident bureaucrats, what passed for a middle class – that their future lay with the forces of order rather than disorder. The fragile alliance began to crumble. The parties of the left, having at last come to see the potential for a radical revolution, became more and more violent in their proclamations and behaviour, causing panic among the faint-hearted. On 2 December the *soviet* (workers' council) in St Petersburg declared that the Czarist government was 'openly at war with its own people', and proposed retaliation through a general strike. The strongest challenge came from Moscow, which came out in open armed revolt (see map).

It was a confrontation which the government was at last prepared to face. In the interval since the issue of the Czar's October manifesto the government had been acting to suppress the disturbances at their most vulnerable, but potentially most damaging, points

Continued on page 84

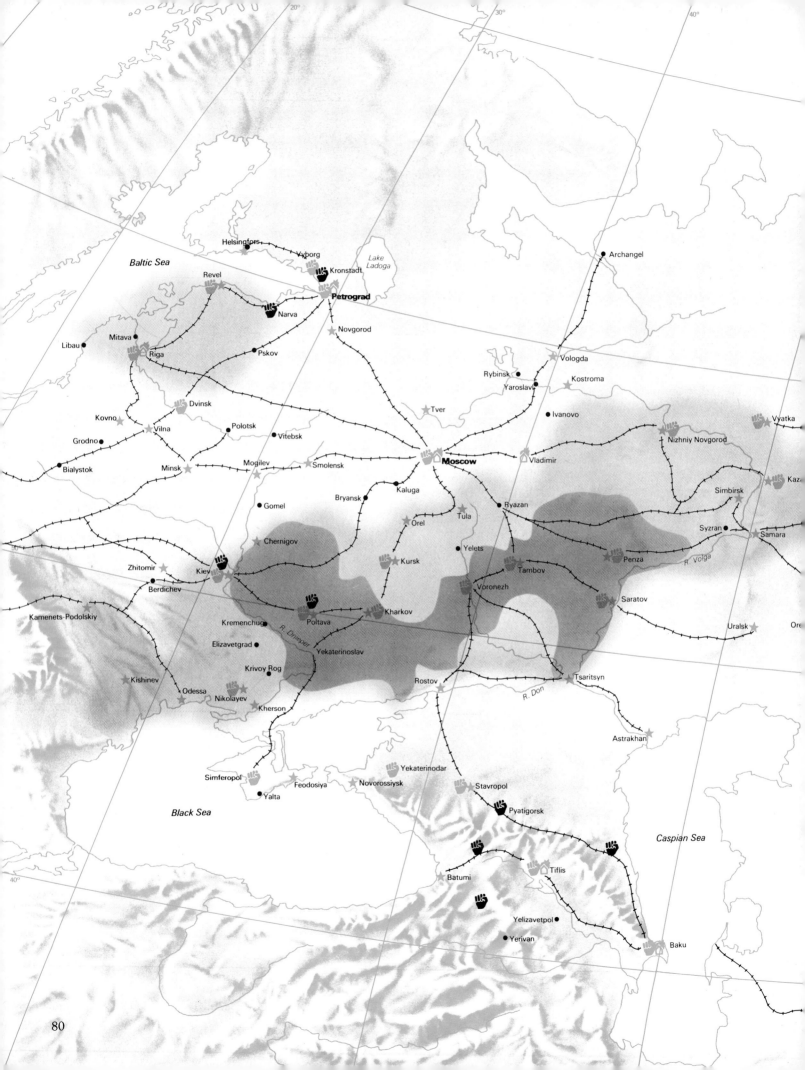

Baltic Sea

Helsingfors
Vyborg
Lake Ladoga
Kronstadt
Archangel
Revel
Narva
Petrograd
Mitava
Libau
Riga
Novgorod
Pskov
Vologda
Rybinsk
Kostroma
Yaroslavl
Dvinsk
Kovno
Ivanovo
Vilna
Polotsk
Tver
Grodno
Vitebsk
Nizhniy Novgorod
Vyatka
Bialystok
Minsk
Mogilev
Smolensk
Moscow
Vladimir
Kaz
Gomel
Bryansk
Kaluga
Ryazan
Simbirsk
Orel
Tula
Syzran
Chernigov
Yelets
Samara
Zhitomir
Kiev
Kursk
Penza
R. Volga
Berdichev
Tambov
Saratov
Kamenets-Podolskiy
Kremenchug
Poltava
Voronezh
R. Dnieper
Kharkov
Uralsk
Ore
Elizavetgrad
Yekaterinoslav
Krivoy Rog
Rostov
Tsaritsyn
Kishinev
R. Don
Odessa
Nikolayev
Kherson
Astrakhan
Simferopol
Yekaterinodar
Yalta
Feodosiya
Novorossiysk
Stavropol
Black Sea
Pyatigorsk
Caspian Sea
Batumi
Tiflis
Yelizavetpol
Yerivan
Baku

80

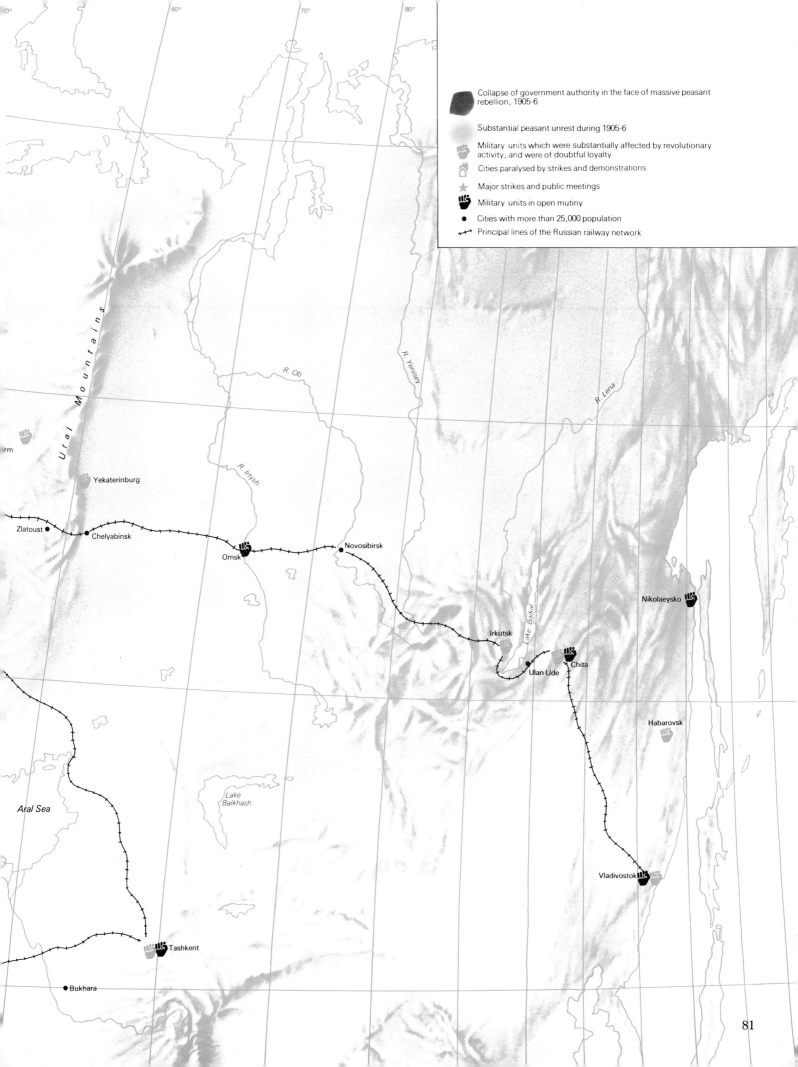

Collapse of government authority in the face of massive peasant rebellion, 1905-6

Substantial peasant unrest during 1905-6

Military units which were substantially affected by revolutionary activity, and were of doubtful loyalty

Cities paralysed by strikes and demonstrations

Major strikes and public meetings

Military units in open mutiny

Cities with more than 25,000 population

Principal lines of the Russian railway network

Ural Mountains

R. Ob

R. Yenisey

R. Lena

R. Irtysh

Lake Baikal

Lake Balkhash

Aral Sea

Yekaterinburg

Zlatoust

Chelyabinsk

Omsk

Novosibirsk

Irkutsk

Ulan Ude

Chita

Nikolaeysko

Habarovsk

Vladivostok

Tashkent

Bukhara

Windau Station

Nicholas Station

Kazan

Race Course

Alexander Station

Nagankovskoe Cemetery

Post Office

Pokrovski Barracks

Governor General

Arsenal

KREMLIN

Alexander Military Academy

Alexander Garden

Imperial Foundling Hospital

Bryansk Station

Saratov Station

R. Moskva

Po
Mag

Military Prison

Moscow 1905

On 7 December 1905 a general strike began in Moscow which paralyzed the economic life of the city as well as halting communications by rail through much of Russia. The authorities were largely inactive, despite their fear that the revolution would spread to the troops of the garrison. One detachment – the 2nd Rostov Grenadiers – had already mutinied. On the following day the governor of the city, F.V. Durnasov, ordered the police and a core of loyal troops to arrest the ringleaders. This provoked the strikers to take militant action and barricades were thrown up all over the city, but the insurrection had no real chance of success. The population as a whole was largely indifferent, and while the revolutionaries dominated the areas around the centre they could make no impression on the central area dominated by the Kremlin and other major buildings. However, the governor did not have the resources to attack the revolutionaries; on 12 December, he telegraphed for reinforcements: 'The situation continues to be serious: a network of barricades is constricting the city ever more tightly; there are clearly not enough troops for counteraction. It is absolutely essential to send a brigade of infantry from St Petersburg.'[1] The revolutionaries had not succeeded in blocking the railway, or in taking control of all the stations, and on 15 December the Semeonovsky Guards, together with artillery and supporting infantry, arrived at the Nicholas Station and moved to attack the revolutionary stronghold. They shelled the Presnya district in the west mercilessly, and executed many of the prisoners they took. On 19 December the strike and the revolution collapsed. It had been a virtual re-run of the Paris Commune, with the revolutionary forces failing to take basic military precautions, and then collapsing in the face of a superior and professional armed force. Over a thousand died in the course of the fighting and many thousands were exiled to Siberia. It revealed once again that the city could easily become a killing ground for revolutionary ambitions.

mile
0   1
0   1000
metres

The core of the revolutionary resistance to the final Czarist assault

Barricades set up by the revolutionary workers

Barracks where the troops joined the revolution

Artillery batteries established by Czarist troops to shell the workers

Held by troops loyal to the government, in addition to the main Kremlin complex

Czarist reinforcements brought in by rail

The final assault by Czarist forces

and strong military forces had been sent to 'pacify' the countryside. The provinces of Saratov, Penza, Tambov, Kursk, Voronezh and Chernigov were the first to suffer. Village by village the army, usually the Cossack regiments, demanded the surrender of known troublemakers. In any village where the rebels were not surrendered, exemplary punishment was borne by the whole community. It was the classically effective technique of quelling rural unrest: hang the ringleaders, flog the rank and file, terrorize the innocent. The next to feel the lash of the *nagaika* (the Cossack whip) or even the forbidden *knout* were the minority regions of the Baltic and Poland. In the Baltic provinces more than two thousand were executed and there were countless fines and floggings. The suppression of the more distant areas of the rebellion came after the conquest of the revolution in St Petersburg and Moscow. The greatest resistance was found among the troops in Siberia, where the mutineers were caught between punitive expeditions sent one from the east and one from the west. When the mutiny in Chita finally collapsed towards the end of January 1906, the government brought troops back from the east to occupy and purge the dissident provinces of the west.

In the end, it was the methods of Ivan the Terrible, or at least Peter the Great, which provided the key to the situation. Despite the mutinies and the surly resentment in the army, the Czar possessed sufficient loyal troops to overcome any internal enemy foolish enough to confront him. Until December 1905 the revolution was not a revolution but a mass protest; Nicholas could not accept more Bloody Sundays on a national scale. Moreover, there were doubts whether the troops would obey. But in December, it was clear that the government was going to be faced by both rural and urban insurrection. The troops had been blooded in suppressing the peasants, and these successes began to restore the government's confidence. But the key to success was the government's capacity to move its loyal regiments by rail to overwhelm any nodule of opposition. The railway strike began to break down early in December, and many railwaymen, the élite of Russian workers, had no interest in violent insurrection. With the support of some railway workers and officials, plus the aid of its own railway battalions, the government was able to reinforce the garrison in Moscow, while the revolutionaries there received a pitiful degree of practical support from revolutionaries elsewhere (see map).

Order was restored, the guilty were punished, and most of the old system was reimposed. However, the constitutional concessions could not simply be abandoned, and in February 1906, a new set of Fundamental Laws was issued. In these it was stated that 'To the Emperor of All the Russias belongs the supreme autocratic power', not as before 'the supreme *and unlimited* autocratic power'.[5] The *Duma* existed, as did the State Council, and those who wished to

were able to see a new dawn breaking. Such confidence was illusory. It was summed up neatly in the Almanach de Gotha, which before 1906 classed Russia as an 'absolute monarchy' and after as 'a constitutional monarchy ruled by an autocrat'. The change was formal and fictitious. What was not fictitious was the concerted effort made by Peter Stolypin to remedy some of the grossest inequities in rural life, and to encourage the process of modernization generally. Between the 1905 Revolution and the First World War, great economic advances were made, and by the time that Nicolas celebrated the 500th anniversary of Romanov rule in 1913, he could congratulate himself that not only had he preserved his autocratic inheritance, but that Russia seemed more tranquil and prosperous than it had done within living memory. 1905 became a bad dream.

The revolutionaries, however, did not or could not forget it. It revealed the strength and resilience of the Czarist system, provided it could still call upon armed force to support it. A few regiments had sufficed to take back Moscow from the insurgents, while the total number of arms possessed by the revolutionaries in St Petersburg was about 6000, and many of those were only pistols and revolvers. A workers' militia stood no chance against trained troops. Lenin drew from the experience of 1905 and concluded, citing Marx, that 'insurrection is an art', and that the revolution was lost if it did not possess the initiative: 'The principal rule of this art is that an audacious and determined *offensive* must be waged. . . . We have not sufficiently mastered this art, nor taught it to the masses, this rule of attacking, come what may.'[6] But this passionate insurrectionism, which his enemies were quick to label 'Blanquism' after the French fanatic, carried equal dangers, as became clear in 1917. No one had any real idea what was to be done.

In 1905 the autocracy had lost its nerve and the great army of bureaucrats was rendered powerless by this indecision. There was no policy to carry out, only a series of tentative gestures; and many of them were reluctant to follow a line of policy of which they fundamentally disapproved. Only a few lunatic generals and blood-thirsty reactionaries rejoiced after Bloody Sunday; for most of the government apparatus, from the Czar down, it was a tragedy. When a crisis emerged again in 1917, the bureaucracy proved unreliable. If it was a choice between the Romanov dynasty and national salvation, they were patriots first. Thus the experience of 1905 picked away at the seams of loyalty which bound state and Czar together. For the working classes, 1905 was a proving ground, and one where they discovered the weapon of collective action. The workers' councils – *soviets* – which appeared in 1905 became of incomparably greater importance in the real revolution twelve years later.

The Russian revolution

AT the end of his novel *Dead Souls*, published in 1842, Nikolai Gogol presents an image of Russia wholly unlike the torpid, sullen Russia of his own day: 'And you, Russia – aren't you racing headlong like the fastest *troika* imaginable? The road smokes under you, bridges rattle and everything falls behind. . . . And where do you fly to, Russia? Answer me! . . . She does not answer. The carriage bells break into an enchanted tinkling, the air is torn to shreds and turns into wind; everything on earth flashes past, and casting worried sidelong glances, other nations and countries step out of her way.'

By 1914, Mother Russia was fulfilling Gogol's vision. The country surged ahead in a fury of industrialization which amazed her competitors. Foreign experts were brought to install plants and develop new industries, while Russia began to copy the products of the West; enlarged industrial regions around Moscow, north to Ivanovo and Yaroslavl in the Urals, around the capital St Petersburg, and in a great sweep south of Kharkov to the lands of the Dnieper and Don rivers, began to transform the country. The new urban working class was at most a generation old, and the majority were only a few years off the land. The bond and contact between city and countryside was unusually close.

One factor which had encouraged an even greater flight from the land were the reforms initiated by Peter Stolypin. By 1913 the rural population was a little in excess of 103 million, and of that figure almost three million were a new class of peasant proprietor, smallholders created by the Stolypin policies.[1] Where the new holdings were created by enclosing and consolidating land formally held communally, it meant that the land tended to support fewer people, although the new proprietors were better off than before.

Once in the towns the former peasants formed a rootless and unstable element. They were prominent in the wave of strikes which rose from a low figure in the immediate aftermath of the 1905 Revolution to more than a million days lost by 1914. For many Russian workers and peasants life was in a state of ferment before the outbreak of war in 1914, and both society and the governmental system were under strain. The pressures generated by war blew the system apart. In many ways it made Russia more modern and economically efficient than ever before. Productivity rose prodigiously, and Russian industry responded to the demands of a war economy. What suffered was the elaborate system of control and manipulation which allowed central authority to function. Before the war Russia had been the most over-governed country in the world, more bureaucratized and tightly controlled than at any previous stage in her history. The transformation of the country into an adjunct of the military system created chaos. Railway transport was requisitioned for military needs, so food could not be sent to the cities in sufficient quan-

tities. Shells and ammunition were produced in profusion, but supplied in the wrong calibre or stockpiled in the wrong place. The countryside was drained of men, not only the millions drafted into the army (and slaughtered on the eastern front), but those who had surged into the cities,[2] many of them into the capital whose name was changed from the German St Petersburg to the Russian Petrograd in a mood of patriotic elation. Inflation rose as the government resorted to any expedient to raise money to finance the war.[3] The government's main effort to exercise control was directed at food prices, and in forcing the peasants to accept artificially low prices for their grain and livestock. The consequence was a passive refusal by the peasants to sell, despite all the pressure which the rural authorities could bring to bear, except to the increasingly flourishing black market. By 1917 the cities were on the point of starvation, while the armies, badly led and the victims of logistical chaos, were on the point of mutiny. The Czar, who had taken up the active role of Commander-in-Chief in 1915, remained at the General Staff Headquarters at Mogilev, largely insulated from the accelerating collapse of the system. The ministers who remained in the capital existed in limbo, often unable to issue orders on their own account or afterwards finding that they had been countermanded by the military authorities. Uncertainty and disillusion were the norm, and the feeling grew everywhere that the autocracy had failed Russia both on the battlefield and in the wasting paralysis of the home front.

In January 1917, after months of industrial unrest agitators in the working class area of Vyborg roused the workers to 'prepare for a general assault' because 'events were moving with incredible speed'.[4] The final collapse of the system came through mass action by every section of society: when it came to the crunch, virtually no one was prepared to sacrifice themselves for the Romanovs. By mid-February 1917, Petrograd had barely ten days' supply of grain.[5] Moscow and the industrial cities of Vladimir province suffered in the same way. Faced with the threat of starvation, the people rioted; towards the end of the month, mass demonstrations were organized by the political parties and the trade unions. On 24 February, the police opened fire and many civilians were killed or injured. On the following day, when the bridges across the river were blocked by police they crossed the Neva on the ice. Mass meetings were held, and at one, when a mounted policeman aimed his rifle at the speaker, a Cossack trooper spurred his horse forward and sabred the policeman to the ground. If the Cossacks were no longer to be trusted, what reliance could be placed on the loyalty of the rest of the huge Petrograd garrison? But on 26 February the soldiers were brought out against the demon-

Continued on page 88

20°   30°   40°

60°

Baltic Sea

Helsingfors
Vyborg
Kronstadt
Revel
Narva
Petrograd
Novgorod

Lake Ladoga

Archangel

Mitava
Libau
Riga
Pskov
Vologda
Rybinsk
Yaroslavl
Kostroma

Dvinsk
Vilna
Polotsk
Vitebsk
Tver
Ivanovo
Nizhniy Novgorod
Vyatka

Grodno
Bialystok
Minsk
Smolensk
Mogilev
Moscow
Vladimir

Kazan
Simbirsk

Gomel
Bryansk
Kaluga
Ryazan
Syzran
Samara

Chernigov
Orel
Tula
Penza
R. Volga

Zhitomir
Kiev
Kursk
Yelets
Tambov
Voronezh
Saratov

Uralsk

Berdichev
R. Dnieper
Poltava
Karkov
R. Don
Tsaritsyn

Kamenets-Podolskiy
Kremenchug
Elizavetgrad
Yekaterinoslav

Kishinev
Krivoy Rog
Nikolayev
Kherson
Rostov

Odessa

Astrakhan

Simferopol
Feodosiya
Yalta
Novorossiysk
Yekaterinodar
Stavropol

Black Sea

Pyatigorsk

Caspian Sea

Batumi
Tiflis

Yelizavetpol
Yerivan
Baku

40°

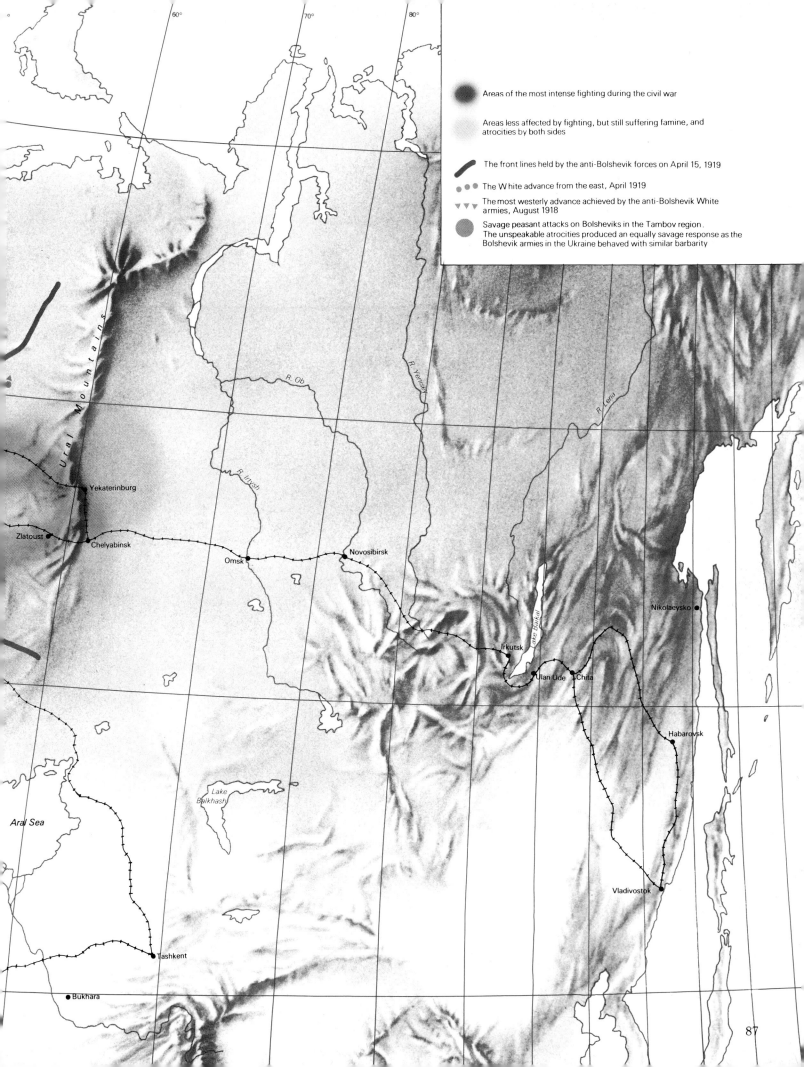

Areas of the most intense fighting during the civil war

Areas less affected by fighting, but still suffering famine, and atrocities by both sides

The front lines held by the anti-Bolshevik forces on April 15, 1919

The White advance from the east, April 1919

The most westerly advance achieved by the anti-Bolshevik White armies, August 1918

Savage peasant attacks on Bolsheviks in the Tambov region. The unspeakable atrocities produced an equally savage response as the Bolshevik armies in the Ukraine behaved with similar barbarity

Ural Mountains

R. Ob

R. Yenisey

R. Lena

R. Irtysh

Yekaterinburg

Zlatoust

Chelyabinsk

Omsk

Novosibirsk

Nikolaeysko

Irkutsk

Lake Baikal

Ulan Ude

Chita

Habarovsk

Lake Balkhash

Aral Sea

Tashkent

Bukhara

Vladivostok

strators and more than forty civilians were killed in Znamensky Square. Afterwards soldiers of the Pavlovsky, Preobrazhensky and Volynsky regiments declared that they would refuse further orders to fire on the workers. Officers who came to bring them to order were shot, and on the following morning the soldiers surged into the streets from their barracks and joined the processions of demonstrators streaming into the city for the fourth day running.

Many joined in the great milling crowd which pressed towards the Winter Palace. The troops in the arsenal had broken open the weapon racks and handed 40,000 rifles into the eager hands of the people. Small pockets of resistance were quickly overcome by the overwhelming force of soldiers and armed workers. Soon, the Comte de Chambrun observed, as he later wrote home to France, 'the Pavlovsky regiment marched from its quarters, with its band playing. I watched the battalions pass in close order, led by their non-commissioned officers. Instinctively I followed them. To my surprise, they marched towards the Winter Palace, went in, saluted by the sentries, and invaded and occupied it. I waited for a few moments and saw the Imperial flag come slowly down, drawn by invisible hands. Soon after . . . I saw a red flag floating over the palace.'[6]

The people had risen, like a repeat of 1905. They demanded, as their banners proclaimed day by day along the Nevsky Prospekt, 'Bread', 'Peace', and 'Down with Autocracy'. In the rising of the 27 February over 66,000 troops had disobeyed their officers, and the remaining two thirds of the garrison could not be relied on.[7] But the revolutionaries, or at least the more alert of them, saw their peril. Rumours grew that a huge army was on its way to take back the city by storm, and the pressing need was to

consolidate the rising. An immediate response was to form a *soviet* which, as in 1905, could co-ordinate the actions of the workers. The *Duma*, which had defied an Imperial order not to hold its sitting, tried to take the leading role. From the steps of the Taurida Palace, where the *Duma* held its sitting, Alexander Kerensky told a milling crowd who demanded 'instructions', 'directives': 'Arrest the ministers, seize the post office, the telegraphs, the telephones. Occupy the railway stations, the government offices.' It was good advice.[8] The *soviet* established later in the evening of 27 February, of which Kerensky and some other *Duma* deputies were members, set up a workers' militia, and launched a revolutionary daily newspaper, *Izvestia*. By dawn on 1 March 1917, the revolution had triumphed in Petrograd.

Power now lay in the streets, controlled, if at all, through the *soviet*. But legitimate authority, in so far as it lay anywhere, resided in the *Duma*, the only popularly elected body. While the *Duma* rallied to form a 'provisional government', the *soviet* struggled to preserve and push forward the revolution. The soviets spread almost spontaneously across Russia as the news of the events in Petrograd became known, workers and soldiers in each locality seeking to take over power. The political complexion of the soviets varied from place to place, for all the left-wing parties were striving to achieve dominance. The strongest group was the Socialist Revolutionaries, followed by the Menshevik wing of the Social Democrats. Much weaker was the Bolshevik wing of the Social Democrats, especially since they had virtually no influence within the army. The Bolsheviks had not made the revolution: no one had, except the angry masses of Petrograd. At best the Bolsheviks had pushed and exhorted where they could. Within three days of the triumph of the revolution in Petrograd, the respectable elements in the *Duma* were seeking to restore calm and order.[9] They dispatched a deputation to Pskov to demand the Czar's abdication. There Nicholas met the delegation and told them he had decided to abdicate in favour of his brother. They were struck by his calm, and his apparent indifference. His brother Michael decided to renounce the throne as well. When this joint abdication was announced to the people of the capital, there was wild rejoicing. In the crowd an officer named Mstislavsky who had sided with the revolution remarked to a friend: 'Now it is finished.' An unseen woman answered him: 'You are wrong, little father. Not enough blood has flowed.'[10]

Petrograd, 1917: the first attempt by the Bolsheviks to take power was defeated in July. Here people scatter with the approach of armoured cars firing their machine guns. In October the Bolsheviks made no mistake

The take-over

VERY late on the night of 3 April 1917, a small group of Bolshevik leaders arrived from exile at the Finland Station in Petrograd. Completely ignoring a welcoming speech – 'We believe that the main task of revolutionary democracy consists *now* of defending our revolution against all attempts against it, internal and external'[1] – Vladimir Ilyich Ulyanov, better known as Lenin, spoke to the crowd beyond the official delegation. His words set the tone for his future actions. He called the soldiers and workers the vanguard of the world proletarian army, and promised a new epoch of world socialist revolution. From the moment he returned, Lenin worked for the overthrow of the cautious and tentative arrangements created in March. He had to struggle not merely against the Russian establishment as embodied in the Provisional Government, but against the revolutionary institutions and parties themselves. The *soviet*, the Mensheviks, the Socialist Revolutionaries, and most of his own Bolshevik party leaders believed that unity in the face of the external and internal enemies was the only course to follow. He recognized that the principal need was to extend the tiny Bolshevik base among the soldiers, and to consolidate their organization in factories and among the workers. Lenin's technique, to call ceaselessly for radical socialist revolution, found an audience, and one which he could not control. On 3–4 July, the radicals among the soldiers, and in particular the ultra-radical sailors from the Kronstadt naval base took to the streets demanding 'all power to the *soviet*'. The soldiers had no intention of following the orders they had received to join the offensive launched against the German armies on 18 June, and determined to throw out the government instead. Lenin was taking a few days' rest in Finland, and in his absence the Bolshevik leadership interpreted the rising as the revolution he had demanded. But the *soviet*, far from accepting power from the hands of the radicals, allowed the remaining troops of the garrison into the streets to suppress them. The Bolsheviks' Military Committee had helped to plan the rising, and the party as a whole was held responsible for it. Lenin's 'insurrectionism' brought the party to the verge of catastrophe as all its enemies united against it. Lenin was accused of having received money from the Germans, and Bolshevik became a synonym for traitor.

While the purges following the failure of the July rising damaged the Bolsheviks' cells everywhere, they were less effective in the provinces and at points distant from the capital. The failure of the vaunted June offensive soon lent weight to the Bolshevik argument that peace, without penalty or annexation, was the only solution, while continued war only threatened the revolution. A number of Bolshevik strongpoints were established, and the party's stock rose immeasurably after the attempted counter-revolution of General Kornilov (26–30 August) implicated many of the 'class enemies' whom they had attacked so remorselessly. The Bolsheviks were also able to make more progress among the peasants by adopting policies, in many cases identical with those of the Socialist Revolutionaries, which chimed in with peasant wishes. Above all this meant the demand for nationalization of the land, although the Bolsheviks harped on the nationalization of the large estates rather than the total nationalization to which Lenin was committed. But the land was being transferred, in action after action as the peasants occupied the land, quite outside the control of anything the authorities in Petrograd might determine.

The Bolsheviks survived the July débâcle, and recovered during August, but they remained extremely wary of Lenin's calls for a new insurrection. At a meeting on 15 September he was turned down flat. The strength of Lenin's position lay in his consistency, advocating what was visionary rubbish in April but by October seemed increasingly plausible. By the autumn the compromises and political structures created by the February revolution were visibly failing. The provisional government was not winning the war to which it had committed itself. The food crisis had not been resolved as it had promised. The peasants had received no satisfaction for their demands, only a bleat of disquiet when they took what they wanted for themselves. The provisional government had failed, as the Bolsheviks had always said it would, and they were the only major group uncompromised by its failure. They offered a radical solution to the problems of Russia.

The only group which could make a revolution were those with arms, and Bolshevik efforts were concentrated on the soldiers and the workers' militias, the Red Guards. Many of the detachments which had come into being in the spring had fallen away in membership and training, and the Bolsheviks took good care to enlarge and revive the organization with their own people. Once again the Kornilov episode was the catalyst, and during September and October the Red Guards' numbers grew in factories throughout the capital and the other cities. Their quality was variable, as was their standard of equipment: in the Vyborg district of Petrograd, only one man in three had a rifle. Although their role in the seizure of power in the capital was secondary to that of the soldiers, in the mining and industrial districts of the southern Urals the factory 'combat squads' were the key to Bolshevik success. The strategy of insurrection depended on the attitude of the army, and more exactly, the large detachments in and around Petrograd.

The progress made by the Bolsheviks within the army was remarkable. On the south-western and Romanian fronts, there had been seventy-four Bolshevik groups in July.[2] By November 1917 there were 280. In Petrograd, radical ideas were very strong

Continued on page 92

Petrograd 1917

The takeover in Petrograd was a creeping occupation of the strategic points of the city rather than a lightning coup, as the timetable makes clear.

October 24 before dawn
Rumours circulate that provisional government is massing troops to take over Petrograd. Cadets occupy *Trud* printing press, which produces radical newspapers.

9.00 am Detachment of Litovsky Regiment and Sixth Engineers, both strongly revolutionary, retake *Trud* on orders of the Military Revolutionary Committee of the Petrograd *soviet*. Trotsky heads the MRC. Bolshevik Central Committee is in permanent session in Smolny Institute, headquarters of *soviet*.

noon Troops loyal to Provisional Government – women's Shock Battalion and cadets – reinforce garrison in the Winter Palace, seat of the government. During the afternoon, Kerensky tries and fails to rally support.

2.30 pm Cadets attempt to occupy Liteiny Bridge, driven off by armed workers. Soldiers occupy smaller Grenadersky and Samsonevsky bridges linking the Vyborg and Petrograd side for the MRC. Cadets succeed in beating Red Guards at Nikolaevsky bridge. Palace Bridge held by Shock Battalion and cadets for the government.

4.00 pm Cycle troops withdraw from the Winter Palace.

5.00 pm The MRC takes over the Central Telegraph Office. Cadets fail to retake it at 8.00 pm.

9.00 pm MRC takes over the Petrograd Telegraph Office.

9.00 pm Ismailovsky Guards take over Baltic Station to prevent reinforcements for Provisional Government arriving from Gulf of Finland. Troitsky Bridge occupied by soldiers.

late evening Lenin arrives at Smolny after perilous journey from the Vyborg side.

October 25 midnight
Sailors take over cruiser *Aurora* in Petrograd docks, and move up the river Neva.

2.00 am Sixth Engineers occupy Nikolaevsky Station. MRC takes over Petrograd electric station and cuts power to the Winter Palace. Take-over of main post office.

3.30 am Cruiser *Aurora* moves up to Nikolaevsky Bridge and sailors take it from cadets.

6.00 am Sailors occupy State Bank, while soldiers guarding it remain neutral.

7.00 am Keksgolmsky Regiment occupies main telephone exchange. Cuts all lines to provisional government and the military command.

8.00 am MRC takes command at Warsaw Station, the last of the main termini. Kerensky, having failed to win over the Cossacks by a last appeal; prepares to leave the capital.

noon Bolsheviks imprisoned in the Crosses Prison are released.

2.00 pm Ships arrive from Kronstadt to support the rising, carrying a large detachment of armed sailors. Approaches to the Winter palace are sealed off. Emergency session of the Petrograd *soviet* begins at Smolny.

6.15 pm Garrison begins to desert the Winter Palace. Artillery cadets leave.

8.00 pm 200 Cossacks leave the Winter Palace for their barracks.

9.40 pm *Aurora* fires a blank shell; many more leave the palace.

11.00 pm Shelling of the palace begins.

October 26 2.00 am
Revolutionary troops enter the Winter Palace, by now almost entirely deserted. The remaining ministers are arrested.

5.00 am The marathon session of the *soviet* ends with a large majority in favour of Lenin's manifesto declaring the end of the provisional government. Those opposing him, the Mensheviks etc., have already left in disgust.

VASILIEVSKY ISLAND

180th Infantry Regiment

Finliandsky Regiment

Franco-Russian shipyard

NARVA DISTRICT

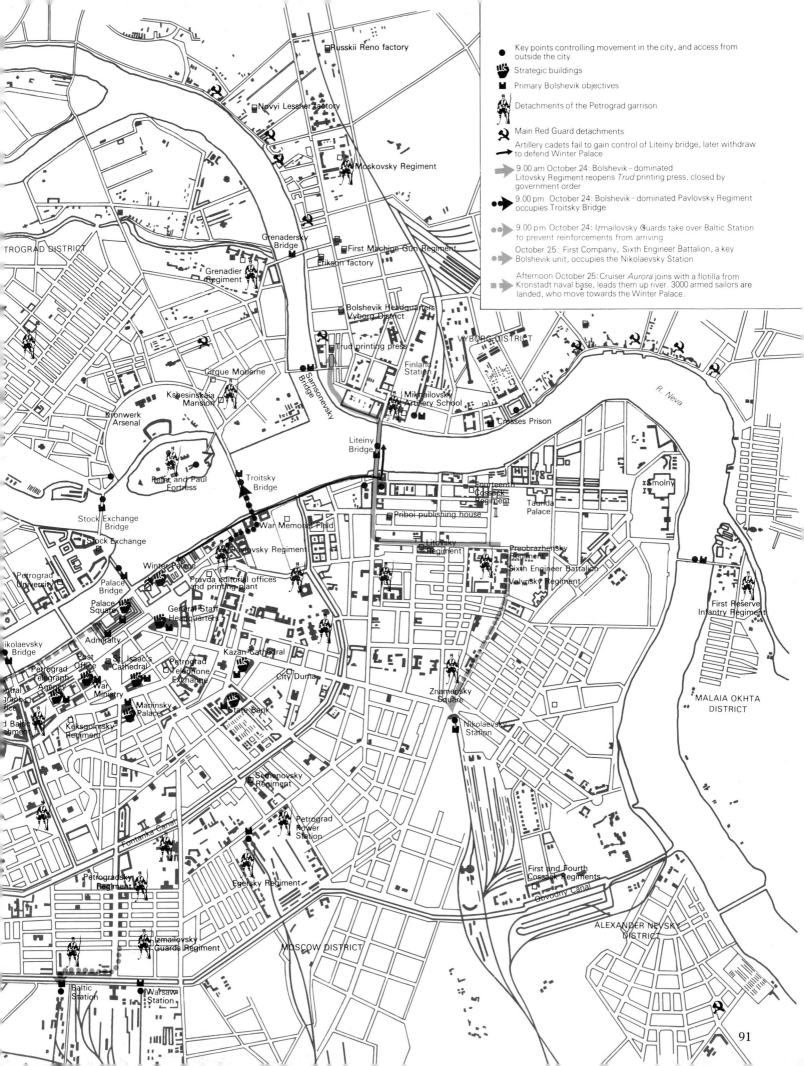

Russkii Reno factory

Novyi Lessner factory

Moskovsky Regiment

Grenadersky Bridge

First Machine Gun Regiment

Grenadier Regiment

Erikson factory

Bolshevik Headquarters Vyborg District

VYBORG DISTRICT

Trud printing press

Finland Station

R. Neva

Cirque Moderne

Kshesinskaia Mansion

Mikhailovsky Artillery School

Crosses Prison

Kronwerk Arsenal

Smolny

Liteiny Bridge

Peter and Paul Fortress

Troitsky Bridge

Fourteenth Cossack Regiment

Taurida Palace

Stock Exchange Bridge

Priboi publishing house

Stock Exchange

War Memorial Field

Winter Palace

Pavlovsky Regiment

Litovsky Regiment

Preobrazhensky Regiment

Sixth Engineer Battalion

Petrograd University

Pravda editorial offices and printing plant

Volynsky Regiment

Palace Bridge

Palace Square

General Staff Headquarters

First Reserve Infantry Regiment

Nikolaevsky Bridge

Admiralty

Kazan Cathedral

Post Office

St. Isaac's Cathedral

Petrograd Telephone Exchange

City Duma

Petrograd Telegraph Agency

War Ministry

Znamensky Square

MALAIA OKHTA DISTRICT

Mariinsky Palace

State Bank

Keksgolmsky Regiment

Nikolaevsky Station

Semenovsky Regiment

Fontanka Canal

Petrograd Power Station

Egersky Regiment

First and Fourth Cossack Regiments

Petrogradsky Regiment

Obvodny Canal

ALEXANDER NEVSKY DISTRICT

Izmailovsky Guards Regiment

MOSCOW DISTRICT

Baltic Station

Warsaw Station

Key

● Key points controlling movement in the city, and access from outside the city

✊ Strategic buildings

■ Primary Bolshevik objectives

Detachments of the Petrograd garrison

Main Red Guard detachments

→ Artillery cadets fail to gain control of Liteiny bridge, later withdraw to defend Winter Palace

9.00 am October 24: Bolshevik–dominated Litovsky Regiment reopens *Trud* printing press, closed by government order

9.00 pm October 24: Bolshevik–dominated Pavlovsky Regiment occupies Troitsky Bridge

9.00 pm October 24: Izmailovsky Guards take over Baltic Station to prevent reinforcements from arriving

October 25: First Company, Sixth Engineer Battalion, a key Bolshevik unit, occupies the Nikolaevsky Station

Afternoon October 25: Cruiser *Aurora* joins with a flotilla from Kronstadt naval base, leads them up river. 3000 armed sailors are landed, who move towards the Winter Palace.

PETROGRAD DISTRICT

among the soldiers, but couched in terms of loyalty to the *soviet*. Many Bolsheviks feared any insurrection would be a repetition of the July catastrophe unless the rising came about with the support of the *soviet*. The dangers posed by counter-revolutionary generals and by attempts to transfer radical troops out of the city, forced the *soviet* Executive Committee to create a Military Revolutionary Committee to control military matters. Through this ostensibly non-party group, the Bolsheviks were able to prepare a rising which would be executed in the name of the *soviet*, rather than merely the Bolsheviks acting alone. It would provide legitimacy in the eyes of the non-Bolshevized regiments, on whose acquiescence any rising would depend. If the bulk of the garrison remained friendly or neutral, then a rising in the capital could succeed. From mid-October, frantic efforts were made to win over the regiments. A garrison conference was established to sound out opinions among the units, and to win them over to the notion of radical action, if it became necessary. At the 21 October meeting of the garrison conference, after a stirring speech by Leon Trotsky, a member of the Military Revolutionary Committee and the architect of the insurrection, 'the representative of the 14th Don Cossack Regiment caused a sensation when he declared that his regiment would not only not support any counter-revolutionary moves, irrespective of whence they came, but would fight the counter-revolution with all its strength. . . .'[3] On 23 October, the last major obstacle, the crucial garrison of the Peter and Paul fortress whose guns dominated the capital, fell in line behind the Committee; their support also gave the radicals control over all the arms in the arsenal.

Through all this careful planning and propaganda, Lenin was proclaiming his litany of insurrection *now*, without more work, more planning, more consolidation within the army and the factories. Had it not been for his immense powers of persuasion it is unlikely that the terrifying leap in the dark would have been taken. But, equally, had he had his way in September or early October, the result would almost certainly have been another dismal failure. The revolution which began early on 24 October succeeded because no one attempted to stop it. The sole armed resistance came from officers, military cadets, some bicycle troops, and a woman's battalion. The plan called for the seizure of the bridges, capture of the railway stations and the telegraph and telephone offices, while the ships from Kronstadt joined the cruiser *Aurora* which was refitting in Petrograd dockyard, and moved to dominate the administrative heart of the city. Once the plan had succeeded – and the control of the bridges was crucial, for the river was not iced over as in February – the outlook for the resistance on behalf of the Provisional Government in the area of the Winter Palace was dismal. 'What will happen to the palace if the *Aurora* opens fire?'

asked one anxious cabinet member. 'It will be turned into a heap of ruins,' was the laconic reply of Admiral Verderevsky, who was in a position to know.[4] At the Council of Soviets in the Smolny Institute, where Lenin had arrived in heavy disguise after a dangerous trip across the city, the radicals needed a quick kill, before the forces of constitutional order, the *Duma* and the supporters of the provisional government could rally. The Mensheviks were outraged at the turn of events. At 2.00 am in the early morning of 26 October the Winter Palace was occupied, and the remaining members of the provisional government were arrested. The Second All-Russian Congress of Soviets, representing workers, peasants and soldiers throughout the nation fell in behind Lenin and the Bolsheviks. The seizure of the instruments of power was complete. But could they now hold them? There were rumours of avenging armies of counter-revolutionaries advancing on the capital, while on 29 October military cadets seized various buildings in Petrograd, attempting a counter-coup. None of the regiments joined them; the pact of neutrality held and the cadets were quickly suppressed. But beyond the city lay real armies dedicated to the destruction of the revolution, and the events of 1917 were prolonged into years of civil war.

The civil war

THE revolution of October 1917 was followed by four years of civil war more savage and bitter than almost any other civil conflict within modern history. The new Bolshevik regime was faced by all those forces from whom it had taken control of Russia in October. In terms of military expertise, and certainly with the intervention of the Allied forces against the revolution from the summer of 1918, in terms of equipment, the White armies seemed to have the advantage. But they were a ragbag of assorted interests united only by their hatred of the Reds. The White armies attacked the Reds from all points of the compass, but the Reds held the core of Russia, the central ground. The inner lines of communication were to prove vital as Trotsky created his Red Army from a motley collection of Red Guards, former soldiers, peasants and conscripts. The main problem was food, for the Whites dominated the areas which had formerly supplied the urban areas of Russia with much of their grain. The scanty rations which had helped to provoke the October rising in Petrograd were abundance compared with what was available in the summer of 1918. Frequently there was no bread at all. The answer of the Bolsheviks was to press much harder on the peasants to disgorge the grain they had hoarded or were feeding to their livestock. In the poor and relatively unproductive agricultural areas within the control of the new government the peasants were pressed hard. On occasions their resentment expressed itself in revolt, as in Tambov province, where almost unspeakable atrocities were inflicted by peasants on Reds unfortunate enough to be captured by them. The Red armies responded in kind – as they did everywhere.

The consequence of the civil war was massive loss of life and devastation, and the final expulsion of the White armies, leaving Lenin and the Bolsheviks in undisputed control of a prostrate country. They tidied up the remnants, like the revolutionary anarchists of Nestor Makhno who had been occasional allies in the region south of Kharkov, and slapped down the hotheads, like the revolutionary sailors at Kronstadt. The national minorities, whom they had encouraged to think and behave independently, were once more brought under the dominion of central authority. For a time Lenin thought exclusively in terms of a worldwide revolution springing from a Russian core. By November 1920, a new tone was creeping in: 'It has transpired that neither one side nor the other, neither the Soviet Russian Republic nor the whole remaining capitalist world, has won a victory or succumbed to defeat, and at the same time it has transpired that, although our predictions have not been fulfilled simply, quickly and directly, they have been fulfilled to the extent that they have given us the main thing, and the main thing was to secure the possibility of the existence of proletarian government and the Soviet republic even in the event of the delay of the socialist revolution in the entire world.'[1]

The stage was set for 'socialism in one country', with world revolution to be achieved by other means. The civil war brought even Lenin down from his high peaks of fantasy to what was possible.

The dissolution of Czarism and the rebuilding of Russia in a new image was not accomplished by steady progress, but in a series of flurries and retreats. The destruction of the army as a means of enforcing the will of government, either the Czar's or the provisional government, was an act of fundamental importance. The army was not united, and the front soldiers often despised the 'slackers' in garrison to the rear as much as they did the ostensible enemy. But front and rear *were* united in their rejection of the old blind and unquestioning obedience – an attitude legitimized by the first decree issued by the Petrograd *soviet*. Order Number One, issued on 1 March 1917, established soviets in military units as among the workers, and denounced the structure of absolute obedience which had previously bound the army to its officers.[2] From 1 March in Petrograd, and soon afterwards at the front and elsewhere in the country, officers could only issue orders with the consent of their soldiers. From that point, the army was an unknown quantity, the instrument of whichever group could manipulate it. After Order Number One groups of officers began to plan what became first the Kornilov *putsch*, and then the White movement.[3] From that point also began the steady Bolshevization of the army units, which was to be the key to the success of the October rising in Petrograd and in the seizure of power throughout Russia.

The spread of Bolshevism. Commissars from Moscow arrive in Kharkov and are greeted by local Bolsheviks. All over Russia, Lenin sought to extend central control where possible: the commissars were the eyes and ears of the party

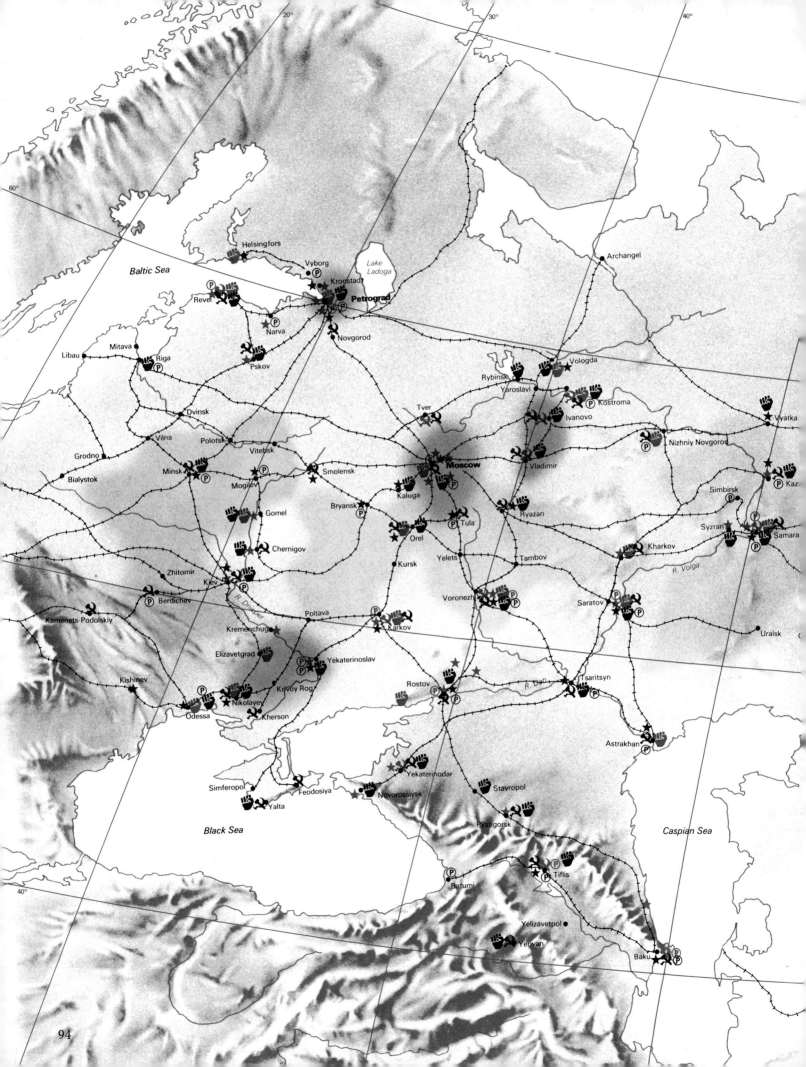

Baltic Sea

Helsingfors
Vyborg
Kronstadt
Petrograd
Revel
Narva
Novgorod
Lake Ladoga
Archangel

Mitava
Libau
Riga
Pskov

Grodno
Bialystok
Vilna
Dvinsk
Polotsk
Vitebsk
Smolensk
Tver

Minsk
Mogilev
Gomel

Berdichev
Zhitomir
Kiev
Chernigov
Bryansk
Kaluga
Moscow
Vladimir
Ivanovo
Kostroma
Rybinsk
Yaroslavl
Vologda

Kamenets-Podolskiy
Kremenchug
Poltava
Orel
Tula
Kursk
Yelets
Tambov
Ryazan
Kharkov
Simbirsk
Syzran
Samara
Vyatka
Nizhniy Novgorod
Kaz

Kishinev
Elizavetgrad
Yekaterinoslav
Krivoy Rog
Kharkov
Voronezh
Saratov
Uralsk
R. Volga

Odessa
Nikolayev
Kherson
Rostov
R. Don
Tsaritsyn
Astrakhan

Simferopol
Feodosiya
Yalta
Novorossiysk
Yekaterinodar
Stavropol
Pyatigorsk

Black Sea

Batumi
Tiflis
Yelizavetpol
Yerivan
Baku

Caspian Sea

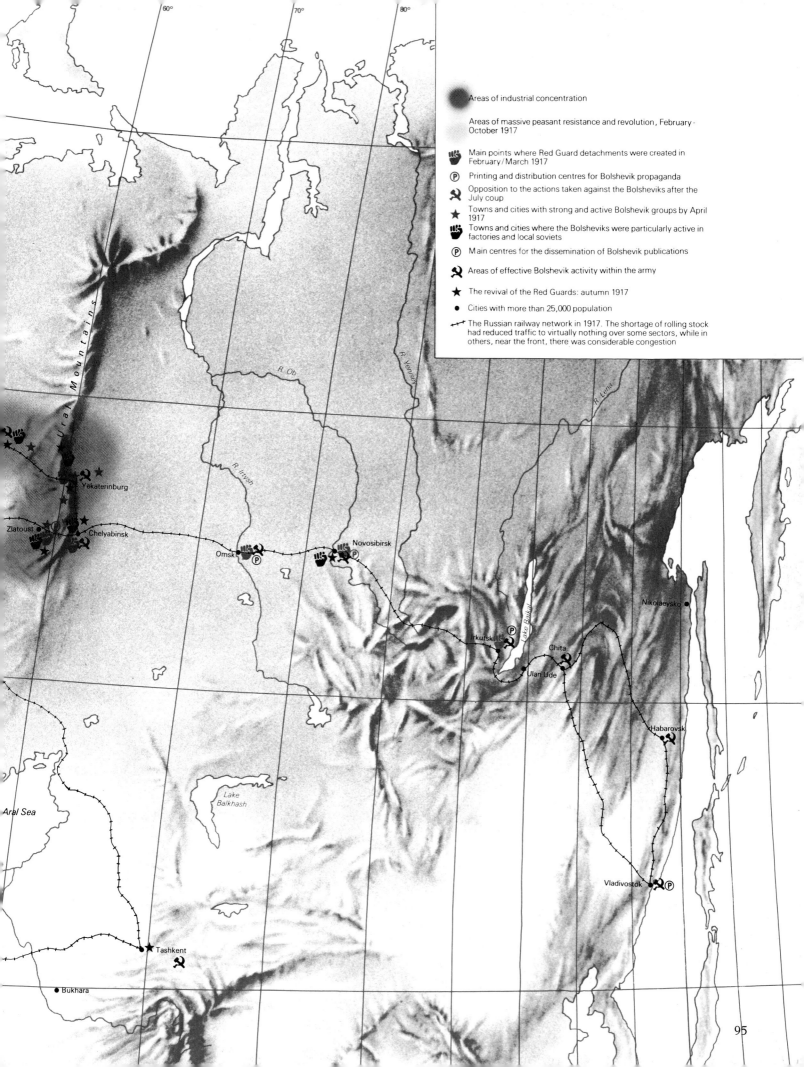

Areas of industrial concentration

Areas of massive peasant resistance and revolution, February–October 1917

Main points where Red Guard detachments were created in February/March 1917

Ⓟ Printing and distribution centres for Bolshevik propaganda

Opposition to the actions taken against the Bolsheviks after the July coup

★ Towns and cities with strong and active Bolshevik groups by April 1917

Towns and cities where the Bolsheviks were particularly active in factories and local soviets

Ⓟ Main centres for the dissemination of Bolshevik publications

Areas of effective Bolshevik activity within the army

★ The revival of the Red Guards: autumn 1917

• Cities with more than 25,000 population

The Russian railway network in 1917. The shortage of rolling stock had reduced traffic to virtually nothing over some sectors, while in others, near the front, there was considerable congestion

Ural Mountains

R. Ob

R. Yenisey

R. Lena

R. Irtysh

Yekaterinburg

Zlatoust

Chelyabinsk

Omsk

Novosibirsk

Lake Baikal

Irkutsk

Chita

Ulan Ude

Nikolaevsk

Habarovsk

Aral Sea

Lake Balkhash

Vladivostok

Tashkent

Bukhara

95

The rebirth of Turkey

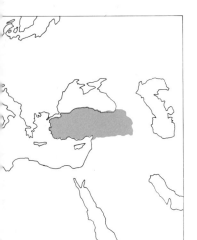

THE Ottoman empire was, by general agreement, an anachronism, certainly in the eyes of the eminent politicians who came to France to create a peace settlement after the First World War. It was a supra-national state, intolerant of minorities and subject peoples. As Caliph, the Ottoman sultan was titular head of all Islam, and thus compromized the interests of a number of the great powers. The 'Islamic card' had been played against the British during the war, producing unrest among India's Moslem population. France and Italy had territorial ambitions in the eastern Mediterranean. The United States had been subjected to a barrage of propaganda from an Armenian lobby strongly represented in the USA: they were concerned with the claims to independence advanced by both the Armenians and the Kurds of eastern Anatolia. The radical dismemberment of the empire found favour with all.

In this plan for partition virtually no consideration was given to the Turks as a nation. The cosmopolitan character of the empire had disguised the Turkish component, with its territorial heartland in Anatolia. Political power was held by Greeks, Albanians, and latterly by a military group of predominantly Macedonian origin which had seized control of the government in 1908. The 'revolution' of 1908, which replaced the sultan Abdul Hamid II with his more pliant younger brother, had as its objective the reform and strengthening of the multi-national Ottoman empire. It was in pursuit of this imperialism that the Ottoman Empire entered the First World War as an ally of Germany and Austria-Hungary. It was not surprising that the victorious Allies, in stripping the Ottoman empire of its domains in the Arab lands, extended the programme of partition to Anatolia: there was no articulate claim for *Turkish* nationhood.

The essence of the revolution created by Mustafa Kemal (Ataturk) was that he forged the notion of a Turkish state. While the revolutionaries of 1908 (of which he had been one) had thought of themselves exclusively as Ottomans, Kemal shed the inheritance of the former empire both geographically and intellectually. In fostering the notion of a *Turkish* state in Anatolia and on the European side of the Bosphorus, he made the claim that the Turks should be treated like any other nationality freed from the shackles of the Ottoman Empire. In doing so he clashed with the interests of France, Greece, Britain and Italy, as well as the ambitions of the nascent Bolshevik state in Russia. To these enemies could be added the Ottoman establishment, now firmly under Allied occupation in Constantinople, and much of the religious hierarchy, obedient to the Caliph-Sultan. Against this opposition, Kemal had two sources of strength. He was the most successful soldier in the former Ottoman army, the hero of the Gallipoli campaign in 1915, and moreover, a number of his potential military allies were located in the east of Anatolia with their troops, far away from the occupying Allied

troops to the west. In April 1919 Kemal secured a post as Inspector of the Ninth army, based at Samsum on the Black Sea, arguing that Anatolia was falling into chaos and required a firm hand. Before the Allies were fully aware of the danger in letting so powerful a nationalist slip from their control, he had sailed from Constantinople in a British freighter, on 16 May 1919. Three days later Kemal stepped ashore at Samsum in Asia Minor. The day before he sailed, the Greeks, impatient to reap the gains in Anatolia to which they felt their support for the Allied cause had entitled them, began a war of conquest at Izmir (Smyrna). It was this invasion by the traditional enemy which gave point to the nationalist demands which the new Inspector began to make. While the authorities in Constantinople seemed to connive at the occupation of Anatolia, Kemal made it clear he intended to throw the Greeks into the sea and he had the soldiers of the Anatolian army standing with him.

While the first stage of the revolution was a military campaign waged with extraordinary tenacity by the nationalists, the political objectives of an independent Turkish state were developed at a series of congresses, beginning at Erzurum and Sivas in the summer and autumn of 1919. From the outset, while many of the nationalists were fearful of cutting the ties of the past (some of Kemal's closest associates, like Rauf Bey and Refet Pasha, believed that 'there can be no form of government other than the Sultanate and Caliphate'[1]), Kemal aimed for a complete break with the past, using existing institutions only insofar as they were useful. Strategic considerations dictated that he should base himself in the heart of Anatolia, at the railhead of Angora (Ankara). In December 1919 he established the nationalists in the centre of peasant support for the nationalist cause, although to the north and east lay strong areas of Moslem fanaticism ready to obey the demands issuing from the Caliphate for the destruction of a rebel and heretic. Kemal, a loyal Moslem when it suited him, declared that he was fighting in 'the Holy War which we have entered upon for the independence of our country'.[2] When the *ulema* (religious council) of Constantinople pronounced against him, he was to persuade the *ulema* of Angora to declare the decrees of Constantinople invalid, since they were issued under the duress of enemy occupation. The nationalists faced three sets of enemies: Turks loyal to the Ottomans, national minorities – the Kurds and the Armenians – and external enemies – the Greeks and the other allies. Against both he adopted a revolutionary style of war. Guerrilla attacks were launched behind enemy lines, and these centres of resistance were so effective against the occupation in the south that the French forces were withdrawn in February 1920. Against his internal enemies, he launched both his regular military forces and a series of emergency 'revolutionary tribunals' which purged rebellious zones with extreme efficiency and ferocity. Where regular troops were not available, he used bandits and irregulars. But in the first six months of 1920 the position of the nationalists in Angora was precarious since Kemal was in effect fighting a civil war as well as facing the more powerful regular armies of the European powers.

In June 1920 the Allies presented the Constantinople politicians with the blueprint of their future, embodied in the Treaty of Sèvres. It was so antithetical to Turkish interests that it provided a charter for the nationalists. The Ottoman politicians who had signed the Treaty, a 'ministry of marionettes' in Winston Churchill's phrase, were utterly discredited, and with them the whole apparatus of power in the capital. The civil strife of Turk against Turk died down, and Kemal was left to face the thrust by the Greek armies into Anatolia. City after city fell to the Greek armies, and the nationalists fell back in panic. Kemal's strategy was to allow the Greeks to lengthen their lines of communication, and draw them further and further into the hostile heart of Anatolia, dependent on the railway for all their supplies and support. The campaign was costly, but the tide turned at the prolonged battle on the Sakarya river, and the Greek armies began to retreat. The retreat became a rout when, almost a year after the victory at the Sakarya, the Turkish armies broke through the Greek defensive line (August–September 1922). The Greek armies fled to Izmir, devastating the land as they went, and repeating the cycle of murder and atrocity which had always marked wars between Greek and Turks. Western observers were horrified by the burning of Izmir which followed the Turkish occupation; Kemal dismissed it as 'a disagreeable incident'.[3] But the image of the 'savage Turk', deserved or not, had a strategic value. As the Turkish armies raced up the coast towards the zone occupied by the British around Chanak, public opinion in Britain (which had never had much interest in the Turkish question) was convulsed by the prospect of hostilities in defence of the Treaty of Sèvres. The most ardent advocate of the Greeks, the Prime Minister David Lloyd George, was turned out of office by his coalition partners; their leader Bonar Law declared: 'we cannot act alone as the policeman of the world.'[4] Thus the fragility of the Allied position which lay behind the Sèvres proposals was exposed. Kemal, having defeated the Greeks, was pushing at an open door. A new peace conference was summoned to Lausanne in November 1922, and after nearly eight months of Turkish intransigence, stalemate and actual breakdown in negotiations, a new treaty was signed on 24 July 1923. The first stage of the revolution was complete. In October Turkish forces entered Constantinople following the Allied evacuation and a week later on 9 October, the Turkish quality of the new state was made clear to the world, when the old capital of Constantinople was abandoned for Angora, now to be known as Ankara.

The achievement of nationhood had taken almost four years; the accomplishment of the social revolution which Kemal had in mind was to occupy the remaining sixteen years of his life. The revolutionaries of 1908 had aimed to 'westernize' the Ottoman Empire, along the lines that progressive Turks had advocated since the 1870s. But change could not be accomplished by mere legislation, or cosmetic changes in, for example, education or the status of women in society. Kemal's attitude stemmed from his belief that while the new Turkey was geographically part of Asia, it was the centuries of Ottoman heritage which bound it culturally to the east. He rapidly secured the extinction of the sultanate and the proclamation of a republic (1923), the abolition of the caliphate and the religious courts which dominated social life (1924), and in the following year accomplished a sweeping campaign against vestiges of the old regime. He toured the most backward and obdurate areas of the country, decreeing the suppression of Islamic sects, places of pilgrimage, and the brimless hat, the fez, which had become the symbol of the Moslem in Turkey. He proclaimed the equality

Mustafa Kemal, who later took the name Ataturk. The outstanding Turkish general of the First World War, he launched a nationalist revolution and swept away the last vestiges of the Ottoman Empire. An autocrat by nature, he forced his country into his vision of modernization. This photograph was taken on the day of his final offensive to drive out the Greek invaders in 1922

of women in civil life, a civil code of law (1926), and in 1928 the introduction of a Latin alphabet for the Turkish language. With this change it became possible to mount a drive against illiteracy, since the new script was much easier to learn than the old Arabic form.

All these changes were pushed forward by the ceaseless energy of Kemal, who in 1935 took the surname Ataturk, 'Father of the Turks'. Nor was the revolution accomplished by reason alone: Kemal Ataturk repressed all opposition with the ruthlessness (and a good deal more efficiency) of the sultans he succeeded. None of his associates had the same zeal for change, and many fell away, often ending their lives on the gallows as victims of the revolutionary tribunal. But like the great Sultan Suleiman the Magnificent, with whom many compared Ataturk, he used the power of repression to achieve a new legal and social structure for his country. What he could not achieve was any political structure to succeed him. The sole element of stability within Turkish society, then and now, was the army. Kemal had no political philosophy beyond Turkish nationhood, and his attempts to develop a political theory for the Turkish nation, rooted in a rather spurious view of the Turkish past, have borne no fruit.

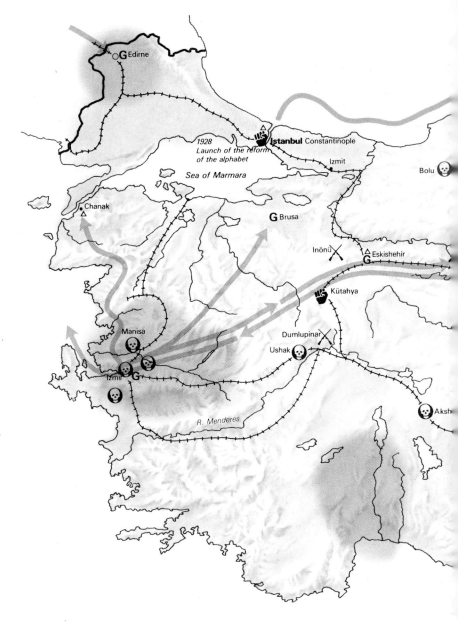

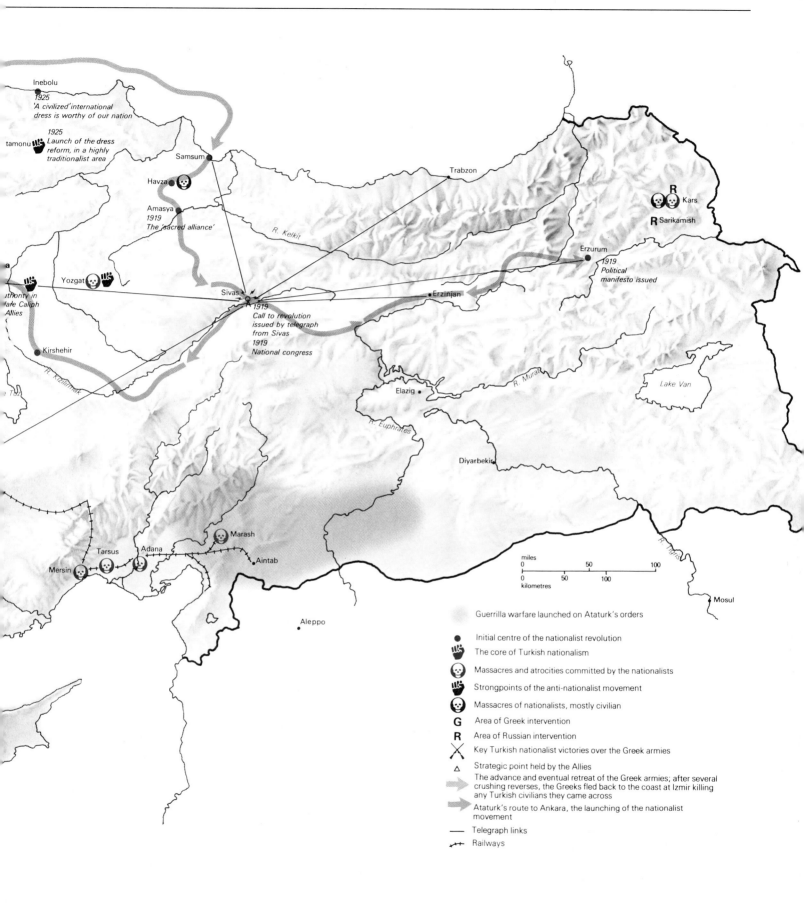

Inebolu
1925
'A civilized'international
dress is worthy of our nation

tamonu 1925
Launch of the dress
reform, in a highly
traditionalist area

Samsum

Havza

Amasya
1919
The 'sacred alliance'

Trabzon

R. Kelkit

Erzurum
1919
Political
manifesto issued

R Kars
Sarikamish

a

thority in
ate Caliph
Allies

Yozgat

Sivas
R 1919
Call to revolution
issued by telegraph
from Sivas
1919
National congress

Erzinjan

Kirshehir

R. Kizilirmak

e Tuz

Elazig

R. Murat

Lake Van

R. Euphrates

Diyarbekir

Marash

Adana
Aintab

Tarsus

Mersin

R. Tigris

miles
0   50   100
0   50   100
kilometres

Mosul

Aleppo

Guerrilla warfare launched on Ataturk's orders

Initial centre of the nationalist revolution

The core of Turkish nationalism

Massacres and atrocities committed by the nationalists

Strongpoints of the anti-nationalist movement

Massacres of nationalists, mostly civilian

G   Area of Greek intervention

R   Area of Russian intervention

X   Key Turkish nationalist victories over the Greek armies

△   Strategic point held by the Allies

The advance and eventual retreat of the Greek armies; after several
crushing reverses, the Greeks fled back to the coast at Izmir killing
any Turkish civilians they came across

Ataturk's route to Ankara, the launching of the nationalist
movement

—   Telegraph links

+++   Railways

'Bolshevism is gaining ground everywhere'

IN the course of the First World War the European states discovered a weapon potentially more devastating than mustard gas or military aviation. Both Germany and the Allies discovered the strategy of subversion.[1] Germany conveyed Lenin back to Russia, with cosmic consequences, but the same style of subversive war had been tried elsewhere. Money was given to nationalist movements in Nyasaland, Ireland, Indo-China and Morocco; agents were active in India, Afghanistan and Persia. They also provided considerable resources for the dissident nationalities within Russia. The Allies could point to the many successes against the Turks, notably by T.E. Lawrence, and to propaganda among the Slav peoples of the Habsburg Empire. The lessons read into the Russian Revolution and the triumph of the Bolsheviks were about the fragility of social stability. Revolution was in the air and no one was safe from its contagion. Behind every murmur of anti-colonialism or demand for radical reform was seen Bolshevik gold.

Revolutionary Russia was happy to foster the spread of revolution with men and money, but not every revolutionary incident could be traced directly back to Moscow. In the last days of October 1918, the war effort of Germany and Austria-Hungary was on the point of collapse. On the Italian front, the Czechs in the Austrian forces began to desert, while the Hungarians marched home to defend their own country. The Adriatic fleet mutinied at Pola. In Germany, events moved so quickly that the Emperor Wilhelm II could not believe that his army would no longer obey him and continue the war. Had they not sworn an oath on the Colours (*Fahneneid*) to follow him? He was told that oaths were now meaningless, even the oath on the Colours – 'only an idea', without substance. But German society was so centralized that the collapse of central authority in Berlin and the provincial capitals would lead to anarchy. Government was pushed into the unwilling hands of the most powerful social group, the Social Democratic party, in the hope that they had sufficient authority to hold the danger at bay. Revolution was not what they wanted. As good Germans, who had co-operated in the war effort, they had a considerable stake in the stability of society. Their leader Friedrich Ebert spoke for almost all of his party when he said: 'social revolution . . . I do not want it – in fact, I hate it like the plague.'[2] On the extreme left wing of the Social Democratic Party however, was a faction which anticipated the revolution with eagerness: a group led by Karl Liebknecht and Rosa Luxemburg, the 'Spartacists'. But the revolution among the war-weary soldiers and sailors was undirected: even the Spartacists, who were closest to the workers of all the forces on the left had no part in its genesis. One of the shop stewards who led the Berlin rising, recounted that 'the characteristic feature of this rising lay in the elemental force with which it broke out'[3]; what was true of Berlin was also true of the sailors' mutiny in Kiel on 3 November, and the take-over by workers and soldiers of towns throughout Germany in the days that followed. No instructions were given, nor was there any central direction. The take-over was spontaneous and largely aimless.

The shaky transfer of power from the monarchy to the Social Democrats was constitutionally invalid, and the only hope they had of controlling events was through the remaining parts of the old Imperial army. As the revolution spread, the troops returning from the front simply ceased to obey their officers; it was like a re-run of February 1917 in Russia. For the extreme left, it seemed that the moment of decision had arrived. But Liebknecht was no Lenin, and there was no clarity in their objectives. As Karl Kautsky observed: 'Our party presented a grotesque appearance, as perhaps no other party has done in the history of the world. Its right wing was in the government, and its left wing worked for the downfall of that very government.'[4]

The small radical group around Luxemburg and Liebknecht severed its links with the Independent Social Democrats at the end of December 1918; thereafter they styled themselves the German Communist Party (Spartacus League), the self-declared nerve centre of the German revolution. Within a fortnight, the Spartacists had allowed themselves to be sucked into a futile, hopeless and unnecessary insurrection in Berlin, ending in the brutal murders of Liebknecht and Luxemburg. They neglected the advice of a much harder-nosed revolutionary, Karl Radek, to abandon the workers who had launched the Berlin rising on 6 January. As he said, even 'if the government should fall into your hands as a result of a coup d'état within a few days it would be cut off from the rest of the country and would be strangled.' But Luxemburg, who had scorned 'insurrectionism' in the past was now writing in a fever of passion: 'Act! Act! Courageously, decisively and constantly. . . . Disarm the counter-revolution, arm the masses, occupy all positions of power. Act quickly!'[5]

The suppression of the Spartacists in Berlin was accomplished by a new military power which had, miraculously, come into the government's hands, a small professional force of ex-officers and NCOs, the *Freikorps*. The precision and callousness with which they suppressed workers in Berlin was seen on every occasion when they were used. By the end of January 1919, there were some dozen of these groups, never more than a few thousand strong. Their loyalty to the new republic was questionable, but the Social Democrats had no alternatives. On 2 February the *Freikorps* were turned on Bremen, then Wilhelmshaven, Cuxhaven, Bremerhaven and Hamburg. In March there was a new rising in Berlin, which was suppressed with more difficulty: the lessons of January had been learned. But the *Freikorps* had artillery and armour, and there was no body of armed workers

NORWAY

Oslo

SWEDEN

Stockholm Ⓟ

DENMARK

Copenhagen ★

UNITED
KINGDOM

Glasgow Ⓟ ★

Belfast ★

Yorkshire
coalfield ★
Liverpool Ⓟ

Nottingham Ⓟ
Leicester Ⓟ

London Ⓟ

NETHERLANDS

BELGIUM

Flensburg
Schleswig
Cuxhaven Rendsburg Kiel ▲
Wilhelmshaven ▲ Brunsbüttel
Hamburg Lübeck Rostock
Oldenburg Parchim
Bremen Lüneburg

GERMANY

Hanover

Bielefeld Brandenburg
Essen Brunswick Berlin 💀 Ⓟ
Krefeld Mansfeld Magdeburg Posen
Rheydt Düsseldorf
Kassel Halle Leipzig Glogau
Eisenach Erfurt Dresden 💀 Görlitz
Koblenz Neustadt Leuna Liegnitz Breslau
Frankfurt Chemnitz
Mainz Königsberg Plauen
Mannheim Bayreuth Plauen
Nuremberg

POLAND

Prague Ⓟ

CZECHOSLOVAKIA

Brno Ⓟ

Stuttgart

Augsburg Passau
Munich 💀 Vienna ★ Ⓟ Bratislava Ⓟ
Rosenheim

AUSTRIA

Berne Ⓟ

SWITZERLAND

Budapest Ⓟ

HUNGARY

FRANCE

Lyons ★

Bergamo ★

Milan ★

Turin ★

Venice Ⓟ
Trieste Ⓟ

Toulouse ★

Genoa Ⓟ

Pola

Marseilles
Toulon ★

R. Po

YUGOSLAVIA

Belgrade Ⓟ

R. Danube

ITALY

Sofia Ⓟ

miles
0   100   200

0   100   200
kilometres

● The main workers' and soldiers' councils set up in November 1918

✊ Spartacists and left wing radicals in control

✊ Right wing violence and coup d'état

★ Major strikes and street demonstrations

Ⓟ Mass protests against allied intervention in Russia

▲ Naval mutinies

💀 The violent suppression of revolution

which could withstand them in battle. The final confrontation came in Bavaria. A radical Soviet Republic had been established in Munich by a small Independent Socialist group led by a theatre critic, Kurt Eisner. Eisner was murdered on 21 February by a young right-wing fanatic after a period of most erratic rule. With his death, power was taken by a *troika* of Communists: Towia Axelrod, Max Levien, and Eugen Levine. They created a much tighter organization than the eccentric Eisner, and on paper, a Red Army totalling about 20,000 men. Facing them was a *Freikorps* 'army' of some thirty thousand; by April 1919, the *Freikorps* had expanded to total some 400,000 throughout Germany. The Red Army melted away, and the few who remained made a final stand in a complex of buildings near the main railway station. Final resistance was destroyed with artillery and flame-throwers. In their last hours, the Munich Commune had murdered a number of hostages which they held, about twenty in all. The *Freikorps* 'cleansed' Munich as a reprisal, in the words of one *Freikorps* officer: 'It's better to kill a few innocent people than to let one guilty person escape.... You know how to handle it ... shoot them and report that they attacked you or tried to escape.'[6] With the Munich massacres, the government realized that their mercenaries were beyond control. In the new Provisional Reichswehr, they hoped that they would have a force which could tame them. In the event, when the *Freikorps* turned against the German Republic, the army would do nothing. The generals told

the Defence Minister, Noske: 'Do you intend, Herr Minister that a battle be fought before the Brandenburg Gate between troops which have fought side by side against the common enemy....'[7] But the Kapp *putsch* in Berlin in March 1922 revealed the limitations of these private armies. They could take a city by storm, but they could not control a population, much less run a city paralyzed by a general strike. In due course they disbanded, many of them eventually to re-emerge in a new uniform, the brown shirt and forage cap of the SA. Hitler gave them purpose and an objective. In their brief existence, they had virtually exterminated a generation of German radical leaders, and given the workers a taste of fear which they never lost. Part of the incapacity of the workers' parties to resist the Nazis stemmed from their experience in 1919–22.

The tide of revolution swept through Germany, touched Austria briefly, and on into Hungary. A Soviet Republic was created by an emissary of Lenin, Bela Kun. Hungary was the one area where the Russian model briefly took root. The Allies were in terror, predicting that Austria, the new state of Czechoslovakia, and the other former Habsburg domains in the Balkans, would succumb to Leninism.

The Communist republic in Hungary, despite an initial surge into Slovakia, was short lived. Bela Kun set up his government on 21 March. Early in April, the Romanians invaded from the east, and at the beginning of August, Bela Kun was in flight, on his way back to Russia. The hopes of International Revolu-

The German revolution, 1919. Mutinous troops carry the Red flag through the streets of Berlin

tion began to fade. But in the minds of the governments of the West the Red menace seemed to be growing rather than receding. Northern Italy was paralyzed by a series of strikes, as was France and much of England and Scotland. There was rioting in Glasgow, and threats of mutiny among British troops both in France and at home. As early as 1919 the British government believed that revolution was on the cards.

Nowhere, not even in Germany and Hungary, had the conditions of Russia reproduced themselves. The revolutionaries of the West forgot the long and tortuous manoeuvres by which the Bolsheviks emerged from a minor part in February 1917 to take centre stage in October. They ignored the setback of July, and also gave little thought to the prolonged process of 'sovietization' in the factories and the creation of a Red Guard. And, even despite the lengthy preparations, and the battles fought by Lenin to enforce *his* view, the revolution would have failed had it met determined armed resistance. Insurrection *is* an art, and neither Liebknecht nor Luxemburg were prepared to learn it. The German revolution was a spontaneous creation, without any controlling intelligence, street violence on a massive scale with a superficial layer of political purpose. Both Germany and Hungary showed, not that Bolshevism was gaining ground everywhere, but the exact contrary. 'Socialism in one country' was not made for export.

The forces of repression: the *Freikorps* in Berlin to support the Kapp Putsch, 1920. This is the infamous Ehrhardt Brigade, which still bore its old Imperial German standard. The *putsch* failed and the *Freikorps* split up. Many of them re-appeared in the ranks of the Nazi SA

The 'dynamic minority'–Mussolini & the Fascists

LIBERAL government in Italy was one of the casualties of the First World War. There was a very strong feeling that Italy should stay out, and politicians who saw in the war a means of resolving the country's internal problems cannily waited until they were certain which side to back. The war party claimed that victory would solve everything, at a stroke. Certainly defeat had just that effect, but not in the way they had hoped. Italy was on the winning side, and took her places with the victorious allies in dismembering the defeated enemies, but it was a 'mutilated victory'. Italy had been humiliated on the battlefield, losing over 300,000 prisoners at the battle of Caroretto in 1917. Even the final successes were only achieved at great cost. Even the promise of a new Italian empire in the Mediterranean and the Adriatic seemed likely to be frustrated. The disgust at the failure and betrayal by the politicians was felt most strongly by the young ex-soldiers, whose patriotism had been dishonoured, they believed, by a craven peace.

For established society, in Italy as throughout Europe, the danger to society came from the Red menace. Socialists had already convulsed the country with strikes – Red Week in June 1914, riots in Turin in 1917 – and behaved in a thoroughly unpatriotic fashion throughout the war. With the war over, they carried confrontation into the streets, provoking endless incidents with the police. By contrast, public opinion looked with favour on the young patriots who were led by the poet Gabriele d'Annunzio to seize Fiume, which was to be allocated by treaty to the new Yugoslavia. The 2000 ex-soldiers saw themselves, or at least their leader did, as warriors in the Garibaldi tradition, taking to arms to right a wrong. When other young ex-soldiers, many of them members of the élite wartime group of shock troops, the *arditi*, began to battle with the socialists in the streets, they were applauded as a 'dynamic minority' tackling the 'Red beast'. Many army officers including those at the most senior level favoured the 'fascists' in their black shirts; the General Staff even issued a circular recommending them.

While the fears of the politicians were exclusively focussed on the enemies to the left, the fascist party grew. Its leader was a young journalist, the son of a smallholder in the Romagna. Benito Mussolini possessed ferocious energy and no fixed principles. He was by turns a socialist, a patriot and a revolutionary. He had no political ideas, except a mish-mash of radical syndicalism, socialism and a dose of violent nationalism; he had no consistency and veered wildly from one extreme to another. By the end of the war he had established his own newspaper, *Il Popolo d'Italia*, in Milan. He described himself as 'an adventurer for all roads' who felt that he had his finger 'on the pulse of the masses'.[1] He was a remarkably good journalist, in a racy, biting kind of style, and he soon gathered a group of supporters. Many of them were in the

Association of Arditi, and he found a ready-made body of fighters who would follow him anywhere. Mussolini's great strength over the other wild men of the extremist nationalist parties in Italy lay in his capacity to organize. By the summer of 1919 he was building support all over the north of Italy: 'armed groups of 200–250 sure, well-tried and well-armed individuals', as he described them. But as so often, his imagination ran away with him. These bands were usually collections of young thugs, aimless and anxious to try conclusions with the socialists. Their weapon was the *manganello*, a short heavy club, and what they lacked in equipment they made up in extreme viciousness. The blackshirts were rightly feared by all on the left.

The fascists found their recruits in those areas where the parties of the left were already strong. The two centres of the fascist movement – Bologna and Milan – were also strongholds of socialism. Fascism was initially an urban movement and Mussolini, who knew the attitudes and inertia of the peasantry, felt that it was destined to remain limited to the cities. One contemporary writer, Agostino Lanzillo, identified the men who made up the new movement: 'Fascism is composed in the large cities of new men. They formed the crowd which before the war watched political events with indifference and apathy and which has now entered the contest. Fascism has mobilized its forces from the twilight zones of political life and from this derives the unruly violence and juvenile exuberance of its conduct.'[2]

The breakthrough came when fascism took root in the countryside. In the Po valley, in Emilia and Romagna, the left had been active in unionizing the rural workers. The victims of this process were the small farmers and small holders, often not far from poverty themselves. To them, as to those in the cities who had been crushed by the rise of working-class power, fascism had a definite attraction. The fascist creed spread through the countryside as the squads of blackshirt fighters moved into the rural regions around the cities, converting where they could and destroying the power base of the left. Apostles of fascism moved up into the Appennines and the hills of central Italy from the cities of the plain where they were already powerful, and it was this creation of a voting base which gave the fascists, who had no parliamentary seats after the elections of 1919, 35 seats in the election of 1921. But they were never able to break the pattern of Italian politics entirely, for they had little or no support in the south. The only natural centre of fascist support in the south was in the area around Foggia, where the pattern of agriculture and society was more like that of the north; elsewhere, the semi-feudal power of the landlords who delivered the vote remained undisturbed.

Mussolini was interested in power, but the natural appeal of fascism to the electorate was limited. Against him stood the Church and its political grouping, the liberals and the middle-class vote, and the solid phalanx of the left. With the votes of the south committed elsewhere, he had no chance of achieving major electoral success. The alternative, and one which came more naturally to him, was to achieve power by the use of force and deception. By 1921 the fascists had discovered that the socialist menace feared by the middle classes was a toothless tiger: 'I am convinced that they will never make a revolution,' wrote one leading fascist to Mussolini.[3] The army looked benignly on the movement, and the politicians were too preoccupied with internal squabbles to take much notice of the blackshirts. In fact they were more mesmerized by d'Annunzio than by Mussolini, who had begun to build a working coalition of the right. His lack of fixed principles, or of any political programme, was an asset. In February 1921 he declared firmly that 'Fascism is not a church. It is more like a training ground. It is not a party. It is a movement . . . we are the heretics of all the churches.'[4] The central control of this band of heretics was feeble, and Mussolini could only hope to tame the wild men of the party, themselves commanders of powerful private armies, by delivering success. He was under pressure to succeed in a hurry. The fascist movement could not sustain a prolonged period without tasting the rewards of power, and he knew that the electoral geography was weighted against him, however much he terrorized the streets.

Even he, however, was surprised by the feebleness of the state's resistance to the advance of fascism and to outright provocation. In the summer of 1922, fascists in a number of cities, notably Bologna, Ferrara, Cremona and Milan, began to put pressure on administrators and politicians, sometimes throwing them bodily out of their offices. The only response was a series of whining complaints from Rome and, encouraged, the fascist leadership began to think of a takeover of the state. The central group met on 16 October, and Italo Balbo, one of the most ardent revolutionaries, put the point succinctly: 'Today we enjoy the benefit of surprise. No one yet believes seriously in our insurrectionary intentions. . . .'[5] Mussolini agreed and planning went ahead at a furious pace. On 24 October final plans were settled at a meeting in Naples. Public buildings were to be seized during the first wave of attacks throughout northern and central Italy. Then three columns were to converge on Rome, halting at S. Marinella, Monterotondo and Tivoli on the outskirts. It was a bold plan, but one which depended more on the weakness of the enemy than on fascist strength. It was weak on detail: the objectives were stated but the means left hazy. The great 'March on Rome' was a fine piece of political symbolism, but no one had given much thought to the logistics of the operation, or as to what they would do when they got there. Faced with the 12,000 troops of the Rome garrison, under a commander loyal to the King, they would be utterly powerless.

Benito Mussolini and his blackshirts at the point of the 'seizure of power' in 1922

The fascists did not so much win as the authorities give up. The latter already knew, from the espionage service run by the Prefect of Naples, what the fascists intended within two days of their meeting, but they made no effective plans to resist it. There was no attempt to co-ordinate a military response in the provinces, or even any willingness to see the threat as anything more than a police problem. They pushed responsibility back onto local officials. This passed the initiative back to the fascists, for as one former official wrote in disgust: 'The uncertainty is greatest among the police and prefectoral authorities . . . the Government does not see the insurrectionary character of this whole movement, since in such a case, it cannot be a mere matter of the police, but of a real movement which should be treated as such, and therefore the arrest of the leaders, military government etc. . . . At Rome they don't understand a thing, and what is worse they give contradictory and uncertain information.'[6] When the rising took place on 28 October, with fascists storming the centres of government in the major provincial cities, the same indecision persisted. The person most deeply affected by the tide of revolutionary success was the King, Victor Emmanuel III. He saw the spectre of civil war looming, and the fragmentation of the state his family had worked so hard to create. He had no particular liking for his ministers, and no aversion on principle to the fascists, as he would have done to the socialists. He consulted the leading military figure of the nation, Marshal Diaz (himself friendly towards the fascists),

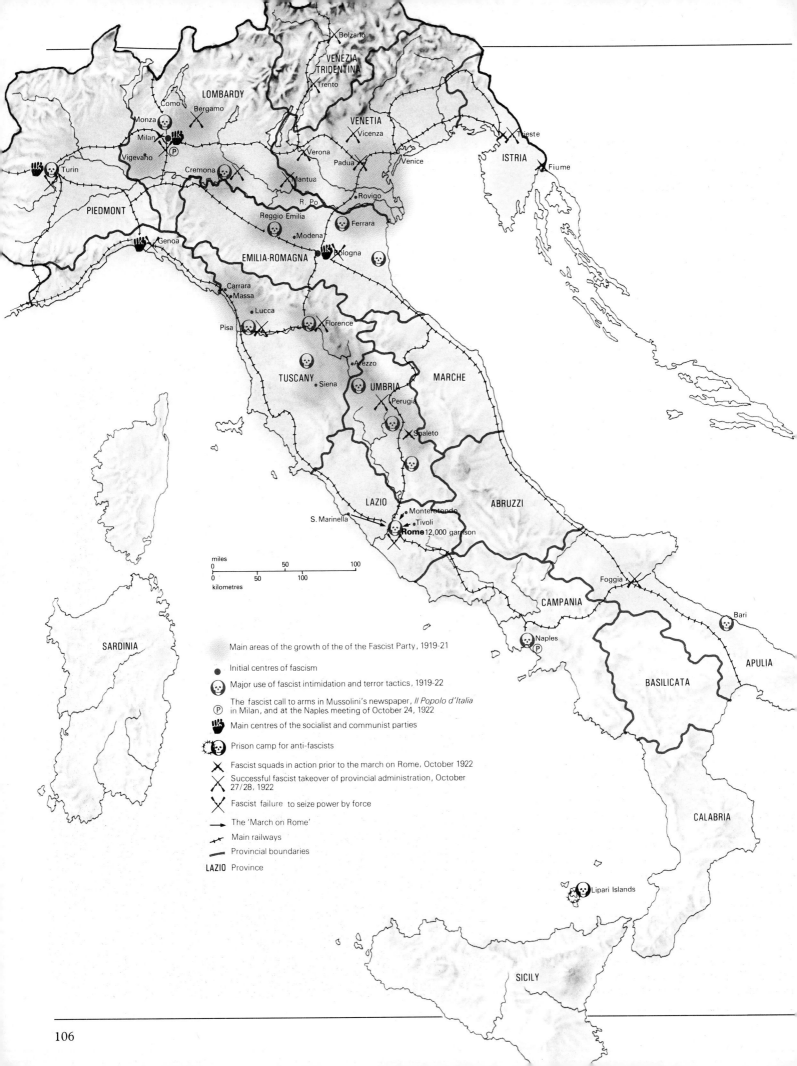

Bolzano

VENEZIA
TRIDENTINA

Trento

LOMBARDY

Como
Bergamo

Monza
Milan

Vigevano

Turin

PIEDMONT

Cremona

Mantua

Verona

VENETIA

Vicenza

Padua

Venice

Trieste

ISTRIA

Fiume

R. Po

Rovigo

Reggio Emilia

Ferrara

Modena

Genoa

EMILIA-ROMAGNA

Bologna

Carrara
Massa

Lucca

Pisa

Florence

Arezzo

TUSCANY

Siena

UMBRIA

Perugia

MARCHE

Spoleto

LAZIO

ABRUZZI

S. Marinella

Monterotondo
Tivoli

Rome 12,000 garrison

miles
0   50   100
0   50   100
kilometres

CAMPANIA

Foggia

Bari

Naples

APULIA

SARDINIA

BASILICATA

Main areas of the growth of the of the Fascist Party, 1919-21

Initial centres of fascism

Major use of fascist intimidation and terror tactics, 1919-22

The fascist call to arms in Mussolini's newspaper, *Il Popolo d'Italia*
in Milan, and at the Naples meeting of October 24, 1922

Main centres of the socialist and communist parties

Prison camp for anti-fascists

Fascist squads in action prior to the march on Rome, October 1922

Successful fascist takeover of provincial administration, October
27/28, 1922

Fascist failure to seize power by force

The 'March on Rome'

Main railways

Provincial boundaries

LAZIO   Province

CALABRIA

Lipari Islands

SICILY

as to whether the army would stand by the monarchy. He received the disturbing reply: 'Majesty, the army will do its duty; however, it would be as well not to put it to the test.' With, as he said afterwards, the determination 'to avoid bloodshed, given the news that the provinces are already in the hands of the fascists',[7] the King decided to send for Mussolini.

On 29 October, proudly wearing his black shirt, Mussolini arrived in Rome by train, and went to his interview with the king; he emerged as prime minister of Italy, a thirty-nine year-old superseding the octogenarian liberal Giolitti. The party of youth and febrile energy had occupied, if not as they liked to claim, *seized* power. A 'seizure' was in fact staged for the benefit of the cameras and the history books, but there was nothing to seize, for fascism had already been invited into office. Mussolini's task was to consolidate fascist power and make it unassailable. He used the same weapons as he had used before, terror and intimidation, but now with the acquiescence of the established and legal government. Many of the fascist squads were incorporated in a national militia, which was to be the physical basis of his power. 'He who touches the militia will get a dose of lead', was a typical Mussolini aphorism. He talked of 'the transformation of fascism into an organ of administration';[8] what he meant was a monopoly of power. The fascists worked hard to strengthen their position. Legislation was prepared to modify the existing structure of proportional representation, so as to give two thirds of the seats to the party with the largest number of votes. An unprecedented campaign, with millions of leaflets, assassination of opponents, intimidation by the *manganello* or massive doses of castor oil got the opposition parties on the run. In the election of March 1924, the fascists received overall some 60% of the votes. In some regions they achieved more than 100% of the votes, such was the zeal of local officials. With the election of 1924, fascist dictatorship was given legal clothing. Parliamentary government and the whole apparatus of liberal democracy had failed.

Mussolini, *'il Duce'*, the leader, created the model for the fascist state, with its emphasis on uniforms, political symbolism and the suppression of all opposition. He was himself an attractive figure, and people tended to blame others for the failings of his state. But he was never in as complete control as Hitler would be in Germany, nor was Italian fascism ever so effective or comprehensive as its German equivalent. Mussolini presided not over a united fascist party as he liked to pretend, but a sometimes uneasy partnership of many different political tendencies. It was necessary for him to maintain a balance between them, and to this end he ran an elaborate spy system, with tapped telephones, constant surveillance and daily reports on his colleagues and all who might pose a threat. This intelligence system provided him with a vital edge over his rivals. His area of greater if theor-

etical vulnerability lay in the manner of his appointment. He was, at base, a prime minister appointed by the King. If the King and the army were to act in a concerted way, the legal basis (and the military basis) of his power would disappear. At the height of his power, this was an interesting constitutional curiosity. After failure in war and the invasion of Italy by the Allies in 1943, it became a decisive factor. On 25 July 1943, he had his usual meeting with the King, who after a few moments told him that Marshal Badoglio was to take over as prime minister; as he left the audience Mussolini was arrested. By the following day, fascism had collapsed throughout Italy.

Mussolini as 'il Duce', an expression of his own self-image. He is seen standing on a box to give him height. His office desk was similarly elevated to enable him to loom over his visitors

ARX OMNIVM NATIONVM

The vocabulary of violence

THE National Socialists did not come to power by stealth. As Josef Goebbels wrote in his Berlin newspaper before the election of 1928: 'We enter Parliament in order to supply ourselves, in the arsenal of democracy, with its own weapons. . . . We do not come as friends nor even as neutrals. We come as enemies. As the wolf bursts into the flock, so we come.'[1]

In National Socialist vocabulary their success was a 'Machtergreifung' – a seizure of power – a concept pregnant with force and threatened violence. The Nazis were a party of youth: when Hitler took office as Chancellor in 1933, he was under forty-five, in a political society where the octogenarian Field-Marshal Hindenburg held sway. In the election of September 1930, the 18–30 age group provided the largest percentage of the party's voters.[2] The appeal of the party was couched in energetic, youthful and vigorous terms declaring their impatience with the failures of the past. The party was seductive not only in what was said, but in the passion and vocabulary with which it was expressed.

The first attempt by the nascent National Socialist Workers' Party to take power by force was a débâcle. It was, however, not a wholly irrational move. Bavaria in the period after the First World War was in ferment. The Communist regime set up in 1918–19 was short-lived, suppressed bloodily by a *Freikorps* (Free Corps) led by a former officer, Ritter von Epp – who immediately became a hero in the conservative pantheon. Bavaria, the haven of many right-wing parties which had no future elsewhere in Germany. In Bavaria Hitler found an acceptable political culture within which to grow. There was a strident Bavarian nationalism, rabidly anti-semitic and declaring undying hatred for the 'Marxist north'. These nationalists believed that Bavaria could become a 'cell of order' which would multiply to take over the rest of Germany. All of which chimed in exactly with Hitler's objective for his new National Socialist German Workers' Party: 'The new movement aims to provide what the others have not: a nationalist movement with a firm social base, a hold over the broad masses, welded together in an iron-hard organization, filled with blind obedience and inspired by a brutal will, a party of struggle and action. . . .'[3]

Hitler's Munich *putsch* of 1923 was indeed a fiasco. The Nazis were unlucky: they had a national hero in their ranks, General Ludendorff, and the tacit support of many of the other right-wing organizations in Bavaria. However, had the *putsch* succeeded, there is no reason to think that there would have been risings elsewhere in Germany as Hitler had hoped: the few hundred who demonstrated in Berlin and elsewhere did not indicate much overall support. The failure of the *putsch* and its consequences – Hitler's imprisonment in Landsberg – provided a political education for the Nazis. They turned towards patient organization, the achievement of a local power-base.

Although they still spoke and wrote in the language of the street fighter, it was subtly adjusted for the ears of a mass national audience. The first task of the winning of the masses was accomplished within Bavaria. It was in Coburg where the Nazis first achieved local political power, in a town set in the Thuringian hills and hitherto a stronghold of the left. It was also in Bavaria that the Nazis discovered the peasantry as a political force and began to tailor their policies to flatter a peasant audience. Their main effort was channelled into a feverish battle for recruitment, a drive handicapped by the fact that, after his release from prison in February 1925, Hitler was banned from public speaking until the spring of 1927. But the energy of the Nazis was phenomenal: in 1926 the party in Bavaria held 2370 mass meetings and 3500 discussion evenings, as well as issuing a torrent of written propaganda.[4] Support was slow in coming, but it soon proved that the most fertile ground for the Nazis was in the Protestant towns and countryside of Franconia, north of Munich. They quickly discovered that saturation was the best technique, with a concentration of effort that none of the other parties cared to match.

The electoral structure of the Weimar republic made the feverish vote-grubbing which the Nazis adopted a worthwhile strategy. The system of proportional representation reinforced success, allocating a number of seats to the larger parties on the basis of their vote. Getting votes could be achieved by a number of means. Hitler introduced a national structure of party regions or *Gaue*, with each area given a degree of freedom within the limits of party doctrine, to expand the electoral base by whatever means seemed best. Party workers also proliferated, with the consequence that the Nazis were able to put far more workers on the ground than the opposing parties. In addition to the party workers, a disciplined and well-organized group of party fighters was built up, to dominate the streets, and to make clear that opposition to the Nazis would be a dangerous business. The militant arm of the party, the SA, was made a much more effective fighting force under a new commander, Ernst Rohm, who was brought back from serving in the Bolivian army to take command early in 1931. Under Rohm, a former Imperial army officer, the SA was given a military structure, and proper training. Hitler recognized that violence was only of use if tightly and properly controlled; his success as a politician depended on his capacity to curb those who had not learned the lessons of 1923.

The great motive force which lay behind the sudden accession of votes by the Nazis in the elections of 1930–32, up from 2.6% of the vote in 1928 to 37.3% in July 1933, was the collapse of the world economy, and the growth of unemployment in Germany.[5] In September 1929, 1.32 million Germans were out of work. Two years later that figure was 4.35 million, rising to over six million in the spring of

1932. The Nazis promised hope, as one propaganda leaflet declared in the 1933 election: 'Adolf Hitler has said, "Within four years unemployment will be removed". . . . What an Adolf Hitler promises, he keeps to.'[6] Police reports made it clear that popular opinion was swinging to the Nazis as a protest. In Starnberg, Bavaria in December 1931, they noted: 'the Nazi party is now the reservoir for all currents of discontent and unsatisfied elements, hence its rise in votes. . . .'[7] There were four Reichstag elections in the space of four years, and the cost both in time and money for the Nazis was prodigious. In the election of November 1932 their share of the vote slumped, and they returned to the Reichstag with fewer seats than they had left it. Many had expected the party to be called to take power after the July election had left them the largest single party in the Reichstag; with the decline in November, many felt that the Nazis had peaked in popularity and were on a downward path.

The politicians conspired to keep the Nazis out of office, yet they could not ignore them, or the chaos they could create in the streets. Attempts had been made to curb the SA, and their Communist counterparts, with a ban placed on uniforms and private armies. The SA relinquished their brown shirts for white ones, and formed themselves into sports clubs and cultural associations. Neither the President, Hindenburg, nor the army was prepared to run the risk of civil war to suppress the SA; but short of an armed response, the state was incapable of destroying them. On the fourth of January 1933 Hitler reached an accord with Franz von Papen, who had been Chancellor and now sought to do down his rival, Kurt von Schleicher. Hitler agreed to take office as Chancellor, with minority Nazi representation in the cabinet.[8] Papen arranged for donations from some industrial companies to swell the depleted Nazi funds. Papen now worked to sell the package to the President, who eventually agreed to withdraw his support from Schleicher on 28 January 1933. Two days later the Papen–Hitler group took office.

Papen was well pleased. He had inveigled the Nazis into government on his terms. Of Hitler, he said, 'Don't worry, we've hired him.'[9] Three Nazis held Cabinet office: Hitler as Chancellor, Goering as Minister without portfolio, and acting Prussian Minister of the Interior, and Frick as Reich Minister of the Interior. All the rest of the Cabinet were Papen's 'safe men'. Hitler, however, knew where real power resided. He held all the 'security' posts, both in the largest state, Prussia, and nationally. While the army was controlled by an independent, General von Blomberg, Hitler knew that it would not intervene against him, since he now constituted the legal government in Germany under the President. In a stormy party meeting in December 1932, Hitler had come out forcefully against an armed uprising, and showed his audience how firmly he grasped the reali-

ties of power politics. He recounted a conversation with Colonel von Reichenau: ' "If your columns [the SA] march against the law, the Reichswehr would be compelled to shoot and would carry out its orders even though its heart would bleed to do so. If you were Reich President and the Reichswehr was under oath to you, we would obey your orders in just the same way and shoot at the enemies of your State if you gave the order. We are unpolitical, obey the law and keep the oath we have given. I urge you to keep within the law. One day power will fall into your lap." ' And Hitler added: 'In the past the police have invariably obeyed the existing political power in the state completely irrespective of the political tendency within the state.'[10] From January, he represented the forces of law and the army stood behind him. The lawful authority over the police lay with the Nazis.

From the end of February 1933, the Nazis monopolized power within the state, both legal and illegal power. The power of the state was now used to sanction the use of illegal power, or to conceal its exercise. The SA was let loose in Prussia on all possible enemies of the Nazis. Provisions for 'protective custody' were misused to allow detention on a massive scale. Goering in Prussia purged the police of all senior officers unsympathetic to the Nazis, and on 22 February ordered the establishment of an auxiliary police force, in which the SA and the SS predominated. Two days later the police claimed to have uncovered Communist plans for a revolution, and on 27 February the

SA men being searched for arms. At one point there was a vain attempt to break up para-military organizations and ban uniforms. The SA responded by wearing white shirts and forming cycle clubs and ramblers' associations . . .

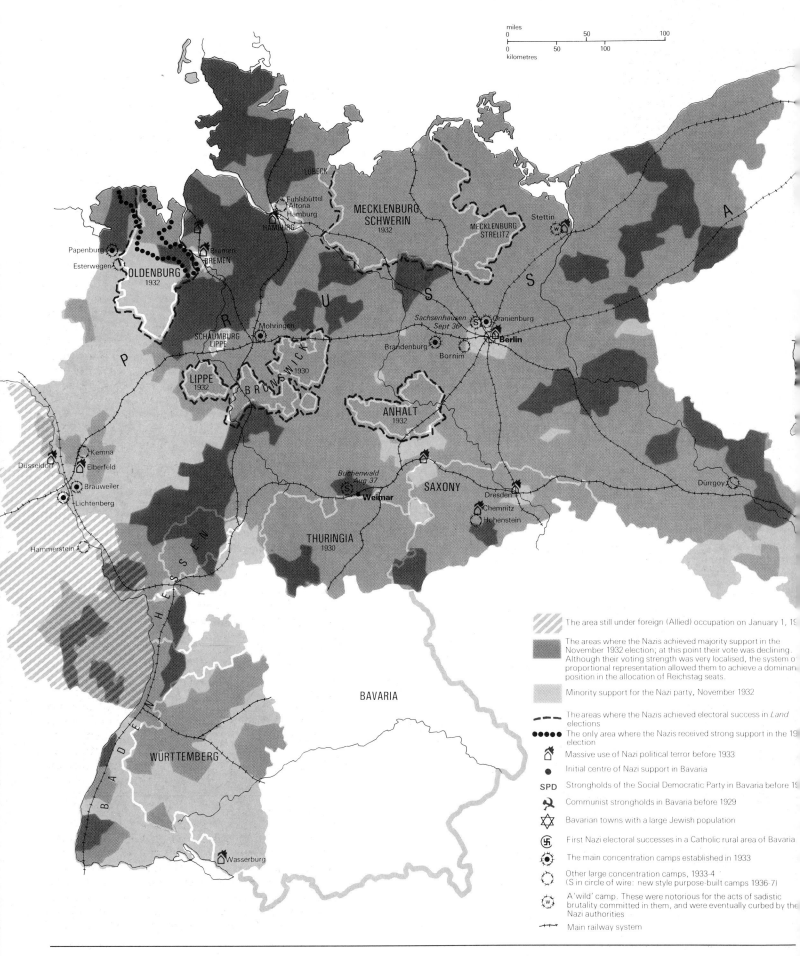

miles
0   50   100
0   50   100
kilometres

LÜBECK

Fuhlsbüttel
Altona
Hamburg
HAMBURG
1932

MECKLENBURG
SCHWERIN
1932

MECKLENBURG
STRELITZ

Stettin W

Papenburg
Esterwegen
OLDENBURG
1932

Bremen
BREMEN

P R U S S I A

Mohringen

SCHAUMBURG
LIPPE

Sachsenhausen
Sept 36
S
Oranienburg

Berlin

LIPPE
1932

BRUNSWICK
1930

Brandenburg
Bornim

ANHALT
1932

Kemna
Düsseldorf
Elberfeld
Brauweiler
Lichtenberg

Buchenwald
Aug 37
S
Weimar

SAXONY

Dresden
Chemnitz
Hohenstein

Dürrgoy

Hammerstein

H E S S E N

THURINGIA
1930

B A D E N

WÜRTTEMBERG

BAVARIA

Wasserburg

The area still under foreign (Allied) occupation on January 1, 19

The areas where the Nazis achieved majority support in the
November 1932 election; at this point their vote was declining.
Although their voting strength was very localised, the system of
proportional representation allowed them to achieve a dominan
position in the allocation of Reichstag seats.

Minority support for the Nazi party, November 1932

The areas where the Nazis achieved electoral success in *Land*
elections

The only area where the Nazis received strong support in the 19
election

Massive use of Nazi political terror before 1933

Initial centre of Nazi support in Bavaria

SPD   Strongholds of the Social Democratic Party in Bavaria before 19

Communist strongholds in Bavaria before 1929

Bavarian towns with a large Jewish population

First Nazi electoral successes in a Catholic rural area of Bavaria

The main concentration camps established in 1933

Other large concentration camps, 1933-4
(S in circle of wire: new style purpose-built camps 1936-7)

A 'wild' camp. These were notorious for the acts of sadistic
brutality committed in them, and were eventually curbed by the
Nazi authorities

Main railway system

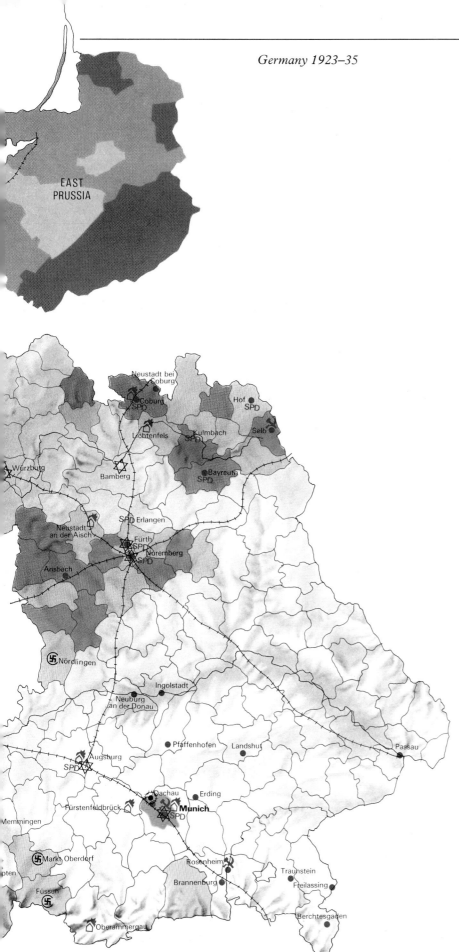

EAST
PRUSSIA

Reichstag was set on fire. Armed with this evidence, Hitler had little difficulty in persuading Hindenburg to grant him wide powers to suspend the provisions of the constitution 'as a defensive measure against Communist acts of violence'. Armed with emergency powers, a pliant police force and a neutral army, the Nazis began to demolish the independence which the constitution gave to the states. In March and April 1933, over 16,000 people were taken into custody in Prussia alone; as the other states were brought into line, the wave of arrests extended throughout the nation.[11] Special camps were set up to accommodate the prisoners, mostly run by the SA, which became the instrument of the terror; some, known as *wild camps*, were especially notorious for the atrocities committed there. The intention of the terror was to allow the Nazis to achieve majority rule through the ballot box in the elections; all leading opposition figures were imprisoned before the voting on 5 March 1933. Hitler remarked to his Cabinet on 28 February that 'as a result of the Reichstag fire I no longer doubt that the Reich Government will gain 51 percent in the elections'. He was to be disappointed: the overall Nazi vote was 43.9%, and only in East Prussia, Pomerania, Breslau, Liegnitz, Schleswig Holstein, East Hanover, and Chemnitz Zwickau, did they pass the magic figure of fifty percent.[12]

On 6 July 1933 Hitler declared that the revolution had officially ended. Certainly the purge of German society was accomplished with great rapidity, backed by the threat of the concentration camps and of unlimited terror. The purge extended to the Reichstag, which dutifully passed enabling legislation which allowed Hitler to rule by decree (24 March 1933). The only element chafing against party control was the SA, and a year after the revolution was officially ended, the 'Night of the Long Knives' (30 June 1934) destroyed any capacity the SA might have to oppose Hitler. On 2 August 1934 Hindenburg died, and within an hour of his death the office of President was merged with the Chancellorship in the person of Adolf Hitler. Von Reichenau's prophecy was fulfilled.

Hitler, a man given to bold strokes, had correctly surmised that the mechanisms of power in Germany could only be taken with the sanction of lawful authority: the German political system was entrenched in notions of legality. But he also realized that the most potent weapon to brandish at his opponents was the threat of anarchy, of controlled violence and disorder. By this means he became the intermediary between the forces of disorder (which he himself had created) and the established authority of the state. The legal fiction was that he had achieved power through the ballot box, and to a degree this was true. But as the Nazis never tired of proclaiming, the Weimar constitution and the ballot box were irrelevancies. The pursuit of power, expressed in Hitler's *Mein Kampf*, followed a determined and logical path.

The holy war – Spain's twin revolutions

SPAIN has never corresponded to the social and political patterns of the rest of Europe. Beyond the Pyrenees, the conventions of European politics underwent a subtle transformation. Alone of the countries of western Europe, Spain had acquired a tradition of direct military intervention in politics, of the army leaving its barracks, replacing the civil administration in a bloodless coup, and then returning to barracks. The whole vocabulary for this type of political action, the *pronunciamiento*, the *cuartelazo*, the *grito*, had no equivalent in other European languages.[1] While the working-class movement in Europe developed on socialist or more avowedly Marxist lines, in Spain the most active political force of the left was anarchism of the kind advocated by Count Mikhail Bakunin, as an actively insurrectionary group. Neither the army nor the anarchists operated on normal lines of self-interest. The army was mesmerized by its sacred duty to preserve the elusive quality of *Hispanidad*, best summed up in the words of Major Bruno Ibañez, on the point of launching a terrifying bloodletting on the people of Cordoba: 'Everything for Spain. The homeland demands it, and those who do not feel the love that every good son must feel for the fatherland are not worthy of living in it. . . . I shall work without rest to ensure that in our capital and its villages there remains not a single traitor who can in any way hinder the self-sacrificing tasks which the army and militias are undertaking to . . . place us amongst the most civilized of nations that, with blind Christian faith, are full of ambitionless hopes. . . .'[2] Across the country, the anarchists were declaring in Barcelona: 'Comrades, the revolution must not drown us in blood. Conscious justice, yes! Assassins, never!'[3] Both were gripped by an utter conviction that what was needed was a total purging and rebuilding of society, a holy war waged for very different gods.

Although Spain was always turbulent, the political system seemed to have achieved stability with the restoration of the monarchy in 1874. Forty years of chaos had made Spaniards long for an end to internal disorders, and the army found politicians willing to observe their requirements. In consequence, there were no *pronunciamientos*. But by the end of the First World War, from which Spain wisely kept aloof, a new generation was coming forward in political life, with no memory of the civil wars of the nineteenth century. The power of the workers, in the socialist *Unión General de Trabajadores* (UGT) and the anarchist *Confederación Nacional del Trabajo* (CNT), made them an interest group almost as potent as the army. In the north, the Basque and Catalan peoples, who saw themselves as separate nations within the Spanish state, were becoming more truculent in their nationalism. The old political order was breaking down, and was incapable of absorbing a final blow. In July 1921, the colonial war in Morocco, which had already caused conscription riots in Spain and was

wildly unpopular, turned into a disaster. The army of Morocco was outwitted by the Rif tribesmen, and at Anual lost 12,000 dead with many wounded and others taken prisoner. The army, following the old routine, rose to save Spain, and in September 1923, after endless attempts to find a political solution, General Primo de Rivera took power, as 'the iron doctor'.

Primo de Rivera took power until 'the country offers us men uncontaminated with the vices of political organization', and as an outsider, he was able to initiate changes beyond the capabilities of conventional politicians. Like many officers, he was impatient with the posturings of intellectuals and respected power. An Andalusian from Jerez, devoted to the pleasures of the flesh, he combined earthiness with a mystic sense of Spanish destiny. 'I have no experience in government. Our methods are as simple as they are ingenuous. They are the methods which the good of the *patria* dictates and our resolutions are taken while we are kneeling at the shrine of the national spirit.'[4] In whatever posture he arrived at his decisions, they were imbued with sound common sense. He bought off labour unrest with concessions, and gained the ready acceptance of the UGT for his reforms. Their co-operation widened the split between the revolutionary anarchists and the socialists who had a definite stake – with investments, pension plans, and office buildings – in the existing social structure. But eventually Primo de Rivera's balancing act collapsed, and within fourteen months of the general resigning in January 1930, the king had gone too. For the second time, Spain was a republic.

Primo de Rivera had fallen because he was unable to resolve all the conflicting interests within Spain. The army felt he had worked against it, and he could not bring himself to conciliate the separatists. The new republic had three phases. In the first, from June 1931 to November 1933, it stood for reform and progress. From November 1933 to February 1936, the disunity of the left allowed a ramshackle right-wing coalition to take power, a position reversed between February and July 1936, when the leftwards tendency was renewed. Late in July came the military uprising in Morocco which developed into the Spanish Civil War. The republic existed only because nothing else could fill the vacuum of power, but it attracted very little royal support. The anarchists would have nothing to do with it, the army was divided in its view but certainly looked upon it with no affection. That neutrality rapidly turned to hatred as the reforms, especially those aimed at the position of the Church, were seen as striking at the roots of 'Spanishness'. Even the UGT which supported the first phase of the republic and battled against the right in the second, had lost interest in the republic by the third. The Basques and Catalans were interested only insofar as it would grant them autonomy.

Both left and right tested the resilience of the republic by armed insurrection. In August 1932, General Sanjurjo declared 'Long live Indivisible Spain' and waited for the army to rally to him.[5] He waited in vain. The unions declared a general strike and the soldiers stayed in their barracks. A much more bloody confrontation came from the left in October 1934, when there was a rising at Oviedo in Asturias and, more briefly, in Barcelona. The savage repression of the Asturian miners by the Army of Africa was an omen of what was to come two years later. The principle on which the army operated was expressed by General Mola: 'indiscipline is justified when the abuses of power constitute an insult and a shame, or when they lead the nation into ruin'.[6] By the spring of 1936, with the left restored to control of the republic, a number of officers had decided that the moment had arrived. Throughout this period, the anarchists, both in the CNT and in its purist offshoot, the *Federación Anarquista Ibérica* (FAI) pressed for total revolution, not the timid reformism which the republic was prepared to offer. The CNT had stated unambiguously in 1933 that anarchists remained 'in open war with the state. We are confronted by the Constituent Cortes (the parliament) as we would be by any power that oppresses us.'[7] The pressure for immediate revolution came from the incorruptibles of the FAI. Many of the members of the CNT in the towns and cities were less keen on the purging flame of destruction which declared that if the cities did not come into line 'it will be preferable to wipe them off the face of the earth. The rural municipalities will absorb their reactionary plague and purify it.'[8] It was wild and dangerous talk, for the anarchists had no more notion of how to make the revolution than they had of the post-revolutionary world. But through all the strands of anarchist thought about the post-revolutionary society, one element was always present. The Church would be destroyed, utterly.

The army and the parties of the right stood equally unambiguously: for Traditional Spain, Catholic Spain. Some, like the Carlists of the Basque country, would add 'Monarchical Spain', other right-wing groups, such as the Falange founded by the son of General Primo de Rivera, Jose Antonio, declared, 'Our ideas are revolutionary – not evolutionary.' The right in Spain rallied behind the banner of Church and Nation. Its territorial base lay in the ancient heartland of Spain, Old Castile, Leon, Navarre, and parts of Galicia. Here the right-wing parties found the bulk of their votes. The power of the anarchists was concentrated in the poorest regions of the south along the Mediterranean coast, and in the industrial complex of Barcelona. If there was a town which could be described as the 'capital' of anarchism, it would be Zaragoza in Aragon. The socialists were in strength in the cities, especially Madrid, but in the years of Primo de Rivera they had also begun to make substantial inroads into the countryside, especially in New Castile. The strongpoint of the army was located

not in Spain itself, but in Morocco where the republic sent many of the officers of doubtful loyalty. It was in Morocco that the *golpe del estado* (coup d'état) to destroy the 'godless republic' began to fester.

From the middle of 1917, the army had begun to re-discover its love of conspiracy. By the third phase of the republic, after a number of failed attempts, it was clear that the old form of symbolic *pronunciamiento* could no longer succeed. In the past, the threat of the army had been sufficient (usually) to bring the politicians to heel. Now, like the Holy Office of the Inquisition, it was a question of burning the heresies from the body of Spain. On the mainland, the organization of the uprising was in the hands of General Mola, the former commander of the army in Morocco, who was transferred to Pamplona in March 1936. His new base gave him access to the right-wing parties, and he entered into discussions with the Falange of Jose Antonio Primo de Rivera, with the Carlists, and other extremist factions. The aim was to give the rising a wide basis of popular support, so that it could plausibly be claimed that the army *and* the people were acting in concert. Furthermore, this new style of *golpe* was intended to be a mass takeover of all the centres of power throughout Spain. The planning went on throughout the early summer, frustrated by the fears of many officers that the republic would take savage reprisals if there was one more coup attempt by the army. The plotters were

A dramatic image of the clashes of societies in Spain. A party of militiamen shoots at the huge statue of Christ standing on the outskirts of Madrid. They sought to destroy what they saw as an emblem of the corrupt old Spain. The Nationalists, by contrast, fought for traditional Catholicism and a traditional Spain: 14 August 1936

a small minority within the army, although many more would join them once a measure of success was achieved. One of those doubters was Francisco Franco, the most talented soldier in the army and Spain's youngest general. He had already been posted to the isolation of the Canary Islands by a suspicious government. The rapidly rising tide of political and social violence as the summer progressed convinced him that a rising was essential 'to save Spain'. Even convinced republicans were becoming convinced that drastic action was necessary. One of the founding fathers of the republic, Miguel Maura, was writing in June that 'peaceful citizens now believe the laws are a dead letter'.[9]

The military rising came on 17 July in the cities of Spanish Morocco. The rising there set the pattern for the mainland. There was short and often bloody resistance, overcome by superior force, which was followed by a concerted drive to round up and kill all those with known leftist sympathies. This task was often left to armed right-wing civilians, assisted by the army. The key to the rising in Morocco, General Franco arrived from the Canary Islands in a secretly chartered plane. On the day following the first events in Morocco, risings began in the mainland cities, beginning with Seville, the capital of Andalucia. They succeeded, with few exceptions, where traditionalist sentiment was already strong and there was general

Continued on page 117

El Ferrol
Gijón
Corunna
Oviedo
Pontevedra
Ponferrada
Léon
Vigo
Vallado
Zamora
Salamanca
Cáceres
Badajoz
Radio Sevilla
Seville
Huelva
Tetuan to Seville
Jerez
Cádiz
Lora del Rio
Algeciras
from Ceuta

GALICIA
1936 — 1964
ASTURIAS
1937 — 1953
NAVARRE
1937 — present day
LEON
1936 — 1948
CATALONIA
1939 — 1963
OLD CASTILE
1936 — 1956
ARAGON
1936 — 1961
NEW CASTILE
1940 — 1952
ESTREMADURA
1936 — 1949
VALENCIA
MURCIA
1938 — 1952
ANDALUSIA
1936 — 1956

Low intensity guerrilla activity continuing after the civil war

Routes taken by guerrilla bands through Spain after 1939

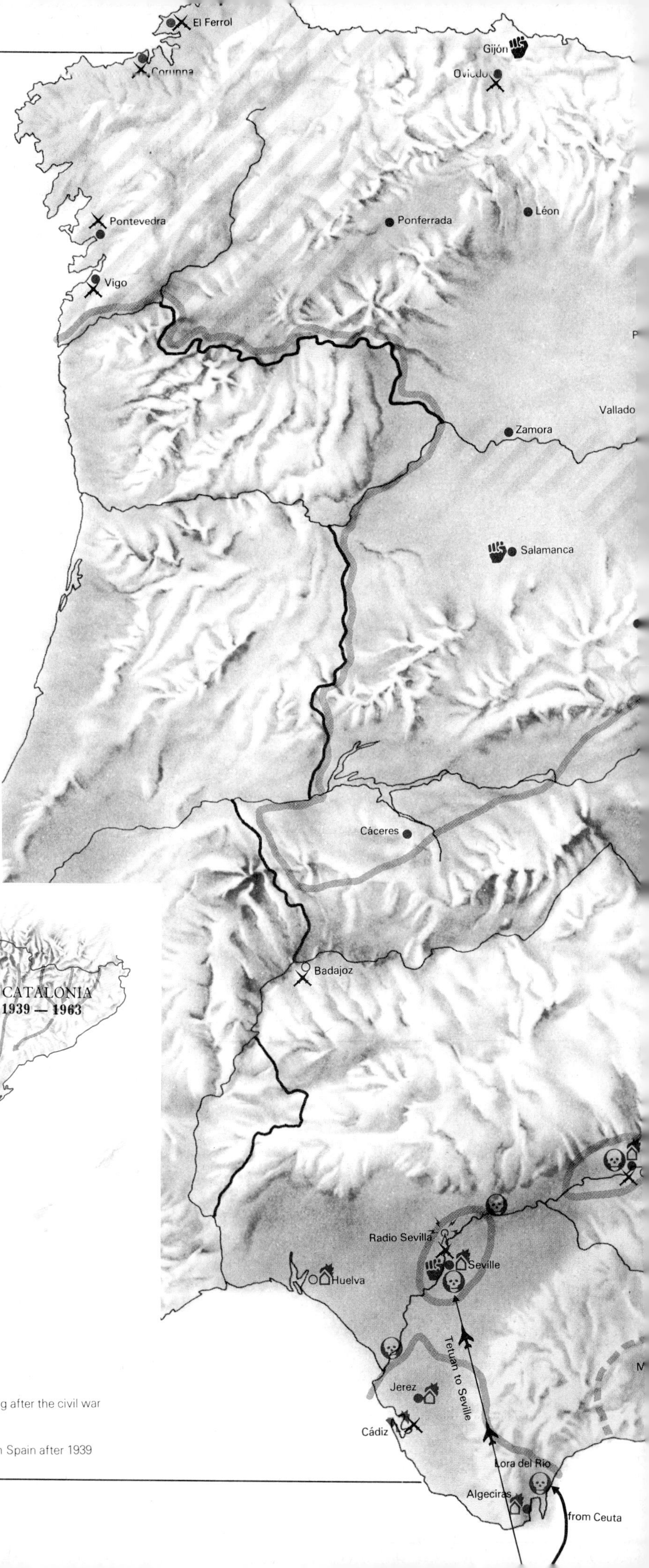

114

Bilbao

San Sebastián

Vitoria

Pamplona

Jaca

Radio Burgos

Huesca

Zaragoza

Radio Barcelona

Barcelona

Guadalajara

Madrid

Alcalá de Henares

Teruel

MINORCA

MAJORCA

Albacete

Valencia

IBIZA

Jaén

Cartagena

Granada

Almería

miles
0   50   100
0   50   100
kilometres

Strongly Anarchist areas which favoured violent revolution

Strongly Catholic areas which gave ready support to the rebels

●   Early successes of the rising — July 19/20, 1936

○   Failed risings

Massacre or atrocity by the Nationalist rebels — July 17-30, 1936

Nationalist rebel strongpoints

First attacks by the rebels — July 17/18, 1936

Nationalist transmitters

'Red vengeance': main concentrations of leftwing terror — July 18-30, 1936

Government strongpoints

Government radio

Skirmish

Troop reinforcements turn the tide in Seville

Moorish and Legion contingent arrives in Spain

Territory taken by the nationalists before the end of July 1936

Radical revolution in the countryside

115

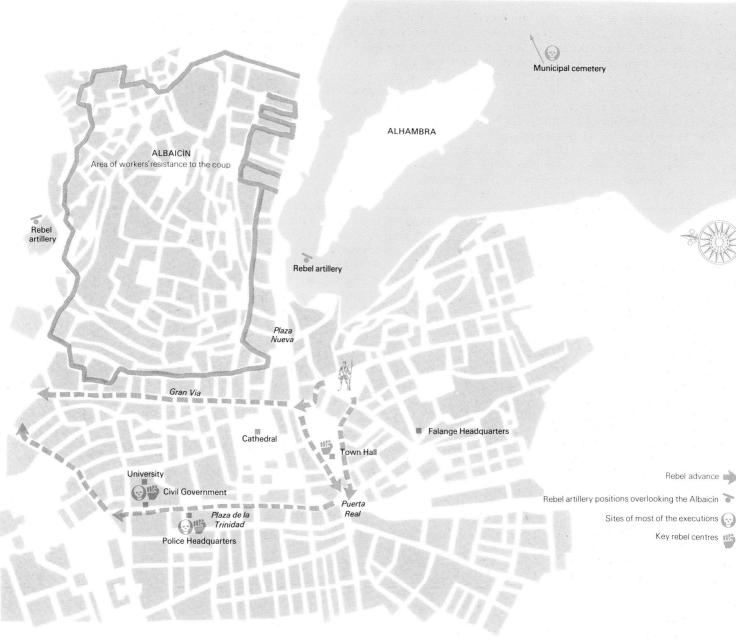

Municipal cemetery

ALHAMBRA

ALBAICÍN
Area of workers' resistance to the coup

Rebel
artillery

Rebel artillery

Plaza
Nueva

Gran Via

Cathedral

Falange Headquarters

Town Hall

University

Civil Government

Puerta
Real

Plaza de la
Trinidad

Police Headquarters

Rebel advance

Rebel artillery positions overlooking the Albaicín

Sites of most of the executions

Key rebel centres

The takeover of Granada

Unlike Seville, which fell on the first day of the Nationalist rising, Granada, the greatest city of eastern Andalucia, remained in a state of uneasy calm during the first forty-eight hours of the rebellion. The paralysis of the authorities mirrored the inaction of those in Madrid, while the left-wing parties also failed to take any defensive measures. There was no doubt that Granada would rise; the only doubt was *when*. The rising, when it came on 20 July, was

textbook. The Governor was taken prisoner by his deputy, who had mobilized the garrison. The conspirators had secured the support not only of the Civil Guard, but of the Assault Guards, a more Republican-minded police force. At 5.00 p.m. troops moved down to take control of the Town Hall and other public buildings as well as the central telephone exchange. The central areas were quickly occupied, and parties of troops were sent to secure the main road out of the town and access to the railway. Workers were seen

in the streets coming down from the Albaicín, but were driven back by gunfire. Patrols were sent to secure the two strategic points on the outskirts, the airport at Armilla to the south and the explosives factory to the north of the city at El Fargue.

On the following day, after the workers' organizations had fortified the Albaicín as best they could, two artillery batteries were set up on the Alhambra hill and the northern outskirts of the quarter; they then opened fire. Troops moved in through the

narrow streets and there was some hand-to-hand fighting. By that night all resistance was crushed and the purge began. According to available figures, 4500 were killed in the space of a few days, most of them at the wall of the municipal cemetery above the Alhambra. Some estimates put the total number of deaths in the city as high as 25,000. This was a white terror, with no preceding revolutionary violence.

Granada remained in the front line for the whole of the Civil War, with guerrilla

bands in the Sierra Nevada and the Alpujarras to the south. When the war ended, the guerrilla bands remained, fighting an increasingly feeble campaign against the Civil Guard. Granada, the setting of *Carmen*, has never been a stranger to violence but the events of July 1936 have seared the popular imagination

popular approval for military action. In Barcelona and Madrid, workers seized arms and overcame the rebels; in other cities either the army refused to rise, or it was a half-hearted affair, easily quashed. In some places, of which Granada is an example, there was a delay in the outbreak of the rising which could have allowed the government to redeem the situation. In the event, the cabinet dithered, and saw their power pass effectively to the masses in the streets or to the rebels. On 24 July General Mola, secure in rebel Burgos, declared: 'The government which was the wretched bastard of liberal and socialist concubinage is dead, killed by our valiant army. Spain, the true Spain, has laid the dragon low, and now it lies, writhing on its belly and biting the dust.' The death throes he so hopefully described were to last for three bitter years.[10]

On the day that the right rose in rebellion in Morocco, the CNT in Barcelona were proclaiming: 'Only by making the social revolution will fascism be crushed.'[11] While the forces of True Spain were exterminating the left in the zones which they controlled, the anarchists, and to a lesser degree the socialist groups, were freeing the new society from the clutches of its enemies. In Andalucia, the revolution became the excuse for resolving local feuds or killing 'class enemies'. In Catalonia the process was slightly more orderly. Everywhere the principal targets were priests, known right-wing sympathizers, or those too well dressed or too well spoken. Private property was made communal property, in some places money was abolished. The revolutionaries of the left believed that it was necessary to accomplish the revolution before turning to its defence. This was the long awaited moment and the anarchists would not allow it to pass. But even in this moment of extremity, the working class pursued antagonistic goals. The socialists, and even more the small Communist party, were concerned with the military defeat of the rebels; in them the beleaguered republic found natural allies. The anarchists, true to their faith, pursued other goals as well.

By the end of July the battle lines had been drawn between the republic and the 'Nationalists', as they now called themselves. The territory which the republic held until the end of the war was contained in a block constituted largely by the south-eastern quarter of the country. The fighting was concentrated in the north and centre of Spain, especially after the nationalists failed to capture Madrid in their first major campaign of the war. In many of the republican areas revolution was the objective. On the nationalist side, the aim was a new society, inspired by the 'eternal verities' of True Spain. What the rebels sought was not merely recognition of the army's interests as had been the case in the past, but the creation of a new authoritarian society. Their ideas, if ill-formed, were positive rather than merely reactionary. On the left, libertarian anarchism was equally dominated by a vision of a new world. The earnestness of their convictions found expression in their mutual determine to 'cleanse' society of its human impurities. 'Shedding of blood is the inevitable consequence of a revolution, which in spite of all barriers, sweeps on like a flood and devastates everything in its path, until it gradually loses momentum.'[12] These could be the words of an anarchist *or* a nationalist. 'Pardon and amnesty must disappear from the Spanish dictionary.'[13] Left or Right? The anarchist Diego Abád de Santillán, who wrote the first, and General Queipo de Llano, who had the second as a catchphrase, shared, if nothing else, a belief that the revolution could only be bought through blood. In point of numbers, the nationalists killed more than the left, but largely because they were more efficient.[14] On the other hand, the anarchist areas of southern Spain were quickly overrun, so the violence was concentrated over a shorter time and a more restricted area. As the war developed, propaganda on both sides began to cloud the truth. On the left, the revolutionary violence in the autumn of 1936 was not Communist-inspired, nor was the republic 'red or Bolshevik'. The dominance of the Communist party came later.[15] Nor were the Nationalist 'Fascists', as they were universally portrayed by the left, part of some international conspiracy. They were revolutionaries of the right, in an exclusively Iberian formulation. Nor did the war end in 1939, as is commonly supposed. It persisted in a guerrilla war for another four decades,[16] finding rebirth in the violence of the Basque ETA.

Part 3

FREEDOM, NOW!

INDIA 1905–47

Violence and non-violence

THE last ninety years of British rule in India were conditioned by memories of the Mutiny of 1857. British governments were not insensitive to Indian feelings of injustice, and there was a spirit of paternalism underlying most legislation affecting India. But Indian political aspirations were not treated seriously. The foundation of the Indian Congress Party in 1885 was approved by the British authorities as a vent for the political feelings of what the Viceroy, Lord Dufferin, described in 1888 as a 'microscopic minority'[1] of Indians. Indians resented the arrogance and hypocrisy of British paternalism, a paternalism which had made India poorer rather than richer. At the 1891 meeting of the Congress held at Nagpur, a delegate put the matter succinctly: 'Free trade, fair play between nations, how I hate the sham. What fair play in trade can there be between impoverished India and capitalist England?'[2]

It is the habit of governments everywhere to suspect conspiracy and subversion, and from the murder of two British officers at Poona in 1897 by two fanatical nationalist brothers, there were fears that another widespread uprising was being planned.[3] The rule of Lord Curzon as Viceroy from 1899 to 1905 was a key element in transforming a small movement dedicated to terror into mass opposition to the British. Curzon proceeded with major programmes of legislative and administrative reform. He despised his officials – 'the Government of India is a mighty and miraculous machine for doing nothing'[4] – and treated, as the wife of his successor described it, 'the three hundred million people as puppets'. He infuriated the nationalists as he whittled away what advances had been made. 'We cannot take the natives up into the administration. They are too crooked-minded and corrupt. We have got therefore to go on ruling them and we can only do it by being both kindly and virtuous. I daresay I am talking rather like a school master but, after all, the millions I have to manage are less than school children.'[5] In this letter is the essence of his approach towards Indians.

The response to the Curzon legislation, in particular his decision to divide the historic province of Bengal into two in the interests of easy administration, was mass violence. Hindu nationalism was led into violence by Bal Gangadhar Tilak, firstly in Bengal and then in his area of greatest strength, in the provinces inland from Bombay. After Curzon's resignation in 1905, the movement gathered pace rather than receded until a broad band across northern and central India was dominated by violent protests and boycotts of British goods, following the success of the Calcutta boycott campaign. Until the return of Mohandas K. Gandhi to India in 1915, the men of violence dominated the movement for Indian nationhood.

Gandhi spent his life in India after 1915 in an effort to restrain violence. His concept of non-violence ('satyagraha') developed, during the years in which he practised it in South Africa and in India, from an individual creed of civil resistance into an ethic for a mass movement. In South Africa it had forced a degree of flexibility from the authorities in their attitudes towards Indians, when backed by strike action from Indian workers. But in South Africa, Indians were a tiny minority in the population, and the possibilities of mass non-obedience were limited. The same precepts, if effective in India, would be working with the whole population. The principal outcome of the non-violent campaigns in India was to perplex the authorities, as it had in South Africa. Gandhi's own sincerity and selflessness won over many government and judicial officials. He accepted imprisonment and privations eagerly, and became a focus of world attention. He developed a whole range of techniques of disobedience. Economic boycott, national strikes, refusal to obey British laws over salt monopolies, forest taxes, and land settlements, withdrawal from any contact with the British structure of administration, were all used to play the same tune. The British rule was unjust and Indian home rule must be conceded.[6]

Gandhi and his immediate band of supporters had the strength of purpose to undertake non-violent non-cooperation. For the masses, it was a difficult notion to comprehend, and in many cases, when non-violence was attempted on a mass scale, it turned towards violence.

Insurrectionary violence continued in parallel with Gandhism. In 1919 the Government had sought to prolong wartime emergency legislation against freedom of speech and assembly. Gandhi immediately demanded a national *hartal*, a complete economic strike, to be followed by disobedience on a mass scale. But throughout India the call to non-violent action turned into riot and murder after the initial success of the *hartal*. The most extreme British attitude towards Indian protestors, violent or non-violent, came with the massacre organized at Amritsar by the military commander, General Dyer. On 13 April 1919, after a number of murders of Europeans and a proclamation against processions and meetings, a large crowd gathered for a peaceful meeting. It was dispersed by ten minutes of aimed gunfire fired into a crowd in an enclosed space which made it difficult to escape. The casualties were 379 dead, and 1137 wounded. In the subsequent enquiry, Dyer indicated that he would probably have used the machine guns on his armoured cars had he been able to bring them to bear. Dyer's intention was to cause terror: 'I thought I would be doing a jolly lot of good'[7] was his reported remark. Nor did the matter end there. Villages surrounding Amritsar were bombed and machine-gunned from the air, while in the city, three days before the massacre, he had flogged any Indians who would not crawl along the road at a point where a white woman had been attacked. It was all reminiscent of the British response to the horrors of the mutiny. The reaction of international disgust which followed Amritsar made it difficult for the British to use the same degree of force in the future, although they were never gentle with the practitioners of non-violence. Amritsar pushed Gandhi into the politics of the Congress movement which, after the death of Tilak in 1920, he was able to win over to the cause of non-violence. But this was difficult to achieve. An attempt to launch a campaign of civil resistance near Bombay in 1922 was withdrawn by Gandhi when he heard that a mob of demonstrators at Chauri Chauri, some eight hundred miles to the north, had turned on the police and killed them all. He argued: 'Suppose the non-violent disobedience at Bardoli was permitted by God to succeed and the Government had abdicated in favour of the victors of Bardoli, who would control the unruly elements that must be expected to perpetuate inhumanity upon due provocation?' It was not a question he was ever able to answer. As a means of mass protest, *satyagraha* needed to develop in less dangerous areas. Gandhi was at his most successful when he created symbols of resistance. Congress members abandoned Western dress and imported

cloth. Homespun cloth became a symbol of resistance to the British; Jawaharlal Nehru described it as 'the livery of our freedom'. From his hermitage – *ashram* – near Ahmadabad, Gandhi wrote articles for the newspaper *Young India*, and also received a stream of visitors. The episodes for which he became famous – the fasts, imprisonment, the campaign in March 1930 where he symbolically broke the law against private production of salt by taking a pinch of it on Dandi beach – have overshadowed his patient political work. Gandhi aimed for a free and united India, while the Moslems were increasingly thinking in terms of a separate Islamic state. Much of Gandhi's time was spent in preserving a framework of unity within the independence movement.

The British eventually came to see that Gandhi was an interlocutor who stood between them and an increasingly turbulent India. Neither violent repression, as in the police attack on the salt marchers at Dharesana near Surat, nor imprisonment of the non-violent protestors, seemed to have any effect. And administratively, government was becoming more difficult without the co-operation of educated Indians. A hundred thousand 'political' prisoners had swamped India's jails by the end of 1931. After the India Act of 1935 was passed, Congress achieved dramatic success in the elections, particularly in rural constituencies, indicating how deeply Gandhian politics had struck home. British intelligence officers reported that 'village voters bowed before the Congress candidate boxes as a mark of respect to Mahatma Gandhi'. With the outbreak of war against Japan in 1941, the British attempted to engage India's

Mahatma Ghandi on his slow march from the *ashram* near Ahmadabad to the sea near Bombay. There he symbolically broke the law that none but the government could produce salt, by taking some grains from the shore. All over India campaigns of law-breaking began. Ironically, Ghandi himself never used salt: March 1930

active support, through a mission led by Sir Stafford Cripps offering concessions once the war was ended. For Congress it was too little and too late. The All India Congress Committee held on 8 August 1942 called on Britain to quit India. After the proposal was passed, Gandhi himself spoke. 'I want freedom immediately, this very night, before dawn if it can be had. Freedom cannot wait for the realization of communal unity. . . . Nothing however should be done secretly. This is an open rebellion. In this struggle secrecy is a sin. A free man should not engage in a secret movement. Freedom has to come not tomorrow, but today.'[8] In the early hours of 9 August he and the leading members of Congress were arrested. India erupted into rebellion to a degree not seen since 1857. It required over fifty battalions of troops to suppress the disorders. Hundreds of miles of railway track were destroyed and according to the government 940 were killed and 1630 injured. Congress estimates exceeded 15,000.[9] The truth probably lay in between. An active opposition, supported by the Japanese, began to recruit Indians for the liberation of the homeland from among prisoners held in Japanese prison camps. The extent of the rebellion of August 1942, which was not suppressed in some areas until 1944, revealed the degree to which India could become ungovernable. The *satyagraha* could not be suppressed, as successive viceroys had discovered. It was even more difficult to hold down an angry people prepared to take armed action. In terms of economics, India had also become a liability: war debt had made India a creditor of Great Britain. The defeat of the Conservatives in the British election of 1945 pushed Churchill out of office. He who in 1930 had been disgusted by 'the nauseating and humiliating spectacle of this one-time Inner Temple lawyer, now seditious fakir, striding half naked up the steps of the Viceroy's palace, there to negotiate and to parley on equal terms with the representative of the King-Emperor',[10] was the single most effective opponent of concession in India. With his departure, realism replaced political romanticism.

The independence of India was granted, on terms which Gandhi rightly feared would result in atrocities on a massive scale committed by both Moslems and Hindus. Partition was a recipe for catastrophe, the antithesis of his life's work. An Islamic Pakistan could only be achieved by removing millions of Hindus and Sikhs; while in India there were 42 million Moslems. Conflict between the communities had been endemic throughout the growth of Gandhi's movement, which had glossed over the divisions between Hindu and Moslem. The demand for a separate Moslem state were voiced stridently by Mohammad Ali Jinnah and the Moslem League. Jinnah, intransigent and haughty where Gandhi was conciliatory and amiable, achieved his objective. India was partitioned, down to the last of the Viceroy's teaspoons.

The influence of non-violence as a means of political action depended on an opponent who had a reputation to lose. The British believed in the rule of law, and on the whole abided by the letter if not the spirit of the law. Gandhi was imprisoned many times, often under obscure and antiquated legislation, but always in accordance with legal process. However inconvenient he might have been, there was never any attempt by the British to dispose of him; his eventual murderer was a Hindu nationalist. Non-violence depended, too, on theatricality for its full effect. Many violent suppressions of rural *satyagrahas* and forced evictions of *satyagrahis*, who withheld rent or refused to pay fines, went unrecorded. The Congress leaders and Gandhi himself underwent repeated martyrdom in the full light of the world's press. In the United States in particular, Britain's intransigent imperialism met with incomprehension, and eventually undisguised opposition. The other element in the relative success of non-violence in India was its novelty. The British in India were attuned to violence. Indeed, the whole ethos of post-Mutiny India was predicated upon it. But non-violence, especially expressed so articulately and so warmly by a man as likeable as Gandhi, had no obvious remedy. Or, to be more precise, no remedy which the British were prepared to contemplate. Elsewhere, and at other times, an answer was found.

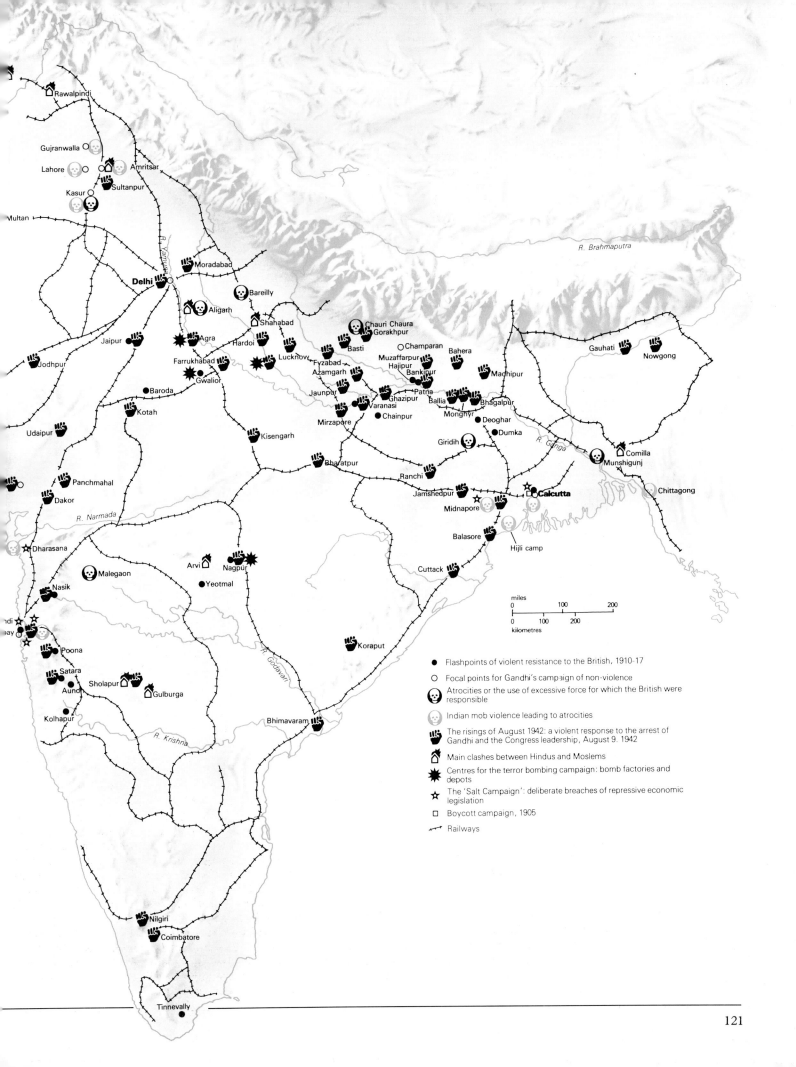

Rawalpindi

Gujranwalla
Lahore
Kasur
Multan

Amritsar
Sultanpur

Moradabad
Delhi
Bareilly
Aligarh
Shahabad
Chauri Chaura
Gorakhpur
Agra
Hardoi
Basti
Champaran
Jaipur
Lucknow
Bahera
Jodhpur
Farrukhabad
Fyzabad
Muzaffarpur
Gwalior
Azamgarh
Hajipur
Madhipur
Baroda
Jaunpur
Bankipur
Kotah
Ghazipur
Patna
Varanasi
Ballia
Bhagalpur
Udaipur
Kisengarh
Chainpur
Monghyr
Gauhati
Nowgong
Mirzapore
Deoghar
Panchmahal
Bharatpur
Dumka
Dakor
Ranchi
Giridih
Comilla
Munshigunj
Jamshedpur
Chittagong
Dharasana
Midnapore
Calcutta
Malegaon
Arvi
Nagpur
Balasore
Nasik
Yeotmal
Hijli camp
Poona
Cuttack
Satara
Aundh
Sholapur
Koraput
Gulburga
Kolhapur
Bhimavaram

R. Yamuna
R. Brahmaputra
R. Ganga
R. Narmada
R. Godavari
R. Krishna

Nilgiri
Coimbatore

Tinnevally

miles
0   100   200
0   100   200
kilometres

● Flashpoints of violent resistance to the British, 1910-17

○ Focal points for Gandhi's campaign of non-violence

Atrocities or the use of excessive force for which the British were responsible

Indian mob violence leading to atrocities

The risings of August 1942: a violent response to the arrest of Gandhi and the Congress leadership, August 9. 1942

Main clashes between Hindus and Moslems

Centres for the terror bombing campaign: bomb factories and depots

The 'Salt Campaign': deliberate breaches of repressive economic legislation

□ Boycott campaign, 1905

⊢⊣ Railways

SOUTH EAST ASIA 1945–62
Bandits or freedom fighters?

ON 7 December 1941 the Japanese navy attacked the United States Pacific fleet in Pearl Harbor. The 'day of infamy' was the first step in a pre-emptive strategy which would enable Japan to secure the oil resources of the Dutch East Indies and political dominance throughout the Pacific. To the United States and to the colonial powers of South East Asia – the French, British and Dutch – the Japanese were aggressors. The attitudes of the subject peoples in Indo China, Malaya and Indonesia were less clear-cut.

The war provided an interlude for the colonial peoples in which they became aware of the relative weakness of their former overlords. In Malaya, a small guerrilla army under Ching Peng was trained and armed by the British, and portrayed itself as the 'Malayan Peoples Anti-Japanese Army', fighting alone for the liberation of the country. In the Philippines, there was substantial resistance, partly organized by the Americans and their Filipino regiment and partly made up from peasants in the Luzon area, known as the Hukbalahap. In Indonesia, the Japanese sponsored a number of self-defence initiatives, which became a secret nationalist army. In each of the occupied areas Communists soon came to take a leading role in resistance to the Japanese, and many nationalist leaders saw the danger of too close a coincidence of interest between Communism and nationalism. With the end of the war in the Pacific, the intention of the Allies was to return to the colonial position as it existed before the Japanese invasion. In every case a nationalist movement was in place to oppose the return of the colonial power. The effect of the war had been to provide nationalism, firstly, with a plausible programme, and secondly, with the physical potential to accomplish it.

Although the process of ending colonial rule – decolonization – seemed to move forward along set lines in the two decades after the war, this was an illusion. There was no general trend, nor even a coherent policy on the part of each of the colonial powers. Each campaign for national freedom evoked different responses in the home governments. When the Philippines were recovered from the Japanese, the United States was quick to grant independence on terms which matched American interests, both commercial and strategic. The Dutch, by contrast, were determined to recover their possessions and to hold them as they had before. The British, now governed by a Labour party with a strong anti-colonial bias, was prepared to grant independence but only if it could save face while doing so. Thus India and Burma were relinquished (1947–48), while in Malaya the old system was perpetuated in a new 'federation' established in February 1948. The position which the Dutch advanced was the least plausible. Although Dutch forces re-invaded Java and the other main islands of the East Indies, and were able to inflict military defeats on the nationalist armies, they found it more difficult to achieve a political acceptance of their reborn empire. Their military task was made easier by a split between the nationalists under Sukarno and the Communists which was only resolved by a civil war while the struggle with the Dutch was still in progress. But the bulk of Javanese opinion – by far the most populous and significant section of the population – was solidly against the Dutch, and this opposition found an echo in the newly created United Nations. Nehru, the Prime Minister of India, speaking at the United Nations in July 1947, expressed the general feeling against the military solution adopted by the Dutch: 'The spirit of Asia will not tolerate such things. No European country, whatever it may be, has any business to set its army in Asia against the peoples of Asia. When it does, Asia will not tolerate it.'[1] The Dutch had always dealt unfeelingly with Indonesian political feelings. Only one minority group, the islanders of Amboina in the South Moluccas (who had provided most of the police and internal security under colonial rule), could be relied upon to support any Dutch initiative. The strategy adopted by the government in The Hague was to outbid the nationalists, and to offer independence not to Indonesia as a whole, but to all the elements within it individually. They believed that the resulting federation would be so weak as to allow continuing Dutch 'guidance'. It was a subtle and ingenious plan which recognized the weakness of the nationalist schemes. Why, argued the Dutch, replace the benign rule of the Netherlands with Javanese imperialism? Indonesia was an accident, a collection of territories composed of different peoples, religions and objectives, and all their interests should be recognized in any independence settlement.

The complex of factors which finally forced the Dutch to yield independence were both local and international. Guerrilla pressure against the Dutch forces had not ceased since their re-occupation, and although much of the nationalists' time was spent in fighting among themselves, they were, potentially, a formidable military opposition. Internationally, financial support for the Dutch economy from the United States was being questioned as the colonial campaign dragged on. The settlement satisfied no one and the elaborate federal structure was soon swept away by the new Republic of Indonesia. Many of the malcontents from the South Moluccas emigrated to the Netherlands, inducing an element of social and racial tension into the colonial homeland. In Indonesia, although the new state was launched with a great accolade as the triumph of an oppressed people, the tensions of the vast new state had only been temporarily held in check. Communism, militant Islam, and separatism all threatened, as they still do, the unity of the new Indonesia.

In Malaya the British were faced with a less intricate set of problems. Where the Dutch had been able to count on only a small minority group for local support, British rule was accepted by the bulk of the majority people, the Malays themselves. The federation established in 1948 was a concession to established Malay political opinion, a half-way house to nationhood. The nationalist opposition to British rule came most strongly from the minority Chinese population, led by a small but well-organized Communist party. Military action came as a last resort, after a campaign to rally political support against the new federation was a complete failure. The primary aim of the revolt was to disrupt the economy and build an anti-British network in the villages, backed by a guerrilla army of about five thousand. Many false lessons have been drawn from the guerrilla war which began in earnest in June 1948 and lasted until the official end of the emergency in July 1960. The theory of 'anti-insurgency' was born in the experience of Malaya, and has been generalized into many other situations. Some points are well known. The Communist 'Malayan Races Liberation Army' was isolated, racially, from the bulk of the population, and British actions reduced still further the areas in which they could operate. Furthermore, the logistical superiority of the 'anti-insurgent' forces was enormous. The army totalled 40,000 men, the police 67,000, and there was a Home Guard of 350,000. More than 525 million leaflets were dropped into the jungle. Informers were paid on a huge scale, and money was paid, literally as well as figuratively, on the heads of the guerrillas. Re-education was not a synonym for torture, but a subtle process of psychological pressure. On the ground the British persuaded the Malay princes to allocate land for landless peasants to be re-settled. The 'New Villages' programme held out advantages to those who were to be re-settled, as well as military benefits to the security forces. The troops were well led, and under General Sir Gerald Templer, who took control in 1952, all the government forces were infused with his conviction that the 'terrorists' were going to be defeated. The strongest card in his hand was the declaration that only terrorism stood in the way of independence. He stated clearly: 'You can and should have independence if you can help me get rid of Communism'. By 1955 the guerrillas were in retreat, and when the promised independence came in August 1957, there were only some 1300 still active inside Malaya.

The key to the Malayan situation lay in the fact that *only* the British could gratify nationalist demands, and were willing to do so. The Communists were left with a narrow range of support from those who wanted a socialist as well as a national state. While the successes of the anti-insurgency campaign could be applied elsewhere in terms of techniques and technology, the political context could not. Templer's catch phrase, 'You've got to offer people in trouble a big carrot',[2] became meaningless if all that could be offered was the stick. The Communist threat was defeated rather than abolished. Their

command structure was set up just north of the Thai border, and limited operations continue to be mounted in the northern states of Malaysia. But they have nothing to offer and remain, like the remnants of the nationalist Chinese armies in the borderlands of Burma, a by-blow of history.

In Malaya, the grievances – land hunger, national independence – were resolved and insurgency became dormant. In the Philippines the national issue was resolved after a fashion, but none of the other grievances. In consequence, insurgency which began in the years after the war has never died down and continues to unbalance the state system. It was convenient to label the Huk movement which developed from the resistance to the Japanese as Communist, but its appeal was much wider than any exclusively Marxist party would have been in the context of rural Luzon. It gained strength from brutal government attempts to repress the movement in the villages of the Luzon plain. The Huks retreated into the *sierra*, where they had established camps and training grounds, moving into the plains at night.

Young Indonesian nationalists, with arms they have taken from the Dutch and Japanese, on parade after the re-occupation by the Dutch forces, 1947. Many of them went on to fight a hit-and-run war against Dutch forces. Others were involved in savage internecine rivalries within the nationalist cause

The war edged backwards and forwards, and there was a belief around 1953–4 that the movement had been defeated, with the Manila government offering political concessions to erode their support. But the concessions never materialized and the peasants, locked into a cycle of poverty and exploitation, turned again to the Huks as the only possible source of redress. Like many peasant-based movements, it remains localized, as does the other body of resistance, that of the Islamic Moro movement in southern Mindanao and the islands to the west. The Moros, with a tradition of resistance to authority, were only barely suppressed by the United States army in their occupation of the Philippines in 1903–5; no succeeding government has been as successful. In the Philippines a tradition of insurgency now extends over generations.

In difficult terrain, the balance of advantage still lies with the insurgent rather than the forces of order, which are forced to defend what they already possess as well as seek out those who wish to take it from them. The dimension so often missing from doctrines of anti-insurgency is *time*. For a war of national liberation to last for thirty years is not unknown, and at the end of that time the revolutionaries have emerged with their programme and ideology relatively intact. To sustain an anti-insurgent war for that length of time would be to induce impossible social tensions accompanied by demands for political change. No state has successfully accomplished it.

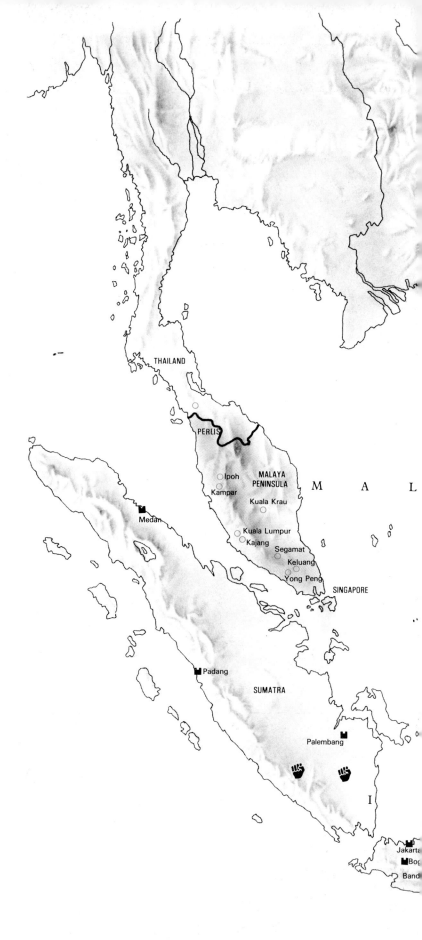

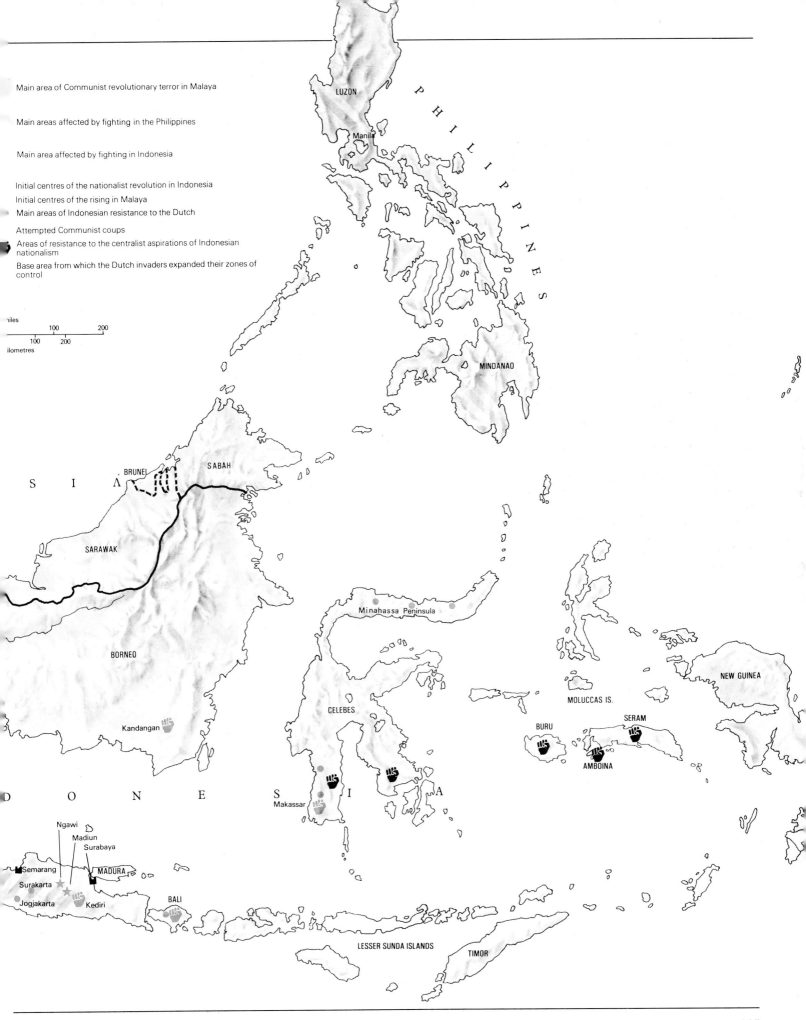

Main area of Communist revolutionary terror in Malaya

Main areas affected by fighting in the Philippines

Main area affected by fighting in Indonesia

Initial centres of the nationalist revolution in Indonesia
Initial centres of the rising in Malaya
Main areas of Indonesian resistance to the Dutch

Attempted Communist coups

Areas of resistance to the centralist aspirations of Indonesian nationalism

Base area from which the Dutch invaders expanded their zones of control

miles
100   200
100   200
kilometres

LUZON

Manila

P H I L I P P I N E S

MINDANAO

S   I   A

BRUNEI   SABAH

SARAWAK

BORNEO

Kandangan

Minahassa Peninsula

CELEBES

Makassar

D   O   N   E   S   I   A

Ngawi
Madiun
Surabaya

Semarang
Surakarta
Jogjakarta   Kediri

MADURA

BALI

MOLUCCAS IS.

BURU   SERAM

AMBOINA

NEW GUINEA

LESSER SUNDA ISLANDS   TIMOR

Mau Mau

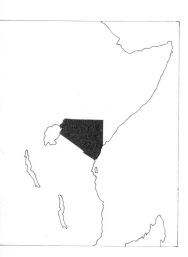

IN 1938 Jomo Kenyatta dedicated his study of the Kikuyu nation, *Facing Mount Kenya*, to the 'perpetuation of communication with ancestral spirits through the fight for African Freedom. . . .'[1] The animating spirit behind the Kenyan nationalist movement was religion and culture, as it had been with the *maji maji* rebellion in Tanganyika before the First World War, but the key issue was land. Land and Kikuyu culture were inextricably intermixed, for as Kenyatta wrote, 'it is the key to the people's life; it secures them that peaceful tillage of the soil which supplies them material needs and enables them to perform their magic and traditional ceremonies in undisturbed serenity, facing Mount Kenya'.[2] The disputes over land and land rights went back to before the First World War.

Between the wars the nationalist movement grew more articulate, focussing on white attempts to 'subvert' local customs, in particular female circumcision, which became a totem of the nationalist movement. Unlike many other seemingly atavistic tribal movements, the Kikuyu were vociferous and enterprising, capable of fighting the British government and the white settlers through the press and the courts. Although the issues which were raised – tribal customs and tribal land – were traditional, they were expressed in the framework of Kenyan nationalism.

The Kikuyu Central Association (KCA) headed by Kenyatta rejected the whole concept of white domination, even in the benign paternalism which the British government began to push, the view that Africans are 'and must be, for a long time yet, wards in trust'.[3] Through a number of African papers, mostly centred on Nairobi which was becoming the dominant centre of Kenyan nationalism, nationalist views were widely spread throughout the country. They received their strongest response in the Kikuyu areas close to the capital, where the mission schools had created a larger literate population than elsewhere in the country. The Kenya African Union (KAU), which was formed during the war after the KCA was banned as being subversive, became the main vehicle after Kenyatta returned to Kenya in 1946 and united the two bodies. He had spent, in all, sixteen years out of Kenya and had married an English wife in 1942. He knew the way the British political system operated and he was also acquainted with many leading figures in Parliament and the press. Yet despite the Western veneer, he had not lost sight of the motivations which dominated the Kikuyu peasantry. He had been born one of them.

Although the Kikuyu were not what the British liked to describe as one of 'the martial races', many of them had served in the British Army during the war. They had returned with their eyes opened. An official British report of 1943 warned that the post-war African 'will not be generally content with the low standard with which most Africans were content before the war'.[4] A number of these former soldiers formed an association called the 'Forty Group' in Nairobi, and began to act as a pressure group for African rights. In 1949, the Electors' Union, representing the white settlers, published a plan which made it clear that they intended to remain the dominant political force in the state, with the Africans permanently subordinate. The response by the Kikuyu leaders was to transform their base of support into a mass movement. The *thenge* (oath) was traditional in Kikuyu society, a means by which a complete commitment could be made. Breach of an oath involved not only whatever sanctions the oath contained but social ostracism as well. By this means it was possible to create a dedicated and committed nationalist movement, firstly among the political and traditional leaders, and then on a mass scale. Oathing did not, of itself, involve any commitment to violence, but in the countryside, where passions were roused, it was followed by arson and cattle maiming. In the towns, mass meetings were held – over 25,000 at one meeting in Nyeri in July 1951. In October 1951, the Kenyan government, in an effort to prevent the spread of oathing which they rightly saw as extremely dangerous, proscribed an organization called 'Mau Mau'. In fact, there was no such organization, the name being a mis-hearing of a Kikuyu phrase. But there *was* a concerted nationalist campaign based on oath-taking which was very rapidly spilling over into violence.

The heart of the violent resistance lay in the Kikuyu Native Reserves, and in Nairobi. On 7 October a leading African moderate and government spokesman, Chief Waruhiu, was murdered near Nairobi. Thirteen days later a state of emergency was declared, and a war launched on militant Kenyan nationalism. On the next day Kenyatta was arrested, as were the other leaders of the KAU. Operation 'Jack Scott' was designed to make a pre-emptive strike and sever the 'Mau Mau' from their leaders. It succeeded, but the trial at Kapenguria from November 1952 to March 1953 placed the Mau Mau issue on the international plane. What many had considered to be a little local colonial difficulty now had considerable press interest focussed upon it. In time, as the government adopted more and more extreme measures to quell the rising, this turned into an indictment of British policy. The move to put the leaders on trial precipitated rather than held back violence and murder. Most of the attacks were directed at Africans loyal to the British rather than at Europeans. During the whole of the period of the Emergency, only 95 Europeans were killed, a figure which included both military and civilians. Over the same period, more than 1920 'loyal' Africans were killed. Of the Mau Mau and those believed to support them, more than 11,500 were killed. More than 90,000 were also processed through camps set up to weed out likely supporters of Mau Mau and those who had taken an oath. The level of planned military activity by Mau Mau was imited. The most dramatic exploits, an attack on the police station at Naivasha, and a massacre of Kikuyu loyal to the government at Lari, both on 26 March 1953, were exceptional. For the most part, the Mau Mau fighters were untrained, and with only home-made arms. The weapons captured at Naivasha represented almost their entire armoury, and even then they had little ammunition. Most attacks were made with spears, *pangas* and *simis*, no match even for the firearms possessed by the settlers. On one occasion, an elderly lady drove off an attack at a lonely farm with a few accurate pistol shots.

The British responded to Naivasha and Lari, and a crescendo of complaints from settlers, with massive reinforcements and a comprehensive strategy. They tackled the emergency on two levels. On the first, substantial troop reinforcements purged the cities and the reserves of Mau Mau. Wholesale population movements were sanctioned, standing crops des-troyed, and settlements were concentrated on 'loyal-ist' villages defended by Kikuyu Home Guard. The same resolute tactics were used on Nairobi. The second level was to win the battle for the 'mind' of the Kikuyu. The government, advised by psychol-

Kenya, 1954: one of the most effective techniques used by the British in the Mau Mau war was the mass round-up of suspects. The whole of Nairobi was emptied at one point. Those cleared were released, while suspects were given much more rigorous treatment. At Hola camp there were deaths from excessively severe treatment which amounted to torture

ogists and expert anthropologists, among them the archaeologist Louis Leakey, came to see Mau Mau as a perversion of traditional Kikuyu beliefs and values.

A special programme of 'counter-magic' was devised, which involved ritual cleansing from the Mau Mau oath, and the taking of a new oath. But for true Mau Mau, nothing could wipe out the *thenge* they had taken, and they were happy to take the government oath to achieve their freedom. In the end these plausible but largely ineffective schemes for mass conversion were abandoned.

The Mau Mau groups were now faced with a free fire zone in the native reserves, their main source of food and support, while their sanctuary in the Aberdare forest was physically cut off from the reserves by a deep ditch or dyke dug by forced labour. Behind it lay a scorched earth zone and regular patrols from the new fortified posts which dotted the countryside. The Mau Mau groups in the reserves, grandly called the Levallation Army, dwindled to nothing. By 1955, the British had begun to penetrate into the dense bamboo forests which clothed much of the Aberdare ranges. They used counter-gangs, often made up of former Mau Mau, to hunt down the small groups in the forest, as well as conventional military sweeps and the use of air power to spot camp sites and to bomb and harass.

The forest was a sanctuary for many in the reserves who were not Mau Mau by conviction, but feared the British. At its peak the numbers in the forests of the Aberdares and around Mount Kenya totalled 16,000. As British pressure increased, and it was made easy to surrender safely, the numbers dwindled. But the forest was also a trap, for the Mau Mau fighters dared not move outside it and the British steadily reduced the safe areas within it. Periodic captures were made of Mau Mau leaders, such as General 'China' and Dedan Kimathi. The 'armies' which they commanded were little more than small bands of frightened men and women, who had been forced to abandon the larger camps for smaller emergency camps in which life was almost impossibly difficult. Outside the forest, life in the detention camps was dominated by the demands of the rehabilitation programme, where compliance brought pardon and eventual release. There were also a number of unofficial camps where settlers abandoned such kid-glove methods and killed many suspects. Even the government found that persuasion would not work with the hard core of convinced Mau Mau. The tough cases were concentrated at Hola Camp in late 1958, where they were subjected to such pressure that a number died. The international outcry against 'lawless violence', the words of a committee of inquiry, convinced many in Britain that repression in Kenya was now counterproductive. Eventually, they came to sit at the same conference table with Kenyatta, who had been released from prison in 1958 and was confined under house arrest until 1961. Two years later Kenya achieved independence under his leadership.

As guerrilla movements go, Mau Mau was insignificant. Of the 12,000 fighters in the Aberdares, and perhaps 4000 near Mount Kenya, few were active guerrillas. In the native reserves, where some 30,000 were thought to give aid and assistance to the fighters, the British policy of rehabilitation destroyed their effectiveness in the space of a few months. But more than their military effectiveness, Mau Mau became a symbol of Africans fighting colonialism. In Kenya its appeal was to a section of one tribe, the Kikuyu, and not at all to the other major tribes; in other African countries, Mau Mau became the vanguard for future liberation movements. But even the feeble efforts of the 'Land and Freedom Armies' frightened the settlers of Kenya and made them realise that 55,000 whites in a population of eight million Africans were vulnerable. In the end, they came to see their best guarantee of stability in Kenyatta and the educated leaders of the KAU.

Mei Mathatthi Army
Mount Kenya

Mbura
Ngebo
Army

Ituma
Ndemi
Army

Kenya
Levallation
Army

Kenya
Inoro
Army

Gikuyu Iregi
Army

NANYUKI
DISTRICT

NYERI
SETTLED
DISTRICT

Meru

MERU
DISTRICT

Ihuruhu
Centre

MOUNT
KENYA

Nyeri

NYERI
DISTRICT

Embu

Guru River Valley

EMBU DISTRICT

MWEA Plains Camps

FORT
HALL
DISTRICT

Fort Hall

Kikuyu Reserve

Hola Camp

Matara

CENTRAL PROVINCE

Lari

Thika

THIKA
DISTRICT

Kiambu

Athi River Camp

KIAMBU
DISTRICT

Nairobi

SOUTHERN PROVINCE

R. Athi

R. Tana

Abedare Forest

NAIVASHA
DISTRICT

Mombasa

20   40
40

ncipal area affected by the rising

tial centres of Mau Mau activity

in Mau Mau camps in the Aberdare Mountains.
en attacked by British bombers and foot
rols, the groups split up and used
aller camps

all camps in the Aberdare Mountains

au Mau attacks on whites and native leaders.
ese attracted widespread international attention

ass attacks by Mau Mau forces

y political trials which the British hoped would discredit the
tionalist aims of the movement

in camps for interrogation and 're-education' of Mau Mau
soners. The methods used often amounted to torture

se areas for the Mau Mau armies. The thick bamboo forests
de them a haven

e 'scorched earth' zone on the edge of the forest. This prevented
fighters in the forest receiving food from the native reserves

in area of European settlement

'Algérie française'

WHEN France first came to Algeria in the 1830s she found an independent Islamic state of great antiquity, nominally ruled by the Ottoman Empire, but in fact in the hands of local clans and great families. The acquisition of Algeria took the French seventeen years, and for a century thereafter they engaged in building an extension of the homeland across the Mediterranean. The occupation of Algeria became not an exercise in colonialism, but the remodelling of a society. France overturned the customary pattern of landholding on which the fabric of Islamic social and economic relationships were based, with the consequence, as was observed to Emperor Napoleon III, that by this means France would 'civilize, perfect and gallicize the Arabs'.[1] The best land along the coastal strip was created by French settlers, who built thriving cities – Algiers, Oran, Philippeville, and Bône – largely from the re-invested profits and the economic activity generated by a productive agriculture. The colonists came from the poor arid lands of the Massif Central and Languedoc, as well as refugees from Alsace after the German conquest of 1871. Others were the surplus population of many Mediterranean lands – Spaniards, Italians, Corsicans, and Maltese. Poor themselves, they saw in the Moslem natives enemies and competitors for the few resources which existed. Where the Algerians had used the land for pasture before expropriation, they grew vines, and wine eventually comprised over half of Algeria's total exports. There was no point of contact between the Christian and Moslem populations, no community of interests. The *colons*, or *pieds noirs* (black feet) as they were more derisively known, largely regarded the Arabs as naturally inferior, but also people to be feared. The white minority lived in a state of perpetual anxiety towards the Moslem majority.

This insecurity was heightened when the Algerians in Sétif rose in a wild and savage rebellion during the celebrations for the victory in Europe on 8 May 1945. The brutality which was to mark the war of liberation was evident in the rebellion and the reprisals which followed. Men, women and children were massacred, with many mutilated and tortured. The European casualties were numbered in the low hundreds, while the reprisals killed many thousands, including the bombing and wholesale destruction of villages where no incidents had taken place. There has never been a satisfactory explanation for the initial Moslem rising, but the repression hardened the attitudes of both *colons* and Algerians.[2] Many of the leaders of the new nationalism were Berbers from the mountains of Kabylia and the Aurès, a region where Europeans had never bothered to penetrate. The core and inspiration of the Algerian revolution lay in these mountaineers, the toughest and most enterprising elements of the peoples of Algeria. The Kabyles lived on the margin of both Arab and *colon* society, and in fact the French admired their capacity for hard work and ability to learn. Many Berbers received higher education in France, while many also served in the French armies during the Second World War. The nationalists possessed a reserve of natural guerrilla fighters and a favourable terrain. What they lacked was money and equipment.

The impetus to organize a national revolution came from outside Algeria. The nationalist movement, now headed by the Comité Révolutionnaire d'Unité et d'Action, usually abbreviated to CRUA, saw the catastrophes which had submerged the French in their war in Indo China, and they believed that the French capacity to resist a rising in Algeria would be reduced. Throughout the summer of 1954 feverish planning and recruitment went ahead, and the rising was planned for All Saints Day, 1 November 1954. The antennae of the French intelligence network soon received news that a major rising was at hand, but the authorities ignored the warnings. When, on 1 November, Cairo Radio broadcast the announcement of the new Front de Libération National, the nationalists achieved almost complete surprise. However, despite attempts to create an insurrection all over Algeria, their only real success was in the Aurès and Kabylia. The enthusiastic revolutionaries believed that France would not be capable of waging a major campaign against them, but they forgot the 'special relationship' of Algeria with metropolitan France. Another factor was the signing away of Indo China in the peace treaties of December 1954. The French government was determined not to suffer another humiliation in Algeria. The full weight of the French army was channelled into the war in Algeria. The FLN and its military wing (the Armée de Libération Nationale), faced with overwhelming military superiority, were forced more and more into irregular warfare. The conflict in Algeria, from Sétif onwards, was a catalogue of atrocities. The FLN sought to use revolutionary terror to intimidate its enemies, both Moslem and Christian. The 'Kabyle smile', signifying the gaping wound of a slit throat, became a trademark of the nationalists. On the French side, the paratroopers who fought the FLN for control of the streets of Algiers, discovered torture and the fiendish uses to which the electric generator of a field telephone could be put when attached to a sensitive part of the body. It was a very dirty war.

When the French were well led, and they were able to use superior technology – helicopters, telecommunications – they had the measure of the nationalists. But while they could defeat them in open combat, they could not exterminate the guerrilla fighters. The FLN had begun the war with pitifully few arms, but they captured many from the French. The bulk of their supplies came through Tunisia where many training bases were established close to the border. This outlet was closed in September 1957 when the French completed the Morice line, an eight-foot electric fence with a fifty-yard minefield on either side.

The 'Battle of Algiers' was won by a combination of police detection methods and wholesale torture by the French army. The FLN began a bombing campaign which the French paratroops and Foreign Legion ended by a reign of terror. Algiers was divided up into sectors and strict controls were imposed on movement within the city

This barrier, which was regularly patrolled, ran from the sea to the desert in the south, and it proved virtually impenetrable for the FLN. The cities were 'pacified' by the French, the bomb factories destroyed and the urban guerrillas flushed from their hideouts in the casbah. The most notable of these urban campaigns, the battle of Algiers, lasted from January to March of 1957. It demonstrated how completely a well-trained and ruthless military force could contain urban violence in a way which was impossible in the countryside. It was a lesson largely lost on revolutionaries elsewhere. The French had other successes too: in October 1956, they had hijacked an airliner heading for Tunis which contained a number of the leaders of the FLN, including Ahmed Ben Bella, its most inspirational figure. Yet despite these considerable successes, France was not winning the war. The conflict had spread to the large Algerian population in France, and the well-attested stories of atrocities committed by the French troops were turning world opinion against France. French participation in the Suez episode of 1956 generated further discredit and made it easier for the FLN to gain international support. All the efforts of the French army, all the excesses which could be justified only by a 'quick kill' and an end to the rising, could not destroy the independence movement.

There was no compromise. From the outset the FLN behaved like a revolutionary government. The country was divided into *wilayas*, operational areas for the Armée de Libération National, and *mintaquas*, on which FLN civil administration was to operate. FLN areas were often better administered than those in French hands. But neither France nor the nationalists could win the war. France proceeded to lose it by the collapse of the home front. French political institutions proved incapable of sustaining another unpopular war, or of solving the riddle posed by Algeria. The key issue was France's attitude towards the *pied noir* community. No French politician could bring himself to admit that the only solution was exile for the *pieds noirs* and independence for Algeria. And there was a further complication with the discovery of oil in the Algerian desert, which made the territory infinitely more worthwhile as a part of metropolitan France.

The answer to all these problems was found in the imposing figure of General Charles de Gaulle, who had been waiting for a decade to receive the call to save the nation. De Gaulle's answer was to think the unthinkable, and to accomplish it. He wooed the army, who had united with the *pieds noirs* in defence of the status quo, and then duped them. He began serious talks with the FLN disguised by a series of *ex cathedra* declarations against independence – justifying the nickname given to him of 'the prince of ambiguity'.[3] From his accession to power in May 1958, de Gaulle pursued a zig-zag path, but it led

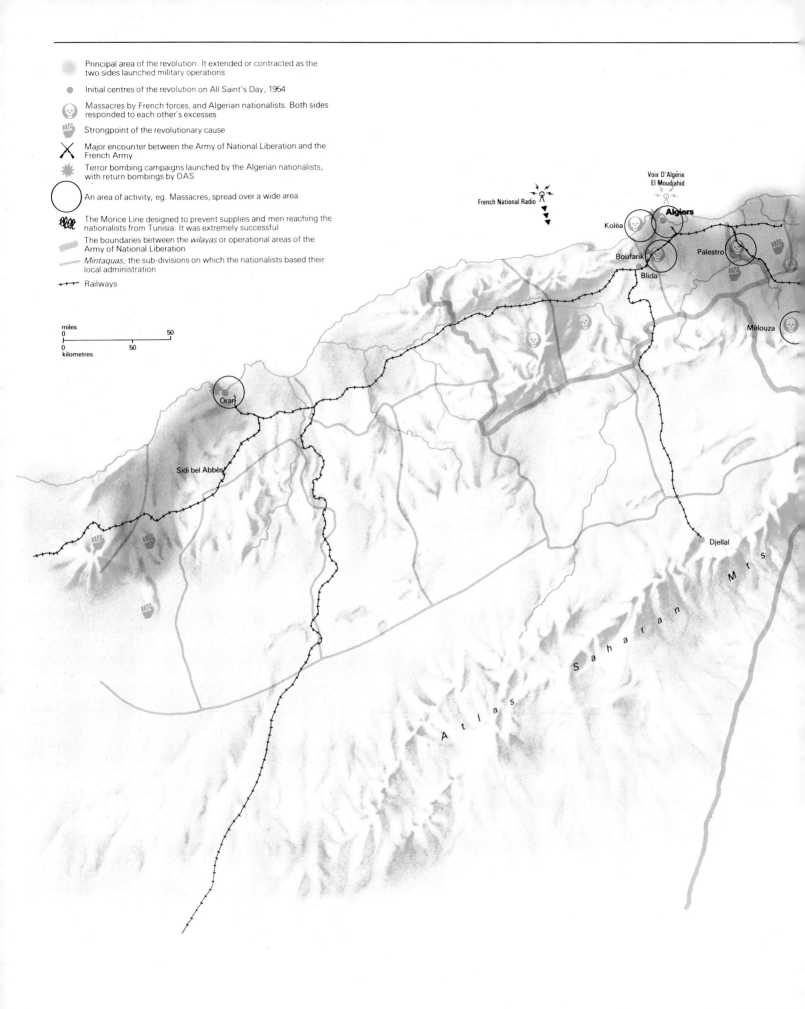

Principal area of the revolution. It extended or contracted as the two sides launched military operations

Initial centres of the revolution on All Saint's Day, 1954

Massacres by French forces, and Algerian nationalists. Both sides responded to each other's excesses

Strongpoint of the revolutionary cause

Major encounter between the Army of National Liberation and the French Army

Terror bombing campaigns launched by the Algerian nationalists, with return bombings by OAS

An area of activity, eg. Massacres, spread over a wide area

The Morice Line designed to prevent supplies and men reaching the nationalists from Tunisia. It was extremely successful

The boundaries between the *wilayas* or operational areas of the Army of National Liberation

Mintaquas; the sub-divisions on which the nationalists based their local administration

Railways

miles
0   50

0   50
kilometres

French National Radio

Voix D'Algérie
El Moudjahid

Algiers

Koléa

Boufarik

Blida

Palestro

Mèlouza

Oran

Sidi bel Abbès

Djellal

Atlas Saharan Mts

inexorably towards independence. At the same time he launched a more effective attack on the FLN strongholds – Operation Binoculars against Kabylia (July 1958) – than had ever been attempted before. In pursuit of this plan over a million Moslem villagers were concentrated in what were called 'regroupment camps', and vast areas of the country were devastated to prevent supplies reaching the fighters in the mountains. De Gaulle's attitude towards Algeria, as far as it can be discerned in the cloud of dis-information which he exuded, remained constant. As he expressed it in June 1958: 'L'Afrique est foutue, et l'Algérie avec' ('Africa is done for, and Algeria with it').[4]

The cities of Algeria went to the barricades, and the *pieds noirs* vowed a war to the death. The OAS, Organisation de l'Armée Secrète, began a bombing campaign in Algeria, and a terror campaign in France in the autumn of 1960. After the French electorate voted for de Gaulle in January 1961, the army prepared a coup to replace him. But when the mutiny was enacted in April 1961, it quickly collapsed. By French national radio de Gaulle appealed to the conscript soldiers and the NCOs not to follow their mutinous officers. Only those units like the paratroops and the Foreign Legion, dedicated to their officers, followed the call to revolt. With the defeat of the mutiny and public support at home, de Gaulle proceeded towards granting independence. The mindless atrocities committed by the OAS killed any residual sentimental attachment to Algeria in French minds, and the final negotiations, although protracted because of the nationalists' refusal to compromise, reached their inevitable conclusion in July 1962.

Few wars of national liberation have been marked by so much savagery on every side. Once the *pieds noirs* had left, to Spain, Canada, Israel and Argentina, as well as over a million to France, the killing of those Moslems who had supported France began. The OAS continued its war, for motives of revenge alone, now that Algeria had gone. France was the main beneficiary of peace. The last great colonial sore had been excised, and de Gaulle had found the technique of dealing briskly with other colonial embarrassments. The French economy, released from the burdens of a huge military budget, leaped ahead. Algeria, the new nation, continued its revolution in private. The lessons of Algeria have been widely publicized, and the overall conclusion that it was a political rather than a military victory for the nationalists is correct. But the conduct of the war, with the determined use of terror as an instrument of policy, a terrain which never allowed the complete annihilation of guerrilla resistance, and a remarkable capacity to absorb appalling setbacks over a long period, should have taught other revolutionaries a lesson they failed to learn.

A thirty years' war

THE empire which France assembled in Indo China in the last half of the nineteenth century was a perpetual source of trouble. Resistance and conspiracy seemed to be second nature to the Viet peoples of the eastern coastal area, while the inhabitants of the hills and mountains had never succumbed to outside rule by anyone. The French administered Vietnam through the native kingdoms of Tonkin and Annam in the north and the colony of Cochin China in the south, with its capital in Saigon. Regionalism was an immensely strong historical tendency exaggerated by the facts of geography, for at its narrowest point, the country is less than fifty miles wide, from the border with Laos to the sea. The core of Viet culture was to be found in the north and centre of the country, as was the long tradition of resistance to outside pressure, whether from China or, more recently, from France. The southern part of the country was settled much later than the north, and the settlers developed a society very different from that centred on the Red River.

During the 1920s and 1930s there were a number of sporadic eruptions against the French, mostly the work of the Vietnamese Nationalist Party, founded in 1927 in Hanoi. But it was a tiny group – never more than 1500 strong, about the same size as the Communist party. The Communists themselves were riven by internal disputes, and one insurrectionary attempt to create village soviets was quickly disposed of by the French. One consequence of this débâcle was the rise to power of Ho Chi Minh, who did not favour this style of adventurism.

The Communists found it easier to make converts in the more relaxed political environment of the north than in the more strictly supervised French colony in the south. By the time of the Japanese entry into Vietnam in September 1940, the Communists had formed the Viet Minh (the League for the Independence of Vietnam) ostensibly a nationalist organization appealing to all patriots but in fact dominated by a largely Communist leadership. Its main claim for popular support was its confident aim of launching a guerrilla war to drive out the French. There were only 35,000 Japanese troops occupying the whole of the country, while the remaining French Vichy forces were not willing to undertake major campaigns. These proved perfect conditions in which to build a clandestine army in areas not under the direct control of either Japan or Vichy France. The core area of the guerrilla army was in the Cao Bang region close to the Chinese border, but Viet Minh control had spread by the end of the war through much of the mountainous Thai Nguyen and adjoining provinces.

Ho Chi Minh arrived in Thai Nguyen in 1944, and set up his headquarters in a group of limestone caves secure from French interference. By then, the Viet Minh groups had also established bases in the lowlands of the Red River delta. On 9 March 1945 the Japanese interned the remaining French officials and soldiers and turned the administration over to the Vietnamese, and thus the Viet Minh rapidly achieved a dominant position in the north, avoiding clashes with the Japanese. When the surrender came suddenly in August 1945, the Viet Minh were taken by surprise, but quickly rallied and seized power, securely in the north and less so in the south where other groups of nationalists were still strong. On 2 September 1945 Ho Chi Minh proclaimed the Democratic Republic of Vietnam. Power seemed to have fallen into his hands like a ripe apple.

The plans of the Allies were very different. By agreement, the French were to be restored to possession of their colonies, and detachments of British troops began to arrive in Saigon early in September. The north, by virtue of the Potsdam Agreement, was to be recovered for France by Chinese forces, which quickly occupied the country of north and central Vietnam. They were faced by a Viet Minh army swollen with eager if ill-trained recruits. This army, under its commander Vo Nguyen Giap, had taken possession of both the Japanese and French arsenals, providing some 60,000 rifles, 3000 light machine guns and some artillery, together with plentiful ammunition. It was not, as the French would find in Algeria, an insurrection equipped with a few old sporting guns, but an army equipped with modern military equipment. This treasure trove of arms led both Giap and his French adversaries into a series of misapprehensions. Giap mistook men armed with modern equipment for a force capable of defeating the French in conventional warfare, while the French fell into the opposite error and equated the Viet Minh with bandits or terrorists to be subdued with superior western technology.

When the long-expected conflict began in November 1946 in Haiphong, the French drove the Viet Minh from the city, while the bulk of Viet Minh troops were withdrawn to the guerrilla bases south of the Red River delta and into the mountain redoubt of Thai Nguyen, known as the Viet Bac. Defence of Hanoi was left to local Viet Minh militia, who when overwhelmed by the French simply merged into the population. For almost two years, each side jockeyed for position. The Viet Minh set in motion a hectic campaign of propaganda and recruitment in the countryside, all the time trying to consolidate a position among the population. In both north and south, while the French held the towns and cities, the countryside belonged to the Viet Minh. They concentrated on building up base areas, along the lines advocated by Mao Tse Tung, in inaccessible zones, while guerrilla operations were mounted continuously but on a limited scale to probe the weak points of the French. By 1949 the French forces in Vietnam numbered more than 150,000, yet there was no visible enemy for them to fight. In October 1949 the Red Army finally triumphed in China and Ho Chi Minh now

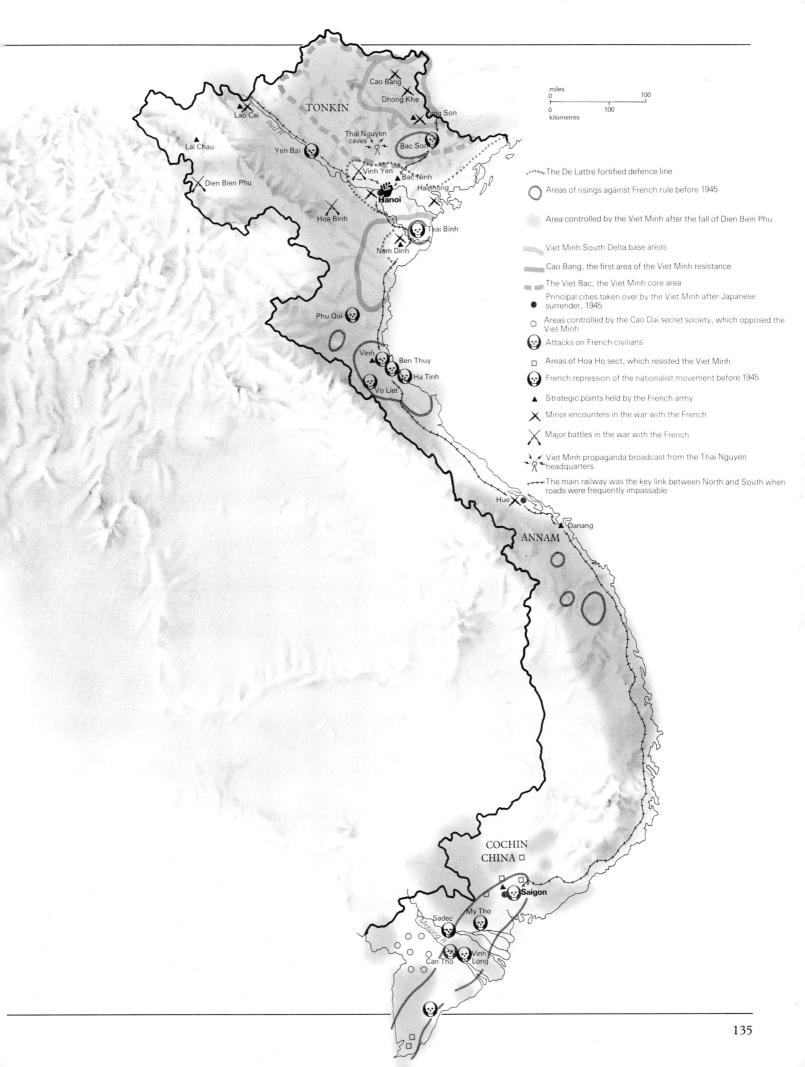

TONKIN

Cao Bang

Dhong Khe

Lang Son

Lao Cai

Thai Nguyen caves

Bac Son

Lai Chau

Red R.

Yen Bai

Vinh Yen

Dien Bien Phu

Bac Ninh

Haiphong

Hoa Binh

Hanoi

Nam Dinh

Thai Binh

Phu Qui

Vinh

Ben Thuy

Ha Tinh

Vo Liet

ANNAM

Hue

Danang

COCHIN
CHINA

Saigon

My Tho

Sadec

Mekong R.

Can Tho

Vinh
Long

miles
0   100
0   100
kilometres

.... The De Lattre fortified defence line

◯ Areas of risings against French rule before 1945

Area controlled by the Viet Minh after the fall of Dien Bien Phu

Viet Minh South Delta base areas

Cao Bang, the first area of the Viet Minh resistance

The Viet Bac, the Viet Minh core area

● Principal cities taken over by the Viet Minh after Japanese surrender, 1945

○ Areas controlled by the Cao Dai secret society, which opposed the Viet Minh

☠ Attacks on French civilians

☐ Areas of Hoa Ho sect, which resisted the Viet Minh

☠ French repression of the nationalist movement before 1945

▲ Strategic points held by the French army

✕ Minor encounters in the war with the French

✕ Major battles in the war with the French

Viet Minh propaganda broadcast from the Thai Nguyen headquarters

The main railway was the key link between North and South when roads were frequently impassable

135

possessed an open border with a major ally at his back. With artillery supplied from China, Giap began a series of operations in early 1950 to clear the forward French positions from the highland areas. These attacks were not entirely successful, but the French, rather than be cut off, eventually withdrew their bases. These easy victories encouraged the Viet Minh to think that the French could be pushed back with equal ease from the cities of the delta. In January 1951 Giap threw 22,000 men into battle against 10,000 French for control of the southern delta. Of the 22,000 over 6000 were killed with another 7000 wounded, many of them by the French use of air-power to strafe and bomb the massed formations with napalm. It was a catastrophic rate of loss. On the French side the new French commander General de Lattre de Tassigny recognized how narrow the margin of victory had been, and decided to construct a major fortified line to protect the heartland of the delta. It was a major enterprise, fully in the impressive French tradition of Vauban and the great fortresses of the seventeenth century. Critics condemned it as being a new Maginot line. Both judgments had an element of truth. It succeeded in protecting Hanoi, Haiphong and the delta until almost the end of the war, but it took the offensive edge off the French army in doing so. Twenty battalions were required to garrison it. Equally unfortunately, a Viet Minh base area was included in the protected zone.

Both sides seemed to seek the type of encounter at which they were least successful. Giap continued to mount conventional large-scale attacks on French prepared positions, while the French tried a sudden sally to take Hoa Binh west of Hanoi, and were nearly cut off when the Viet Minh severed their lines of communication. The same happened to the massive 'Operation Lorraine' of October 1952, launched by de Lattre de Tassigny's successor, General Salan. A long armoured column pushed forward along the river valley until it reached 100 miles north-west of the de Lattre line, but it too was ambushed and forced to retreat in some haste. Salan's replacement, General Henri de Navarre, found that of his 190,000 troops, 100,000 were tied down in defensive positions, and that the initiative lay with the Viet Minh. He gambled on creating at Dien Bien Phu a strong defensive position that would fester in the heart of Viet Minh country, drawing their forces to attack it, and preventing their use either in the delta or in an invasion of Laos. It was the old Verdun gambit, the hammer and the anvil. Unfortunately, it was his troops and not the Viet Minh who were trapped upon the anvil. The plans to supply the base depended on air transport to supply the 15,000 crack troops placed there. The valley in which the camp lay was vulnerable to heavy artillery fire, but Navarre believed (wrongly) that the Viet Minh only possessed light guns. The dense vegetation on the sides of the valley and the hills made it impossible to strafe enemy supply columns from the air. Even the strategic plan behind the operation was cloudy; the local commander wanted to use it as a base for counter-guerrillas, with whom the French had achieved considerable success further north.

The loss of Dien Bien Phu after an epic siege of 55 days was a military catastrophe for the French, although the Viet Minh lost more – 8000 dead, and more than 20,000 casualties overall. It was the last card the French army had to play, and the first major positional battle which the Viet Minh had won. The French lost because they were not able to use what technological advantage they possessed in terms of air power, and because the supply advantage lay with the Viet Minh. The result of this victory in the field was the Geneva Conference in which France reluctantly conceded independence to all her territories in Indo China, in agreements which came into force in July 1954. Vietnam was to be partitioned into two states, much against the wishes of the North Vietnamese. Ho Chi Minh was persuaded that the country would be reunited with the elections which were to be held within a year of the agreement. But since neither the new government of South Vietnam nor the United States were party to this agreement, such thinking was largely wishful. More reasonably, the Viet Minh had gained the independence of the north, where the bulk of their army and support lay. Northerners had never had much interest in the south, and

The army of North Vietnam in action near Quang Tri, South Vietnam, 9 May 1972. After the entry of the American ground forces in 1965 the North Vietnamese regulars took an increasing part in the war for the South

although many cadres were secretly left behind in the south after the official withdrawal of Viet Minh units from below the 17th Parallel, support was very localized. In a number of areas the Communists remained in control as much after 1954 as they had before, but these were in the base zones peripheral to the main centres of power in the south. The new republic of North Vietnam had neither the resources nor the will to mount a full-scale war for the south in the aftermath of the Geneva accords.

The key instrument of change was the position of the United States. The Americans had declined French pleas for assistance, but the USA was not prepared to see South East Asia fall to Communism, as President Eisenhower expressed it in April 1954 in an uncharacteristically graphic phrase, 'like a set of dominoes'. The new government of South Vietnam, nominally under the former Emperor of Annam, Bao Dai, became the recipient of Eisenhower's version of President Roosevelt's 'All aid short of war' to beleaguered Britain. The strong man around whom the new South Vietnam would coalesce was a Catholic politician, in exile since 1949, Ngo Dinh Diem. With the financial backing of the United States he was able to create a power base, to curb the secret societies who had run much of the south in the last years of the French, and to neutralize the fragments of old nationalist parties. Diem was able to reverse many of the land redistribution programmes set in hand by the Viet Minh and to restore land to the original landlords. In time he clashed with almost every interest-group within the state, but he was able, for the most part, to bend them to his will. What he failed to do was provide any counter to the renewal of Communist agitation in the countryside which began in 1957, after he had cancelled the reunification elections in the previous year.

The United States was well aware of the need to secure the countryside, and sought to pour money into various schemes for rural indoctrination and stabilization. The British, experts in counter-insurgency, advised on a 'strategic hamlets' programme similar to the one found so successful in Malaya. It was a failure in Vietnam, largely because the government refused to offer anything positive. Indeed, it demanded both extra taxes and labour service from the villagers. Moreover, the comparison with Malaya was false. There the scheme had been aimed largely at landless sharecroppers, who were given land of their own. In Vietnam the tightly knit village societies were disrupted and often transported to farm inferior or unbroken ground. It was a policy dictated from above by men who would not know one end of a hoe from another, administratively logical but utter failures in practical terms. The NLF, National Liberation Front, as the new Communist-dominated nationalist group was known, operated on different premises. Propaganda was conceived to appeal at the village level. Teams travelled from village to village,

flattered villagers, performed little plays with a political message as well as good entertainment value. Frequently, group leaders came from the locality and could pitch their propaganda in specific local terms. The constant theme was that, through struggle, the villagers could eventually achieve a social revolution for themselves. Making converts was the prime activity even for guerrilla fighters, most of whose time was taken up by political work in the villages. The military technique of the NLF was initially to split guerrilla groups into small sections who lived and worked in the villages until they united for an operation. In consequence the NLF had remarkably good intelligence which was able to direct when terror tactics should be applied against government sympathizers or officials. The armed struggle was used to demonstrate the feebleness of the government. The war for the countryside was lost before the United States committed its ground forces to action in 1965.

The NLF in the south was not simply a puppet controlled by the Ho Chi Minh government in the north. There were occasions when the NLF forces on the ground failed to follow the course of action laid down by Hanoi. The real control exercised by the north was logistical. The movement in the south depended for its growth on the supplies passed down the Ho Chi Minh trail in Laos and Cambodia and then moved across the frontier to the groups in south Vietnam. The Americans located their main bases in enclaves on the coast which could be supplied (or evacuated) by sea. The inland positions tended to be held by élite or specialist troops. The most effective United States effort was in the air, both tactical support for ground forces and strategic raids against North Vietnam designed to disrupt communications and economic life. Following US intervention, the

The Communist philosophy of guerrilla war concentrated on persuading the people to take part in their own 'struggle for freedom'. Active guerrillas were used for political work to stimulate the peasants to become active supporters or militia: 1967 regular army of North Vietnam became more and more involved in the struggle for the south, especially around the border area with the north, known somewhat ironically as the De-Militarized Zone (DMZ). This became one of the main killing grounds, both for the Americans and for the NLF and North Vietnamese regulars. But nothing the Americans could do by the application of military power altered the basic fact that the NLF controlled most of the countryside in the south, and in some cases had done so since 1945. The campaign organized by the US Special Forces to train the *montagnard* peoples, traditional enemies of the Vietnamese, had some success, but as a group they were difficult to exploit in a major way by foreigners. The NLF had their own campaign among the *montagnards*, but using *montagnard* tribesmen trained in the north. In fact the *montagnards* proved a doubtful weapon both for the Americans and the NLF.

In the period from the death of Diem in 1963, which was organized with the connivance of the American government to whom he had become a political liability, to the death of Ho Chi Minh in 1969, the war moved from a guerrilla and low-intensity campaign to a full-scale war waged in a number of styles and over a number of fronts. The indirect or guerrilla style continued, but the brunt of the fighting was taken over by regular forces. In January 1968 the strength of the NLF and the Vietnamese People's Army – the regular forces of the north – revealed itself in the south in the Tet offensive, which took place at the New Year season when hostilities were traditionally at a low ebb. For the first time, the northerners showed their hands in the cities. In one sense they failed, for they failed to topple the government in the south, but they also demonstrated the strength of the revolutionary movement on the ground. The propaganda of the southern government had pushed the line that in alliance with the United States, the greatest military power in the world, they were bound to triumph. Tet sowed strong seeds of doubt, and the NLF achieved a dominant psychological advantage over the army of South Vietnam.

In America the human cost of the war roused a surging wave of hostility, and the American military began to look for operations which would achieve a decisive result. In July 1969 President Nixon indicated that the USA would in future avoid entanglements like Vietnam, although he remained committed to victory. The process of grudging concession had begun. Bombing of North Vietnam had been suspended, largely because of international opposition, in October 1968; in March 1969 the massacre of villagers at My Lai by American troops again branded the Americans as warmongers. The assault on the NLF strongholds by the Cambodian border undertaken in May 1970 was an attempt to strike a blow at a key point with maximum force. The Cambodian episode achieved limited local success, and dented the NLF supply system, but it was not a major reverse. An incursion into Laos by the army of South Vietnam with American support in February 1970 was even less successful.

The disentanglement of the United States from Vietnam was accomplished in stages during 1972. The last American ground forces guarding the Danang base ceased operations in August 1972. Great efforts were put into training the army of South Vietnam to hold the Communist forces on their own. For a time they maintained the *status quo*, but the attempt to organize a phased withdrawal in 1974–5 became a rout, and in the spring of 1975 the thirty years' war ended in complete victory for the armies of the north and the NLF. Certainly the NLF was more authentically the voice of the southern country people than the government in Saigon. Once the north triumphed in 1975, many of the southerners prominent in the NLF were purged. Unification meant rule from Hanoi.

In writing about the war Vo Nguyen Giap, the military mind behind it, declared: 'The War of Liberation is a protracted war and a hard war in which we must rely upon ourselves – for we are strong politically but weak materially while the enemy is very weak politically but stronger materially. . . .'[1] The society of the north had been waging wars of resistance for centuries, and had the discipline and cohesion, brutally enforced by mechanisms controlled by the Communist party, to withstand the strains of the war with America. The United States, susceptible to so many internal and international pressures, was not able to fight for a generation in a cause which became as unpopular as Vietnam did. Ultimately the war was won by those with the will to win.

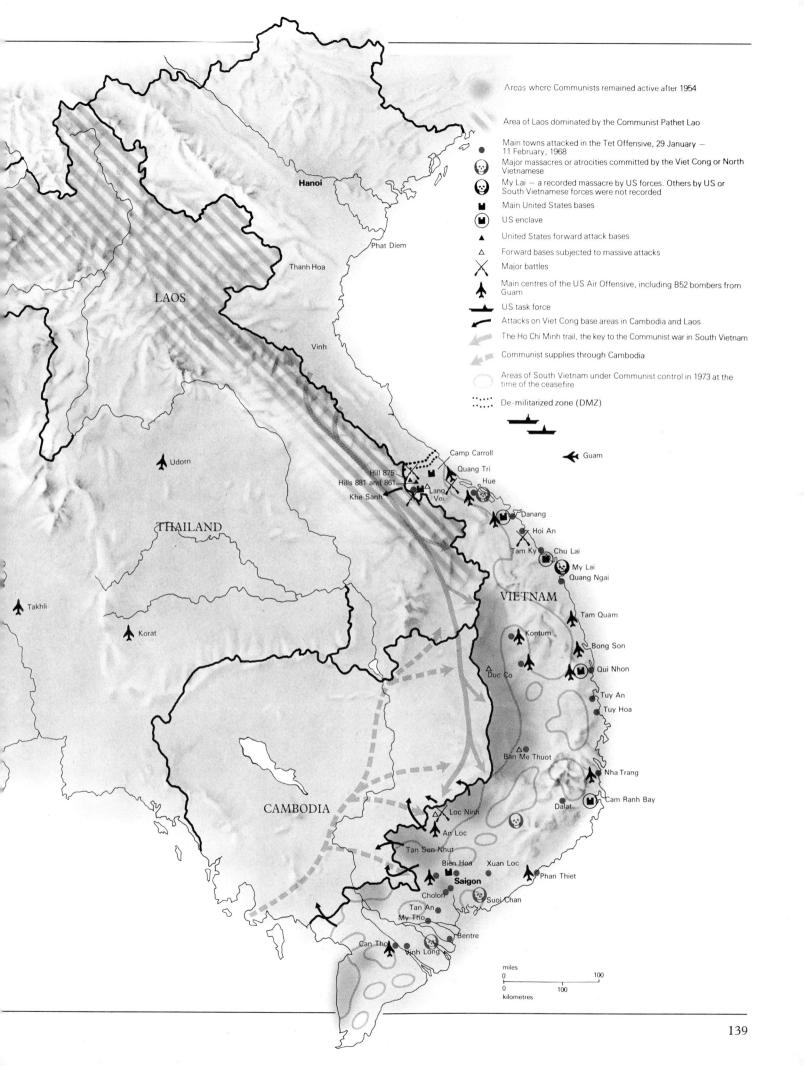

Areas where Communists remained active after 1954

Area of Laos dominated by the Communist Pathet Lao

● Main towns attacked in the Tet Offensive, 29 January – 11 February, 1968

☻ Major massacres or atrocities committed by the Viet Cong or North Vietnamese

☻ My Lai — a recorded massacre by US forces. Others by US or South Vietnamese forces were not recorded

▆ Main United States bases

⊕ US enclave

▲ United States forward attack bases

△ Forward bases subjected to massive attacks

✕ Major battles

✈ Main centres of the US Air Offensive, including B52 bombers from Guam

━ US task force

↵ Attacks on Viet Cong base areas in Cambodia and Laos

➡ The Ho Chi Minh trail, the key to the Communist war in South Vietnam

⇢ Communist supplies through Cambodia

◯ Areas of South Vietnam under Communist control in 1973 at the time of the ceasefire

⋯ De-militarized zone (DMZ)

Hanoi

Phat Diem

Thanh Hoa

LAOS

Vinh

THAILAND

✈ Udorn

✈ Takhli

✈ Korat

✈ Guam

Camp Carroll

Hill 875
Hills 881 and 861
Khe Sanh
Lang Vei
Quang Tri
Hue

Danang
Hoi An
Tam Ky ✕ Chu Lai
My Lai
Quang Ngai

VIETNAM

Tam Quam

Kontum
Bong Son
△ Duc Co
Qui Nhon

Tuy An
Tuy Hoa

△ Ban Me Thuot

Nha Trang

Cam Ranh Bay
Dalat

CAMBODIA

✕ Loc Ninh
An Loc

Tan Son Nhut

Bien Hoa   Xuan Loc
Saigon   Phan Thiet
Cholon
Suoi Chan
Tan An
My Tho
Bentre

Can Tho
Vinh Long

miles
0 ———————————— 100
0 ———————— 100
kilometres

The struggle for *enosis*

BRITAIN occupied Cyprus in 1878, deftly removing the island from the nerveless grasp of the Ottoman Empire, but more in the interests of strategic tidiness than of imperial expansion. Cyprus dominated the whole of the Eastern Mediterranean in an arc from Anatolia to Egypt, and it had been a pawn in Mediterranean politics for more than two thousand years. The main political theme of the island was a desire among the Greek population for a union with Greece, hundreds of miles to the northwest. The minority Turkish population traditionally played no part in politics. The emotional force of the call for 'enosis' – Union – was recognized by the British who even offered the island to the Greeks in 1915 as a bribe to persuade them to enter the war on the Allied side, an offer which was not taken up by Athens. Britain's sole interest in the island rested on its strategic value. There were few commercial issues to defend, no expatriate settler communities to complicate the political issues. 'Enosis', however, was seen to threaten fundamental British military commitments in the Middle East and elsewhere. It was tacitly acknowledged that over 95 per cent of the Greek population had voted, in a poll taken in 1950, for union with Greece; Britain's answer was a complete denial that *enosis* would ever be possible. The Minister of State for the Colonies, Henry Hopkinson, declared in July 1954: 'It has always been understood . . . that there are certain territories in the Commonwealth which, owing to their particular circumstances, can never expect to be fully independent . . . the question of the abrogation of British sovereignty cannot arise. . . .'[1] In his reply for the Opposition, Richard Crossman predicted the course of future events with grim accuracy: 'The tragedy of the Middle East is that there is not a country whose people got their rights from the British without murder.'[2]

Faced with British intransigence, the leaders of Cypriot society, in particular the Orthodox Church under Michael Mouskos, Archbishop Makarios III, began to think in terms of a campaign of violence to force the British to the conference table. Makarios stood for *enosis*, the banner behind which Greek Cypriots would rally, but eventually he came to accept independence without *enosis* as an alternative. Unlike the leader of the guerrilla fighters, George Grivas, whose dedication to *enosis* was fanatical and total, Makarios was a realist prepared to take what he could get.

George Grivas was Cypriot by birth, but had taken Greek nationality. His experience of guerrilla warfare began in Anatolia in 1921, continued through the Second World War against the Germans, and continued after the war with a subversive group called χ (Khi) which attacked Communists and any others whom Grivas decided to proscribe. He began to lay plans in 1948 for the violent liberation of the land of his birth and the achievement of *enosis*, but he found it difficult to raise much support on the island for a guerrilla war. The furthest Makarios would go was to accept that sabotage could be used. From the days of planning and organization onwards, Grivas worked against rather than with the Cypriot hierarchy around Makarios; only when he faced them with a guerrilla war as a *fait accompli* did they fall in reluctantly behind him.

Grivas was a meticulous planner. A small quantity of arms were smuggled into the Paphos area, which was by tradition the most militant and violent part of the island. He recognized that in a small island guerrillas would always be at a disadvantage if they could not become invisible within the population. Even the Troodos Mountains, where many guerrilla bases were to be located, was small enough to be combed through by troops. Grivas' technique was based on small groups dedicated to sabotage and guerrilla warfare, based in safe houses and camps in the countryside but operating within the towns and against lines of communication. The terrain and patterns of occupation posed definite limits on the scope of any revolutionary action. EOKA, as the nationalist force called itself, was designed to destabilize British rule, and to force the British into the type of repressive measures which would brand them as oppressors of colonial minorities before world opinion. Actions which might be dismissed as insignificant pinpricks individually would become a major irritation when they occurred continuously. It was a war waged to achieve a propaganda effect. This limited, instinctive terror was a peculiar talent of Grivas'. When larger-scale operations were attempted, such as an economic boycott of British goods, they were a dismal failure. Bombings of soft targets, assassination and intimidation were the preferred EOKA tactics, since they corresponded to their limited numbers and equipment. Their main targets were Greek Cypriots, especially community leaders hostile to EOKA. Even more important were the Greeks in the Cyprus police who would be crucial to any British counter to EOKA terror tactics. Thus, of the 238 civilians killed between April 1955 and March 1959, 203 were Greek Cypriots.[3] All policy was determined by Grivas, but his contact with the twenty-two EOKA sub-regions which covered the island was limited. Much of their political as opposed to military effort was devoted to rousing young Greek Cypriots to revolt, and some schools were hotbeds of nationalist activity. Demonstrations were organized often with the purpose of provoking a violent British response. The British reaction, after the experience of Malaya and Kenya, was both precise and reasonably effective. Huge concentrations of troops were used to clear areas, like the 25,000 soldiers used to break up the guerrilla bases in the Troodos and Paphos mountains. Communities were fined for guerrilla activity in their locality, while rewards were offered for information. They sought to decapitate the political leadership by removing Makarios, as they had done with Kenyatta in Kenya.

But short of the programmes of population re-loc-ation which had been undertaken in Kenya and Malaya, and which the French had found successful in Algeria, the pinpricks of urban terror were impossible to contain. EOKA fought back with more terror and more denunciation of the British camps for EOKA prisoners – Camp K near Nicosia, Platres, and Omorphita – as 'British Belsens'.

The most serious element in the war was the rousing of the Turks. They were strong in the police force, and more Turkish than Greek police were killed. The Turkish community began to feel embattled, Turks began to arm, and a Turkish version of EOKA, the TMT, was set up: 'The day is near when you will be called upon to sacrifice your life and blood in the PARTITION struggle.... All Turkdom, right and justice and God are with you. PARTITION OR DEATH!' were the words of a pamphlet circulated in Larnaca in May 1958.[4] On 12 June, Turks massacred a group of Greek Cypriots near the village of Geunyeli, and inter-communal strife spread into the cities. Partition was held up as the alternative to *enosis*, and there were strong appeals for Turkey to intervene. EOKA now turned its forces on the Turks and a civil war seemed likely. Under these circumstances the rather languid British attempts to negotiate a settlement were inspired with a new sense of urgency. In fact, the strategic significance of Cyprus had diminished, and furthermore, neither the Turkish nor Greek Governments wanted to be dragged into confrontation over the Cyprus question. All the main protagonists had an imperative need to reach a settlement. On 19 February 1959, after prolonged negotiations, an agreement was signed in London for an independent Cyprus. On 1 March Makarios returned from three years of banish-

April 1956: searches near the Troodos mountains for EOKA guerillas. Note the EOKA slogan on the building: the whole area was fervent in its support for the movement

ment to a hero's welcome. Grivas and EOKA wanted to fight on, to achieve *enosis*, but in the face of the determination of the Greek government to accept the independence solution, *enosis* was not on offer. The new republic of Cyprus came into being on 16 August 1960, with a complex electoral system guaranteeing both Greek and Turkish interests.

Peace, however, did not come with independence. The passions roused by the guerrilla campaigns, and the fears of the minority, did not disappear. The party for *enosis* prepared for an attack on the enemy, the Turks, and in August 1964, Grivas returned to lead them. Despite the involvement of the United Nations, the situation drifted by stages towards open war, a process hastened by the seizure of power by the Greek colonels in 1967. Their covert dedication to *enosis* gave an impetus to Greek nationalism in Cyprus. EOKA began to see in Makarios an obstacle to the longed-for union with the motherland, and in July 1974, the Cyprus National Guard led by Greek army officers mounted a coup against him. Makarios was replaced by an ex-EOKA man. But the Archbishop escaped his pursuers, reached the Troodos Mountains and eventually the safety of one of the British sovereign bases, whose existence he had agreed to in the treaty of independence. While he attacked the usurpation, Turkish troops landed in the Kyrenia area to establish partition. Since July 1974 the island has been divided.

Superficially, the course of the war in Cyprus seems routine. There were relatively few casualties and the guerrilla movement was feeble by comparison with the contemporary movements in Vietnam or Algeria. The significance of Cyprus was that it showed, almost for the first time, that wars could be waged, not for ground, but for public opinion and the political will of an opponent. Britain's interest in Cyprus was practical, not emotional. As the war in the island developed it seemed likely to precipitate a crisis in NATO and the collapse of the eastern strategy which the island base existed to support. At the outset of the war, British opinion was indifferent except for a small left-wing minority opposed to the British approach. The tactics of terror, especially the murder of British soldiers' wives in Famagusta in October 1958, produced violent responses by British soldiers. After the Famagusta episode, 256 Cypriots

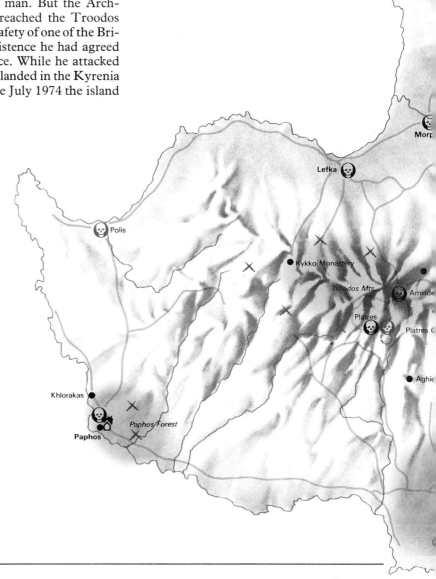

were injured in the course of a round-up of about 1000 suspects. Some regiments like the Parachute Regiment were renowned for having short tempers, and the commandos and paratroopers were notorious for their rough handling of suspects.[5] This random and usually unplanned violence was used by EOKA to mount a campaign against British brutality which was reflected in the British and foreign press. The effect on Britain was to rouse public opinion from torpor to anger, and then to a desire to be finished with Cyprus. On the international scene, it forced Britain on to the defensive. In the end the British yielded nothing of substance. The agreement for two bases totalling 99 square miles corresponded neatly to Britain's revised strategic needs, and at a much lower cost. The lesson of Cyprus was that terror alone, in the right context, is not just a weapon of last resort, but a preferred tactic.

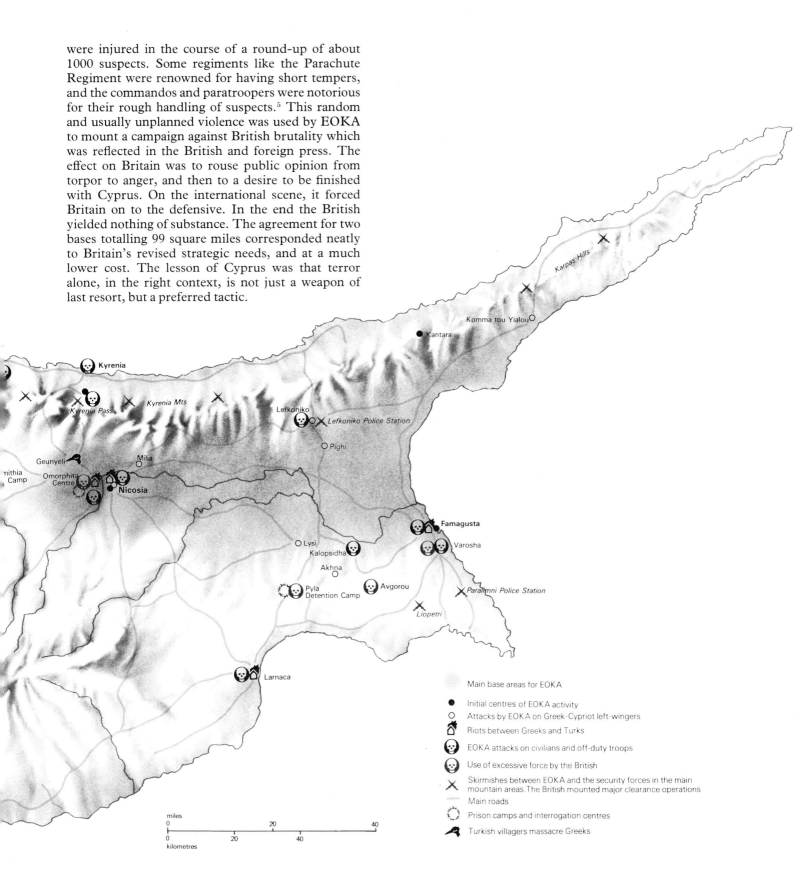

Main base areas for EOKA

● Initial centres of EOKA activity

○ Attacks by EOKA on Greek-Cypriot left-wingers

Riots between Greeks and Turks

EOKA attacks on civilians and off-duty troops

Use of excessive force by the British

✕ Skirmishes between EOKA and the security forces in the main mountain areas. The British mounted major clearance operations

Main roads

Prison camps and interrogation centres

Turkish villagers massacre Greeks

miles
0   20   40

0   20   40
kilometres

Part 4

THE REVOLUTIONARY MIRAGE

CHINA 1923–76

Forging the Communist revolution

WHEN nine future leaders of the Communist party – among them the son of a Hunan peasant, Mao Tse Tung – met in an upper room of a deserted girls' school in the French sector of Shanghai in July 1921, China had effectively been partitioned. The revolution of 1911, which had removed the Manchu from the throne of China and ushered in a Republic, had simply redistributed power to the provinces. Every governor, or leader of a substantial minority community, sought to set himself up as a warlord. The lack of any central authority created large areas of China outside the direct control of any external authority, except when a band of soldiers raided into the countryside to collect taxes, kidnap potential recruits, or wage war against neighbouring warlords. More effectively policed but still outside Chinese control were the foreign enclaves where dissidents could find refuge. This fragmentation was to prove the eventual salvation of the Communist movement in China. But at the meeting in Shanghai, later described as the First Congress of the Chinese Communist Party, the essence of the debate turned on the political question of how best the Communist party could survive and grow in an era of great opportunity. The conclusion, that the Communist party should join hands with the Kuomintang, the national revolutionary party established by Sun Yat Sen after the 1911 revolution, was an attempt to ride on the coat-tails of the more powerful organization.

The Communists were successful in attracting a considerable following among industrial workers and among the miners around Hankow, where the young Mao Tse Tung recruited many members. Communist cells were set up in many cities, but they met with much less success in making converts among the peasants. In 1925 Sun Yat Sen died, and his successors were determined to rid the Kuomintang of its Communist parasites. The military success of the Kuomintang (KMT) had been built on the powerful support of the Soviet Union.

The Russians were attempting a very delicate balancing act. They wished to preserve the vital link with the new leader of the KMT, General Chiang Kai-shek, but also to retain the Chinese Communist Party as the eventual vehicle for creating a Communist China. When in April 1927, Chiang began to suppress the Communists, first in Shanghai and then in the other areas under his control with the aid of a number of Triad societies, he continued to profess friendship for the Soviet Union. This crocodile dance continued while KMT and the Soviet Union manoeuvred for advantage. The principal losers were the Chinese Communists, forced to leap this way and that as the Russians sought to maintain their toehold in China. By 1927 the party was split into numerous factions. Mao Tse Tung, who had been entrusted with liaison with the peasants, saw that a rural base was essential, especially since China was in the throes of a spontaneous peasant rising. Yet his attempt to co-ordinate a military movement against the KMT in Hunan was a failure, and he was forced to flee with the remains of his troops into the mountains of Chingkangshan, a traditional bandit fastness. The failure of this insurrection led to his censure and removal from the *politburo* of the party.

Mao's Autumn Harvest Rising had failed, but not so devastatingly as an urban rising in Canton, which was intended to spark off revolution throughout Kwangtung province. The Communists succeeded in holding the city for two days, and in the reprisals which followed its recapture, anyone bearing the stain of having worn the red kerchief which had identified the rebels was shot out of hand. The American vice-consul watched while 'execution squads patrolled the streets and on finding a suspect, they questioned him, examined his neck for tell-tale red. If found, they then ordered the victim to open his mouth, thrust a revolver into it and another coolie came to the end of his Communist venture. . . .'[1] Another American official reported that 'the slaughter continued for four or five days during

144

Mao Tse Tung in 1938. The architect of Communism in China, Mao was frequently opposed and outvoted in the 1920s and early 1930s. The Long March of 1934–6, although immensely costly in terms of lives, was seen as the salvation of Chinese Communism, and Mao's position became unassailable. The theoretical lessons he drew from the war with the Nationalists and the Japanese were formulated into classic statements of the art of guerrilla warfare

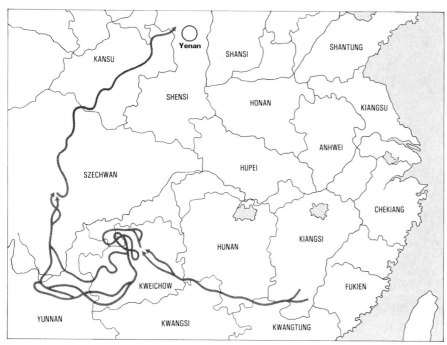

The main route of the epic Long March from south and central
China to Yenan, 1934-5. This was the key formative
influence in the creation of the Communist revolution

miles
0   100   200
0   100   200
kilometres

which some 6000 people, allegedly Communists, lost
their lives in the city of Canton.' The *politburo*, which
had declared confidently before the Canton rising
that they were 'profoundly convinced that all the conditions for victory were joined, and that with good
technical and political technique, victory was as-
sured', were left in a dangerous position by the defeat.
While Mao with his peasants' and workers' army was
relatively secure in the mountains far from any centre
of authority, the Canton refugees were trapped in
Kwangtung at the heart of nationalist power. Only
by degrees could they slip through the enemy lines
to northern Kwangtung and then to join Mao to the
north.

In his base area, Mao was formulating an approach
radically different from that being planned by the
party *politburo* under guidance from Moscow. In his
Problems of Strategy in China's Revolutionary War,
written in 1936, he was later to indicate that the Russians and their Chinese associates tried to apply the
precedents of the Russian revolution and civil war to
Chinese conditions. He described the power of the
Nationalists: 'There is a world of difference between
the Kuomintang army and the Red army. The KMT
controls the key positions or lifelines in the politics,
economy, communications, and culture of China; its
political power is nationwide.' Of his army he said:
'Our political power exists in scattered and isolated
mountainous or remote regions and receives no outside help whatsoever . . . the Red army has no really

consolidated base areas. But . . . our base areas, small
as they are, are politically very powerful and stand
opposed to the enormous KMT régime, while mili-
tarily they place great difficulties in the way of Kuomintang attacks . . . the Red army has great fighting
capacity, because its members are born of the agrarian revolution and are fighting for their own interests.
The KMT, on the other hand, presents a sharp contrast. It opposes the agrarian revolution and therefore
has no support from the peasantry. Though it has a
large army, the KMT cannot make its soldiers and
the many lower-ranking officers . . . risk their lives
willingly for it.'[2] At one point the Red Army under
Mao and Chu Teh had shrunk to about three thousand men, but following the strategy of retreating in
the face of a superior enemy they kept the army in
being, or in Mao's phrase, 'the Red flag flying'. New
bases were created and became magnets for Communists, deserters from the Nationalist armies, disgrun-
tled peasants, all of whom saw the revolutionary base
areas as a point of refuge.

The tactic of retreat lay at the back of the most
remarkable of all the decisions of the war, to begin
a march from the base areas in central China, which
were being regularly subjected to Nationalist campaigns of encirclement, to an area far from the centre
of Nationalist power where they could begin to build
a counter-state. The decision to undertake the Long
March to Yenan was the point at which Mao Tse
Tung and his supporters established a dominant position within the party against the factions supported
by the Soviet Union, which were constantly seeking
to force the path of the revolution into conventional
warfare with the Nationalists and a return of the campaign in the cities. In October 1934 the Red Army
began to move out of central China. In their tortuous
trail to Yenan they crossed eighteen mountain ranges,
passed through twelve provinces, occupied sixty-two
cities, and fought their way past the armies of ten separate warlords, as well as the pursuing armies of
Chiang Kai-shek. Eventually the Red Army reached
Pao An in Shensi, a mere fragment of the 130,000
who had set out, and in December 1936 they established their base in Yenan.

In July 1937 the long-standing quarrel between
China and Japan turned into open war. The consequences of Japanese aggression – the investment of
Shanghai and the seizure of Manchuria to the north-
east of China proper in 1932 – had been a series of
humiliations for the Nationalists and pressures
within the Nationalist camp forced Chiang to abandon his single-minded pursuit of the Communists in
the interests of a united campaign against the common enemy. The Red Army, from its new bases in
Yenan, was well placed to attack the Japanese in the
flank while the Nationalists were pressed back by the
remorseless and well-equipped Japanese army.

Continued on page 150

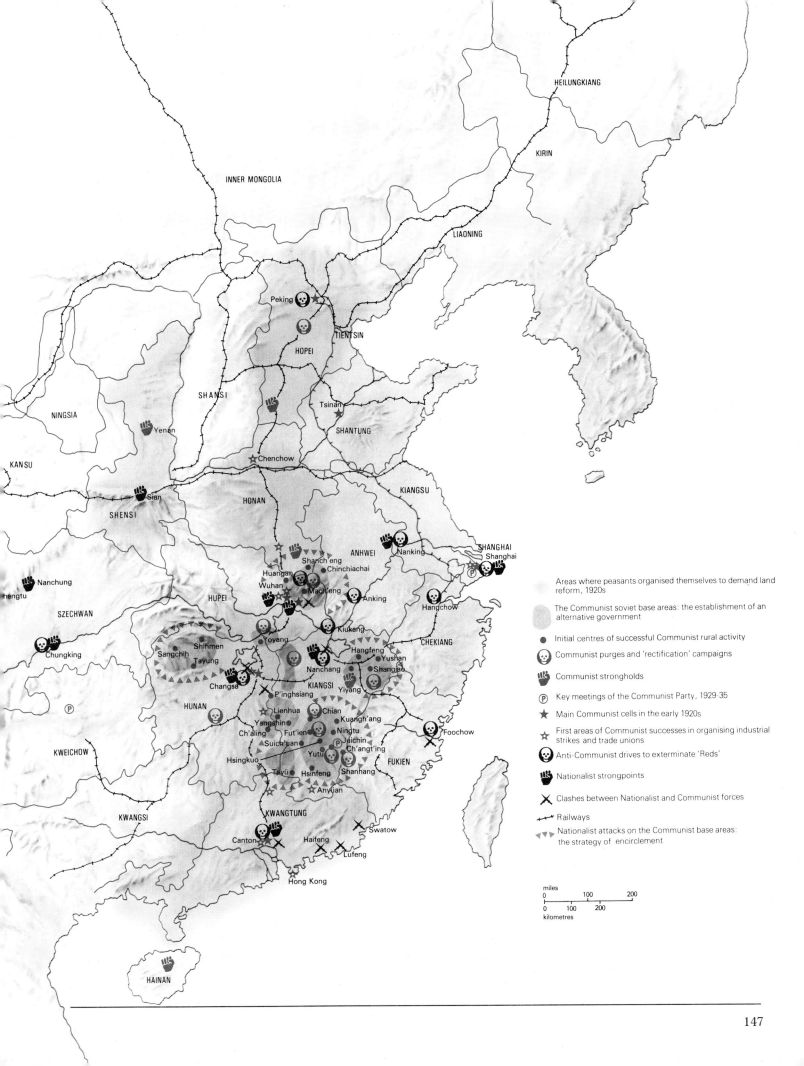

HEILUNGKIANG

KIRIN

INNER MONGOLIA

LIAONING

SHANSI

NINGSIA

Yenan

HOPEI

Peking ☠ ★

☠

TIENTSIN

✊ Tsinan ★

SHANTUNG

KANSU

✊ Sian

SHENSI

Chenchow ☆

HONAN

KIANGSU

ANHWEI

✊ ☠ Nanking

SHANGHAI
Shanghai ☠ ✊

ⓅShanch'eng ✊
Huangan ● Chinchiachai
Wuhan ☠☠ Mach'eng ☠
HUPEI ✊☠ ●Anking
Kiukang ☠

Nanchung ✊

☠hengtu

SZECHWAN

Hangchow ☠

CHEKIANG

☠ Chungking

Yoyang●
Shihmen●
Sangchih Tayung●
Changsa ✊☠
P'inghsiang ✕

Hangfeng ●
Yushan●
Nanchang ☠ Shangjao●
KIANGSI Yiyang ☠

Foochow ☠

HUNAN ☠

Lienhua ☆ Chian ☠
Yangshin ● Kuangh'ang●
Ch'aling ● Fut'ien● Ningtu●
Suich'uan ● ⓅJuichin●
Hsingkuo ● Yutu Ch'angt'ing●
Tayü● Hsinfeng●
Anyüan ☆ Shanhang●

FUKIEN

KWEICHOW

KWANGTUNG

Canton ☠✊ ✕ Haifeng
✕ Swatow
✕
Lufeng ✕

KWANGSI

Hong Kong

HAINAN ✊

Areas where peasants organised themselves to demand land reform, 1920s

The Communist soviet base areas: the establishment of an alternative government

● Initial centres of successful Communist rural activity

☠ Communist purges and 'rectification' campaigns

✊ Communist strongholds

Ⓟ Key meetings of the Communist Party, 1929-35

★ Main Communist cells in the early 1920s

☆ First areas of Communist successes in organising industrial strikes and trade unions

☠ Anti-Communist drives to exterminate 'Reds'

✊ Nationalist strongpoints

✕ Clashes between Nationalist and Communist forces

╋━ Railways

▼▼▼ Nationalist attacks on the Communist base areas: the strategy of encirclement

miles
0 ___ 100 ___ 200
0 ___ 100 ___ 200
kilometres

June 1949: the Red Army
arrives in Nanking,
photographed by Cartier-
Bresson

The advance of the Communists 1945-9. At the end of the war the
Communists held the darkest areas, where they consolidated all
their troops from South and Central China. They concentrated on
winning back Manchuria, which the Nationalists took over in the
wake of the Japanese. Through 1946 and early 1947, the Red Army
took over in much of Manchuria and in Shansi and Shensi,
isolating the Nationalists. By the spring of 1948, the Nationalists
had been driven back into enclaves around the main cities in
Manchuria, and by the autumn, the Communists controlled all of
North and Central China. They then pressed south on a broad
front. By September 1949, the front had reached almost to Amoy.
The Nationalists evacuated to Formosa, leaving their western
armies to flee in Burma and Indo-China.

⬤⬤⬤⬤⬤ The maximum territory held by the Japanese, 1945

✗ Skirmishes

✗ Battles

miles
0   100   200
0   100   200
kilometres

HEILUNGKIANG

INNER MONGOLIA

KIRIN

SINKIANG

✗ Mukden

Chengteh ✗   ✗ Chinchow

Kupehkow ✗
✗ Miyun

Peking ✗

Paoting ✗

HOPEI

TIENTSIN

KOREA

✗ Taiyuan

SHANSI

✗ Tsinan
SHANTUNG
Tsingtao ✗

NINGSIA

Yenan ✗

Ichwan ✗

✗ Linfen

KANSU

Loyang ✗   ✗ Kaifeng

Sian ✗

SHENSI

HONAN

Suchow ✗
Suhsien ✗

KIANGSU

Nanking ✗

Chengtu

SZECHWAN

R. Yangtze

HUPEI

ANHWEI

Shanghai
SHANGHAI

Chunking ✗

✗ Hangchow

CHEKIANG

✗ Changsa

KIANGSI

KWEICHOW   ✗ Kweiyang

HUNAN

FUKIEN

NNAN

KWANGSI

R. West

KWANGTUNG

Canton ✗

Amoy

FORMOSA

HAINAN

149

The war against the Japanese allowed the Communists to consolidate and to create an army. They formed an anti-Japanese alliance with the Nationalists. The relationship was never an easy one, and in 1941 open hostilities broke out briefly between them, leaving 5000 Communist and almost 20,000 Nationalist casualties after an eight-day battle. In fact, much of the war was spent in preparing for a final confrontation between the two implacable enemies. Where the Communists had begun the war after fleeing from their bases in central China, by 1944 they had achieved a dominant position. The Chief of United States Military Intelligence noted in 1944: 'From control of about 35,000 square miles with a population of about 1,500,000 people at the beginning of 1937, the Communists have expanded their control to about 225,000 square miles with a population of some 85 million people.'[3] At the end of the war, the Japanese had driven the Nationalists back west of Nanking, and into an area inland from the ports of south China, while the Communists controlled a solid zone in the north and guerrilla forces who roamed through much of south and central China behind Japanese lines. With the Japanese surrender, the Nationalists surged forward to occupy all the land they had lost, and with the help of the United States, sent an army north to occupy Manchuria. The Communist strategy was the reverse. They contracted from all outlying points into the northern redoubt, shortening their lines of communication and concentrating their resources. The Nationalists attempted too much, and in the wild grab for territory took more than they could hold. Many of the areas which they took over had never been under Nationalist control before, and they had no basis for support among the people. The greatest disaster was the attempt to preempt the Communists' plan to move into Manchuria.

The four years of war saw a simple strategy on the part of the Communists. They resisted attacks by much larger Nationalist armies from the south while they attacked the KMT armies in Manchuria, first cutting their lines of communication to the south, and then isolating the armies from each other, in enclaves around the major cities. Once the northern flank had been secured, they began to attack all along the southern front throwing back the Nationalists in battle after battle. Peking was surrendered by the Nationalist general in January 1949 to save the capital from destruction. Possession first of Peking, and then of the eastern capital Nanking, gave greater legitimacy to the Communist cause. On 15 October 1949, the Communists took Canton and the main remnant of the Nationalist armies took ship for Formosa, while those trapped in the south-western provinces slipped over the border into Burma and Indo China. The Communists had won, and the revolution was about to begin.

The task facing the Communists was equalled only by that which had confronted Lenin and Stalin, but the methods and the objectives were different. Many died in the course of the revolution and its aftermath, but nothing approaching the twenty million or more who were sacrificed to make Russia Communist in the 1930s. By his conquest of China, Mao had inherited the mandate of heaven, and the Chinese tradition was of submission to the legitimate ruler. On 5 March 1949, he had made clear that the accomplishment of the new China would involve efforts which would dwarf all the exertions they had made before. He had already, characteristically, expressed his beliefs in a version of the old Chinese fable of the Foolish Old Man who removed the Mountains. The fable told how, with his two sons, he set to dig up two great peaks. When he was told it was impossible, the old man replied: 'When I die, my sons will carry on; when they die, there will be my grandsons and then their sons and grandsons, and so on to infinity. High

An ardent Red Guard in Shanghai, birthplace of the movement

as they are, the mountains cannot grow any higher, and with every bit we dig, they will be that much lower. Why can't we clear them away?' Mao believed that the people of China would be roused to join the Communist party in digging up the mountains of imperialism and feudalism. 'If they [the masses of the Chinese people] stand up and dig with us, why can't these two mountains be cleared away?'[4]

For the remainder of his life, the best part of three decades after the victory in the civil war, Mao tried to impress his notion of the continuing struggle on to the Chinese people. He had been opposed by the party throughout his political career, and all his later attempts to rouse the spirit of revolution again met with opposition from those in the party who wanted to enjoy the fruits of success, or felt conscientiously that consolidation not revolution was the right road. Mao wished for a continual ferment and a new gene-

ration of revolutionaries to remould and reform the state established by the victory of 1949. In 1964, he declared that 'successors to the revolutionary cause of the proletariat come forward in mass struggles nd are tempered in the great storms of revolution'.[5] This was the justification for the Cultural Revolution, launched as the last in a long line of purges, *cheng feng* movements for 'ideological remoulding': Mao had set the first in motion in Yenan in 1942. There had also been the Great Leap Forward of 1958, which was designed to galvanize China's economy by bringing the notion of productivity down to commune units. It was an economic disaster. But in Mao's vision it was a political and ideological triumph; he admitted his own faults in launching the campaign, but he answered his critics: 'Have we failed? . . . No, our failure has been only partial. We have paid too high a price, but a gust of Communist

Young Red Guards on the move through the countryside seek to rally peasants with the words of Chairman Mao. The Red Guards were frequently attacked and sometimes killed by peasants, who resented them: 1969

wind has been whipped up and the country has learned a lesson.'[6] So in 1965, he prepared to launch a whirlwind, the ultimate *cheng feng* which would burn false thinking from the heart of the party.

The Cultural Revolution began in Shanghai in the autumn. With the active support of Mao, who arrived in Shanghai in October, and the army under Lin Piao, a mass purification movement carried forward by young Red Guards spread through much of China. It began as an attack on false intellectuals, but they were merely a cover for the figures in the Communist party whom Mao wished to destroy or to neutralize. By the end of May 1966 the revolutionaries had taken control of the party propaganda machine, which was used to fan the flames to a white heat. Criticism gave way to physical attacks, and Red Guards began to remove or kill worthy and effective members of the administration. It was a negative campaign and left profound disorder in its wake. In some areas the local bureaucracy was strong enough to resist the Red Guards and either to divert them or to disperse them forcibly; but by August 1967, after almost two years, the Great Proletarian Cultural Revolution had become an internal war, with the youth stealing weapons and waging pitched battles with those who opposed them. In September Mao, by now disillusioned with the consequences of the purification campaign, turned to the Red Army as the guardian of the nation's political virtue. Ten months later, in July, the leaders of the Red Guards were told by Mao: 'You have let me down and, moreover, you have disappointed the workers, peasants and soldiers of China.'[7] In early August, in an exquisitely symbolic gesture, Mao sent a basket of mangoes, not to the Red Guards as he would have done a year earlier, but to workers and peasants engaged in converting students to Maoist doctrines. It was treated with extreme reverence by the recipients, who placed it on a red table in the midst of the campus. When the fruit began to rot, it was preserved in formalin, like a sacred emblem. It made clear that Mao now reposed his confidence in the workers and peasants, and the army of workers and peasants, while the students and Red Guards were to be controlled and re-educated. By 1969 the process of recovery was well advanced, and one method of neutralizing the former Red Guards was the movement of 'sending down' urban youth to toil in the fields. They were split up and dispatched, year by year, to work in provinces far from home. It was wildly unpopular but very effective, and it did succeed in achieving part of its avowed aim, of increasing the level of mature skills available in the rural areas.

In the end Mao's initiative had failed. The principal consequence of the revolution was widespread revulsion from further turmoil, and an increasingly dominant role for the army within the political structure. He had fought to prevent the Communist party becoming the new mandarins, standing above the masses. In his little red book, *Quotations from Chairman Mao Tse Tung*, he had posed the question: 'Who are our enemies? Who are our friends?'[8] He accepted rapprochement with the United States, and received President Nixon after a near-lifetime of denouncing America and her capitalist running dogs. At the end of his life, Mao had no clear vision of the future, for the present represented an antithesis to most of his life's work.

OUTER MONGOLIA

HEILUNGKIANG

Harbin

KIRIN

Shenyang
LIAONING

INNER MONGOLIA

KOREA

Huhehot

HOPEI
Fangshan
Peking

Tientsin
TIENTSIN

Taiyuan
Shihchiachung
Linyi

SHANSI
Tsingtao

SHANTUNG

Hwang Ho (Yellow R.)

NINGSIA
Yenan
base

Chengchow

Lanchow
Loyang

HONAN

ANSU
SHENSI

KIANGSU

Nanking

ANHWEI

Shanghai
SHANGHAI

SZECHWAN

Hanyang
July 1967
July
1967
Wuchang

Yangtze R.

HUPEI

August
1967
Chengtu

Hangchow
July 1967

August
1967
Chunking

August
1967

Nanchang

CHEKIANG

Ipin

Changsa

Wengchow

KIANGSI

HUNAN

Fuchow

KWEICHOW

Kweilin

FUKIEN

April
1968

TAIWAN

Liuchow

April
1968
Wuchow

June
1967
Canton

KWANGTUNG

KWANGSI

West R.

Nanning

```
                                    miles
          200        100       100    0
          200        100       100    0
                                    kilometres
```

Areas most affected by Red Guard agitation.
Government was frequently brought to a standstill

Clashes between Red Guards and the army,
or workers and peasants

Provinces with very active Red Guard mass-movements

Areas most fervent in their support of the Cultural Revolution

Urban youth 'sent down' to the provinces 1974-6 for
agricultural work

Railways, much used by young Red Guards to
move around the country

Open conflict between revolutionaries and 'reactionaries'

HAINAN

Revolution in one country

GUERRILLA (meaning 'little war') describes perfectly both the scale and style of the Cuban revolution. In December 1956 Fidel Castro began his attack on the largest military forces in the Caribbean and Central America with a force of twenty men. Yet within a little over two years the Cuban dictator Fulgencio Batista, who had been the dominant force, in and out of office since the 1930s, had fled from the island, leaving the somewhat disparate forces of revolution in undisputed control. The Batista regime had had every advantage in its struggle against the revolution: considerable financial resources, an effective secret police and paramilitary force, much feared, and the general if grudging support of the United States. Most of the opposition groups in the cities were entirely ineffective, and usually penetrated by Batista's intelligence agents. The general level of anti-government feeling was not especially high, save in some university and intellectual circles.

The significance of the Cuban Revolution lies not so much in the bitterness or savagery of the struggle – for the action on the ground was spasmodic and the forces involved minuscule – but in the way in which it fulfils the romantic notion of the revolution and the revolutionary. In South America, most revolutions are created by the military, in the fashion of the Spanish *pronunciamiento*. Batista himself was an army sergeant. The residue tend to be peasant risings, fuelled by fundamental grievances like famine, landlord oppression, or land hunger. In Cuba the intellectuals were a strictly urban minority, with little knowledge of, or concern for, the countryside. With Castro, an urban radical took to the hills, and by doing so created a new pattern. A small group of men, without military training, ill-equipped and in terrain as strange to them as to their enemies, were able to survive, attract recruits to their cause and eventually to triumph. In retrospect, the very speed and thoroughness with which the moral cohesion of their enemies decayed helped to create the myth of the inevitability of the revolution. It was this belief in the Cuban model, with a revolutionary 'focus', a small group of ardent activists who would act in Che Guevara's phrase as the 'seed-corn of the revolution', which lay behind the many Cuban-inspired revolutionary movements on the mainland in later years. Yet although they followed the Cuban example, most were abject failures; Guevara himself met his end after a minor encounter with the Bolivian army in 1967. The Cuban revolutionary method was not for export, for it developed from particular circumstances: the success of Castro made for an inspiring legend, but it proved a bad primer for future revolutions.

The island of Cuba lies almost equidistant from the southern tip of the United States at Key West and the furthest extremity of Central America on the peninsula of Yucatan. But when Fidel Castro was born in 1927, the son of a wealthy but self-made farmer of Spanish origin and a Cuban servant girl, Cuba had been a virtual dependency of the USA for a generation. American imperialism had replaced the rule of Spain and the exchange was to the advantage of Cuba. Under American control the economic substructure of the country was rebuilt, with the consequence that by the time of Castro's revolution Cuba ranked fourth among the twenty countries of Latin America by the usual measures of economic and social advance. Yet within Cuba there were marked inequalities, especially in the far east of the island in Oriente province (Castro's birthplace), where the dominance of American-owned agricultural enterprises was particularly strong. Oriente had already experienced an extremely bloody rising in 1912, which was only ended when government forces came under pressure from Washington to end it. Peace was restored with the loss of some three thousand lives. Castro had his roots there and knew the potential for unrest and discontent in the region. It was also the area of Cuba most remote from the power of the Havana government, with rugged terrain in the Sierra Maestra and the Sierra Cristal, well wooded and ideal for insurgency. Oriente functioned for Castro as Yenan had done for Mao Tse Tung – a secure provincial base whence the revolution could be launched. Castro was only one among many groups in Cuba working for the overthrow of the Batista regime, and not the most widely favoured. But all the others were based in the cities of the plain, vulnerable to the attentions of the SIM, Batista's intelligence service. Castro's only experience of an urban uprising had been the ill-fated attack on the Moncada barracks at Santiago de Cuba on 26 July 1953. This fiasco left Castro a prisoner (although he was lucky not to be murdered or mutilated, the fate which befell a number of his companions); but he was freed in a general amnesty some two years later. He began to plan a new attack on the regime, but this time based on a rural revolt. From the foundation of his new revolutionary movement – named the 26th of July Movement – until his triumphal entry into Havana on 8 January 1958, Oriente lay at the heart of his thinking.

On 2 December 1956 eighty-two men landed from a shabby motor cruiser called the *Granma* on a remote beach in Oriente province. The landing was either betrayed to the Cuban army, or else they suffered from extraordinary ill-luck, but many of them were killed on the beach and still more in a series of running fights in succeeding days. The Sierra Maestra, with its highest point at the Pico Turquino at more than 6000 feet, was the area which Castro had already selected as his headquarters. When the bare dozen, the bedraggled survivors of the *Granma*, arrived in the mountains, he asked a peasant: 'Are we already in the Sierra Maestra?' On being told that they were, he declared: 'Then the revolution has triumphed.'

Fidel Castro en route to Havana after the collapse of the Batista government. Castro had spent the guerilla war in his base on the Sierra Maestra, moving forward in the last stages to take Santiago de Cuba. He then turned to travel the whole length of the Central Highway to the capital. On the way he made stirring speeches, as here at Santa Clara

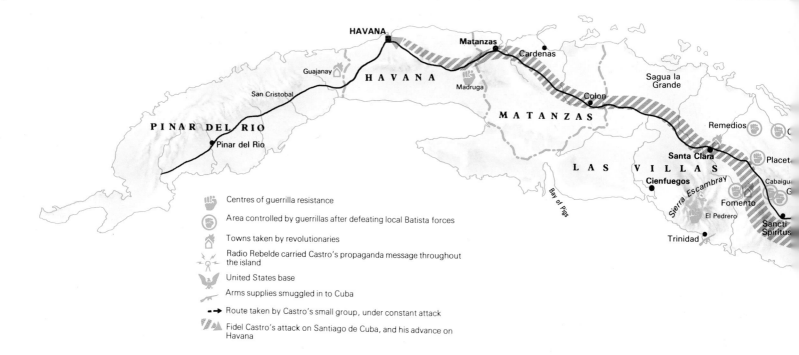

Centres of guerrilla resistance

Area controlled by guerrillas after defeating local Batista forces

Towns taken by revolutionaries

Radio Rebelde carried Castro's propaganda message throughout the island

United States base

Arms supplies smuggled in to Cuba

Route taken by Castro's small group, under constant attack

Fidel Castro's attack on Santiago de Cuba, and his advance on Havana

Given his slender resources – by the spring of 1957 his band had only grown to eighty, many of them without arms and untrained to the life of the guerrilla – it might seem an outrageous statement. Yet it contained a strong element of shrewd practical sense. In the Sierra the revolution proved to be invulnerable, both to the land forces which Batista sent against Castro and to air attack. The trees and deep valleys of the mountain range gave the revolutionaries almost complete cover from the air, while the army was never willing to penetrate very deep into the fastness. Neither soldiers nor officers had much taste for close fighting, and the preferred tactic was a feeble attempt to encircle the guerrilla redoubt. But Castro evaded the army and dispatched small teams which attacked vulnerable targets in the east of the island, notably economic objectives. The success of these operations was broadcast (and exaggerated) throughout the island over Radio Rebelde. Castro, still secure in the *sierra*, was able by radio to reach deep into the cities. In the urban areas the supporters of the revolution developed an oral network of news and rumours, known as *bolas*, which effectively undermined the crude propaganda efforts of the central government. In earlier days a rebellion in Oriente would have been a simple provincial disturbance, remote from the centres of power. The Castro revolution managed to transform a provincial irritant into a running sore. The mythology of the revolution has tended to emphasize the rural revolt to the exclusion of the urban movement, which owed less to Castro's efforts. In the cities the successes of the revolutionaries were fewer, given the efficacy of the SIM, but their efforts served to erode the confidence of the regime as much as the successes in the Sierra.

During 1958 the revolutionary columns, notably that of Raul Castro in north-east Oriente and that led by Che Guevara, which penetrated deep into central Cuba, attacked more substantial targets and paralyzed communications; but there were few pitched battles. The collapse of the Batista regime came from within, rather than from the growing power of the revolution. In the last days of December 1958, Batista decided to cut his losses. On 1 January 1959, he and his close associates flew out of the island taking with them a heavy cargo of valuables, to add to the vast fortune which Batista had already secreted in foreign banks. On that day Castro made his only advance of the war, and took Santiago de Cuba, his target in the ill-fated rising of 1953. It was left to the other commanders to push along the length of the island, taking city after city in a headlong advance on the capital. There was resistance at Santa Clara, and in some other cities on the Carraterra Central, and the revolutionaries settled old scores as they advanced on Havana. But by the time that Fidel Castro set out from Santiago, the battles had been won, and his was a triumphal progress rather than a military campaign.

Castro's victory was based on patience and caution and not the airy flamboyancy which he affected in the hour of victory. Although the odds against him were enormous, much of Batista's army was preoccupied with preserving internal order in the cities and provincial towns. The free portion available for action against Castro probably numbered no more than ten thousand, and almost all were unwilling conscripts. Nor was the officer corps entirely unsympathetic to him. The 26th of July Movement attracted covert support from many elements in the army, as well as the vast bulk of the more enlightened and educated element in the island. Castro's revolution had an attractively middle-class face, led by a man who had been a student of outstanding brilliance, and whose radio manner inspired in a way which neither Batista himself nor any of his associates could match.

There was nowhere in Latin America which re-

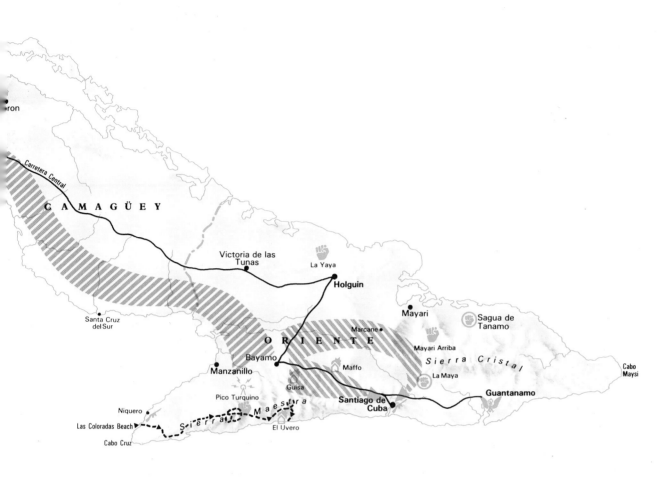

flected the same pattern of development as Cuba, nowhere where the sense of general grievance was so great and the government so universally unpopular. The Cuban model of revolution was not for general export, and the generation which tried to transfer it to the mainland paid with their blood. For Castro himself, although he was delighted, and not a little flattered, that the Cuban Revolution should become the engine-room for revolution throughout the sub-continent, his concerns were exclusively for Cuba.

The failure of revolution

IF an epitaph were wanted for the failure of revolution in continental Latin America, the remark of one of the few survivors of Che Guevara's Bolivian adventure could not be bettered: 'Peasants are always with the forces of power and strength.'

As Guevara found when he and his group infiltrated the eastern region of Bolivia near Santa Cruz in 1966, it was impossible to rouse peasants who regarded every move with suspicion, and who were eventually to betray the whole group to the Bolivian army. The whole theory of the *foco*, of the ardent revolutionary core which would ignite revolution by some process of spontaneous combustion, was shown to be disastrously wrong. The revolution involved wish-fulfilment, in Guevara's own words: 'What is decisive is the determination to struggle which is maturing daily, the awareness of the need for revolutionary change and the certainty of its possibility.' Determination and conviction were not enough.

The Cuban example was not, as was confidently believed, the magic formula for a successful revolution in Latin America, but a very special and misleading case. The geography, and the social and political structure of Cuba, its history and pattern of political relationships, made it unique. The pattern of rural revolution which Castro formulated after events had marooned him in the Sierra Maestra was not to be copied elsewhere. Until 1898 Cuba was still a colony of Spain, and since that date had been a virtual dependency of the United States. On the Latin American mainland the war for independence had been fought two generations before 1898, and for the whole of the nineteenth century the states of Latin America had fought among themselves and within each country for social and territorial dominance. The political lines were harshly drawn, for classes which had experienced revolution and counter-revolution, and suffered from it, then fought viciously to maintain their position. The largest element in the population of some Latin American countries, like Bolivia and Peru, were Indians who had lived in a state of permanent subjection to white society. They often spoke nothing except their own Indian dialect.

In much of Latin America potential revolutionaries confronted military governments, or states in which the military by tradition exerted a dominant role. They were not facing a flabby dictatorship like Batista's in Cuba, nor a free and easy democracy. But there was a deep belief that revolution was inevitable. The seductive lure – that nothing can hold back an idea 'whose time has come' – pulled revolutionaries in every country into a morass. In most cases the type of guerrilla campaign was determined by the terrain. In predominantly urban Uruguay, the revolutionaries had to operate in Montevideo and the cities, while in Argentina, bombing and kidnappings, although concentrated in Buenos Aires and the principal cities, also spread out into the small towns and the provinces. Only in the sub-Andean region of Argentina and in the Sierra de Cordoba was it possible to mount a Cuban-style guerrilla campaign, with the men of the mountains descending to raid the plain. The terrain of Uruguay provided virtually no cover at all. In Brazil the revolutionaries were faced with a dilemma. The bulk of the influential population was concentrated in the coastal belt of towns and cities. It would have been perfectly possible to have created a revolutionary army deep in the heart of Amazonia, but it would have been so peripheral to the main political centres that the government could have ignored it. The revolutionaries in Brazil devised an urban solution, as exemplified by the veteran Communist leader Carlos Marighella, in his 'Minimanual of the Urban Guerrilla'. He detailed with glee the methods of bombing, the taking of hostages, targets for assassination, and the methods of bringing pressure to bear on governments. He assumed that it was possible for the urban guerrilla to hide among the people, to disappear into the crowd. He underestimated the skill and ruthlessness of his opponents. They had no more compunction about making mass arrests and sanctioning torture and murder to expose the guerrillas than they would have had about setting fire to a forest to flush out wild beasts. There are no secrets in a city and the urban fighters were tracked down and destroyed as the police discovered the location of their bases.

Latin America spawned more theorists on revolutionary war than successful revolutions. A respected theorist, Abraham Guillen, could write confidently in his 'Philosophy of the Urban Guerrilla': 'Today the epicentre of the revolutionary war must be in the great urban zones, where the heavy artillery is not as efficient as in the countryside for annihilating guerrillas tied to the land.' Yet only a few pages later, he was saying: 'In order to defeat imperialism . . . one has to master revolutionary strategy. . . . It is necessary to lure imperialism into ground fighting deep into the interior of a continent, in zones without communication, in order to destroy its infantry and to annul the effect of heavy weapons and atomic weapons where there are no easy targets.' He is off target in both cases. The weapons of the counter-revolution are not 'heavy weapons', let alone 'atomic weapons'. They are: systematic intelligence, the use of information technology, confession, terror and torture, bribery, *agents provocateurs*, and above all a ruthlessness and capacity to behave without scruple which equals or exceeds that of the revolutionary. Such devices are easiest to use in the city where the guerrilla is trapped within the cordon of buildings. If the Latin Americans wanted a model for an urban guerrilla war, they should have looked to the Battle of Algiers during the Algerian Revolution. The utter defeat of the revolutionaries, better organized and more determined than many of their Brazilian, Uruguayan or Argentinian counterparts, was a sobering lesson. It is not possible to wage an urban guerrilla war simply by transposing

A young Salvadorean girl who has become a refugee in Nicaragua. The human cost of the war in El Salvador is appalling: 1982

all the attributes of the rural war to the city. In an urban environment there is no security, no safety at any time of day or night when facing an enemy totally devoted to your extermination. The urban guerrilla must accept a short life expectancy.

The war against society stood its best chance in those areas where the terrain was favourable and the power of the enemy not too great. In the highlands of Colombia, in parts of Venezuala, in the Ayacucho province of Peru, revolutionaries have not succeeded, but they have survived, and show spasmodic signs of life. *Sendero Luminoso* in Peru and FARC, ELN, and M19 in Colombia have all shown a flurry of activity in the last two years. Further north, in Central America, the revolutionaries have actually triumphed. Here the Cuban example is relevant. In the small republics of Central America, power and wealth was concentrated in the hands of a tiny group, while the domination by United States interests – Honduras was the original 'banana republic' – was analogous to the Cuban situation. Certainly the USA has responded with outrage and concern at revolutionary movements in central America. The mountainous terrain makes possible a guerrilla war launched from the relative security of the 'zones without communication', but because the countries are small – a notable case being El Salvador – the guerrilla can strike into the heart of enemy territory at will. Moreover, unclear borders have given sanctuary to many guerrillas among the thousands of refugees who have crossed the frontier in search of safety. Even co-operation between Central American governments can do little to resolve the problem.

The most unusual and sinister aspect of revolution in Latin America is the degree to which it has bred vigilantism, or death squads, often with official encouragement. Even governments insensitive to world opinion or to the international human rights lobby prefer not to be branded as bestial. To be described as a 'torture state' and then to be seen to do nothing about it can have dangerous consequences for the aid programme. Military and financial aid from the United States in particular is dependent on at least a little cosmetic attention to violations of human rights. Often the death squads, as in Brazil and Argentina, have simply been the security forces acting out of uniform and unofficially. This cover has now been exposed and the practice is of diminishing value. But some of the death squads have been genuine expressions of class or political hatred, staffed by civilians and outside the direct scope of government control. These will continue to be a valuable asset to states seeking to wage a counter-terror without restraint. The quality of life in such countries would be hard to imagine, for the real loss in the war which has been waged in Latin America since 1960 has been the system of social values built up over generations. Nowhere is this more true than in Chile, once advanced as evidence that a balanced, pluralist and generally democratic state could exist in the Latin American context. The replacement of the Allende regime in 1973, whatever its many faults, has led to something infinitely worse in terms of human rights for the majority of the population. The events of the last two decades cannot be reversed anywhere in the continent. The future is grim.

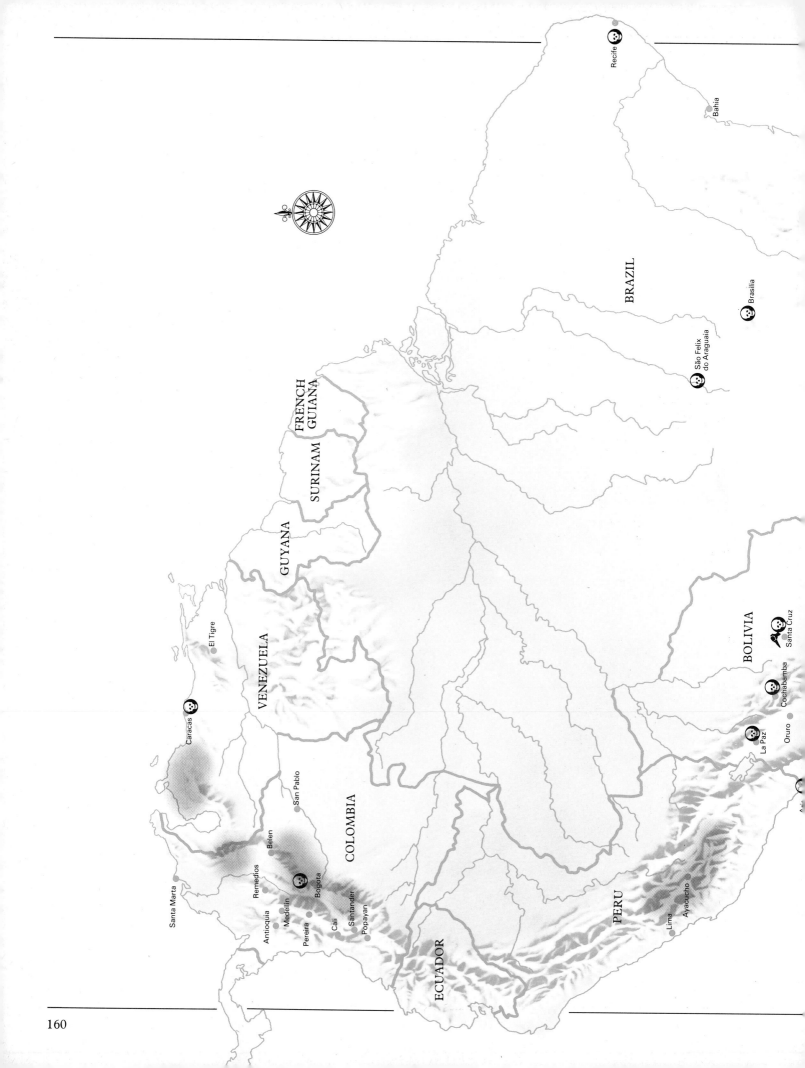

BRAZIL

Recife

Bahia

Brasilia

São Felix
do Araguaia

FRENCH
GUIANA

SURINAM

GUYANA

VENEZUELA

El Tigre

Caracas

COLOMBIA

San Pablo

Belen

Remedios

Bogota

Santa Marta

Antioquia

Medellin

Pereira

Cali

Santander

Popayan

ECUADOR

PERU

Lima

Ayacucho

BOLIVIA

Santa Cruz

Cochabamba

La Paz

Oruro

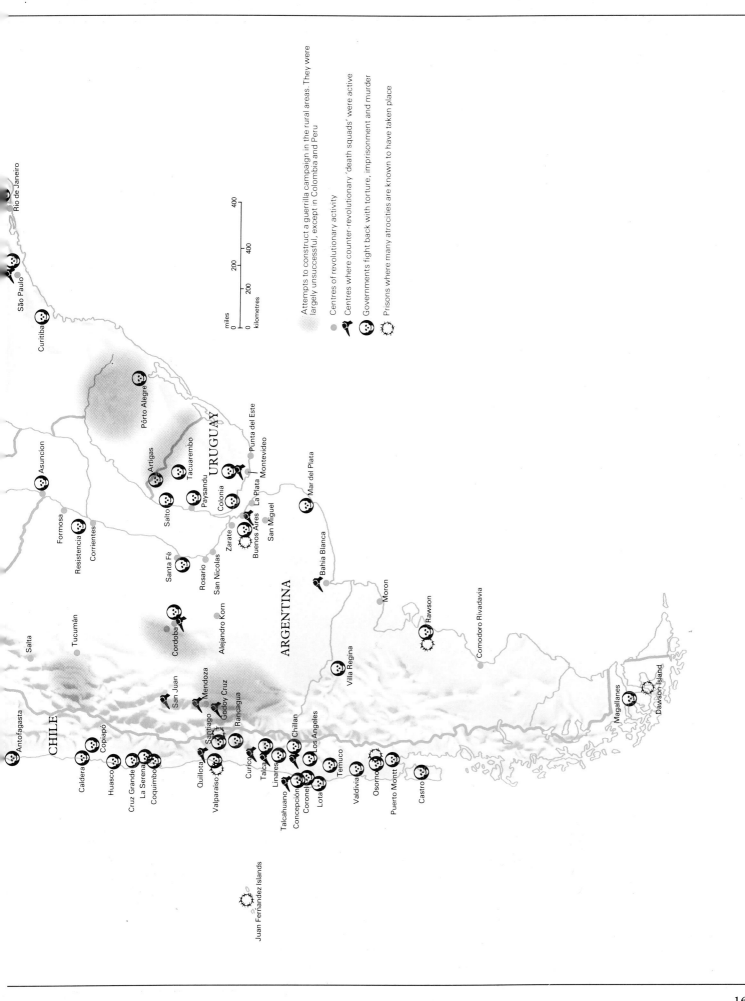

Attempts to construct a guerrilla campaign in the rural areas. They were largely unsuccessful, except in Colombia and Peru

● Centres of revolutionary activity

🗡 Centres where counter-revolutionary 'death squads' were active

😖 Governments fight back with torture, imprisonment and murder

☼ Prisons where many atrocities are known to have taken place

miles
0   200   400
0   200   400
kilometres

Rio de Janeiro

São Paulo

Curitiba

Pôrto Alegre

Asuncion

Artigas

Tacuarembo

URUGUAY

Punta del Este

Paysandu

Salto

Colonia

Montevideo

La Plata

Formosa

Corrientes

Resistencia

Santa Fé

Rosario

San Nicolas

Zarate

Buenos Aires

San Miguel

Mar del Plata

Bahia Blanca

ARGENTINA

Moron

Tucumán

Salta

Cordoba

Alejandro Korn

Villa Regina

Rawson

Comodoro Rivadavia

San Juan

Mendoza

Godoy Cruz

CHILE

Antofagasta

Santiago

Rancagua

Chillan

Los Angeles

Caldera

Copiapó

Quillota

Curico

Temuco

Huasco

Valparaiso

Talca

Linares

Cruz Grande

La Serena

Coquimbo

Talcahuano

Concepción

Coronel

Lota

Valdivia

Osorno

Puerto Montt

Castro

Magallanes

Dawson Island

Juan Fernández Islands

Central America

While the flashpoints of the 1960s and 1970s were in the major states of Latin America, during the 1980s the centre of action has shifted to the small states of Central America. The shift is more apparent than real, for the countries of Central America, notably El Salvador, have traditional patterns of revolution and counter-revolution. In 1932, a largely ineffectual Communist revolution in the cities of western El Salvador, which killed no more than thirty civilians, produced a counter-revolution which killed between 20,000 and 30,000, most of them guilty only of being Indians, or having vaguely liberal ideas. Since then the military has exercised a dominant influence in the government of El Salvador. In Nicaragua, a rebellion led by Augustino Sandino in 1931 was suppressed by the Guardia Nacional, trained by the United States Marines; from that event emerged in 1936 the political system dominated by the Somoza family, which enjoyed the

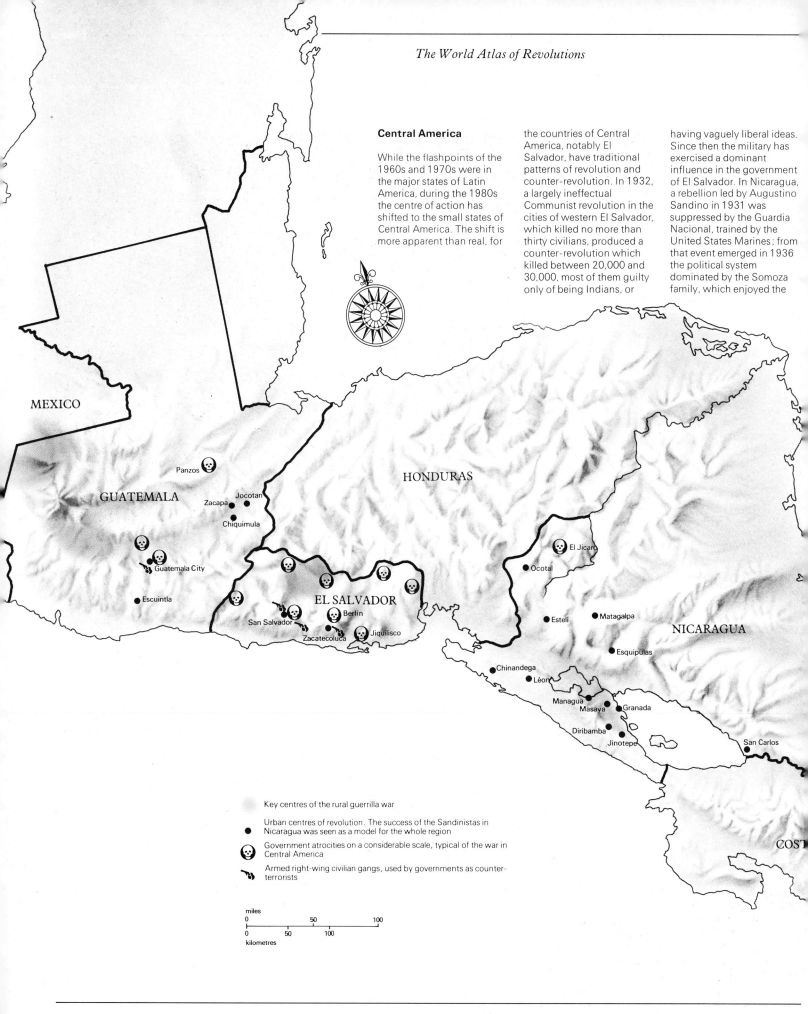

Key centres of the rural guerrilla war

Urban centres of revolution. The success of the Sandinistas in Nicaragua was seen as a model for the whole region

Government atrocities on a considerable scale, typical of the war in Central America

Armed right-wing civilian gangs, used by governments as counter-terrorists

miles
0   50   100

0   50   100
kilometres

ll support of the Guardia acional until it was toppled most forty-five years later y revolutionaries who took e name 'Sandinistas', and ollowed many of Sandino's bjectives. The cycles of epression and revolution in entral America are eemingly endemic to its eoples.

If the left is to succeed in reaking the pattern of ppression on which the rces of the right have ased their regimes, it will ave to adopt the same eprehensible tactics. The ocial revolution' in icaragua is already ecoming a sanguinary ffair. If the revolutionaries ucceed in El Salvador, they oo will need to take their evenge. But this endless avagery on both sides owes ttle or nothing to external rces. Those who blame the vents of 1980–82 on Cuba nd the Soviet Union are verstating the case as much s those who see the nfluence of the United tates behind every epressive act. *Matanza* — laughter — is as native to Guatemala, El Salvador and Nicaragua as are the tactics f the Mafia to Sicily or the acoits to northern India.

Salvadorean soldiers firing at guerrillas who had attacked the funeral procession of two soldiers. The army, rather than the guerrillas, was seen as the enemy by the peasants. It operated by making raids into the country, devastating whatever lay in its path. The rural war in central America was more damaging than anywhere else in Latin America since the beginning of the active revolutions of the 1960s

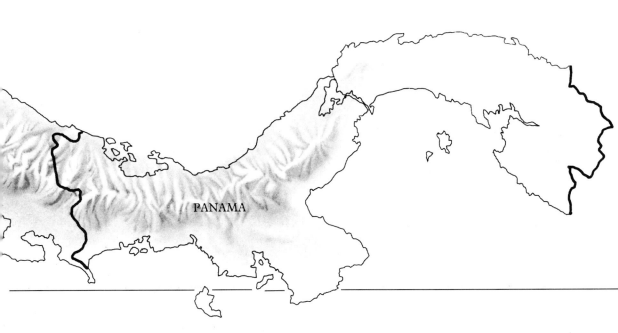

PANAMA

The last redoubt

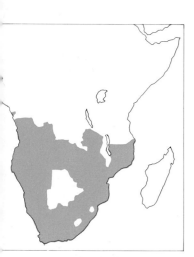

IN the space of three years, 1960–63, Britain and France shed the vast bulk of their colonial empires in Africa, if not without acrimony then certainly without much bloodshed. Even the crisis which enveloped the former Belgian Congo was not a war against the white man to achieve freedom, but a struggle within the nationalist movement for control of the state. By 1964 all the former British territories had become independent, leaving only Southern Rhodesia as an obstinate anomaly. The last redoubts of white rule in the continent were: the Portuguese possessions of Angola and Mozambique and the small territory of Equatorial Guinea; South Africa and the territory of South West Africa; and Southern Rhodesia. The 'war for liberation' in Africa had its first spasm with the Mau Mau rising in Kenya, but it only reached a mature stage after 1960. The first attempt to overthrow the Portuguese in Angola came in 1961 with an attack launched across the border from the newly-independent Congo republic, led by Holden Roberto. The latent antagonism of the Bakongo peasants towards the white farmers flared into a war of extermination, but the massacres carried out by the black revolutionaries were timid by comparison with the terrifying reprisals exacted by the Portuguese. When it was over, the only vestige of the revolution was a small group of guerrilla fighters cut off in wooded country north-east of Luanda, who managed to maintain a precarious existence dodging Portuguese patrols.

Until the withdrawal of Britain as a colonial power there was no safe haven for revolutionaries. With the new independent nations, opposition groups found it possible to set up camps on friendly soil. Zambia and Tanzania were vital to the success of the liberation armies. Guerrilla armies could operate in the field at only a low level of efficiency if they were forced to be entirely self-sufficient. It was possible to wage a war with captured weapons and supplies, and to live off the land. But an inordinate amount of time was then taken up with fulfilling basic needs rather than carrying out military or political objectives. In the base areas in Tanzania and Zambia, and later, as secure areas were captured inside the country being 'liberated', in Angola, Mozambique and Rhodesia/Zimbabwe, there was a steady throughput of equipment and new recruits for the cause. The principal sources of money, equipment and training were the USSR and other countries of the Warsaw Pact, with China acting as the principal competitor. The Soviet Union had taken a special interest in the struggle against colonialism since the days of the 1917 Revolution. At the Congress of the Peoples of the East held at Baku in 1918, a call had been issued for revolution among the peoples of Asia and Africa. In the forty years that followed, the Soviet Union wavered in the details of its approach to the 'enslaved peoples'. Sometimes it actively encouraged revolutionary movements, and on other occasions deliber-ately held them back. What was unwavering was its belief that the peoples of what became known as the Third World were worthy of attention and support, verbal and sometimes practical. In 1960 the Patrice Lumumba University was created in Moscow, and by 1976 over 20,000 students from Africa, Asia and Latin America were studying in Russian institutes of higher education. The consistent approach was reflected in an official statement in 1975: 'The Soviet Union battles persistently for international recognition of the lawfulness of armed struggle for colonial peoples and recognition of their right to self-defence and of the principle of legality and justice, of aid and support to peoples waging a war for national independence.'[1] For forty years the Russians played a long game, sure that in the end events would justify their approach. From the 1960s the years of unrewarded effort began to bear fruit. The Western countries were either colonialists themselves, or in the case of the United States, seen as an active supporter of the worst of the white regimes. The revolutionaries turned to the Communist countries and received a cornucopia of arms, training facilities, and advice. Nor was the political price too high: both Russians and Chinese were concerned to avoid giving the impression that the Africans had merely replaced one master with another.

After the initial failure in Angola, all the liberation movements concentrated on building a more solid base for action. They still had much to learn. The initial guerrilla infiltration across the Zambezi into Rhodesia during 1964–7 was a disaster. In July 1967 the Zimbabwe African People's Union, ZAPU, sent a force into Rhodesia/Zimbabwe near Victoria Falls. They were cornered near Wankie and were all killed or captured. The lesson was quickly learned by the other main nationalist group, the Zimbabwe African National Union, ZANU, who saw that the Zambezi was too easily defended by the Rhodesians and the South Africans who came to help them. The ZANU attack came in 1972 through the heavy cover on the Mozambique border, an area secured by the advance of the Mozambique liberation movement from its first bases in Cabo Delgado province, just beyond the Tanzanian border. Thus the Zimbabwe and the Mozambique campaigns moved in harmony. ZANU and FRELIMO shared many training facilities in Tanzania and Zambia. ZAPU forces remained on their bases in Zambia, and only crossed the border later in the war.

In Angola, the main advance also came after Zambia's independence in 1964, with a slow and painstaking guerrilla advance across the central plains. The situation was complicated by the operation of three separate and largely antagonistic liberation movements. The MPLA was the favoured child of the Soviet Union and Cuba. The UPA which had launched the 1961 rising had become the FNLA, and was strong in the north of the country, while the

UNITA movement, created in 1966, had its main support in the south. The latter two groups took aid from any possible source, including China and, after the triumph of the MPLA, the United States. The MPLA had its strongest support in the coastal region, and the aim of their guerrilla war was to establish themselves there, close to the main cities. But the power base of the MPLA was too small to defeat the other two nationalist movements after the war with the Portuguese had taken its toll. In the spring of 1975 discreet parties of fit young Cubans were arriving clutching large suitcases, large enough to contain their personal small arms. Later in the year this transparent deception was dropped, as more Cuban soldiers arrived in large uniformed groups. By the time the republic was declared on 11 November 1975 there was a sizeable Cuban force which eventually exceeded 12,500 men fully equipped with armour, artillery and air support. This force smashed the FNLA in the north and centre, and drove back the UNITA forces in the south until they were confronted by the South African army advancing from South West Africa/Namibia. An uneasy and uncertain No Man's Land was created.

The steady succession of Portuguese military failures in Guinea and the African Empire undermined the position of the government in Lisbon and produced a bloodless revolution. This collapse on the home front hastened the fall of Angola and Mozambique. The freedom of Rhodesia/Zimbabwe was delayed because of the anomalous constitutional position of the country. Technically it was still British, although in rebellion. Whether the efforts of the British hastened or hindered the final achievement of black majority rule is an open question. Certainly, despite sanctions and extreme international outrage, white Rhodesia continued to flourish if in an increasingly beleaguered state. The real pressure which brought about a settlement was the heavy hand of South Africa, Rhodesia's sole lifeline after the loss of Mozambique in 1975. The South African view was that it was better to do a deal with a moderate black government than to face a victorious guerrilla army. In the event, Rhodesian stubborness produced exactly that result: a government dominated by ZANU led by Robert Mugabe after a massive electoral victory under British supervision. In March 1980 the last bastion had fallen, and white rule was confined to the final redoubt, the Republic of South Africa.

Isolation was no sudden shock to South Africa for she had always expected that it would come one day. An icy realism has dominated South African political thinking ever since the victory of the National Party in 1948 cut away any illusion that South Africa shared the same attitudes as the rest of the Western world. The country possessed an excellent white army and police force, as well as a small but efficient air force and navy. The reserves were well equipped, and by the late 1970s the country was self-supporting in armaments. Mineral and agricultural wealth made the country a powerful force in the world economy, too important to be ignored either as a market or a source of supply. Nor was there any doubt as to where the danger to the country lay. The South African police began to collect detailed information on subversive organizations and individuals in 1922, and the country now possesses the best system of internal intelligence outside the Communist world.[2] Yet although isolation was accepted, South Africa attempted to cushion the effect by forming links with other African countries, such as Malawi, as well as seeking to break up the unity of opposition within the country. With potential enemies like Zimbabwe, Mozambique and Angola, it has supported counter-revolutionary movements like UNITA in Angola and MRM in Mozambique, as well as launching attacks on guerrilla training bases in both countries which were aimed at South Africa. Zimbabwe has a considerable economic dependence on South Africa, and this has forced a degree of circumspection on the ZANU government. It is also likely that South Africa has taken steps to destabilize the Mugabe regime by the use of counter-revolutionary tactics which have already proved successful in the former Portuguese colonies.

Continued on page 168

A propaganda march in which the young children of MPLA members in Angola dedicate themselves to the struggle, clutching wooden guns. It was an out and out war: the Portuguese had not spared women and children, and nor had the revolutionaries. Children not much older than this one had been killed in action with real guns: October 1975

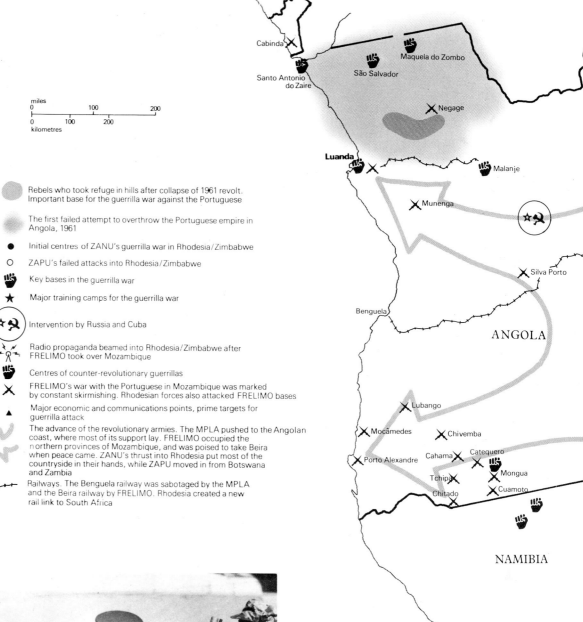

Cabinda ✕

Santo Antonio
do Zaire

Maquela do Zombo 💪

São Salvador 💪

Negage ✕

Luanda 💪 ✕

Malanje 💪

Munenga ✕

☆☭

Silva Porto ✕

Benguela

ANGOLA

Lubango ✕

Mocâmedes ✕

Chivemba ✕

Cahama ✕   Catequero ✕

Porto Alexandre ✕

Tchipa ✕   Mongua 💪

Chitado ✕   Cuamoto ✕

💪

NAMIBIA

Rebels who took refuge in hills after collapse of 1961 revolt. Important base for the guerrilla war against the Portuguese

The first failed attempt to overthrow the Portuguese empire in Angola, 1961

● Initial centres of ZANU's guerrilla war in Rhodesia/Zimbabwe

○ ZAPU's failed attacks into Rhodesia/Zimbabwe

💪 Key bases in the guerrilla war

★ Major training camps for the guerrilla war

☆☭ Intervention by Russia and Cuba

Radio propaganda beamed into Rhodesia/Zimbabwe after FRELIMO took over Mozambique

💪 Centres of counter-revolutionary guerrillas

✕ FRELIMO's war with the Portuguese in Mozambique was marked by constant skirmishing. Rhodesian forces also attacked FRELIMO bases

▲ Major economic and communications points, prime targets for guerrilla attack

The advance of the revolutionary armies. The MPLA pushed to the Angolan coast, where most of its support lay. FRELIMO occupied the northern provinces of Mozambique, and was poised to take Beira when peace came. ZANU's thrust into Rhodesia put most of the countryside in their hands, while ZAPU moved in from Botswana and Zambia

Railways. The Benguela railway was sabotaged by the MPLA and the Beira railway by FRELIMO. Rhodesia created a new rail link to South Africa

June 1976: the embodiment of frustration and hatred. Black rioters protesting against the decision to abolish teaching in English and replace it with Afrikaans. The Soweto riots caused many deaths and thousands of injuries. But the police never lost control and the rioting was contained in the black township

ZAIRE

TANZANIA

★ Mgagao

★ Itumbi

★ Nachingwea

Lake Nyasa (Malawi)

✕ Mkushi

★ Chifombo

▲ Cabora Bassa Dam

MOZAMBIQUE

Moatize ✕

ZAMBIA

Lusaka ✕

R. Zambezi

Kariba Dam ▲

Lake Kariba

Mutarara ✕

● Centenary ● Mount Darwin

Macossa

● Sinoia ✕

■ **Salisbury**

✕ Catandica

✕ Muanza

ZIMBABWE

Goronzaga Mts

▲ Beira oil tanks

✕ Chimoio

✕ Beira

Victoria Falls ▲

Kazangula ○

Mavinga

do

○ Wankie

Beit Bridge ▲

✕ Chicualacuala

R. Limpopo

Gaza

BOTSWANA

✕ Mabalane

SOUTH AFRICA

Voice of Zimbabwe

Lourenço Marques (Maputo)

167

The resistance in South Africa itself antedates all the later liberation movements. The African National Congress was founded in 1912, and after the nationalist victory in 1948, became the main focus of black opposition to the torrent of measures aimed at controlling the blacks and other non-whites. The military wing of the ANC, *Umkhonto we Sizwe* ('the spear of the nation'), was broken up after South African counter-intelligence uncovered its plans in 1963. But a great number of sabotage and arson attacks were launched, and this type of activity has continued to be the traditional style of the ANC: militant but largely ineffective protest. The capacity to engage in mass organization was limited by the willingness of the authorities to put down demonstrations regardless of the human cost, as was seen at Sharpeville and Langa in 1960 and in the disturbances at Soweto township near Johannesburg and in Cape Town in 1976. Faced with the sensitivity of the security services to any whisper of armed action, the most fruitful line of action for the black nationalists has been through trade union organization. But all this is very far from toppling the South African state, especially when the state, understandably, does not hesitate to dispose of those whom it deems dangerous. 'Death in custody' is the South African equivalent of the Mexican *ley de fuga*, 'shot while attempting to escape'. The South African government has its sensitivities. It lays great stress on its competence and capacity to deal with 'terrorism'. The attacks on the SASOL oil production unit, a major strategic target, in 1980, and on the nuclear power plant near Cape Town in December 1982, have dented that reputation.

South Africa is now fighting a war in South West Africa/Namibia, and faces growing internal unrest. On the other flank there have already been guerrilla infiltrations from Mozambique, and a strike against the ANC base near Maputo (Lourenço Marques) provided only a temporary respite. No individual attack can do any major damage to the white redoubt, but if the intensity of both the external and the internal pressure were to increase dramatically, the quality of life for the white population might suffer. The sense of insecurity in the white community is present though still theoretical. But a decade of intense revolutionary terrorism aimed at white society, a campaign aimed at the economic foundations of the state, and a wasting war on the frontiers might shake the foundations of even the strongest fortress.

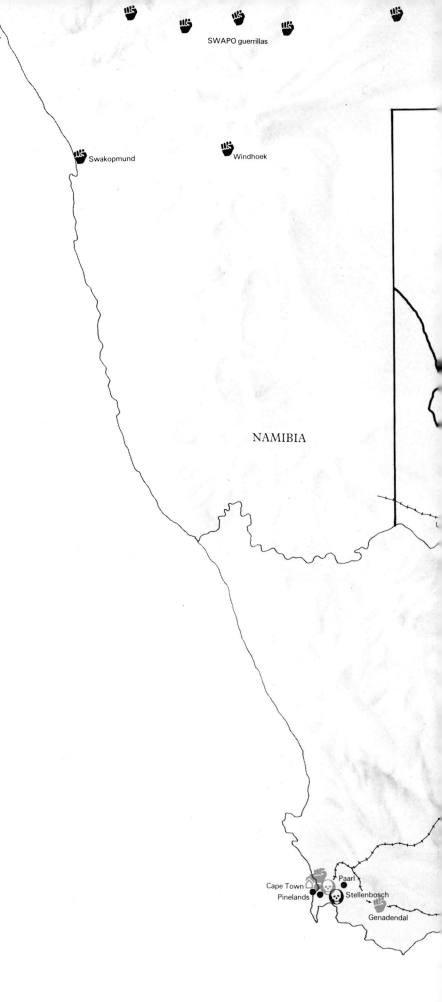

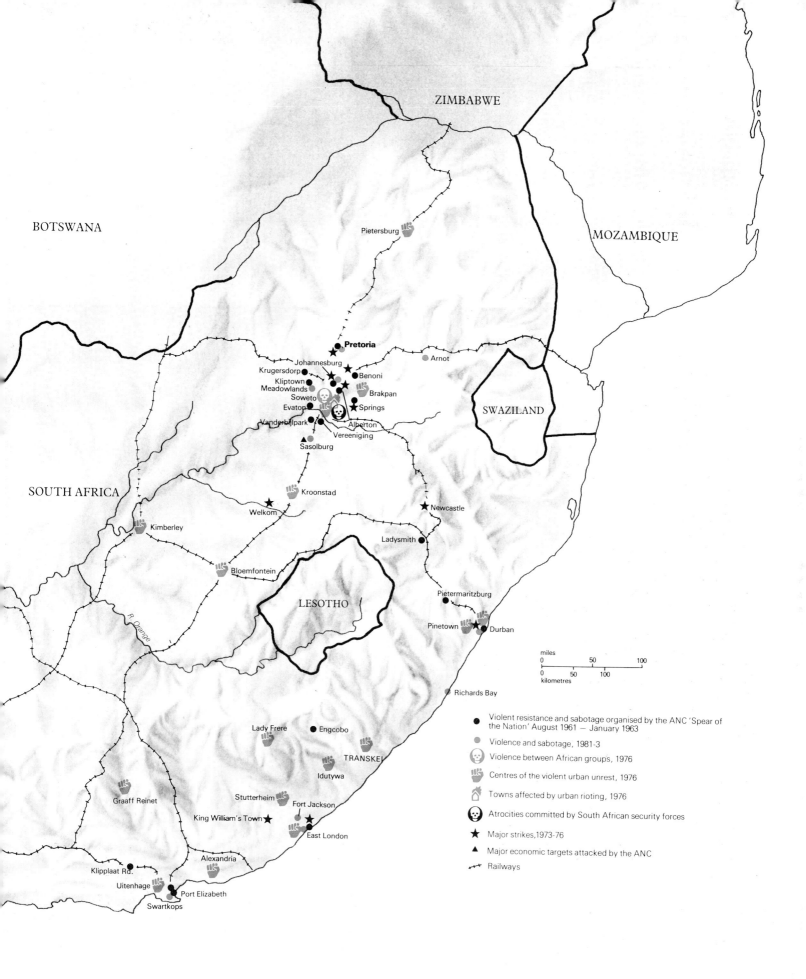

ZIMBABWE

BOTSWANA

MOZAMBIQUE

Pietersburg

Pretoria

Johannesburg
Krugersdorp
Kliptown
Meadowlands
Soweto
Evaton
Vanderbijlpark
Benoni
Brakpan
Springs
Alberton
Vereeniging
Sasolburg

Arnot

SWAZILAND

SOUTH AFRICA

Kroonstad

Welkom

Kimberley

Newcastle

Ladysmith

Bloemfontein

LESOTHO

Pietermaritzburg

R. Orange

Pinetown
Durban

Richards Bay

Lady Frere
Engcobo

TRANSKEI

Idutywa

Graaff Reinet

Stutterheim
Fort Jackson

King William's Town

East London

Alexandria

Klipplaat Rd.

Uitenhage
Port Elizabeth

Swartkops

miles
0   50   100
0   50   100
kilometres

● Violent resistance and sabotage organised by the ANC 'Spear of the Nation' August 1961 — January 1963

● Violence and sabotage, 1981-3

☺ Violence between African groups, 1976

✊ Centres of the violent urban unrest, 1976

⌂ Towns affected by urban rioting, 1976

☠ Atrocities committed by South African security forces

★ Major strikes,1973-76

▲ Major economic targets attacked by the ANC

✕✕ Railways

'We shall overcome, some day . . .'

WHEN the United States army set up its bases in Britain prior to the invasion of Europe in the Second World War, ordinary British people were horrified at the antagonism between black and white GIs.[1] At the small village of Kingsclere, near Newbury, there was even a fire-fight with rifles and automatic weapons in which civilians were killed. What was novel to the British was commonplace in the United States, especially in the southern states where slavery had prevailed until 1865. Even in the northern cities, where poor whites and blacks had migrated during the Depression, elements of racial tension were just as strong, if not so starkly presented. The report of the Congressional Committee on Civil Rights which was published in 1947 pointed to the damage which racism was doing to America's image overseas: 'our civil rights record has been an issue in world politics. . . . Those with competing philosophies have stressed – and are shamelessly distorting – our shortcomings. . . . They have tried to prove our democracy an empty fraud, and our nation a consistent oppressor of underprivileged people.'[2]

Racism in the south depended for its success on a largely static society in which white and black 'knew their place'. In the decade after the Second World War, the economic and social base of the south was changing profoundly. The old rural industries were in decline, and mechanization was beginning to reduce the overall demand for unskilled rural labour. The consequence was a huge migration of black workers from countryside to southern cities, as well as to the cities of the north. The stable, deferential black population which had existed since the 1890s, controlled by a white power structure, was affected by the pressure for black rights which was growing in the cities. The campaign to obtain equality through the courts which had been undertaken by the National Association for the Advancement of Coloured People finally bore fruit in 1954 when the Supreme Court reversed a string of earlier decisions that segregation could be maintained in education provided that the facilities provided were 'separate but equal'. In the following year, southern blacks discovered another weapon available to them in the cities – boycott and economic pressure. In 1955, a middle-aged black seamstress in Montgomery, Alabama, refused to sit in the back portion of a municipal bus reserved for 'coloureds', and took a seat in the white section. She was jailed, and a complete boycott of buses was organized by the black community. Many were imprisoned and fined, but the agitation continued until November 1956 when the bus company, close to financial collapse, conceded the issue. The local ordinance was repealed and a test case before the Supreme Court prohibited segregation on all local buses. The techniques – largely those of Gandhi's satyagrahra campaign in India, active civil disobedience and economic boycott – were opposed by the traditional white weapons of both legal and extra-legal violence. But it was difficult to suppress an urban movement in the full light of national and international publicity. Bombs thrown at black churches in Montgomery were front page news, while upstate, a savage beating by a gang of white men resulting in permanent injury to a black boy barely featured in the local paper. Conditions in the south were known to be shameful, but as Truman's committee pointed out, they were no longer consistent with America's status as leader of the free world. The alliance which presented this shameful face of America for inspection was dominated by articulate, wholesome and often religious men and women. The radicals and communists who had preserved the claim for freedom during the 1920s and 1930s were left on the sidelines. The new campaign was to be a Crusade for Civil Rights, borne along by bible hymns and preaching, a unified bloc of all strands of black opinion.

The prize for which the civil rights workers aimed was not merely to end segregation, but to allow blacks the right to make their power felt through the ballot box. This was the most dangerous threat to white supremacy, since in many localities the blacks had a commanding majority. In 1960, a protest about segregated lunch counters in Greensboro, North Carolina produced mass action all over the south, while in the following year a series of 'Freedom Rides' organized in the north produced routinely violent reactions from both southern police and racist mobs. Federal law specifically prohibited segregation on inter-state buses and the 'Freedom Riders' (blacks and white students for the most part) proved the degree to which federal law was flouted in the south. By 1963, racial tension was at a peak: the Department of Justice recorded 1412 demonstrations for one quarter of 1963 alone.

Racial violence was spreading from the towns and cities out into the countryside.[3] Casual, routine violence by white authority against blacks became more programmatic: civil rights activists were murdered, and those seeking the vote were threatened with death. But electoral registration increased steadily: where in 1952 only 20% of blacks eligible to register had done so, by 1964 the figure had doubled. In the core area of white resistance, however, the figures were less promising. Mississippi had a registered black electorate of 6% of those eligible in 1964, with Alabama around 19%.[4] The consequence of the civil rights agitation in the south, especially as the protests were recorded by press and television, was to heighten the sense of black consciousness among blacks in the north as well, and to rouse them against the poverty and relative oppression under which they suffered. The speeches of Martin Luther King, one of the finest crowd orators of the century, had a message for all minorities in the USA: 'I have a dream that one day this nation will rise up, live out the true

The Freedom March to Jackson, Mississippi in 1966. In the front rank are (l. to r.) Martin Luther King, James Meredith, and Stokely Carmichael (in overalls). While King passionately advocated non-violence, Carmichael moved over to violent revolution. Freedom marches were intended to provoke violent reaction and thereby diminish the south in the eyes of national and world opinion. They also aimed to make the government in Washington enforce the Civil Rights legislation lying unused

meaning of its creed: we hold these truths to be self-evident, that all men are created equal.' In 1967, he wrote: 'A riot is at bottom the language of the unheard'; from the Watts riot of 1965 onwards, all over the United States, the dispossessed discovered a new voice.

Individual violence was commonplace in America, a continuation of the frontier tradition. Mass violence and mass action was feared and regarded as deeply subversive, even when it offered only minimal disruption. In the great wave of riots which afflicted the USA between 1965 and 1968, coupled with the mass movements against the war in Vietnam, a new political radicalism developed, dedicated to the overthrow of traditional American society and its values. There were many attempts both to explain this and to demonstrate a common conspiracy behind it, but none was very convincing. In the course of the investigations, the role of corporate mass violence in the history of the United States was shown in a clearer perspective: riot had once been *the* American way. Wisely, the authorities came to agonize less about curing the causes of mass violence than being concerned with containing its consequences. Police units throughout the country began to train with internal counter-terrorism as one of their likely contingencies. The Federal Bureau of Investigation expended an

inordinate amount of effort in seeking to prove that Martin Luther King was a communist, and that white radicalism was part of a Soviet conspiracy against the United States. Both efforts were largely fruitless, but this pattern of mass investigation with the use of infiltrators and *agents provocateurs* transformed the shape of opposition politics. True revolutionary groups became smaller and more tightly controlled. This made them less liable to penetration. The broad mass movements dwindled as the great issues which had spawned them – civil rights and the American involvement in Vietnam – disappeared. Like other great populist movements which have gripped America, the upsurge of the 1960s left little trace of its passing. And racism, whether directed against blacks, Hispanics or other minorities, remains a uniquely potent force.

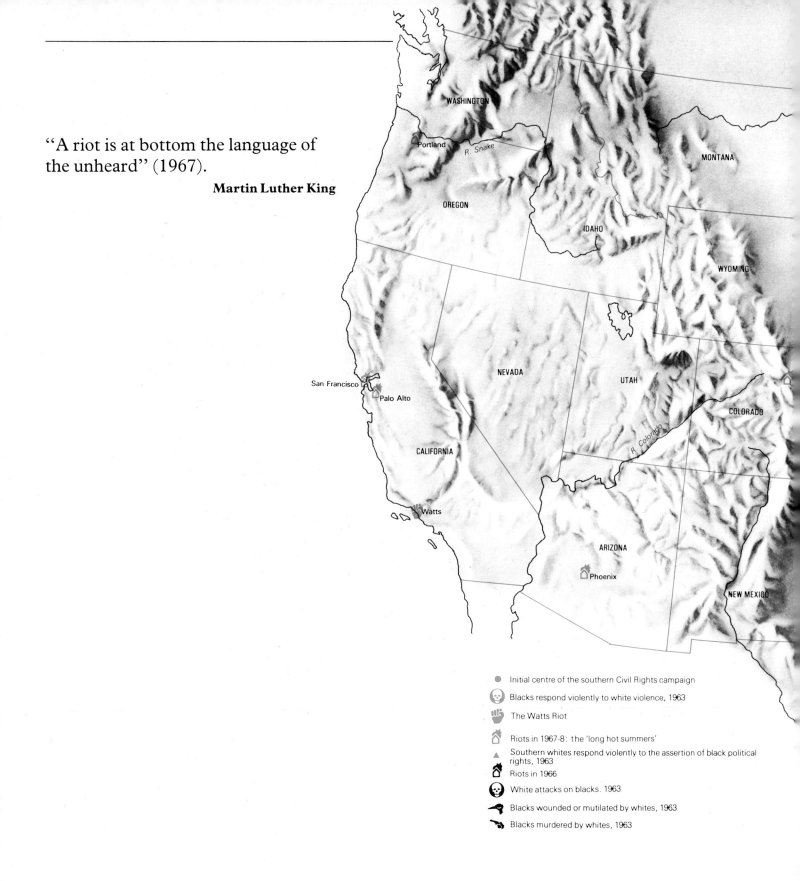

"A riot is at bottom the language of the unheard" (1967).

Martin Luther King

Initial centre of the southern Civil Rights campaign

Blacks respond violently to white violence, 1963

The Watts Riot

Riots in 1967-8: the 'long hot summers'

Southern whites respond violently to the assertion of black political rights, 1963

Riots in 1966

White attacks on blacks, 1963

Blacks wounded or mutilated by whites, 1963

Blacks murdered by whites, 1963

173

Revolutionary chauvinism in world power-politics

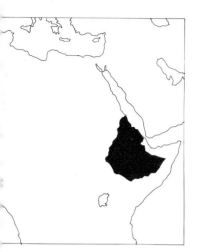

ETHIOPIA was an anomaly in Africa, a monarchy which had resisted the march of colonial expansion and preserved itself independent in a world dominated by white men. This survival was achieved in the twentieth century by Ethiopia's becoming a client of the western world, in the same way as the Roman Empire had attracted a cluster of nominally independent associates on its eastern edge. So the Emperor of Ethiopia, Haile Selassie, was restored to his throne by the British in 1941 after fleeing before an invading Italian army in 1936, and he repaid the debt by remaining a faithful supporter of the west thereafter. Considerable sums of aid were invested during the 1950s and 1960s, and the armed forces were modernized with equipment supplied by the United States on generous terms. The cream of Ethiopia's students were sent for their final education to Britain or to the United States. The bulk of these graduates became state employees, many of them in the army and air force. This was also the destination of the best secondary school graduates. The well-educated – by 1974 totalling 20,000 from the secondary schools, 3000 from the Haile Selassie University in Addis Ababa, and 1500 from foreign universities – formed an isolated elite group within Ethiopian society. Apart from its highly conservative and traditional nature, this society was also marked by a racial divide. In the north were the Christian Amhara clans, and to the south the Oromo, largely Moslem with a Christian minority. On the southern edge of the Oromo provinces were numerous tribes, most of Somali lineage. The dominant power in the state was the Amhara, the group from which the Emperor and the aristocracy were drawn. There was no doubt that the Amhara came out best from the traditional state structure, especially from the system of land holding which existed in the north; and Amhara landlords strongly resisted moves to reform landholding for the benefit of the Oromo. One area of opportunity open to successful Oromo members was the expanding state service. By the 1970s a growing proportion of the junior officer corps, as well as some twenty percent of the senior officers, were of Oromo origin.

For the considerable number of educated Ethiopians who had travelled abroad, the contrast between the outside world and their homeland was stark. The state had ossified under the control of an octogenarian emperor at a time when black Africa as a whole was making remarkable strides, and this point was made by a group of officers of the Imperial Guard in 1960, who staged a half-hearted revolt, declaring: 'The fantastic progress achieved by the newly independent African states has placed Ethiopia in an embarrassing situation. The new government will have as its aim to restore Ethiopia to its appropriate place in the world.'[1] And although the revolt of 1960 fizzled out, there was a growing body of opinion in the armed forces that patriotism demanded a profound change. By 1974 the government was visibly failing. It had

got nowhere with a rebellion in Eritrea, nor with resistance among the Somali trabesmen to the east, or an Oromo uprising in Bale. When a garrison at Nagalle in the southern desert area mutinied in January 1974 against their appalling living conditions, the government dithered, and finally weakly abandoned any attempt to restore discipline. By June, after further mutinous rumblings within the army and air force, a group of officers based at the capital Addis Ababa had formed a Co-ordinating Committee of the Armed Services (*Derg*, in the Amharinya language). This Military Committee contained representatives of every unit of the armed forces, and they found no difficulty in dictating to a spineless government. On 12 September, the Emperor was arrested, and power placed temporarily in the hands of a Provisional Military Administrative Council. The millennial monarchy had come to an end as the Lion of Judah was turned off his throne for the second time. None of this merited much more than a passing mention in the world press, for military coups were commonplace in the Third World.

The leading officers had, for the most part, been educated in the USA, or had visited Western countries. Neighbouring Somalia, with whom Ethiopia was at odds, was in receipt of considerable aid from the Soviet Union, and there seemed no reason why the West should not continue to support Ethiopia, especially since the United States had become increasingly irritated with the inadequacies of the old regime. World interest was roused to a greater degree of interest when the Provisional Council declared itself perpetual and began a bloody purge of the senior officer corps, especially those who had attended the élite Harar Military Academy. Most of the revolutionary officers had the common bond of passing through the junior, and much less prestigious, establishment. This was followed on 1 January 1975 and by stages through the spring by a huge programme of socialist measures: the banks were nationalized, then industry, and finally all rural land. In July all urban land and housing was nationalized. This total transformation of Ethiopian society was proclaimed with very little thought as to how it could be achieved, or the degree of opposition such radical measures might arouse. The only positive step was to dispatch 60,000 radical students, many of them very young, to the countryside to rouse and radicalize the peasants – a textbook and thoroughly amateurish move. The one real sanction which the *Derg* possessed was terror, and it needed to be used increasingly often. The wild surge towards the new rural Ethiopia was carried out against the advice of officials in the Chinese and Yugoslav embassies, as well as the staff of the Soviet mission. They feared that a promising situation would be doomed by recklessness.

The revolution raced ahead, almost out of control. Peasant risings were suppressed with considerable bloodshed, and opposition in the towns was treated equally severely. In February 1977 the movement turned upon itself: the *Derg* was purged of many of its senior members, including its chairman Teferi Benti; and the vice chairman Haile-Mariam Mengistu, was left as the strong man in control. Of the original 126 members of the *Derg*, no more than 80 remained after eighteen months of revolution. Mengistu turned to Russia for assistance in carrying out the revolution effectively and in providing aid to resist the Somalis, whose forces were making great progress in the war over Eritrea. A move towards the

Ethiopia's war with Somalia was largely waged against guerrillas. One is seen here in 1977, proud of his captured Soviet heavy machine gun. Only Russian and Cuban intervention saved the Ethiopians from a humiliating defeat, and Cuban troops remain active in the country

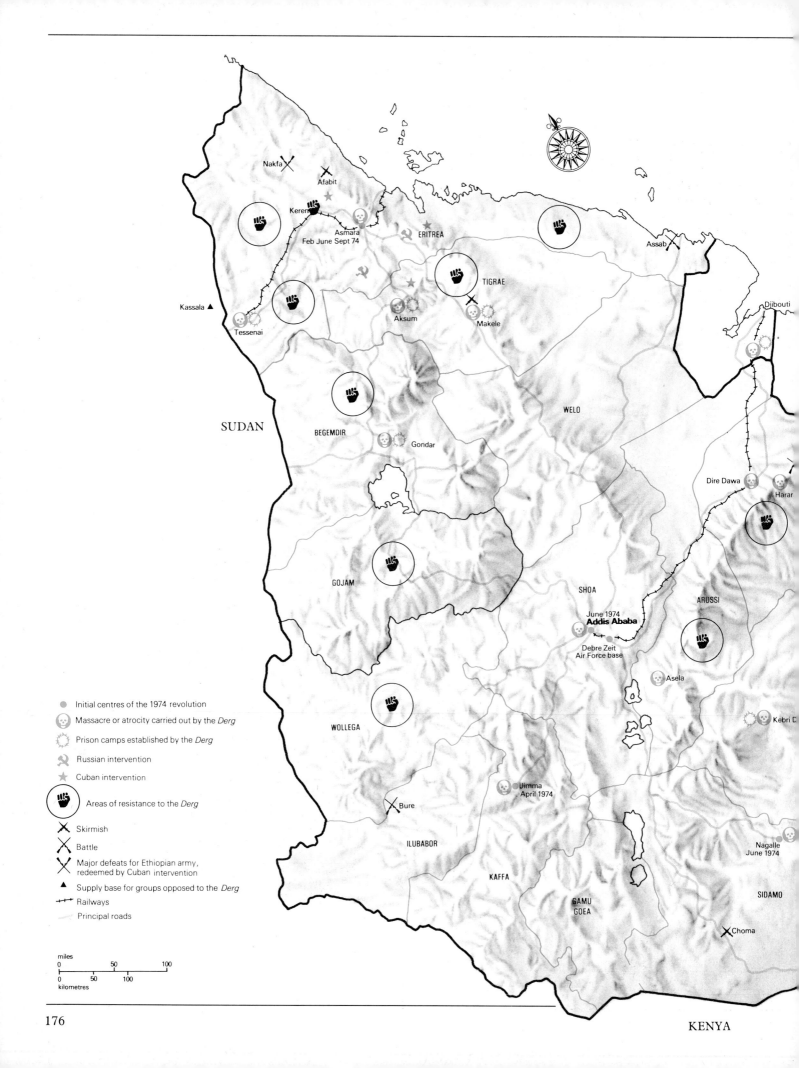

SUDAN

Nakfa
Afabit
Kerem
Asmara
Feb June Sept 74
ERITREA
Tessenai
Kassala ▲

Aksum
TIGRAE
Makele

Assab

Djibouti

WELO

BEGEMDIR
Gondar

GOJAM

SHOA
June 1974
Addis Ababa
Debre Zeit
Air Force base

WOLLEGA

ILUBABOR

Bure

Jimma
April 1974

KAFFA

GAMU
GOEA

Dire Dawa
Harar

ARUSSI

Asela

Kebri D

Nagalle
June 1974

SIDAMO

Choma

Initial centres of the 1974 revolution

Massacre or atrocity carried out by the *Derg*

Prison camps established by the *Derg*

Russian intervention

Cuban intervention

Areas of resistance to the *Derg*

Skirmish

Battle

Major defeats for Ethiopian army, redeemed by Cuban intervention

Supply base for groups opposed to the *Derg*

Railways

Principal roads

miles
0   50   100
0   50   100
kilometres

USSR had been policy since the early stages of the revolution in 1974, with the reluctance coming from the Soviet side. The Russians were suspicious of the wild plans of the *Derg*, and gave verbal encouragement but no commitment. Mengistu went to Moscow late in February 1977 and came back with military and economic aid, on Russia's terms. In March Fidel Castro came to East Africa to patch up the quarrel between Ethiopia and Somalia since both were now recipients of Eastern bloc aid. In the following month the Societ President Podgorny arrived on the same mission. In June the first Russian and Cuban aid arrived and was used in battle against Somali forces. On 13 November 1977 Somalia, having failed either to stop Russian aid for Ethiopia or to obtain more

for herself, expelled all the Russian and Cuban 'advisors', and sought a rapprochement with the United States. Within weeks of that decision, Ethiopia began to receive massive Soviet and Cuban aid: on 26 November flight after flight of Soviet transports brought military equipment into the country, to be followed within a few days by Cuban troops. This gesture of 'fraternal aid' saved the revolution from defeat. Like Angola, Ethiopia was now firmly within the stifling embrace of Soviet power.

The crisis which made the support of the Russians and Cubans essential was the abject failure of the Ethiopians in the war with Somalia in the Ogaden and with the Eritrean nationalist movements. Resistance to the *Derg* within Ethiopia was widespread but becoming muted as terror began to work on the peasants and political opposition. Where the revolution was accomplished, as in the south, it was accompanied by monumental inefficiency and corruption, which brought a further bout of terror between November 1977 and May 1978. The capital was covered, as one visitor noted, with posters carrying the message 'Intensify Red Terror', and the street was littered with bodies bearing placards with slogans such as 'This was a counter-revolutionary', 'We are tired of burying them', 'Red terror will flourish'.[2] But the army was wilting under the attacks of the spreading number of nationalist groups, as the northern province of Tigrae launched its own liberation movement and harassed Ethiopian lines of communication with the forces in Eritrea. Without the support of the Cuban troops and the infusion of Russian arms, the war would have been lost and the revolution with it.

Mengistu is an Ethiopian chauvinist, and utterly unwilling to allow any degree of latitude to the separatist movements, even in areas marginal to the interests of the state or the revolution. He has purged both the *Derg* and the cities of all political groups which advised concessions to the separatists and he has inherited the old tradition of Ethiopian imperialism. So closely has he filled the role that he is widely reputed to be an illegitimate son of Haile Selassie, a belief which has helped to give legitimacy to the regime. The Soviet Union would have preferred peace in the Horn of Africa and its two client states of Ethiopia and Somalia. The current arrangement is fraught with danger, especially since the war in the Ogaden continues, with Cuban and Ethiopian gains but no end in sight. Intervention has brought an open-ended commitment with 8000 Cuban troops still in action, but no clear view as to the eventual outcome. Russia's adventurous 'forward' policy, whether in Africa or Afghanistan, is beginning to turn sour.

The power of militant Islam

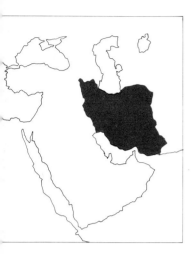

THE two and a half millennia of Iranian monarchy were celebrated in 1971 by Shah Mohammad Reza Pahlevi with unparalleled splendour, but while the monarchy was ancient his family was not. The former dynasty, under Shah Mohammad Ali, had been overthrown in a revolution (1905–9), and the country suffered occupation by both Russians and British until Reza Pahlevi seized power in 1921. In 1941 he was forced to abdicate by the British and his son Mohammad Reza became Shah in his place. In 1953 he too had fled in the face of a nationalist revolution, later to be replaced when the American CIA engineered a restoration.

Two elements have dominated Iran throughout the twentieth century: popular nationalism, as exemplified by the revolution of 1905 and the Mossadeq government of 1951–3, and the power of the mosque, militant Islam led by the mullahs of the holy city of Qum. On the international scene, the Shah radiated power and prestige. He spent vast sums on armaments and had clear aspirations to be the dominant influence in the Gulf. An effective secret police, a widely publicized programme of land reform – 'the white revolution' – and patronage on a vast scale were the means used to stifle or buy off internal opposition. The prize was a modernized, Western-orientated Iran. Both Reza Shah and his son aimed to achieve for Iran what Ataturk had done for Turkey, a secular state free from the domination of traditionalist Islam.

The Shah bought off the more venal nationalists, imprisoned the left and the more principled nationalists, and sought to decapitate the Islamic militants by exiling their leader after a failed insurrection against his 'godless' white revolution in 1963. The leader, Ayatollah Khomeini of Qum, was arrested in the middle of the festival of Muharram, always a highly charged period, and within two hours of his arrest there were riots in Tehran, Mashhad, Isfahan and Shiraz which resulted in thousands of dead.

The Shia sect of Islam which is dominant in Iran revolves around the theme of martyrdom. In countless vivid sermons called *rawdas*, which were dramatic orations on the theme of martyrdom, Khomeini was portrayed as a descendant of the martyred Husayn while the Shah was seen as the image of the arch-tyrant Yazid who slaughtered Husayn and most of his family. This Islamic symbolism was immensely potent in a society which was largely pre-literate, but well versed in the oral tradition of the mosque. The rallying points for religious opposition came to be the many significant festivals of the Shiite calendar. The anniversary of Khomeini's arrest was marked in Qum by fresh unrest, and those killed by the Shah's commandos were added to the list of martyrs. Khomeini, in exile in Iraq, kept in touch with his followers by pamphlets and cassette tapes of his voice smuggled into the country, along with his book on Islamic Government published in 1971. As the Shah was celebrating the long tradition of Persian monarchy in Persepolis, his country was racked by rioting students, striking workers, and demonstrators shouting, 'Long live Khomeini.' Every month murders and guerrilla attacks, arson and bombings increased. Unemployment grew when the wildly optimistic targets for industrial expansion were not met, while in the countryside peasants were squeezed out of the market by the large new businesses set up with state aid.

The 'white revolution' was an abstract modernization, figures on a balance sheet, with monumental opportunities for graft and corruption. It corresponded to a desire to increase the statistics of national well-being – an improved gross national product, more agricultural production, better welfare services – without considering the implications of imposing them on a traditional society. The Shah believed that the application of vast oil revenues and careful paperwork would produce effective progress. Propaganda extolling the 'white revolution' was aimed abroad rather than at home: little attempt was made to prepare the people for the impact of change. The Islamic establishment held to the view that 'what the people want is the result of what they are taught. They can be taught to want what God wants.' From every mosque, from the mouth of every mullah, came a denunciation of the Shah and his works. The people in the streets cried in religious processions, 'O Husayn, save us from this Shah.'

For a revolution to be forced through, regardless of human cost, was quite possible given the military and police resources at the government's disposal, but only in a closed society, cut off from the outside world and indifferent to world opinion. But the Shah was the client of the United States, and the appalling human rights record of his regime was embarrassing to the moralistic administration established by President Carter after 1976. In January 1978, after more rioting in Qum and more deaths at the hands of the police, the leading ayatollah in Qum, Shariatmadari, declared the Shah's government to be against Islam. This had been regularly said by Khomeini in exile, but never since 1963 by so senior an official figure. In February 1978 there was prolonged rioting in Tabriz, and when on 30 March a day of mourning was declared by the Islamic authorities, there was rioting in many of the major cities. Processions and street demonstrations were the traditional method of protest in Iran. Forty days after the riots of 30 March, public demonstrations were renewed, leaving more dead. The cycle of Shiite mourning ritual calls for ceremonies on the third, seventh and fortieth day after death, and this pattern, familiar to all, became the formula for mass protest.

In the face of this activity the Shah's government took no decisive action. The police and troops fired on rioters in response to danger or provocation, but there was no sense of a concerted plan. Even the loyalty of the army itself was coming in question, for

10 December 1978: more than a million people marched through the streets of Tehran, demonstrating against the Shah. They called for the return of their hero, the Ayatollah Khomeini, here on a banner above the heads of his fanatical young followers

the conscripts too were susceptible to social pressures.

From the beginning of the Ramadhan fast on 5 August 1978, virtually no day passed without demonstrations. At a funeral for victims of a cinema fire in Abadan, ten thousand came to the cemetery, chanting, 'Death to the Shah! Burn him! End the fifty years of Pahlevi tyranny!' and, significantly, 'Soldiers, you are guiltless. The Shah is the villain!'[1] On 8 September, martial law was declared and hundreds were killed in a demonstration in Tehran. But strikes and disturbances continued, and the vital oil industry was brought to a halt. The Shah made concessions, lifted martial law, and promised a ruthless suppression of corruption as well as the restoration of civil liberties. This did nothing to check the daily pattern of violence.

In 1978 the religious festival of Muharram, a season pregnant with the blood of martyrs, fell in December and the mass marches had risen to a fever pitch during the previous month. More than a million and a half people marched through the city of Mashhad on 26 November, and there was a general strike throughout the country as well as countless smaller demonstrations. It was widely believed that the political crisis would erupt during the festival. As December progressed the country fell into complete chaos, with millions on the march daily in cities throughout Iran, two million in Tehran alone. Many demonstrators wore white shrouds, signifying that

they would welcome martyrdom, and violence reached a crescendo on both sides. The Shah, in desperation, sought to form a new government headed by a figure not tainted by past associations. At the beginning of 1979 Shahpur Bakhtiar took office and began a major purge of the former officials; most people believed that he intended to depose the Shah. There was a lull in the disturbances and then a succession of largely peaceful demonstrations. On 15 January, the Shah left the country, for a brief 'vacation'. Khomeini continued to denounce Bakhtiar as the Shah's creature and at the end of January declared that he would return home from Paris, where he had been since October 1978. On 1 February 1979 he arrived at Tehran airport, to be greeted by two million people.

The Shah had been destroyed by a national rising of all opposition groups. Khomeini represented the extreme wing of Islamic militancy and was determined not merely to destroy the Shah but to achieve a revolution in Iranian society. Over the space of two years he achieved the elimination of most of the other opposition groups, either by death – 10,000 a month were condemned by Islamic tribunals at their peak of activity – or flight. Since he was impervious to international opinion, as the episode of the American embassy hostages indicated, or to the human cost, a profound transformation was achieved. The land reforms attempted by the Shah were replaced by much

miles
0   50   100
0   50   100
kilometres

○ The main centres of violent reaction to the Shah, 1975–78

☠ The main centres of the Islamic terror, 1979-82

✊ The strongpoints of Islamic resistance to the Shah's policies before 1978

☠ Massacres by the police, armed forces, or groups loyal to the Shah

✊ Areas where national minorities are resisting the Islamic revolution

🏠 Centres of organised left wing and Islamic resistance

more radical measures, and by purging Iranian society of most of its Western consumer attitudes, he has reduced Iran's dependence on oil revenues. Even the war with Iraq has had its advantages in terms of siphoning off national discontent. Where he has failed to achieve decisive results is with the national minorities. They joined the revolution against the Shah, but then demanded autonomy from the new government. Khomeini sought to centralize rather than de-centralize administration, and territorial concessions were not part of his policy. The same terror tactics were used against the Kurds, Baluchis, and Azerbaijanis as against Iranian enemies, with countless deaths resulting from the activities of the revolutionary tribunals. But nationalism has retreated rather than disappeared. The same may be said for the left wing, which with its leaders in exile has now begun to mount more and more effective attacks against the Islamic People's Party established by Khomeini.

Earlier in this century (and in the last) the state was overthrown by an alliance between nationalists and Islamic militancy. On each occassion the alliance broke down and the fundamentalists retreated to the mosque and the *medressah* (religious schools) to take up their traditional role of criticism and exhortation. The novelty of the present arrangement is that the religious militants have not abandoned the political stage, but forced the nationalists and the middle classes from it. Islamic militancy is now an instrument of government, largely peasant and working-class in its bias, and with a fanatical following among the young. It is unique in the history of Iran.

The tradition of resistance

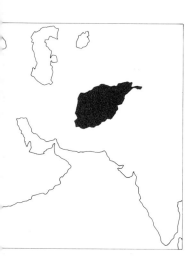

THE position of Afghanistan, between the Russian-dominated khanates of central Asia and the riches of India ruled by the British, made it a prize eagerly sought by both the great empires before the First World War. The Afghans became adept at avoiding entanglements with either power bloc, and resisted various British attempts at military intervention even more strongly. The monarchy was carefully balanced between the various tribal interest groups, and the rulers of Afghanistan disregarded tribal matters of landholding and blood feuds at their peril. This skill at balancing powerful factions proved useful after the Second World War, when Afghanistan touted for aid from all the major donor countries, and was at one time receiving aid from twenty countries, including the USA, Western Europe, the Eastern bloc, China, and an assortment of Middle Eastern states. The major road system which linked all the main cities was built by both the Russians and the Chinese, each hoping for political advantage.

The principal support of the monarchy against the tribes was the armed forces, and in the 1930s Nadir Shah had created an effective army and air force with German assistance. By the 1950s, however, the armed services were becoming antiquated and approaches were made to the United States for a military aid programme. The request was turned down, and the Afghans were forced to turn to the Soviet Union as the only plausible alternative source of supply. The weapons needs related to internal security rather than external defence, and the Russians proved trustworthy and largely undemanding patrons. However, since many of the new officers were trained in Russia, and the equipment was both supplied and serviced by the Russians, it provided the Soviet Union with a controlling interest in the affairs of Afghanistan if they cared to use it. The architect of the rapprochement with the Soviet Union was Muhammad Daoud, a cousin of King Zahir. He fell from office after a quarrel with the king in 1963 after a decade in office. He returned to power ten years later after a coup organized by the Parcham section of the Marxist People's Democratic Party of Afghanistan, using longstanding contacts established in the army and air force. It was not hard to detect the hand of the Soviet Union behind the coup. However Daoud proved less amenable than had at first seemed likely, and he had no intention of being the puppet of a largely middle- and working-class Marxist party. Over the next three years he purged many Marxists from positions of power, and sought to re-establish the broad base of international financial support for Afghanistan that he had achieved in his earlier period in power. On 27 April 1978, a new Marxist coup was launched, this time against Daoud but organized jointly by both the Parcham and Khalq factions of the party, which were usually at each other's throats. Few of the military units, except the air force at the distant Shindand base, rallied to Daoud, and they were too far away to be much use. Yet although the fighting was over quite quickly, over 2000 died in the murders and purges which followed, including Daoud, his entire family, and the residue of the royal house. During the summer and autumn of 1978, the Khalq faction turned on the Parcham group, murdering or imprisoning those whom it could catch. But the Parcham leadership, including Babrak Karmal, its principal spokesman, was safely in Moscow by this time.

The tension between the tribes and the central government had never been resolved under the monarchy, and the kings were careful never to press their claims to practical sovereignty too far. But the tribal chiefs recognized the dynasty as equals; Daoud had been admired as a hard man and an aristocrat in the traditional Afghan style. His replacement, Hafizullah Amin, was a peasant, and completely unacceptable for his origins, let alone his political ideas. An earlier peasant revolutionary, Bacha Saquo, had received a similar reception from tribal leaders in the 1920s. But however much a peasant by origin, Amin, who had forced his way to the head of Khalq, was a man of considerable shrewdness and intellectual gifts. He believed that a slow and painstaking transformation of Afghan society would always be drowned by vested interests. The only hope was a whirlwind revolution, shaking Afghanistan to its foundations. A massive campaign of land redistribution and compulsory education on Marxist lines was announced, and an army of officials dispatched to put it into practice. Within a year of seizing power, Khalq was faced by revolt in almost every province and a total breakdown of governmental authority. In the cities as well as the countryside, Khalq supporters were killed by mobs enraged by the attack on custom and religion. In Herat, almost 5000 were killed in the murders and reprisals which followed. Other towns followed suit and there were mutinies in the army. One of the main targets for vengeance were the numerous Russian advisors, over 5000 of them by the summer of 1979. The Soviet Union tried to have Amin replaced by Nur Muhammad Taraki, a more pliant Khalq leader, but Amin learned of the plot and disposed of Taraki. By the autumn of 1979 the country was in chaos, the army on the verge of disintegration, and Amin, now distrustful of his former Russian allies after the Taraki episode, controlled little more than Kabul with a few loyal troops. His nephew, Asadullah Amin, was appointed chief of the secret police, and he began to use members of his own family in high positions since they were the only people that he felt he could trust. In December 1979 Asadullah was shot by an unknown assailant, and Amin followed the advice of his Russian security advisor that it would be difficult to protect him in the city and he would be safer in the Darulaman Palace on the outskirts of the city. It was there that he and his supporters met their end on the day that the Russians began a massive invasion: 27 December 1979.

The motives behind the Soviet intervention in Afghanistan, and the explanation for the gross clumsiness of their actions, are difficult to understand. At the time, in the West, it was reliably attributed even by quite shrewd analysts to Russia's desire to achieve a 'warm water port'. Diagrams were drawn to show the dangerous proximity of Pakistan's ports to Afghanistan, and the domino theory enjoyed a brief but heady revival. However, the question as to why the Russians should want a port so far from their main centres of production, and accessible only over some of the world's worst terrain, soon put paid to such theorizing. Perhaps a more plausible explanation is poor intelligence, and a fundamental misunderstanding of the country and its peoples. It is likely that the Soviet leadership made some sort of mental equation between the Afghans and the Moslem tribesmen of Soviet Asia. Certainly, their experience of the Marxist Afghans they had met gave them no inkling of a race of guerrilla supermen. Nor did the KGB in Afghanistan have much experience of the rural areas; and it is widely believed that they advised against the invasion.

The military operation for the seizure of the country was immaculately executed, but it took place within a political vacuum. The Parcham faction of the MDPA, under Babrak Karmal, would stand no better chance than Amin of attracting wide popular support, and the Soviet Union was placed in the uncharacteristic position of reinforcing failure, which

had been the role of the United States in Vietnam. A pattern of resistance was already established before the invasion took place, but it was now reinforced by wholesale desertions from the Afghan army, and growing popular support as the weight of the Russian-led repression was felt. Both the terrain and the nature of Afghan rural society made it splendid guerrilla country. The main highway was dominated at almost every point by higher ground, and even the centres of population were close to mountain areas which provided perfect bases for guerrilla fighters. The Russians began their invasion with second-line troops from the Asiatic republics, who were ill-equipped for a long stay or any prolonged fighting. They have, progressively, been replaced with specialists better suited to the terrain, and with equipment adapted to counter-insurgency in rugged terrain. But the zones in which they operate have been limited to areas close to their support groups. The Panjshir valley area and the area around Pagman, both close to Kabul, have seen repeated 'search and clear' operations. But the hinterland, in particular the provinces of Bamiyan and Ghor, has been left secure in rebel hands. Both the Russian and the remnants of the Afghan army hold firmly to the road network: it is logistically difficult to move much beyond it. More than 100,000 Soviet troops are now involved, and by night even the cities are no longer secure.

In fighting their war the guerrilla fighters, *mujahidin*, have followed tradition. They have little political

Afghan warriors buying arms in Pakistan, as they have always done. But now the weapons are for use against the Russian invaders. The Peshawar link is a crucial route for arms supplies to the guerrillas, whose main concern is the cost of ammunition

coherence and their common objectives now focus on forcing the Russians to withdraw. They possess a long frontier with Pakistan and a degree of liberty beyond the Iranian border. From their bases inside Pakistan arms and equipment are smuggled into the country, a traffic which it is difficult for the Russians to prevent. The *mujahidin* have captured much basic equipment from Russian and Afghan soldiers, and learned the best ways either to avoid or to resist Russia's tactical airpower. Their main target has been the main highway, the lifeline of Russian communications, which remains vulnerable. An accident in the Salang tunnel north of Kabul in November 1982 in which hundreds of Russian soldiers were asphyxiated, indicates the ease with which it can be cut. But the *mujahidin* can have no hope of inflicting other than minor reverses on the Russians, whose casualties, estimates of which vary between 2000 and 10000 over a three-year war, compare favourably with those suffered by the United States in Vietnam over a six-year period. While the Russians can hold what they have taken, they have no hope of recovering the whole of the country. Even if they were able to dislodge the guerrillas from their fastnesses close to the cities, and succeeded in closing the border with Pakistan, a style of irregular war which Afghans have carried on for generations from the hills and mountains of the interior, an exalted form of banditry, would still be possible. It was believed at one time that Russia would be able, as she had been in her conquest of the Asiatic khanates in the nineteenth century, to plan a campaign of pacification running over decades. But Afghanistan has international political complications. It has caused great damage to the carefully fostered image of the Soviet Union in the Moslem world and the Third World in general. Moreover, Afghanistan continues to be a major topic of news coverage throughout the world, and Soviet actions take place under the relentless gaze of international opinion. The option existed, before the invasion, of allowing the Marxists to sink and thereafter seeking to re-establish relations with a new Afghan administration which would emerge from the turmoil. It is now probably the only alternative to stalemate.

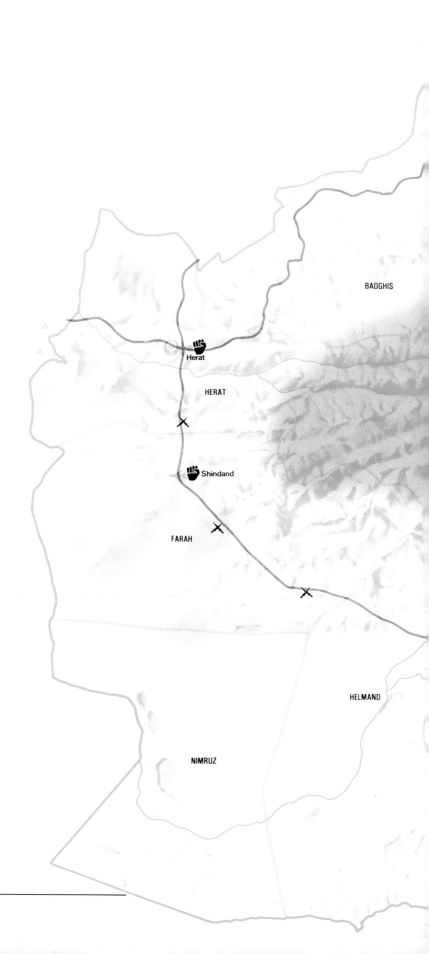

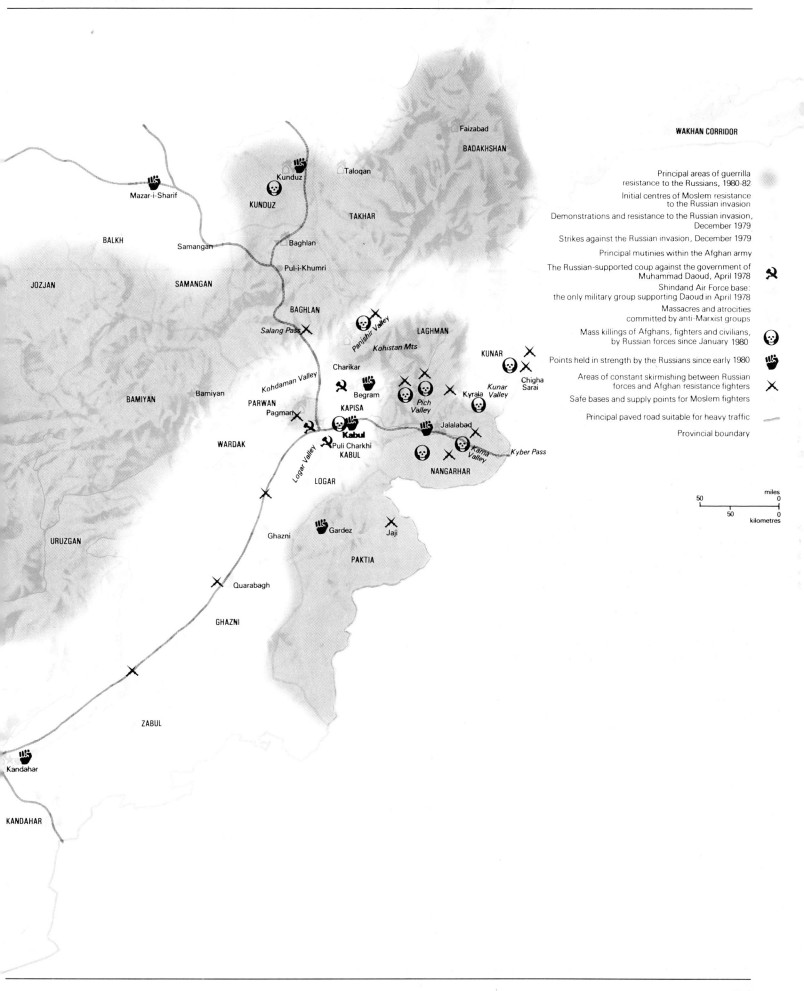

WAKHAN CORRIDOR

BADAKHSHAN

Faizabad

Taloqan

TAKHAR

Kunduz
KUNDUZ

Mazar-i-Sharif

BALKH

Samangan

Baghlan

JOZJAN

SAMANGAN

Pul-i-Khumri

BAGHLAN

Salang Pass

Panjshir Valley

LAGHMAN

Kohistan Mts

Charikar

KUNAR

Kohdaman Valley

Begram

Kyrala

Kunar
Valley

Chigha
Sarai

Bamiyan

BAMIYAN

PARWAN

Pagman

KAPISA

Pich
Valley

Kabul
Puli Charkhi
KABUL

Jalalabad

Kama
Valley

Kyber Pass

WARDAK

Logar Valley

LOGAR

NANGARHAR

URUZGAN

Ghazni

Gardez

Jaji

PAKTIA

Quarabagh

GHAZNI

ZABUL

Kandahar

KANDAHAR

Principal areas of guerrilla
resistance to the Russians, 1980-82

Initial centres of Moslem resistance
to the Russian invasion

Demonstrations and resistance to the Russian invasion,
December 1979

Strikes against the Russian invasion, December 1979

Principal mutinies within the Afghan army

The Russian-supported coup against the government of
Muhammad Daoud, April 1978

Shindand Air Force base:
the only military group supporting Daoud in April 1978

Massacres and atrocities
committed by anti-Marxist groups

Mass killings of Afghans, fighters and civilians,
by Russian forces since January 1980

Points held in strength by the Russians since early 1980

Areas of constant skirmishing between Russian
forces and Afghan resistance fighters

Safe bases and supply points for Moslem fighters

Principal paved road suitable for heavy traffic

Provincial boundary

miles
50   0

50   0
kilometres

185

The matter of Palestine

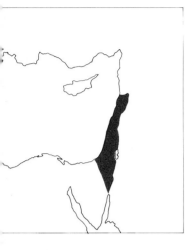

THROUGH the centuries of dispersal, persecution and oppression, there have always been Jews in Palestine. Continuous settlement can be traced back to Biblical times. Equally certain is the fact that Palestine has been an Arab country since the seventh century AD and Jerusalem is as holy to a Moslem as it is to a Jew. The parallelism continues within the twin revolutions which have been mounted, first by the Jews and latterly by the Arabs, both seeking to create a nation-state in the land of Palestine. In 1920, Britain was entrusted with Palestine at the San Remo Conference in which she undertook to create a Jewish national home in accordance with the Balfour Declaration of 1917. After stating that 'His Majesty's Government view with favour the establishment in Palestine of a national home for the Jewish people, and will use their best endeavours to facilitate the achievement of this objective', it continued with the important qualification, 'being clearly understood that nothing shall be done which may prejudice the civil and religious rights of non-Jewish communities in Palestine . . .'[1] These aims were incompatible.

From the beginning, antagonism between Jew and Arab was expressed violently. During the 1920s Arabs killed many more Jews than Jews killed Arabs, but as the Jewish community became better organized for self-defence and the British police and army did more to protect them, the numbers equalized. It was only in 1937, after suffering fifteen years of attacks, that the Jews began to organize reprisals

The British stand between Jews and Arabs during the endless series of riots and murders which characterized the Mandate from 1930–48. The Arabs proved more troublesome than the Jews, until Irgun began their terror campaign in the early 1940s

and counter-terror, although the Jewish National Council denounced any active response or counter-violence against the Arab population. But from the late 1930s, the voice of the militant Zionists led by Vladimir Jabotinsky began to be heard more strongly. At a World Congress in Prague, they declared that Arab terror would be met by Jewish terror and that they opposed any plan 'which would deprive the Jewish people of their right to establish a Jewish majority on both sides of the Jordan'.[2] In fact, the White Paper of 1939, which represented Britain's definitive thinking on the Palestinian question was a catastrophe for the Zionist cause, for it offered only limited Jewish immigration until 1944, and thereafter only with the approval of the Arabs, in effect a total bar to immigration. Under the White Paper there was no prospect of a Jewish majority in any substantial area of Palestine, let alone 'on both sides of the Jordan'.

The Zionist revisionists, already enraged by the White Paper, looked upon the British as murderers, collectively guilty as the evidence of the death camps and Nazi persecution became more widely known. In 1943, the Irgun Zvai Leumi, the most militant of the Jewish self-defence forces, whose members were largely responsible for the atrocities committed following Arab massacres of Jews, declared that it had begun a revolt against the British mandate. Under the leadership of a Polish Jew, Menachem Begin, who had once intended to bring an army of Polish fanatics to take the land of 'Eretz Israel' by force of arms, it launched a campaign of symbolic terrorism designed to provoke the British. They had to be shown not as an honest trustee holding Palestine for the benefit of all, but as a brutal occupying power. The 'war' launched on 12 February 1944 consisted largely of pinpricks – bombing attacks and revolutionary propaganda – all that the tiny, ill-equipped organization could contemplate. Then in September the Irgun began a programme of assassinating British officials, and by mid-October more than fifteen had been killed. Initially the established Jewish authorities assisted the British to stamp out the wild men of the Irgun, but eventually they came to a tacit working understanding with militant Zionism. The terror campaign gathered momentum in 1945, and in 1946 Irgun squads were dispatched to Europe. A bomb damaged the British Embassy in Rome in October 1946. In Palestine, as Irgun prisoners were flogged, the organization promised reprisals. In July 1947, after several Irgun men had been hanged, and 'a death for a death' had been promised, the Irgun executed two captured British sergeants after three Irgun men had gone to the gallows. The outcry in Britain was immediate, and there were attacks on Jewish shops in Liverpool and Glasgow. The majority wanted disengagement, and no further sacrifice of British lives.

Irgun was not the main force behind the creation

The symbol of Palestinian terror tactics. The burned-out wreck of a hijacked airliner at Dawson's Field near Amman. By this means Palestinians sought to make their protest felt throughout the world

of the Jewish state, and its activities were viewed with utter distaste by many Jews. But their violent and symbolic acts, such as the destruction of the King David Hotel in Jerusalem, and the almost daily murders and bombings in 1946–7, raised the political temperature and roused extreme passions. In August 1945 the Officer Administering the Government of Palestine had written to the Colonial Secretary in London: 'The young Jewish extremists . . . know neither toleration nor compromise; they regard themselves as morally justified in violence directed against any individual or institution that impedes the complete fulfilment of their demands. . . .'[3] But remorseless violence did keep the Palestine issue at the centre of world news, and as the leading problem facing British politicians. The concession of the Jewish state was made to the 'responsible' Jewish leaders, who clamped down on Irgun. Begin and his followers transferred their militancy to the Knesset (the Parliament) through the Herut Party. Many Arabs had fled from Palestine in 1948 on the advice of their leaders, and from fears of a Jewish war of atrocity. They had some justification for such a belief, for Irgun massacred 200 Arabs in the village of Deir Yassin near Jerusalem, the bloodiest single incident of the war on either side.[4] In the camps created by the United Nations in the countries bordering the new Zionist state of Israel, the Arabs created their own terror organization to retake the land of Palestine, beginning in 1950 and continuing year by year thereafter.

It is possible to read accounts of Irgun activities in the 1940s and simply by changing the names and places, use them to describe the tactics of the Arab *fedayin*. The pattern was indeed much the same, although it took the Arabs much longer to settle upon effective tactics. The infiltration, which lasted until 1967, achieved limited successes but little international interest. In the aftermath of the 1967 war, the Palestinians decided, as a counsel of despair, to internationalize the conflict, to attack Israel at its weakest rather than its strongest points. The ensuing campaign of international terrorism – aircraft hi-jackings, and symbolic acts of revolutionary terrorism – gained more international attention for the Palestinian cause than years of murders and bombings inside Israel. This culminated with the leader of the Palestine Liberation Organization, Yasir Arafat speaking to the General Assembly of the United Nations dressed not as a politician but as a guerrilla, in battle-fatigue dress, with a pistol on his hip. The history of the Palestinians since 1967 has been of retreat territorially, and advance politically. They were expelled from Jordan in 1970, and have been under pressure in Lebanon since 1976, most especially in the sustained Israeli advance to Beirut in 1982. The various Palestinian military formations are now well armed with equipment supplied by the Eastern bloc and many other countries, well financed both by contributions from Arab nations and the contributions of Palestinians throughout the world.

The issue of Palestine has affected relationships not merely in the Middle East but throughout the world. The Jewish diaspora has given Zionism a voice in many countries, especially in the United States (the world's largest urban Jewish population is to be found in New York not in Israel). But Palestinians have now experienced their own diaspora, and an articulate case for a national homeland is now being made by Palestinians who have achieved positions of importance not merely in the Middle East and Asia but in the Western world. Where at one time only the Zionist voice was widely believed to present a true picture of events in the Middle East, more credence is now being given to the Palestinians. But although they may be winning the argument, Zionism is winning the ground. The west bank of the Jordan is being secured for Israel as Jabotinsky and the revisionists always believed it should be, by Jewish occupation and settlement. The aim of the government of Israel, headed by the same Menachem Begin who devised the Irgun terror, is to achieve majority Jewish control of the whole land of 'Eretz Israel', the historic kingdom given by God to the Jews. This is not peaceful settlement, but war by other means: each settlement has a part in a wider defensive pattern. Thus the Palestinians in exile see their land disappearing, literally, under concrete and tarmac.

Irgun succeeded against the British because the British set limits to the punitive action there were prepared to take. Israel has defeated the Palestinians by making it clear that in defence of the homeland, there are no limits. Such a policy has forced the neighbouring states either to put limits on Palestinian *fedayin*, or to expel them, as Jordan did. In every state, the Palestinian army has brought catastrophe in its wake, and nowhere more so than in Lebanon. Two civil wars, foreign occupation, and many thousands of dead have followed inexorably from the arrival of the Palestinian military command from Jordan, which made Lebanon the 'front-line state' in their war with Israel. The Israeli advance was a military catastrophe for the Palestinians, but it has also closed a number of options for Israel. It was waged for reasons which can no longer be presented as mere defence of the homeland, because no threat existed which required a response on such a scale. The massacres at the refugee camps of Chatila and Sabra were widely seen, rightly or wrongly, as Israel using a vendetta by the Christian Lebanese in the same way that certain Latin American regimes used the independent death squads: elimination of an enemy without personal responsibility for the act. Limits have now been set, in terms of internal Israeli politics as well as of international opinion, on future courses of action.

Irgun and the constellation of the Palestinian resistance organizations have waged the same type of war for the same ground. In his struggle for a Jewish homeland, Begin sought to discredit the British

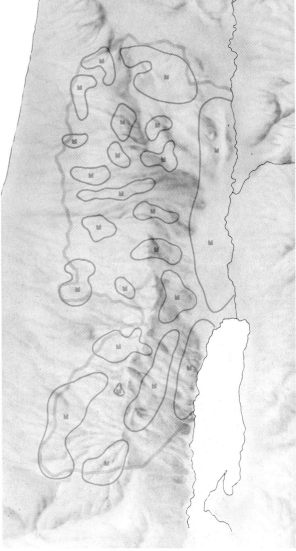

administration: 'History and our observation persuaded us that if we could succeed in destroying the government's prestige ... the removal of its rule would follow automatically. Thenceforward we gave no peace to this weak spot. Throughout all the years of our uprising, we hit at the British Government's prestige, deliberately, tirelessly, unceasingly.'[5] It was a strategy born of weakness and the lack of any plausible alternative. Now the Palestinians are also without any credible strategy in the wake of the war in Lebanon. They could do worse than play the Irgun game.

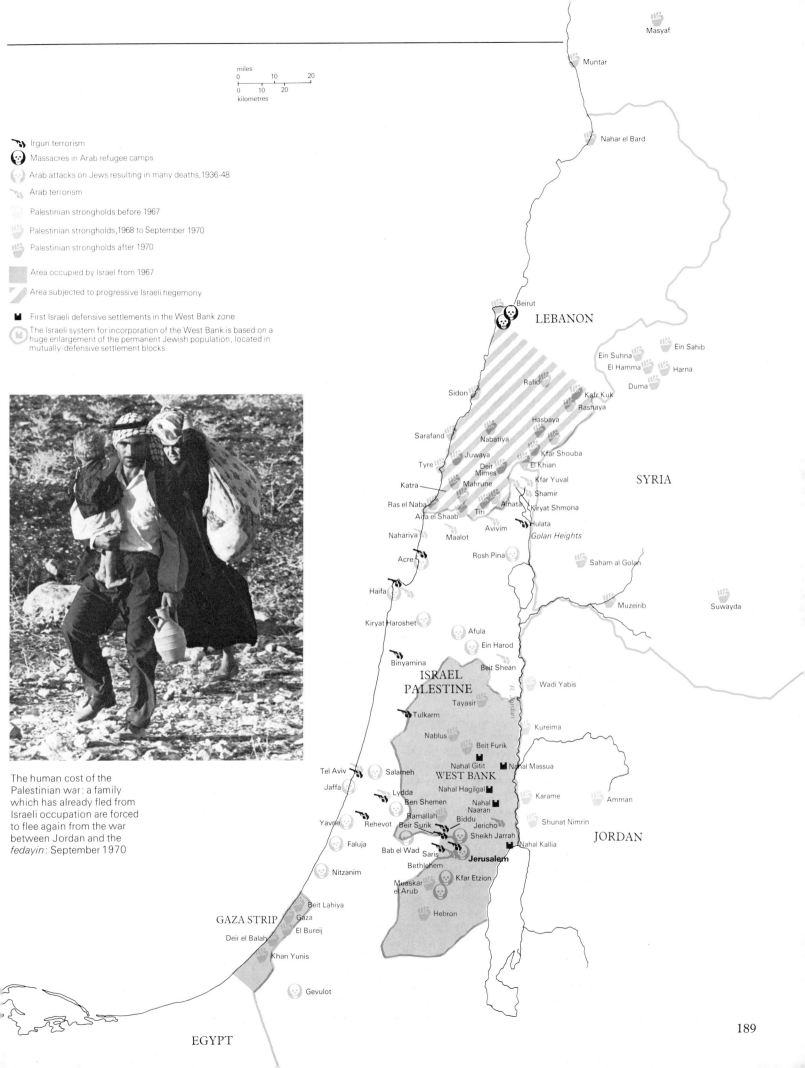

Legend

- Irgun terrorism
- Massacres in Arab refugee camps
- Arab attacks on Jews resulting in many deaths, 1936-48
- Arab terrorism
- Palestinian strongholds before 1967
- Palestinian strongholds, 1968 to September 1970
- Palestinian strongholds after 1970
- Area occupied by Israel from 1967
- Area subjected to progressive Israeli hegemony
- First Israeli defensive settlements in the West Bank zone
- The Israeli system for incorporation of the West Bank is based on a huge enlargement of the permanent Jewish population, located in mutually-defensive settlement blocks

The human cost of the Palestinian war: a family which has already fled from Israeli occupation are forced to flee again from the war between Jordan and the *fedayin*: September 1970

miles
0   10   20
0   10   20
kilometres

Map labels

Masyaf
Muntar
Nahar el Bard
Beirut
LEBANON
Ein Suhna
Ein Sahib
El Hamma
Harna
Duma
Rafid
Sidon
Kafr Kuk
Rashaya
Hasbaya
SYRIA
Sarafand
Nabatiya
Kfar Shouba
Tyre
Juwaya
El Khian
Deir Mimes
Kfar Yuval
Katra
Mahrune
Shamir
Ras el Naba
Ainata
Kiryat Shmona
Aita el Shaab
Tiri
Hulata
Nahariya
Avivim
Golan Heights
Maalot
Saham al Golan
Acre
Rosh Pina
Haifa
Muzeirib
Suwayda
Kiryat Haroshet
Afula
Ein Harod
Binyamina
Beit Shean
ISRAEL
PALESTINE
Wadi Yabis
Tayasir
Tulkarm
Nablus
Beit Furik
Kureima
Nahal Gitit
Nahal Massua
Tel Aviv
Salameh
WEST BANK
Jaffa
Nahal Hagilgal
Karame
Lydda
Nahal Naaran
Amman
Ben Shemen
Biddu
Ramallah
Jericho
Shunat Nimrin
Yavne
Rehevot
Beir Surik
Sheikh Jarrah
Faluja
Bab el Wad
Saris
Nahal Kallia
JORDAN
Bethlehem
Jerusalem
Nitzanim
Muaskar el Arub
Kfar Etzion
Beit Lahiya
Hebron
GAZA STRIP
Gaza
El Bureij
Deir el Balah
Khan Yunis
Gevulot
EGYPT

R. Jordan

The static revolution

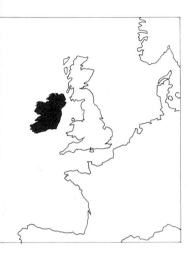

O N 24 April 1916, outside the General Post Office in O'Connell Street, Dublin, a solemn declaration was read to the bemused passersby. It was from 'The Provisional Government of the Irish Republic to the people of Ireland', and began 'Irishmen and Irishwomen: In the name of God and of the dead generations from which she receives her old tradition of nationhood, Ireland, through us, summons her children to her flag and strikes for her freedom.' The futile and pathetic Easter Rising ended for sixteen of its leaders before a British firing squad. In consequence, the Easter Rising became a new symbol in the Irish struggle for independence from the British connection, all the more potent because it is a myth of our own times rather than some relic of the past. William Butler Yeats, who wrote with passion on the martyrs of 1916, expressed the importance of the rising for the future conduct of Anglo–Irish relations:

> But who can talk of give and take
> What should be and what not
> While these dead men are loitering there
> To stir the boiling pot?
>
> (SIXTEEN DEAD MEN)

The Anglo–Irish quarrel has outlasted the settlement which gave independence to the bulk of Ireland because a united and free Ireland has been the central goal of the independence movement since the days of Wolfe Tone; it is a conflict which is frozen by the deeds and misdeeds of the past.

The republicans who fought the British before 1921 then turned on those of their leaders who had accepted the terms for an Irish Free State which had been negotiated with the British government. The war between militant republicans in the Irish Republican Army and the army of the Free State cost some 700 lives, and was marked by its own futile and spectacular gesture – the seizure of the Four Courts in Dublin in April 1922. The outcome followed the same pattern as the Easter Rising – the firing squad at dawn, and a renewed heritage of bitterness. IRA bombings and ambushes continued through the 1920s, accompanied by all the trappings seen in campaigns in Northern Ireland after 1968. There was mass internment of suspects, hunger strikes, demonstrations and protest movements. But popular support for the IRA declined when Fianna Fail, which represented a wide body of opinion opposed to the 1921 settlement, took power after an electoral victory in 1932 under Eamonn de Valera, himself a 'man of 1916'. He repressed both the IRA and the fascist Blue Shirt movement with equal vigour. By the end of the 1930s, the IRA in Northern Ireland had been forced to follow its own line, since the leadership in the south was riddled with government spies as well as feeble and uncertain as to the future course it should follow. There was a strong feeling in the north that it was now the IRA in Northern Ireland which carried the torch on behalf of the dead generations.

The record of the IRA in the sixty-odd years of its existence has been one of failure and a lack of progress. Yet this lack of success has not produced either a growth of new patterns of resistance or new methods of struggle. None of the factions which have grown up since the revival of militancy in Northern Ireland, specifically the Irish National Liberation Army or the Provisional IRA, differs very greatly, except in terms of personalities, from the long tradition of the IRA dating back to the 1920s. There has been only a marginal fragmentation within the nationalist movement. Nor have their tactics changed much from those decades. Hunger strikes, bombing campaigns in mainland Britain, terror tactics aimed at the structure of authority, have all been tried in the past and failed. The IRA has been outside all the political and social developments which have taken place. It had no influence on the development of the Civil Rights movement in 1968–69, which transformed the political situation in Northern Ireland by inducing a political crisis. It was completely ill-prepared to defend the Catholic areas of Belfast and Derry against Protestant attack in August 1969. It has reacted to the pattern of external events rather than generated initiatives of its own. By comparison with the Palestinian revolutionaries, who internationalized their conflict with Israel and captured world attention, the IRA has remained bogged down in the patterns of the past.

IRA ceremonial at the funeral of Bobby Sands, who died on a hunger strike for political status in prison. The hunger strikes succeeded in attracting world attention, and lavish funds from the USA, but political status did not result for the prisoners

While the IRA have hi-jacked no airliners, nor unleashed unlimited terror tactics on the British mainland, they have become remarkably proficient within their chosen arts of terrorism, predominantly bombing and sniping. They have developed an efficient operational structure in specific areas of northern Ireland, although much less effectively in mainland Britain. Finance is raised on a regular basis both in the Irish community in the USA, and through bank raids in Ireland itself. It is a campaign which has grown in intensity within strict limits as the years have passed since 1969. Terror is now aimed specifically at individuals associated with the power structure of the state in Northern Ireland and in Britain, and despite the fact that the steady trickle of deaths and bombings continues at a low level, by comparison with the late 1970s, it is a tempo which can be kept up indefinitely. It is as if the IRA, having survived lean years and virtual extinction, is now prepared to wage a war over decades.

In the past, Britain has always conceded its position to determined revolutionaries with majority support on their side. In Northern Ireland the Catholic community is in a minority, except in parts of Belfast and Londonderry and in specific border areas. But the Catholic birth rate is far higher than that of the Protestants, and since the beginning of the 1980s there has been a considerable increase in middle-class Protestant emigration. To intelligent Protestants, the

LONDON: House of Commons
Old Bailey
Whitehall
N. London
Tower of London
Hyde Park
Dulwich
Campden Square
Oxford Street
Regent's Park
Chelsea Barracks
Kensington Church Street
Hilton Hotel

The bombing campaign in mainland England. There were also attacks on an Army coach on the M62 and on Protestant organisations in Glasgow

long-term prospects are not good. The area of safety in which Protestants can live in security is being reduced by the IRA campaign to the core Protestant area east of the river Bann. A programme of murder aimed against farmers in marginal areas has proved effective, and there has been a discernible flight from the land. To the IRA, all signs are that they are winning, but the strains of a prolonged war are beginning to tell upon their organization. They are a small group of dedicated revolutionaries, with public sup-

Catholic children jeer at a passing army vehicle in the Falls Road, Belfast in 1980. The years of urban unrest in Ulster mean that these children have never known Belfast without a military presence. They are the potential fanatics of tomorrow

port, grudging as well as willing, within their own limited areas. They have never before succeeded in waging so long a campaign of violence, but it is recognized that it may take another ten or twenty years to make the price of holding Northern Ireland unacceptable to Britain. The temptation is to force a crisis and to attempt to shorten the war by waging it at a higher degree of intensity.

For the British government, the war in Ireland has already caused a considerable social cost. The IRA campaigns in England have forced through a pattern of emergency legislation and counter-intelligence which is not popular, and would be less so if the full extent of its operation was widely known. The pub bombings in Birmingham and Guildford and the Regents Park and Hyde Park explosions of 1982 produced a vast public outcry, but no attack on the large Irish community in the United Kingdom. In France, the transfer of the passions of the Algerian war to the mainland had a devastating effect, and a similar danger exists if an all-out terror campaign were to be mounted on targets in Britain. It might be possible

to seal the Ulster border with a system of fortification and to guard the coasts, but the creation of Fortress Ulster would carry an impossibly high political price both nationally and internationally. Thus the approach of all British governments has been to tinker with the security equation, make vague political gestures, and hope that things don't get much worse. Or, if they do, that it is on the other side of the Irish sea. In fact, both the IRA and the British have arrived at a stalemate, which can only be resolved by a dramatic and dangerous change of strategy. It is to be hoped that neither party will take a leap in the dark.

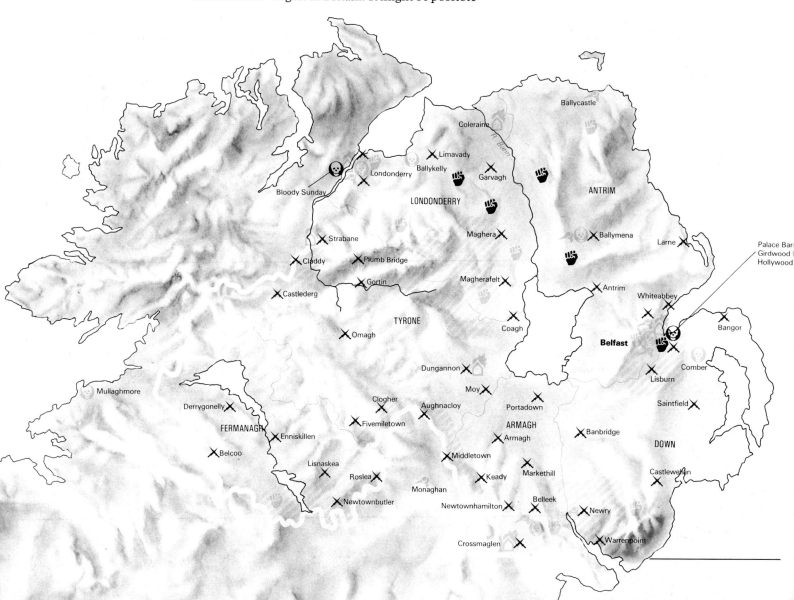

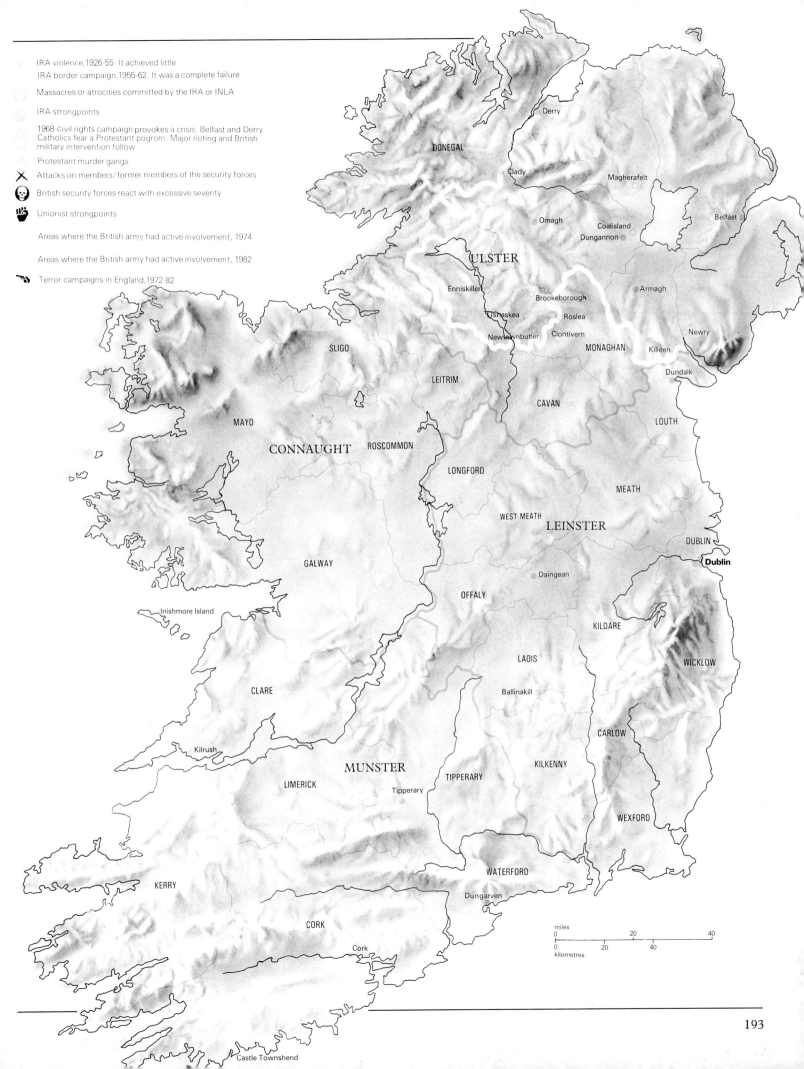

IRA violence, 1926-55. It achieved little

IRA border campaign, 1955-62. It was a complete failure

Massacres or atrocities committed by the IRA or INLA

IRA strongpoints

1968 civil rights campaign provokes a crisis: Belfast and Derry Catholics fear a Protestant pogrom. Major rioting and British military intervention follow

Protestant murder gangs

Attacks on members/former members of the security forces

British security forces react with excessive severity

Unionist strongpoints

Areas where the British army had active involvement, 1974

Areas where the British army had active involvement, 1982

Terror campaigns in England, 1972-82

DONEGAL

Derry

Clady

Magherafelt

Omagh

Coalisland

Dungannon

Belfast

ULSTER

Enniskillen

Brookeborough

Armagh

Tisnaskea

Roslea

Newtownbutler

Clontivern

Newry

MONAGHAN

Killeen

Dundalk

SLIGO

LEITRIM

CAVAN

LOUTH

MAYO

CONNAUGHT

ROSCOMMON

LONGFORD

MEATH

WEST MEATH

LEINSTER

DUBLIN

Dublin

GALWAY

Daingean

OFFALY

Inishmore Island

KILDARE

LAOIS

WICKLOW

CLARE

Ballinakill

CARLOW

Kilrush

KILKENNY

MUNSTER

TIPPERARY

LIMERICK

Tipperary

WEXFORD

KERRY

WATERFORD

Dungarven

CORK

Cork

miles
0   20   40

0   20   40
kilometres

Castle Townshend

The military option

The military take-over, on this occasion in Turkey, but it could be anywhere in the world

IN some countries the military by tradition play a dominant role in politics, while in others they are thought to act as a residual protector of national honour and stability. The training given to officers is designed to instil a respect for order and discipline, the lack of which they may find disturbing in outside society. In many Third World countries a large proportion of the educated and administrative capacity of the state is contained in the armed forces, and here military government may, like the one-party state reflecting the wishes of the majority tribal group, be a realistic approach to national problems. In many states military rule has not been noticeably more tyrannical than that of civilians. The increase in military take-over which has taken place since the 1960s is in part a reflection of the greater pressure which revolutionary movements have placed on political systems. Where the political balance has been disturbed by violent actions and reactions, of which Turkey is an example, stability can only be restored by a powerful outside force, usually the army.

The problems which arise for military governments stem from the fact that deep antagonisms often exist between different military services, resentments which become all the greater when military budgets

Countries which have experienced a military
seizure of power since 1960

REPUBLIC OF KOREA (SOUTH)

INDONESIA

LAOS
BURMA
KAMPUCHEA
BANGLADESH
THAILAND

AFGHANISTAN
PAKISTAN

OLAND

GREECE TURKEY
SYRIA IRAQ
CYPRUS

SOUTH YEMEN
YEMEN

LIBYA

SOMALIA

GER CHAD SUDAN ETHIOPIA

RIA

SEYCHELLES

CENTRAL
AFRICAN
EMPIRE/REPUBLIC
UGANDA

COMOROS

RWANDA
BURUNDI

AL

ZAIRE

MALAGASY
REPUBLIC

OPLES
EPUBLIC
THE CONGO

have to be allocated by the military themselves. Professional quarrels are then projected on to the nation
as a whole. In one instance in Latin America, the air
force bombed and disabled a new ship which it
thought the navy had achieved by unfair pressure.
Officers may be competent within the narrow range
of choices for which they have been trained, but outside them they can only operate with the limited set
of premises with which their education has equipped
them. As military education in most countries has
become clogged with technical knowledge, officers
are probably less well-equipped to exercise a political
and administrative role than earlier generations.

The military are the dominant power group within
the state because they have the monopoly of legal violence. Para-military forces such as the police serve
to complicate the issue still further. But any society
which is dominated by the military is deficient in
modes of political control – deficient either because
they have been destroyed by subversion, or because
they have never existed. The military option has
never yet proved satisfactory in the long term, for
either it destroys the military capacity of the armed
forces, or the efficiency of the state – to say nothing
of the erosion of human liberty.

The uses of terror

TERROR has always been seen as a weapon for use by the weak against the strong, who, like Cain killing his brother Abel, seize whatever weapon lies to hand. It is certainly true today that many who used the weapons of terror against governments themselves aspired to be the rulers, with terror as an infantile stage in the growth of the revolutionary mechanism as it moved to open warfare against the state and finally seizure of the mechanism of power. But there is another line of development, which sees terrorism as a uniquely powerful weapon, more insidious and deadly than victory on the battlefield. It is likely to become more and more significant as the possibility of a revolutionary transformation of many societies becomes more remote: all that remains is the struggle.

In modern times this tradition can be traced back to nineteenth-century Russia and the nihilist group known as 'The People's Will' which organized the assassination of Czar Alexander II. The violence was aimed at specific individuals, but it was also symbolic. It was desirable to kill a czar or a police chief, but as the doctrine developed, it included any public outrage which would lead the people to question the competence of the authorities. In an autocracy such as Czarist Russia, where the state was by definition omni-competent, this approach had a certain logic, although the immediate response was to support authority in suppression of violence. Only when government was shown to be ineffective over a long period did popular fury turn against it to the potential profit of the revolutionaries. But both the People's Will and their spiritual successors, the militant wing of the Socialist Revolutionary Party (SR), failed because the police penetrated their security. Indeed, in a bizarre reversal of roles, the police double agents were instrumental in planning the more successful and spectacular assassinations. Sergei Degaev prepared the murder of his superior, the head of the St Petersburg police, in 1883, while Evno Azev, the head of the SR murder machine, was a uniquely successful terrorist as he betrayed the organization which he commanded.

The terrorism of the 1960s and 1970s had specific objectives. In Latin America, it aimed to create festering sores within the authoritarian states which would grow until the infection took over the body politic. Symbolic violence was the key instrument by which this was to be achieved. Sometimes it was aimed against individuals, sometimes against property, sometimes against symbols themselves, as on the occasion when a guerrilla group hi-jacked an international art exhibition. The abject failure of symbolic violence in Latin America has called in question the presuppositions on which it was based. It was in fact the wrong method for the time and place. Symbolic violence can only work to de-stabilize a society in a subtle and indirect manner. In countries such as Argentina and Brazil, which were fundamentally unstable anyway, it was a pointless exercise. It is possible to argue that the campaign was successful in that it made the governments more obviously tyrannical and less popularly based, but such a judgment can only be made in hindsight. Elsewhere, symbolic violence has been more successful because its targets have been more appropriate and its objectives more limited. The Palestinian campaign, organized principally by the Popular Front for the Liberation of Palestine, involved aircraft hi-jacking and mass murder. It served to raise the issue of a Palestinian homeland from the trough into which it had sunk after the catastrophic defeat of the Arabs in the 1967 war. Few acts of symbolic violence have equalled Black September's taking hostage the Israeli Olympic team at the Munich Olympics in September 1972. After the international outrage had died down, the issue of Palestinian nationalism remained in relief to a degree which would have been impossible but for the terror campaign. The Israeli response, both of counter-terror and of attacks on Palestinian bases in Lebanon and elsewhere, contributed to the destruction of the benign image of the Zionist cause. The Palestinian target was the world's press and television, not the people of Israel, and they were seeking to advertise their message in the only way available to them. In a similar fashion, the other nationalist causes which have successfully used terrorism – the IRA, the Basque ETA, and to a much lesser degree the Corsican and Breton nationalists – have also managed to broaden their publicity base. But terrorism is competitive and a dead policeman in the Falls Road is nowhere near so compelling as a hi-jacked airliner or a mass atrocity. Symbolic violence requires careful management.

There is no example in modern times where the use of terror, by itself, has achieved the objectives for which it was launched. At best, as in Cyprus, it shortened the preliminary political process and brought about an early resolution of the problem. If the effect of terrorism is to accelerate a political process, then the mechanism by which it achieves this is unclear. Is there some threshold at which this effect begins? Or is it a case of the more violence that can be applied, the more rapidly results will be achieved? One consequence of the terror campaigns of the last twenty years is that established societies have developed a clearer understanding of the uses and importance of terrorism. Where once it was classed as mindless violence, it is now seen as being not just a bludgeon, but a subtle and complex weapon. Research now sees it as specifically related to its social context rather than being a universal application. Like Winston Smith's terror of rats which was used to break his resistance in Orwell's *1984*, particular types of terror are effective in different societies. In Algeria the FLN was given to throat-cutting, for it symbolized animal slaughter in a Moslem society, and was a final act of humiliation for its victim and those whom he represented. In China during the Cultural Revolution, the immense pressure for public recantation, which involved self-humiliation and self-abasement, was related to the Chinese context much more than being a *communist* practice. Confession in Nazi or Soviet show-trials served a different purpose. The IRA tradition of hunger striking, 'the blanket protest', was made more potent with its well-publicized filth of smeared faeces on the walls. It was deeply shocking to both British and American societies which practised secrecy and harboured *pudeur* about excretion. Effective acts of symbolic violence or protest must be appropriate both in type and scale.

Western societies have made great advances in the control of conventional terrorism. Many of the terrorists of the 1970s are now dead or in prison, although the social cost of improved security has been very high. Computers, especially the West German system at Wiesbaden, have advanced the whole process of tracking down terrorists and even predicting their future actions. Progress has been made towards identifying future deviants, potential revolutionaries. Certain patterns of behaviour, which would certainly have identified Mao Tse Tung or the young Lenin (whom his sister described as 'choleric'), can be used to specify a deviant personality. Noticed early enough, the power and energy of such individuals can be channelled into socially desirable directions. This type of programme is already used in relation to motor and intellectual skills in the USSR. The increasing efficiency of record-taking in Western societies from birth onwards makes this approach feasible. Much work is being done to construct a profile of a potential revolutionary, and although the image is still relatively crude it may mean that the successful revolutionary of the near future will need to lead a life of unblemished social virtue before the moment comes to throw off the mask.

This is the state at which the theorists of the counter-terrorist offensive would like to arrive, but it remains a chimera while societies continue to be fluid and undocumented. For most of the world outside the Communist bloc, potential revolutionaries will be able to grow up as they always have. Of non-Communist societies, France, Britain and Western Germany are potentially closest to it. The United States, with a huge and unrecorded sub-stratum of illegal immigrants, has a long way to go before a comprehensive data-base could be constructed. If the new machinery does help to control terrorism, it is because it is aimed at frustrating the old style of revolutionary violence. In the same way that improved airport security has reduced the likelihood of an effective hi-jacking campaign, so surveillance and intelligence can counteract the known or potential terrorist with a recognizable pattern of behaviour. What it cannot do is control the single symbolic act, without a previous pattern of deviance. It is conventional wisdom among security services that the lone assassin or a suicide squad can breach the best known systems. The new machinery cannot hope to stop the revolutionary who poisons Israeli oranges, as an Arab claimed to do, or a group which seeks publicity by claiming to have planted poison in a proprietary brand of headache cure. These can be remarkably efficient acts of symbolic violence, given effective publicity, perhaps because they serve to remind people that it is impossible to guard all the areas at risk in a modern Western society.

I have specified a number of areas which I believe will see increased revolutionary violence in the next decade. Some are areas with an established pattern, such as Turkey, where there has been a temporary lull in violence because of resolute government action. Spain has attempted to find a democratic form of political stability, but this may lead even larger numbers of non-democratic groups – of left and right, as well as with a nationalist line – to take violent action. South Africa is beginning to experience a small but growing campaign of successful terrorism, to

The stereotype revolutionary. He is young, fanatical, and he has failed. In this case he is a South Moluccan who has occupied the Indonesian embassy in The Hague in 1970. He himself has never been to the South Moluccas, which his family left before he was born. He is poor, and his group has minimal resources. His answer is to make his protest by political and revolutionary terror

● Principal cities afflicted with terrorism, 1968-83

IRAN Areas experiencing substantial terrorism at the height of the terror campaigns, 1968-80

✹ Bombing

✈ Hi-jacking

☢ Kidnapping

🗡 Assassination

Areas likely to suffer increasing terrorism in the late 1980s

which she is responding with both political and military initiatives. Mainland Britain, which has largely escaped the consequences of violence in Ireland, is likely to suffer the attentions of the IRA and INLA to an increasing degree, especially as they begin to develop new patterns of terrorism. West Germany, which has destroyed the threat of conventional terrorism of the Baader-Meinhof pattern by counter-intelligence and resolute action, is wide open to the random symbolic terror directed against society at large rather than specific political and military targets. The growing fragmentation of the West German political structure will enhance this tendency. Finally, the United States, which is already suffering terror by crime rather than by political groups, is a natural target for new patterns of violence. If, as I suspect, propaganda by the deed becomes the principal means of revolutionary violence, it is the developed world, which has already suffered from the main effects of the terror campaigns of 1960–80, which will bear the full force of the new attack, an assault not on institutions or individuals but on affluence and the whole Western style of life.

RN GERMANY

Stockholm

Hamburg
GERMANY — Cologne
Frankfurt
Munich

Vienna

Islamabad

Istanbul

TURKEY
Ankara
TURKEY

IRAN

Bombay

Nicosia
Tel Aviv
Beirut
Amman

me

Athens

Cairo

MIDDLE EAST

Singapore

an

ITALY

Khartoum

SOUTH AFRICA

S. AFRICA

Sources

MY aim with these source notes is to indicate the source of each quotation. I have not tried to annotate every fact in the text, and would refer the reader to the books in the Select Bibliography for further enlightenment. Where the facts are contentious or the issue is complicated I have also indicated where the reader should look for further detailed elaboration. These sources should be used in conjunction with the bibliography for each section. The author's name is given in capitals. Where he has more than one work cited, then the short title is given, and where there is more than one volume, it is indicated in Roman numerals. Page references are given in Arabic numerals. I have not cited quotations from journals, since these are often difficult for the reader to find. Current information has been drawn from *The Times* and the *Guardian* of London, and the *New York Times* and the *International Herald Tribune* and the *Annual of Power and Conflict* (London). I have tried to restrict the references and bibliography to books in English, or to translations of books published originally in other languages. On one or two occasions, I have found no relevant material in English, in which case I have indicated the foreign language material.

North America, 1765–75
1 YOUNG, 325
2 KNOLLENBURG, 184
3 PAINE (Tom: *Complete Works, II*), 26
4 DAVIDSON, 150
5 Adams to Jefferson in 1815
6 KNOLLENBURG, 192

France, 1789–95
1 LEFEBVRE, *The French Revolution*, 114
2 LEFEBVRE, *The Great Fear*, 75

Ireland, 1798
1 PAKENHAM, 124–7

Spain, 1808–14
1 LOVETT, II, 424
2 Ibid., 468
3 Ibid., 731
4 Ibid., 730
5 Ibid., 736
6 LIDDELL HART, 129
7 LOVETT, II, 445

Greece, 1821–7
1 BYRON, *Childe Harold* Canto II, stanza 73
2 ST CLAIR, 9–12
3 DAKIN, 132 ff.

Latin America, 1808–30
1 LYNCH, 50
2 Ibid., 190
3 Ibid., 212
4 Ibid., 293

Europe, 1848–9
1 MACARTNEY, 313
2 STEARNS, 43–44
3 MACARTNEY, 330
4 STEARNS, 73
5 MACARTNEY, 332–3
6 HOBSBAWM, 15
7 STEARNS, 92; DUVEAU, 180–1
8 MACARTNEY, 402–3; RATH, 361–5
9 HOBSBAWM, 9

India, 1857–9
1 HIBBERT, 59 (Hadow Papers)
2 MAJUMDAR, 609–10
3 LUNT, 163
4 Ibid., 162
5 Ibid., 162
6 MAJUMDAR, 467–94
7 HIBBERT, 210–14; MAJUMDAR, 591–602
8 LUNT, 165

Italy, 1860
1 RIDLEY, 242
2 Ibid., 306
3 Ibid., 411

China, 1850–1911
1 EBERHARD, 48; DAWSON, 297
2 DAVIES, 57–61
3 MEADOWS, 112
4 Ibid., 149–50
5 Ibid., 155–7
6 HIBBERT, 302

Japan, 1865–80
1 AKAMATSU, 291–2
2 Ibid., 225

Mexico, 1810–1920
1 See LYNCH, John, *The Spanish American Revolutions 1808–26*, London, 1973: 309
2 QUIRK, 110

Arabia, 1900–35
1 ALMANA, 243

France, 1871
1 HORNE, 265
2 Ibid., 364
3 Ibid., 413
4 Ibid., 365

Russia, 1905
1 HARCAVE, 93
2 Ibid., 131
3 Ibid., 116–7
4 HOUGH, 91

5 HARCAVE, 249
6 Ibid., 261

Moscow, 1905
1 HARCAVE, 235–6

Russia, 1917
1 KEEP, 11–13
2 STONE, 284–5
3 STONE, 281
4 KEEP, 57
5 STONE, 296
6 FERRO, *Russian Revolution*, 43
7 KEEP, 276–80
8 FERRO, *Russian Revolution*, 45
9 Ibid., 61
10 Ibid., 76–7

Petrograd, 1917
1 FERRO, *Russian Revolution*, 207–8 (see also: WILSON, Edmund: *To the Finland Station*, New York, 1940: 470–72)
2 FERRO, *October*, 83
3 RABINOVITCH, *The Bolsheviks*, 240
4 Ibid., 286–7

Russia, 1917–21
1 FISCHER, 422
2 FERRO, *October*, 70–85; FERRO, *Russian Revolution*, 54–5
3 LUCKETT, 48–9

Turkey, 1918–35
1 LEWIS, 257
2 Ibid., 252
3 KINROSS, 326
4 Ibid., 339

Europe, 1918–23
1 See FERRO, Marc: *The First World War, The Great War 1914–1918*, London, 1974: Chapter 11
2 RYDER, 169

3 Ibid., 155
4 Ibid., 183
5 WATT, 267
6 Ibid., 338
7 Ibid., 506

Italy, 1919–25
1 LYTTLETON, 44
2 Ibid., 67
3 Ibid., 60
4 Ibid., 44
5 Ibid., 83
6 Ibid., 88
7 Ibid., 92
8 Ibid., 137

Germany, 1923–35
1 PRIDHAM, 78–9 (citing *Der Angriff*, 20 April 1928; see also BRACHER, 141–2)
2 SCHOENBAUM, 40
3 PRIDHAM, 9
4 Ibid., 55
5 NOAKES, 116
6 PRIDHAM, 303
7 Ibid., 223
8 TAYLOR, 531–2; NOAKES, 146–50
9 NOAKES, 146–50
10 Ibid., 144
11 KRAUSNICK, 406 & 402
12 NOAKES, 116 & 173

Spain, 1936
1 See CARR, Raymond: *Spain 1808–1939*, Oxford, 1966: 125–6
2 FRASER, 160
3 Ibid., 146
4 CARR, 566
5 Ibid., 619
6 Ibid., 616
7 FRASER, 542
8 Ibid., 543
9 PAYNE, 203
10 THOMAS, 283
11 FRASER, 136
12 BOLLETEN, 41
13 FRASER, 154
14 THOMAS, 264–68;

GIBSON, 171–2: Appendix B

15 For a full treatment of this subject, see BOLLETEN. This has appeared in a heavily revised form as *The Spanish Revolution – The Left and the Struggle for Power during the Civil War* (Chapel Hill, NC, 1979) to which the reader's attention is also directed.
16 PONS PRADES, passim.

India, 1905–47
1 GOPAL, 69
2 Ibid., 72
3 Ibid., 137
4 ROSE, 343
5 Ibid., 345
6 FISCHER, 217
7 Ibid., 204
8 GOPAL, 428
9 MAJUMDAR, 651–79
10 FISCHER, 302–3

South East Asia, 1945–62
1 KAHIN, 215
2 BARBER, 152

Kenya, 1950–6
1 KENYATTA, v.
2 Ibid., xxi
3 ROSBERG, 199
4 Ibid., 194

Algeria, 1949–62
1 WOLF, 214
2 HORNE, 27
3 Ibid., 373
4 Ibid., 378

Indo China, 1945–75
1 PIKE, 34

Cyprus, 1955–60
1 CRANKSHAW, 76
2 Ibid., 78
3 Ibid., 406–7
4 See BELL: *On Revolt, Strategies of National Liberation*, Cambridge, Mass. & London, 1976: 136
5 CRANKSHAW, 245

China, 1923–76
1 NORTH, 104
2 MAO, *Problems*, 27–8
3 NORTH, 165–6

4 MAO, *Thoughts*, 201–2
5 Ibid., 279
6 KARNOW, 121
7 Ibid., 429
8 MAO, *Thoughts*, 12

Latin America, 1960–82
1 See FEIT: *Urban Revolt in South Africa, 1960–64*, Northwestern UP, 1971: 312
2 See DEBRAY, Régis: *Revolution in the Revolution*, New York, 1967: 24
3 HODGES, 233

South Africa, 1960–82
1 GREIG, 55
2 FEIT, 310–2

United States, 1963–82
1 See LONGMATE, Norman: *How We Lived Then, A History of Everyday Life During the Second World War*, London, 1971: 479
2 ZINN, 440
3 Ibid., 447

4 GILBERT, 106

Ethiopia, 1974–82
1 HALLIDAY, 79
2 Ibid., 123

Iran, 1978–82
1 FISCHER, 197

Middle East, 1934–82
1 GILBERT, *Exile*, 108
2 Ibid., 195
3 Ibid., 273
4 See GILBERT, *The Arab Israeli Conflict*
5 BEGIN, 52

Select bibliography

THIS collection of books does not represent my own sources. I have adopted two points of policy in preparing a short list of further reading. Firstly, they are all books which I found useful, although on many occasions I found profound causes for disagreement with them. Secondly, they relate to each text, either supporting or refuting the line which I have followed. With most of the subjects in this book, facts are clouded by prejudice and special pleading, and this list of books reflects this position. Where possible I have also selected books which have a much wider frame of reference than I have space for, so the reader can use them as a point of entry into the huge body of literature on revolutions.

I have found that the problem of categorizing revolutions is insuperable. In general, I have found the definitions laid down by Peter Calvert in his *A Study of Revolution* (London, 1970) very helpful. Three other books of recent vintage have also helped me to formulate the approach I have followed. Theda Skocpel, in *States and Social Revolution* (Cambridge, 1979) has remarkable insight into the 'great revolutions', while I have found all the books by J. Bowyer Bell extremely enlightening and a delight to read. In particular *On Revolt, Strategies of National Liberation* (Cambridge, Mass. and London, 1976) deals comprehensively with the uses and function of terror, mostly aimed at British interests. Ellen Kay Trimberger in *Revolution from Above: Military Bureaucrats and Development in Japan, Turkey, Egypt, and Peru* (New Brunswick, NJ, 1978) is not entirely convincing, but raises important issues about revolutions without a mass popular base.

North America, 1765–75
BAILYN, Bernard: *The Ideological Origins of the American Revolution*, Cambridge, Mass., 1967
BAILYN, Bernard & HENCH, J. B. (eds): *The Press and the American Revolution*, Worcester, Mass., 1980
BREWER, J.: *Party Ideology and Popular Politics at the Accession of George III*, Cambridge, 1976
CAPPON, L. (ed): *Atlas of Early American History: the Revolutionary Era, 1760–90*, Princeton, NJ, 1976
DAVIDSON, Philip: *Propaganda and the American Revolution*, Chapel Hill, NC, 1941
KNOLLENBURG, Bernhard: *Growth of the American Revolution 1766–75*, New York & London, 1975
KURTZ, Stephen G. and HUTSON, James H. (eds): *Essays on the American Revolution*: no 3. Violence and the American Revolution (Brown, Richard Maxwell); no 4. The American Revolution. The Military Conflict Considered as a Revolutionary War (Shy, John), Chapel Hill, 1973
MAIER, Pauline: *From Resistance to Revolution*, New York, 1972
NASH, G. B.: *The Urban Crucible*, Cambridge, Mass., 1979
YOUNG, Alfred: *The American Revolution: explorations in the history of American radicalism*, De Kalb, Ill., 1976

France, 1789–95
BEST, Geoffrey: *War and Society in Revolutionary Europe*, London, 1982

CARON, Pierre: *Les massacres de septembre*, Paris, 1935
COBB, R.: *Police and the People: French Popular Protest, 1789–1820*, Oxford, 1970
GODECHOT, Jacques: *Taking of the Bastille, July 14th, 1789*, London, 1970
GREER, Donald: *The Incidence of Terror during the French Revolution*, Boston, 1935
GREER, Donald: *The Incidence of Terror during the French Revolution*, Boston, 1951
HIBBERT, Christopher: *The French Revolution*, London, 1980
HOBSBAWM, E. J.: *The Age of Revolution, Europe 1789–1848*, London, 1962
JOHNSON, Douglas (ed): *French Society and the Revolution*, London, 1976
LEFEBVRE, Georges: *The French Revolution from its Origins to 1793*, London, 1962
LEFEBVRE, Georges: *The Great Fear of 1789*, Paris, 1932, London, 1977
RUDÉ, George: *The Crowd in the French Revolution*, Oxford, 1959
RUDÉ, George: *The Crowd in History*, London, 1964
SCOTT, William: *Terror and Repression in Revolutionary Marseilles*, London, 1973

Ireland, 1798
PAKENHAM, Thomas: *The Year of Liberty*, London, 1969
DUDLEY EDWARDS, Ruth: *An Atlas of Irish History*, London, 1973

Spain, 1808–14
CARR, Raymond: *Spain 1808–1939*, Oxford, 1966
LIDDELL HART, Basil: *Strategy: the Indirect Approach*, London, 1967
LOVETT, Gabriel H.: *Napoleon and the Birth of Modern Spain* (2 vols), New York, 1965

Greece, 1821–7
DAKIN, Douglas: *The Greek Struggle for Independence 1821–1833*, London, 1973
GORDON, T.: *History of the Greek Revolution* (2 vols), Edinburgh, 1832
ST. CLAIR, William: *That Greece might still be Free*, London, 1972
WOODHOUSE, C. M.: *The Greek War of Independence*, London, 1952

Latin America, 1808–30
LECUÑA, Vicente: *Bolivar y el arte militar*, New York, 1955
LYNCH, John: *The Spanish American Revolutions, 1808–26*, London, 1973
METFORD, J. C. J.: *San Martin the Liberator*, New York, 1950
URIBE WHITE, Enrique: *El Liberador*, Bogota, 1969

Europe, 1848–9
DUVEAU, Georges: *1848: The Making of a Revolution*, Paris, 1965
HOBSBAWM, E. J.: *The Age of Capital, 1848–1875*, London, 1975
MACARTNEY, C. A.: *The Habsburg Empire 1790–1918*, London, 1969
RATH, A. J.: *The Viennese Revolution of 1848*, Austin, Texas, 1957
STEARNS, Peter N.: *The Revolutions of 1848*, London, 1974

India, 1857–9
CHAUDHURI, Sashi Bhusan: *Theories of the Indian Mutiny (1857–9)*, Calcutta, 1965
HIBBERT, Christopher: *The Great Mutiny*, London, 1978

KIERNAN, V. G.: *The Lords of Human Kind*, London, 1969
LUNT, James (ed): *From Sepoy to Subedar*, London 1873 and 1970
MAJUMDAR, R. C. (ed): *The History and Culture of the Indian People, vol IX: British Paramountcy and Indian Renaissance, Part 1*, Bombay, 1963

Italy, 1860
MACK SMITH, D.: *Cavour and Garibaldi*, Cambridge, 1954
RIDLEY, Jasper: *Garibaldi*, London, 1974
TREVELYAN, G. M.: *Garibaldi and the Thousand*, London, 1948
TREVELYAN, G. M.: *Garibaldi and the Making of Italy*, London, 1911

China, 1850–1911
DAVIES, Fei-Ling: *Primitive Revolutionaries of China*, London, 1977
DAWSON, Raymond: *Imperial China*, London, 1972
EBERHARD, Wolfram: *A History of China*, London, 1977
FAIRBANK, J. K. (ed): *The Cambridge History of China, vol X*, London, 1978
HIBBERT, Christopher: *The Dragon Wakes: China and the West 1793–1911*, London, 1970
HSU, I. C. Y.: *The Rise of Modern China*, New York, 1970
MEADOWS, Thomas Taylor: *The Chinese and their Rebellions*, London, 1856

Japan, 1865–80
AKAMATSU, Paul: *Meiji, 1868*, London, 1972
BARR, Pat: *The Coming of the Barbarians*, London, 1967
BEASLEY, W. G.: *The Modern History of Japan*, London, 1973
BEASLEY, W. G.: *The Meiji Restoration*, Stanford, 1973

Mexico, 1810–1920
CUMBERLAND, Charles C.: *Mexico: The Struggle for Modernity*, New York, 1968
QUIRK, Robert E.: *The Mexican Revolution 1914–15*, Bloomington, 1960

Arabia, 1900–35
ALMANA, Mohammed: *Arabia Unified*, London, 1980

France, 1871
EDWARDS, Stewart: *The Paris Commune*, London, 1971
HORNE, Alistair: *The Fall of Paris*, London, 1965
TOMBS, Robert: *The War against Paris, 1871*, Cambridge, 1981

Russia, 1905–21
BRADLEY, John: *Civil War in Russia*, London, 1975
FERRO, Marc: *October 1917*, Cambridge, Mass. & London, 1980
FERRO, Marc: *The Russian Revolution of February 1917*, London & New York, 1972
FISCHER, Louis: *The Life of Lenin*, New York, 1964
GILL, Graeme J.: *Peasants and Government in the Russian Revolution*, London, 1979
HAMMOND, T. T.: *The Anatomy of Communist Takeover*, London, 1975
HARCAVE, Sidney: *First Blood, The Russian Revolution of 1905*, London, 1965
HASEGAWA, Tsuyoshi: *The February Revolution*, Seattle, 1981
HOUGH, Richard: *The Potemkin Mutiny*, London, 1960
KEEP, John L. H.: *The Russian Revolution, A Study in Mass Mobilisation*, London, 1976
LAQUEUR, Walter: *The Fate of the Revolution*, London, 1967
LUCKETT, Richard: *The White Generals*, London, 1971

MELGUNOV, S. P.: *How the Bolsheviks took Power*, Santa Barbara, 1972
PARKER, W. H.: *An Historical Geography of Russia*, London, 1968
PETHYBRIDGE, Roger: *The Spread of the Russian Revolution : Essays on 1917*, London, 1972
PIPES, Richard: *Russia under the Old Regime*, London, 1974
PIPES, Richard (ed): *Revolutionary Russia*, London, 1968
POMPER, Philip: *The Russian Revolutionary Intelligentsia*, London, 1970
RABINOVITCH, Alexander: *The Bolsheviks Come to Power, The Revolution of 1917 in Petrograd*, New York, 1976
RABINOVITCH, Alexander and J. (ed): *Revolution and Politics in Russia*, Bloomington & London, 1973
RADKEY, Oliver H.: *The Unknown Civil War in Soviet Russia*, Stanford, 1976
STONE, Norman: *The Eastern Front, 1914–17*, London & New York, 1975
WILDMAN, A.: *The End of the Russian Imperial Army*, London, 1980

Turkey, 1918–35
KINROSS, Lord: *Ataturk : The Rebirth of a Nation*, London, 1964
LEWIS, Bernard: *The Emergence of Modern Turkey*, Oxford, 1968
ROBINSON, R. D.: *The First Turkish Republic*, Cambridge, Mass., 1963
SMITH, E. D.: *The Origins of the Kemalist Movement*, Washington, 1959
WEBSTER, D. E.: *The Turkey of Ataturk*, Philadelphia, 1939

Europe, 1918–23
Atlas Revoluche Hnuti, Prague
DUKES, Paul: *October and the World*, London, 1979
RYDER, A. J.: *The German Revolution of 1918*, Cambridge, 1967
TÖKÉS, Rudolph L.: *Bela Kun and the Hungarian Soviet Republic*, London, 1967
WATT, Richard M.: *The Kings Depart*, New York, 1968

Italy, 1919–25
CHABOD, F.: *The History of Italian Fascism*, London, 1963
LYTTLETON, Adrian: *The Seizure of Power : Fascism in Italy, 1919–29*, London, 1973
MACK SMITH, D.: *Italy : A Modern History*, London, 1959
MACK SMITH, D.: *Mussolini*, London, 1981

Germany, 1923–35
The Third Reich: Collected essays published under the auspices of the International Council for Philosophy and Humanistic Studies (see TAYLOR, A. J. P.: *The Seizure of Power*), London, 1955
BRACHER, Karl Dietrich: *The German Dictatorship*, New York, 1970
BULLOCK, Alan: *Hitler : A Study in Tyranny*, London, 1962
KRAUSNICK, Helmut (ed): *Anatomy of the SS State*, London, 1968
MALTITZ, Horst von: *The Evolution of Hitler's Germany*, London, 1973
NOAKES, Jeremy & PRIDHAM, Geoffrey (ed): *Documents on Nazism*, London, 1974
ORLOW, Dietrich: *The History of the Nazi Party, vol I*, Pittsburgh, 1973
PRIDHAM, Geoffrey: *Hitler's Rise to Power*, London, 1973
SCHOENBAUM, David: *Hitler's Social Revolution*, New York, 1966
STONE, Norman: *Hitler*, London, 1980

Spain, 1936
BOLLETEN, Burnett: *The Grand Camouflage*, London, 1961
BOOKCHIN, Murray: *The Spanish Anarchists*, New York, 1977
BRENAN, Gerald: *The Spanish Labyrinth*, Cambridge, 1943
FRASER, Ronald: *Blood of Spain*, London, 1979
GIBSON, Ian: *The Death of Lorca*, London, 1973
PAYNE, Stanley G.: *The Spanish Revolution*, London, 1970
PONS PRADES, Eduardo: *Guerrillas Españolas 1936–60*, Barcelona, 1977
THOMAS, Hugh: *The Spanish Civil War*, London, rev. edn.1977

India, 1905–47
FISCHER, Louis: *The Life of Mahatma Gandhi*, London, 1951
GOPAL, Ram: *How India Struggled for Freedom*, London, 1967
LOW, D. A.: *Congress and the Raj*, London, 1977
MAJUMDAR, R. C. (ed): *The History and Culture of the Indian People, vol XI : Struggle For Freedom*, Bombay, 1969
ROSE, Kenneth: *Superior Person : A Portrait of Curzon and his Circle in Late Victorian England*, London, 1969

South East Asia, 1945–62
BARBER, Noel: *The War of the Running Dogs*, London, 1971
BRIMMELL, J. H.: *Communism in SE Asia*, Oxford, 1959
CHALIAND, Gérard: *Revolution in the Third World*, London, 1978
DAHM, Bernard: *History of Indonesia in the Twentieth Century*, London, 1971
FAIRBURN, Geoffrey: *Revolutionary Warfare and Communist Strategy*, London, 1968
KAHIN, George McTurnan: *Nationalism and Revolution in Indonesia*, London, 1952
KERKVLIET, Benedict J.: *The Huk Rebellion*, London, 1977
O'BALLANCE, Edgar: *Malaya : The Communist Insurgent War*, London, 1966
PYE, Lucien W.: *Guerrilla Communism in Malaya*, Oxford, 1956
STAVRIANOS, L. S.: *Global Rift : The Third World Comes of Age*, New York, 1981
THOMPSON, R.: *Defeating Communist Insurgency*, London, 1966

Kenya, 1950–6
BARNETT, Donald L. & NJAMA, Karari: *Mau Mau from Within*, London, 1966
KENYATTA, Jomo: *Facing Mount Kenya*, London, 1938
KITSON, Frank: *Gangs and Counter Gangs*, London, 1960
ROSBERG, Carl G. & HOTTINGHAM, John: *The Myth of Mau Mau : Nationalism in Kenya*, London, 1966

Algeria, 1949–62
GILLESPIE, Joan: *Algeria : Rebellion and Revolution*, London, 1960
HEGGOY, Alf A.: *Insurgency and Counter-insurgency in Algeria*, London, 1972
HORNE, Alistair: *A Savage War of Peace*, London, 1977
HUTCHINSON, Martha Crenshaw: *Revolutionary Terrorism*, Stanford, 1978
WOLF, Eric R.: *Peasant Wars of the Twentieth Century*, New York, 1969

Indo China, 1945–75
MALLIN, J.: *Terror in Vietnam*, Princeton, 1966
McALISTER, John T.: *Vietnam : The Origins of Revolution*, London, 1969
O'BALLANCE, Edgar: *The Indo China War*, London, 1964
O'BALLANCE, Edgar: *The Wars in Vietnam*, London, 1975
PIKE, Douglas: *Viet Cong*, London, 1966
SNEPP, Frank: *Decent Interval : The American Debacle in Vietnam and the Fall of Saigon*, London, 1980

Cyprus, 1955–60
CRANKSHAW, Nancy: *The Cyprus Revolt*, London, 1978
GRIVAS, George: *Guerrilla Warfare and EOKA's Struggle*, London, 1964

China, 1923–76
ATKINSON, Alexander: *Social Order and the General Theory of Strategy*, London, 1981
BERNSTEIN, T. P.: *Up to the Mountains, Down to the Villages: The Transfer of Youth from Urban to Rural China*, London, 1977
CHASSIN, Lionel Max: *The Communist Conquest of China*, London, 1965
HARRISON, James Pinckney: *The Long March to Power: A History of the Chinese Communist Party, 1921–72*, London, 1973
KARNOW, Stanley: *Mao and China: From Revolution to Revolution*, New York & London, 1973
MacFARQUHAR, Roderick: *The Origins of the Cultural Revolution* (2 vols), London, 1974
MAO TSE TUNG: *Problems of Strategy in China's Revolutionary War*, Peking, 1965
MAO TSE TUNG: *Quotations from Chairman Mao Tse Tung*, Peking, 1967
NORTH, Robert C.: *Chinese Communism*, London, 1966
SPENCE, Jonathan: *The Gate of Heavenly Peace*, London, 1982
TRAGER, Frank N. & HENDERSON, William (ed): *Communist China, 1949–69*, New York, 1970
WILSON, Dick (ed): *Mao Tse Tung in the Scales of History*, New York, 1977

Cuba, 1956–60
ATLAS de Cuba, Havana, 1968
DEBRAY, Régis: *Revolution in the Revolution*, New York, 1967
DORSCHNER, J. & FABRICIO, R.: *The Winds of December*, London, 1980
GUEVARA, Che: *Guerrilla Warfare*, New York, 1961
MALLIN, J.: *Strategy for Conquest*, Coral Gables, Fla., 1970
THOMAS, Hugh: *Cuba*, London, 1971

Latin America, 1960–82
ANDERSON, Thomas P.: *Matanza: El Salvador's Communist Revolt of 1932*, Lincoln, Nebraska, 1972
DUFF, Ernest A. and McCAMANT, John F.: *Violence and Repression in Latin America*, London, 1976
GOTT, Richard: *Guerrilla Movements in Latin America*, New York, 1971
HODGES, D. C. (ed): *Abraham Guillen: Philosophy of the Urban Guerrilla*, London, 1973
KOHL, J.: *Urban Guerrilla Warfare in Latin America*, London, 1974
LABROUSSE, Alain: *Urban Guerrillas and Uruguay*, London, 1973
NUNN, Frederick M.: *The Military in Chilean History*, Albuquerque, 1976
QUARTIM, Joao: *Dictatorship and Armed Struggle in Brazil*, London, 1971
SWEEZY, Paul M.: *Revolution and Counter Revolution in Chile*, New York & London, 1974
VEGA, Luis Mercier: *Guerrillas in Latin America*, New York, 1969

Southern Africa, 1960–82
ADELE JINADU, L.: *Fanon: In Search of the African Revolution*, Enugu, 1980
BUTLER, J. (ed): *Change in Contemporary Southern Africa*, London, 1975
CHALIAND, Gèrard: *Armed Struggle in Africa*, London, 1969
DAVIDSON, Basil: *The People's Cause*, London, 1981

FEIT, Edward: *Urban Revolt in South Africa, 1960–64*, Northwestern UP, 1971
GREIG, Ian: *The Communist Challenge to Africa*, Richmond, England, 1977
HIRSON, Baruch: *Year of Fire, Year of Ash: The Soweto Revolt*, London, 1979
HORRELL, Muriel: *Terrorism in South Africa*, London, 1968
MARCUM, John: *The Angolan Revolution* (2 vols), Boston & London, 1969
MARTIN, David & JOHNSON, Phyllis: *The Struggle for Zimbabwe*, London, 1981
WHEELER, Douglas L. and PELISSIER, Rene: *Angola*, London, 1971

United States, 1963–82
BARTLEY, Numan V.: *The Rise of Massive Resistance: Race and Politics in the South during the 1950s*, Baton Rouge, 1969
GILBERT, Martin: *American History Atlas*, London, 1968
GRAHAM, Hugh Davis and GURR, Ted (ed): *Violence in America*, New York, 1969
GRIMSHAW, Allen D. (ed): *Racial Violence in the United States*, Chicago, 1969
MUSE, Benjamin: *The American Negro Revolution*, London, 1968
MUSE, Benjamin: *Ten Years of Prelude: The Story of Integration since the Supreme Court's 1954 Decision*, Beaconsfield, USA, 1964
ZINN, Howard: *A People's History of America*, London, 1980

Ethiopia, 1974–82
BELL, J. Bowyer: *The Horn of Africa*, New York, 1973
HALLIDAY, Fred and MOLYNEUX, Maxine: *The Ethiopian Revolution*, London, 1981
OTTAWAY, David and OTTAWAY, Marina: *Ethiopia, Empire in Revolution*, New York, 1978
POOL, David: *Eritrea: Africa's Longest War*, London, 1979

Iran, 1978–82
AKHAVI, S.: *The Relationship between Religion and State in Iran under the Pahlavi Dynasty*, New York, 1980
FISCHER, Michael M. J.: *Iran: From Religious Dispute to Revolution*, London, 1980
KEDDIE, Nikki: *Roots of Revolution: Interpretive History of Modern Iran*, London, 1981
MOGHTADER-MOJDEHI, J. M.: *Interpreting the Iranian Revolution*, London, 1983
ZABIH, Sepehr: *Iran since the Revolution*, London, 1982

Afghanistan, 1975–82
NEWELL, Nancy Peabody & NEWELL, Richard S.: *The Struggle for Afghanistan*, London, 1981
SEN GUPTA, Bhabani: *The Afghan Syndrome*, London, 1982

Middle East, 1934–82
BEGIN, Menachem: *The Revolt*, London, 1952
BELL, J. Bowyer: *The Long War: Israel and the Arabs since 1946*, New York, 1969
BELL, J. Bowyer: *Terror out of Zion, 1929–49*, New York, 1977
BULLOCH, John: *Death of a Country: The Civil War in Lebanon*, London, 1977
CHALIAND, Gèrard: *The Palestinian Resistance*, London, 1972
GILBERT, Martin: *The Arab Israeli Conflict, Its History in Maps*, London, 1978
GILBERT, Martin: *Exile and Return: The Emergence of Jewish Statehood*, London, 1978
HIRO, Dilip: *Inside the Middle East*, London, 1982
LUCAS, Noah: *The Modern History of Israel*, London, 1974
SAID, Edward W.: *The Question of Palestine*, London, 1979
SOBEL, Lester A.: *Palestinian Impasse*, New York, 1977

Ireland, 1920–82
ALEXANDER, Yonah and O'DAY, Alan (ed): *Terrorism in Ireland*, London, 1983
BELL, J. Bowyer: *The Secret Army: IRA*, London, 1970
COOGAN, T. P.: *The IRA*, London, 1980
DILLON, Martin: *Political Murder in Northern Ireland*, London, 1973

The Military Option, 1960–80
CHORLEY, Katherine: *Armies and the Art of Revolution*, London, 1943
LUTTWAK, Edward: *Coup d'Etat: A Practical Handbook*, London, 1968

The Uses of Terror, 1900–
ALEXANDER, Yonah (ed): *International Terrorism*, New York, 1976
ALEXANDER, Yonah and MYERS, Kenneth A. (ed): *Terrorism in Europe*, London, 1982
BELL, J. Bowyer: *Transnational Terrorism*, Washington, 1975
BELL, J. Bowyer: *A Time of Terror: How Democratic Societies Respond to Revolutionary Violence*, New York, 1978

BELL, J. Bowyer: *On Revolt: Strategies of National Liberation*, London, 1976
CLUTTERBUCK, Richard: *Guerrillas and Terrorists*, London, 1977
DOBSON, Christopher and PAYNE, Ronald: *Terror: The West Fights Back*, London, 1982
FAIRBURN, Geoffrey: *Revolutionary Guerrilla Warfare*, London, 1974
HIBBS, D. A.: *Mass Political Violence*, London, 1973
LAQUEUR, Walter: *Terrorism*, London, 1977
MALLIN, J.: *Terror and Urban Guerrillas*, Coral Gables, Fla., 1971
NIEZING, J. (ed): *Urban Guerrilla*, Rotterdam, 1974
NORTON, Augustus R. & GREENBURG, Martin H.: *International Terrorism: An Annotated Bibliography and Research Guide*, Boulder, Col., 1980
SOBEL, Lester A. (ed): *Political Terrorism* (2 vols), Oxford, 1976
SOBEL, Lester A. (ed): *Political Prisoners*, New York, 1978
WILKINSON, Paul: *Terrorism and the Liberal State*, London, 1977

Photographic sources

Frontispiece: The Bridgeman Art Library
ET Archive, *p. 18*
ET Archive, *p. 24*
ET Archive, *p. 31*
BBC Hulton, *p. 33*
The Wessell Press, *p. 35*
Reproduced by Gracious permission of Her Majesty the Queen, *p. 38*
Reproduced by Gracious Permission of Her Majesty the Queen, *p. 41*
Radio Times Hulton, *p. 43*
The Wessell Press, *p. 47*
ET Archive, *p. 49*
National Army Museum, *p. 51*
Mansell College, *p. 55*
Mansell College, *p. 57*

SOAS/photo Eileen Tweedy, *p. 59*
SOAS/photo Eileen Tweedy, *p. 61*
SOAS/photo Eileen Tweedy, *p. 63*
ZEFA/Photri, *p. 67*
Library of Congress, *p. 68*
The Wessell Press, *p. 70*
The Wessell Press, *p. 73*
BBC Hulton, *p. 74*
Mansell College, *p. 75*
BBC Hulton, *p. 79*
Mansell College, *p. 88*
Eric Baschet/Illustration, *p. 93*
Turkish Embassy, *p. 97*
BBC Hulton, *p. 102*
Bundesarchiv, *p. 103*
Robert Hunt Library, *p. 105*
Rizzoli Editore/Weidenfeld & Nicolson Archives, *p. 107*
Historical Research Unit, *p. 109*

AP, *p. 113*
BBC Hulton, *p. 119*
Cas. Oorthuys, *p. 123*
Popperfoto, *p. 127*
Rex Features, *p. 131*
Keystone, *p. 136*
Keystone, *p. 137*
BBC Hulton, *p. 141*
SACU, *p. 145*
John Hillelson/Henri Cartier-Bresson, *p. 148*
SACU, *p. 150*
SACU, *p. 151*
John Hillelson/photo Burt Glinn, *p. 155*
Network/photo Mike Goldwater, *p. 159*
Network/photo Mike Goldwater, *p. 163*

Rex Features, *p. 165*
Keystone, *p. 168*
Popperfoto, *p. 171*
Keystone, *p. 175*
John Hillelson/photo Keler/Sygma, *p. 179*
Network/photo Judah Passow, *p. 183*
Keystone, *p. 186*
Keystone, *p. 187*
Popperfoto, *p. 189*
Network/photo Judah Passow, *p. 190*
Network/photo Laurie Sparham, *p. 191*
Rex Features, *p. 194*
ANP Foto, Amsterdam, *p. 197*

Index

Abdul Hamid II, Sultan, *96*
Aberdare, Kenya, *126, 128*
Adams, John, *18*
Addis Ababa, Ethiopia, *174*
Adrianople, Peace of, *41*
Afghanistan, *100, 177, 182–5*
Aguascalientes, Mexico, *67*
Ahmadabad, India, *119*
Albania, *96*
Albert, Prince Consort, *46*
Alexander II, Czar, *196*
Alexander III, Czar, *78*
Algeria, *35, 130–3, 142, 158, 192, 196*
Algiers, *130, 131*; battle of, *131, 158*

Ali, Mohammad, Shah of Iran, *178*
Allahabad, India, *51*
Allende regime, Chile, *159*
All Russia Union of Railway Employees & Workers, *78–9*
al Saud, Abdul Aziz ibn Abdul Rahman, *see* Saud, Ibn
Ambala, India, *51*
Amboina (South Moluccas), *122*
American Civil War, *20*
American War of Independence, *14–20, 30*
Amhara, Ethiopia, *174*
Amin, Asadullah, *182*
Amin, Hafizullah, *187*

Amritsar, India, *119*
anarchism, *112, 113*
Anatolia, Turkey, *70, 96, 97, 140*
Andalucia, Spain, *117*
Andes, Army of the, *42*
Angola, *164, 165, 168, 177*
Angora (Ankara), Turkey, *96, 97*
Angostura, Venezuela, *43*
Anhwei, China, *59*
Annam kingdom, S. Vietnam, *134*
Anual, Morocco, *112*
Apure, river, Venezuela, *43*
Arabia, *70–3*
Arafat, Yasir, *187*

Arenas de San Pedro, Talavera, Spain, *34*
Arditi, Association of, *104*
Argentina, *72, 133, 158, 159, 196*
Artawiya, Arabia, *70*
Asgill, General, *31*
Assi, Adolphe, *75*
Ataturk, *see* Kemal, Mustafa
Aurès, Algeria, *130*
Aurora (Russian cruiser), *90, 92*
Austria, *25, 28, 46, 102*
Austria-Hungary, *96*
Axelrod, Towia, *102*
Ayacucho, battle of, *44*
Azev, Evno, *196*

Baader-Meinhof, *198*
Badoglio, Marshal, *107*
Bailén, Spain, *34*
Bakhtiar, Shahpur, *179*
Baku, USSR, *164*
Bakunin, Count Mikhail, *112*
Balbo, Italo, *105*
Balfour Declaration, *186*
Ballinamuck, Ireland, *33*
Bann, river, Ireland, *191*
Barcelona, Spain, *43, 112, 113, 117*
Barrackpur, India, *50*
Basques, *112, 113, 117, 196*
Bastille, *21, 22, 24, 28, 29*
Batista, Fulgencio, *154, 156*
Bavaria, *102, 108*
Begin, Menachem, *186, 187, 188*
Beirut, Lebanon, *187*
Belfast, Ireland, *190, 191*
Belgian Congo, *see* Congo
Bella, Ahmed, Ben, *131*
Bengal, India, *50, 118*
Berhampur, India, *50*
Berlin, *46, 100*; Kapp *putsch, 102, 108*
Bey, Rauf, *96*
Black September movement, *196*
blackshirts, *105*
'Blanquism', *84*
Blomberg, von, General, *109*
Bloody Sunday, *78, 84*
Bogotá, Colombia, *43*
Bolivar, Simon, *42, 43–5*
Bolivia, *42, 44, 158*
Bologna, Italy, *105*
Bolshevism, *78–9, 88, 89–92, 93–5, 96, 100–103*
Bombay, India, *50, 118*
Bonaparte, Joseph, *34, 42*
Bonaparte, Napoleon, *34, 35*
Bourbon dynasty, *34, 36*
Buenos Aires, Argentina, *42, 158*
Bunker's Hill, battle of, *15*
Boxer rising, *59–61*
Boyacá, battle of, *43*
Brazil, *158, 159, 196*
Britain, *34, 46, 134, 137, 170, 174, 178, 182, 197*; and American colonies, *14–20*; and Arabia, *71*; and Cyprus, *140–3*; and India, *50–3, 118–21*; and Ireland, *30–3, 190–3, 198*; and Kenya, *126–9*; and Malaya, *122, 123*; and Palestine, *186–8*; and Southern Africa, *165, 166*; and Spain, *35*; and Turkey, *96, 97*
Burma, *122, 123, 150*
Byron, George Gordon, Lord, *38, 40*

Cadiz, Spain, *34, 36*
Calatafimi, Sicily, *54*
Calcutta, India, *51, 118*
Cambodia, *137*
Camden, Lord, *30*
Canada, *14, 18, 19, 133*
Canton, China, *58, 144, 146, 150*
Cape Town, S. Africa, *166*
Caporetto, battle of, *104*
Caprera, Italy, *57*
Caracas, Venezuela, *43*
Cardenas, Lázaro, *69*
Carlists, *113*

Carranza, Venustiano, *66–7*
Cartagena, Colombia, *43*
Carter, President, *178*
Castro, Fidel, *154*
Castro, Raul, *156, 177*
Cavaignac, General, *47*
Cavour, Count, *47*
Central America, *159, 162*
Chambrun, Comte de, *88*
Charles I, King of Great Britain and Ireland, *14*
Charles Albert, King of Piedmont, *54*
Chartist movement, *46*
Chauri Chauri, India, *119*
Chekiang province, China, *59*
Chiang Kai-shek, General, *144, 146*
Chihuahua, Mexico, *66, 67, 69*
Child, Edward, *77*
Chile, *42, 159*
China, *58–61, 134, 136, 144–53, 164, 166, 182, 196*
'China', General, *128*
Ching Peng, *122*
Chita mutiny, *84*
Choshu, Japan, *62, 63*
Christianity, *22, 25, 28, 29, 50, 62, 66, 130, 174*
Churchill, Sir Winston Leonard Spencer, *97, 120*
Chu Teh, *146*
Clare, Co., Ireland, *33*
Clonmel massacre, Ireland, *30*
Cochin, China, *134*
Cochrane, Thomas, Earl of Dundonald, *41, 42*
colonialism, *14–20, 42–5, 112, 122–5, 164*
Colombia (prev. New Granada), *42, 43, 159*
Common Sense (Tom Paine), *20*
Commune of Paris, *49, 74–7, 83*
Communism, *122–3, 134, 140, 144–53, 197 (see also* Marxism, Bolshevism, Russia)
Communist Party, German (Spartacus League), *100*
Concord, Mass., USA, *15, 18, 19*
Confederacion Nacional del Trabajo (CNT), Spain, *112, 113, 117*
Congo, *164*
Congress of the Peoples of the East (1918), *164*
Constantinople, *38–9, 40, 96, 97*
Cordeliers Club, *25*
Cordoba, Spain, *112*
Cornwallis, Lord, *31*
Cossacks, *79, 84, 85, 90*
Crete, *40*
Cripps, Sir Stafford, *120*
Cromwell, Thomas, *30*
Crossman, Richard, *140*
Cuba, *154–7, 158, 159, 163, 164, 165, 175, 177*
Cultural Revolution, *151, 152, 197*
Curzon, Lord, *118*
Custozza, battle of, *47*
Cyprus, *41, 140–3, 196*
Czechoslovakia, *102*

Danang, S. Vietnam, *138*
d'Annunzio, Gabriele, *104, 105*
Danton, *29*
Daoud, Muhammad, *182*
Dead Souls (N. Gogol), *85*

Declaration of Independence, American, *15*
Degaev, Sergei, *196*
Deir Yassin, Israel, *187*
Delhi, India, *50, 51*
Dharesana, Surat, India, *119*
Diaz, Marshal, *105, 107*
Diaz, Porfirio, *66*
Diem, Dinh Ngo, *137, 138*
Dien Bien Phu, *136*
Drogheda massacre, Ireland, *30*
Dublin, Ireland, *30, 31, 190*
Dufferin, Lord, *118*
Dum Dum, Calcutta, India, *50*
Durnasov, F. V., *83*
Dutch East Indies, *122*

Easter Rising, Ireland, *190*
East India Co., *19, 52*
Ebert, Friedrich, *100*
Ecuador, *42, 43*
Egyptians, *40, 41, 140*
Eisenhower, President, *137*
Eisner, Kurt, *102*
Elizabeth I, Queen of England, *30*
ELN, Colombia, *159*
El Salvador, *159, 162, 163*
enosis, 140–3
EOKA, Cyprus, *140–3*
Eritrea, *174, 177*
Estates General, France, *21, 22, 28*
ETA (Basque separatists), *117, 196*
Ethiopia, *174–7*
Europe, *46–9, 100–3*

Facing Mount Kenya (Jomo Kenyatta), *126*
Falange movement, *113*
Famagusta, Cyprus, *142–3*
FARC, Colombia, *159*
fascism, *104–7, 190*
Federacion Anarquista Iberica (FAI), *113*
Ferdinand, Emperor, *46*
Fianna Fail, Ireland, *190*
Filikia Etaria (Friendly Society), Greece, *38*
Finland, *89*
First World War, *71, 84, 96, 97, 100, 104, 108, 112, 126, 182*
Fiume, Italy, *104*
FNLA, *164, 165*
Foggia, Italy, *104*
Fouché, Joseph, *22*
France, *164, 197*; and Algeria, *35, 130–3, 192*; and America, *15, 19, 22*; and Indo China, *134–6*; and Ireland, *30, 31, 32, 33*; and Garibaldi, *54*; and Greece, *41*; and Revolution of 1789–95, *21–30*; and Revolution of 1848, *46, 47*; and Spain, *34–7, 42*; and Turkey, *96*
Franco, Francisco, *114*
Franz Joseph, Emperor of Austria-Hungary, *47*
Frederick William, King of Prussia, *46*
Freikorps, 100, 102, 108
FRELIMO, *164, 168*
Front de Libération National (FLN), Algeria, *130–2, 196–7*
Fukien, China, *58*

Gage, Thomas, General, *15, 17, 19, 20*

Galicia, peasant rising in (1846), *46–7*
Gallipoli, *96*
Galway, Co., Ireland, *33*
Gandhi, Mohandas K., *118, 170*
Garibaldi, Anita, *54*
Garibaldi, Giuseppe, *47, 49, 54–7, 104*
Gaulle, General Charles de, *131, 133*
George, David Lloyd, *97*
Germany, *46, 96, 100–3, 108–11, 197, 198*
Giap, Vo Nguyen, *134, 136, 138*
Giolitti, *107*
Goebbels, Josef, *108*
Goering, Franz, *109*
Gogol, Nikolai, *85*
Gordon, Charles, General, *59*
Goya, *34, 35*
Granada, Spain, *116, 117*
Granard, Ireland, *33*
Graves, Admiral, *17*
Great Fear, the (1789), *22, 23, 25, 28*
Greece, *38–41, 96, 97*; and Cyprus, *140–3*
Greensboro, N. Carolina, USA, *170*
Grivas, George, *140, 142*
Guadalupe, Black Virgin of, *66*
Guanajuato, Mexico, *66*
Guatemala, *163*
guerrilla warfare; in Cuba, *154–7*; in Cyprus, *140–3*; in Greece, *38–41*; in Italy, *54*; in Kenya, *126–9*; in Latin America, *158–63*; in South America, *43*; in Spain, *34–7*; in Turkey, *96*
Guevara, Che, *154, 156, 158*
Guillén, Abraham, *158*
Guinea, Equatorial, *164, 165*

Habsburg Empire, *46, 47, 100*
Hadow, Dr Gilbert, *50*
Hail, emirate of, *70*
Haiphong, Vietnam, *134, 135, 136*
Hankow, China, *58, 60, 61*
Hanoi, *134, 135, 136, 137, 138*
Harar Military Academy, *174*
Havana, Cuba, *154, 156*
Haynau, General, *47*
Hejaz, Arabia, *71*
Hendrick, Chief of Mohawk tribe, *15*
Herat, Afghanistan, *182*
Hidalgo, Miguel, *66*
Hindenburg, Field-Marshal, *108, 109, 111*
Hindus, *50, 51, 118, 120*
Hitler, Adolf, *102, 107, 108–11*
Hola Camp, Kenya, *127, 128*
Honan province, China, *58*
Honduras, *159*
Hopkinson, Henry, *140*
Hsien-feng, Emperor of China, *58–59*
Huerta, General Victoriano, *66, 67*
Huk movement, *123, 124*
Humbert, General, *33*
Humboldt, Alexander von, *43*
Hungary, *46, 47, 48, 102, 103*
Hung Hsiu-ch'uan, *58*
Hussein, *sherif* of Mecca, *71*

Ibañez, Major Bruno, *112*

Iberian peninsula, *34*
Ikhwan, Brotherhood of, *70–3*
Il Popolo d'Italia, *104*
India, *50–3, 100, 118–21, 122*
Indo China, *100, 122, 130, 134–9, 150*
Indonesia, *122*
IRA, *190–3, 196, 197*
Iran, *178–81, 198–9*
Iraq, *71*
Ireland, *30–3, 46, 100, 190–3*
Irgun Zvai Leumi, Palestine, *186, 188*
Iroquois, Six Nations of, *15*
Islam, *70–3, 96–9, 119, 120, 122, 130, 174, 178–81*
Islamic People's Party, Iran, *181*
Israel, *133, 186–9*
Italy, *46, 47, 54–7, 96, 103, 104–7*
Ivan the Terrible, *78, 84*
Izmir, *96, 97*
Izvestia, *58*

Jabotinsky, Vladimir, *186*
Jacobin Club, *25, 29*
James II, King of England, *14*
Japan, *62–5, 78, 119, 120, 122, 123, 134, 146, 150*
Java, *122*
Jefferson, Thomas, *18*
Jerusalem, *186, 187*
Jhansi, India, *51*
Jidda, Arabia, *71*
Jinnah, Mohammad Ali, *120*
Juarez, Benito, *66*
Junin, battle of, *44*

Kabylia, *130, 133*
Kabul, Afghanistan, *183, 184*
Kagoshima, Japan, *62, 65*
Kansu, China, *58*
Kapenguria, Kenya, *126*
Kemal, Mustafa (Ataturk), *71, 96–9, 178*
Kenya, *126–9, 140, 141, 165*
Kenya African Union (KAU), *126, 128*
Kenyatta, Jomo, *126, 128, 140*
Kerensky, Alexander, *88, 90*
Khomeini, Ayatollah, *178, 179, 181*
Kikuyu tribe, Kenya, *126–9*
Kilcullen Bridge, Ireland, *30*
Killala, Co. Mayo, Ireland, *31, 33*
Kimathi, Dedan, *128*
King, Martin Luther, *170–1*
Komei, Emperor, *62*
Kornilov, General, *89, 93*
Kronstadt, Russia, *89, 90, 92, 93*
Kumamoto, Japan, *65*
Kun, Bela, *102*
Kwangsi, China, *58, 59*
Kwantung, China, *58, 144, 146*
Kyoto, Japan, *62, 63*
Kyushu, Japan, *62*

Lafayette, Marquis de, *28*
Lake, General, *31*
Laos, Asia, *134, 135, 136, 137, 138*
Lari, Kenya, *127*
Larnica, Cyprus, *141*
Latin America, *158–63, 195, 196*; Cuba, *154–7*; Mexico, *66–9*
Lattre de Tassigny, General de, *136*
Law, Andrew bonar, *97*
Lawrence, T. E. (of Arabia), *71, 100*

Leakey, Louis, *128*
Lebanon, *187, 188, 196*
Lenin, Vladimir Ilyich Ulyanov, *75, 78, 84, 89, 90, 93, 100, 102, 103, 197*
Levien, Max, *102*
Levine, Eugen, *102*
Lexington, Mass., USA, *15, 18, 19*
Liddell Hart, Sir Basil, *35*
Liebknecht, Karl, *100, 103*
Li Hung Chang, *59*
Lima, Peru, *43*
Lin Piao, *152*
Londonderry, Ireland, *191*
Longford, Co., Ireland, *33*
Louis XVI, King of France, *21, 25, 28, 29*
Louis Philippe, King of France, *46*
Luanda, Congo, *164*
Lucknow, India, *50, 53*
Ludendorff, General, *108*
Luzon, Philippines, *123, 124*

MacMahon, Marshal, *75*
Madero, Francisco, *66*
Madrid, Spain, *34, 113, 117*
Maggiore, Lake, Italy, *54*
Mahmud II, Sultan, *37, 38, 39, 40*
maji maji rebellion, *126*
Makhno, Nestor, *93*
Malawi, *165*
Malaya, *122–3, 137, 140, 141*
Manchuria, *146, 150*
Manchus, rebellion against, *58–61*
Mani peninsula, Greece, *38*
Mao Tse Tung, *134, 144, 145, 146–53*
Maputo (Lourenço Marques), *166*
Marie-Antoinette, Queen of France, *25, 29*
Marighella, Carlos, *158*
Marsala, Sicily, *54, 57*
Marx, Karl, *84*
Marxism, *112, 123, 182, 184*
Mashad, Iran, *179*
Mass., USA, *15, 18, 19*
Mau Mau, Kenya, *126–9, 165*
Maura, Miguel, *114*
Maximilian of Austria, *66*
Mazzini, Giuseppe, *54*
Meadows, Thomas, *58*
Medina, Arabia, *71*
Meerut, India, *50*
Mein Kampf (Hitler), *111*
Mengistu, Haile-Mariam, *175, 177*
Mensheviks, *78–9, 88, 89, 90, 92*
Mesolonghi, Greece, *40, 41*
Messina, Sicily, *55*
Mexico, *66–9*
Miao tribe, China, *58*
Michael, Prince (brother of Czar Nicholas II), *88*
Middle East, *186–9*
Milan, Italy, *46, 104, 105*
Minh, Ho Chi, *134, 136, 137, 138, 139*
Mirabeau, Comte de, *21*
Mito, Japan, *62*
Mogilev, *78, 85*
Mohammed, Prophet, *70*
Mohawk tribe, North America, *15*
Mola, General, *113, 117*
Moltke, von, General, *74*
Montevideo, Uruguay, *158*
Montgomery, Alabama, USA, *170*
Moro movement, *124*

Morelos, Jose Maria, *66, 67*
Morocco, *100, 112, 113, 114, 117*
Moscow, *77, 78, 79, 82–3, 85, 146*
Moslems, (*see also* Islam), *38, 51, 58, 119, 120, 130, 133, 186–9*
Mouskos, Michael, Makarios III, Archbishop of Cyprus, *140, 141, 142*
Mozambique, *164, 165, 166, 168*
MPLA, *164, 165*
MRM, Mozambique, *165*
Mugabe, Robert, *165*
Munich, *102, 108*; Olympics ('72), *196*
Mussolini, Benito, *104–7*
My Lai, Vietnam, *138*

Nadir Shah, *182*
Nagasaki, Japan, *62*
Nagpur, India, *118*
Nairobi, Kenya, *126, 127*
Naivasha, Kenya, *127*
Namibia, *165, 166*
Nanking, Treaty of (1842), *58, 59, 61, 150*
Naples, Italy, *54, 55, 57, 105*
Napoleon III, *74, 130*
National Assembly, France, (1789), *21, 22, 28* (*see also* National Convention)
National Association for Advancement of Coloured People, *170*
National Convention, France, *22, 28, 29*
National Guard, Paris, *21, 28, 29, 75*
NATO, *142*
Navarre, Henri de, *136*
Nazism, *102, 108–11*
Nehru, Jawaharlal, *119, 122*
Neill, Colonel, *51*
Nejd, Emir of, *70*
Netherlands, *122*
New England, USA, *14, 17, 18*
New Granada (now Colombia), *43*
New York, USA, *14, 15, 17, 18*
Nicaragua, *162, 163*
Nicholas II, Czar of Russia, *78, 79, 84, 85, 88*
Nien Fei movement, China, *59*
Nixon, Richard, *132, 152*
North America, *14–20*
North Vietnam, *136, 137*
Novara, battle of, *47*
Nyasaland, *100*

Oaxaca, province of, Mexico, *66, 67*
Odessa, Russia, *79*
Ogaden, Ethiopia, *177*
O'Higgins, Bernardo, *42*
Oriente province, Cuba, *154, 156*
Orinoco, river, *43*
Oromo (tribes), Ethiopia, *174*
Orthodox Church, Greek, *38*
Orwell, G., *196*
Ostolaza, Blas, *36*
Otho, King of Greece, *41*
Ottawa tribe, North America, *15*
Ottoman Empire, *38, 40, 96–9, 130*

Pacific war, *122*
Paez, Jose Antonio, *43*
Pakistan, *120, 183, 184*
Palermo, Sicily, *55*

Palestine, *186–9, 196*
Papen, Franz von, *109*
Paphos, Cyprus, *140*
Paris; Commune of, *49, 74–7, 83*; Peace of (1763), *19*; revolutions, *21, 22, 25, 26–7, 28, 29, 46–7*
Pasha, Ali, *38, 39*
Pasha, Ibrahim, *40, 41*
Pasha, Refet, *96*
Pasha, Reshid, *41*
Patras, bishop of, *38*
Patrice Lumumba University, Moscow, *165*
Pearl Harbor, *122*
Peking, *59, 60, 61, 150*
Pennsylvania, USA, *14, 18*
Pennsylvania Evening Post, *20*
Pennsylvania Journal, *18, 19*
Perry expedition (1854), *62*
Peru, *42, 43, 44, 158, 159*
Peter the Great, *84*
Petrograd, *78, 79, 83, 84, 85, 88, 89–92, 93*
Philadelphia, USA, *14*; Continental Congress in (1774), *19, 20*
Philhellenes, *40*
Philippines, *123, 124*
Piedmont, *47, 54*
PLO, *187, 196*
Podgorny, President, *177*
Poland, *84*
Pontiac, Chief (of Ottawa tribe), *15*
Poona, India, *118*
'Porfirismo', *66*
Portugal, *35, 164, 165*
Potemkin (battleship), *79*
Potsdam Agreement, *134*
Prague, *46, 47, 186*
Problems of Strategy in China's Revolutionary War (Mao Tse Tung), *146*
Prussia, *25, 28, 46, 74, 109, 111*

Qum, Iran, *178*
Quotations from Chairman Mao Tse Tung, *152*

Radek, Karl, *100*
Ram, Sita, *50, 51*
Rancagua, battle of (1814), *42*
Rashid, Abdul Aziz ibn Mutaib, *70*
Red Army, Russia, *93, 102*; China, *134, 146, 152*
Red Guards, *89, 90, 93*; in China, *151, 152*
Reichenau, von, Colonel, *109, 111*
Revere, Paul, *15*
Reza, Mohammad Pahlevi, Shah of Iran, *178–81*
Rhodesia/Zimbabwe, *164, 165, 166, 168*
Rio de Janeiro, *54*
Rio de la Plata (Argentina), *42*
Rivadavia, Bernadino, *42*
Rivera, José Antonio *Primo de*, *113*
Rivera, Primo de, General, *112, 113*
Riyadh, *70*
Roberto, Holden, *165*
Robespierre, Maximilian, *22, 25, 29, 36*
Roch, Father Philip, *31*
Roehm, Ernst, *108*
Roland, Madame, *25*
Romagna, Italy, *104*
Rome, Italy, *54, 105*

Romania, *46, 102*
Rowdhat Muhanna, Arabia, *70*
Rozaz, Calvo de, *34*
Russia, *38, 39, 171, 196, 197*; war
    with Turkey, *41*; (1905), *77,*
    78–84; (1917), *77, 85–8*; and
    Petrograd, *89–92*; and Civil War
    (1917–21), *93–5*; and Europe,
    100, 102; and China, *50, 144,*
    146, 163; and Southern America,
    164; and Ethiopia, *174–7*; and
    Afghanistan, *182–5*

Sachi, Prince, *62–3*
Saigon, *134, 138*
Sakarya, river, *97*
Salan, General, *136*
Salerno, Italy, *55*
Samsum, Asia Minor, *96*
samurai, *63, 65*
San Antonio, *54*
Sandino, Augustino, *162–3*
Sanjurjo, General, *113*
San Martin, Jose de, *42–3*
San Remo Conference (1920), *186*
sans-culottes, *22, 25, 28, 29*
Santa Clara, Cuba, *150*
Santiago de Cuba, *154, 156*
Santillán, Diego Abad de, *117*
Saragossa, Spain, *35*
Sardinia, *54, 55*
SASOL, South Africa, *166*
Satsuma, Japan, *62, 63*
Saud, Ibn, *70*
Schleicher, Kurt von, *109*
Scotland, *46, 103*
Second World War, *130, 170*
Selassie, Haile, *174, 177*
Sendero Luminoso, *159*
Sétif, Algeria, *135*
Seven Years War (1759–63), *15*
Seville, Spain, *114, 116*
Sèvres, Treaty of, *97*
Shanghai, *59, 144, 146, 152*
Sharpeville, South Africa, *166*
Shawnee tribe, North America, *15*
Shensi, China, *58*
Shimonoseki, straits of, *62*
Siberia, *78, 84*
Sicily, *54–5*
Sierra de Cordoba, *158*
Sierra Maestra, Cuba, *154, 156, 158*
Sikhs, *50, 51*

Silesia, *46*
Sipri, India, *51*
Smolny Institute, Petrograd, *90, 92*
Smyrna, Asia Minor, *38, 41*
Social Democratic Party, Russia,
    78, 88
Social Democratic Party,
    Germany, *100*
Socialist Revolutionary Party,
    Russia, *78, 88, 89*
Society of the Friends of the
    Constitution (Jacobins), *28*
Somalia, *174, 177*
Sonora, Mexico, *67*
Soto, Diaz, *67*
South Africa, *164–7, 197–8*
South America, *42, 54, 66–9, 154,*
    (*see also* Latin America)
South East Asia, *122–5*
South Vietnam, *136, 137*
Southern Africa, *164–9*
Southern Rhodesia, *164*
soviets (workers' councils), *84, 88,*
    89, 90, 92, 93
Soviet Union, *see* Russia
Soweto, South Africa, *166, 168*
Spain, *66, 133, 197*; (1808–14),
    34–7; (1936), *112–7*; Carlist
    Wars, *36*; Civil War, *36*; and
    South America, *42–5*
Spanish America, *42–5*
'Spartacists', *100, 101*
Stalin, Josef, *150*
Starnberg, Bavaria, *109*
Stolypin, Peter, *84, 85*
St Petersburg, *see* Petrograd
Styria, *46*
Suez, *131*
Sukarno, *122*
Suleiman the Magnificent, Sultan,
    98
Sun Yat Sen, *61, 144*

Tabriz, Iran, *178*
Taif, Arabia, *71*
Taiping (movement), *58, 59, 60, 61*
Takashima Shuhan, *62*
Tambov province, Russia, *93, 95*
Tandy, Napper, *33*
Tanganyika, *126*
Tanzania, *165*
Taquari, Brazil, *54*
Tara Hill, Ireland, *30*

Taraki, Nur Muhammad, *182*
Tea Act (1773), *19*
Tehran, Iran, *178, 179*
Templer, Sir Gerald, *123*
Tennis Court Oath, France, *21*
Terror, Reign of (1793–4), *22, 25,*
    29
terrorism, *198–9*
Thai Nguyen, *134*
Third Estate, France, *21, 28*
Tientsin, China, *59*
Tilak, Bal Gangadhar, *118, 119*
TMT, Cyprus, *141*
Tocqueville, Alexis de, *47–8*
Tokugawa family, Japan, *62–5*
Tone, Wolfe, *30, 31, 190*
Tonkin, kingdom, N. Vietnam, *134*
Topia, Tantia, *51, 53*
Torres, Jose Antonio, *66*
Troodos Mts., Cyprus, *140, 142*
Trotsky, Leon, *78, 90, 92, 93*
Truman, Harry S., President, *170*
Tseng Kuo-Fan, *59*
Tuileries, *25, 28, 29*
Tumusla, battle of, *44*
Tunisia, *130*
Turkey, *38–41, 96–9, 140–3, 194,*
    197

Ulster, Ireland, *30, 192*
Union General de Trabajadores
    (UGT), Spain, *112*
UNITA, *165*
United Nations, *122, 142, 187*
United States of America, *14, 96,*
    120, 122, 124, 136, 150, 158, 164,
    165, 166, 170–3, 174, 177, 182,
    188, 191, 197, 198–9; and
    Vietnam, *137–9*; and China, *152*;
    and Cuba, *154*; and Latin
    America, *159, 162, 163*; and
    Iran, *178–81*
Uruguay, *54, 158*

Valera, Eamonn de, *190*
Velletri, Italy, *54*
Vendée, France, *29, 35*
Venezuela, *42, 43, 44, 159*
Venice, Republic of, *47*
Veracruz, Mexico, *67*
Verderevsky, Admiral, *92*
Versailles, France, *21, 28, 75*
Victor Emmanuel II, King, *57*

Victor Emmanuel III, King, *105,*
    107
Victoria, Queen of the United
    Kingdom, *46*
Vienna, Austria, *46, 47, 48*
Viet Minh, *134–9*
Vietnam, *134–9, 142, 171, 184*
Villa, 'Pancho', *67, 69*
Vistula, river, *46*
Voronezh, Russia, *78*

Wahhab, Mohammad Ibn Abdul,
    70
Warsaw, Poland, *78*
Waruhiu, Chief, *126*
Watts Riot (1965), USA, *171, 172*
Weimar Republic, *108*
Wellesley, Sir Arthur (1st Duke of
    Wellington), *35*
West Germany, *197, 198*
Westmeath Co., Ireland, *33*
Wexford, Ireland, *31*
White Army, *93*
White Lotus Society, Honan
    province, China, *58*
Wiesbaden, West Germany, *197*
Wilhelm II, Emperor, *100*
Wilhelmshaven, *100*
Wilkes, John, *19*
Windichgrätz, General, *47*
Winter Palace, Petrograd, *88, 90,*
    92
Wuchang, China, *58, 59, 60, 61*

Yangtze, river, *58*
Yeats, William Butler, *190*
Yedo (Tokyo), Japan, *62, 64, 65*
Yenan, *146, 151*
Yokohama, Japan, *62*
Yoshinabu, *62, 63*
Young India, *119*
Yuan, Shih-Kai, *61*
Yugoslavia, *104*

Zahir, King, *182*
Zambia, *175*
Zapata, Emiliano, *66, 67, 69*
Zaragoza, Aragon, Spain, *113*
Zimbabwe African National Union
    (ZANU), *164, 168*
Zimbabwe African People's Union
    (ZAPU), *168*
Zionism, *186–9, 196*